YOUR MBA

Proven Strategies for Getting Into the Top Business Schools

GAME PLAN
THIRD EDITION

By

OMARI BOUKNIGHT

and

SCOTT SHRUM

CAREER PRESS

Pompton Plains, NJ

YOUR MBA GAME PLAN, THIRD EDITION
EDITED BY JODI BRANDON
TYPESET BY EILEEN MUNSON
Original cover design by Rob Johnson
Updated by Jeff Piasky
Printed in the U.S.A.

To order this title, please call toll-free 1-800-CAREER-1 (NJ and Canada: 201-848-0310) to order using VISA or MasterCard, or for further information on books from Career Press.

The Career Press
220 West Parkway, Unit 12
Pompton Plains, NJ 07444
www.careerpress.com

Library of Congress Cataloging-in-Publication Data

Bouknight, Omari, 1977-
    Your MBA game plan : proven strategies for getting into the top business schools / By
    Omari Bouknight and Scott
    Shrum. -- 3rd ed.
                    p. cm.
    Includes bibliographical references and index.
    ISBN 978-1-60163-182-4 -- ISBN 978-1-60163-644-7 (ebook) 1. Master of business
administration degree--United States. 2.
Business education--United States--Planning. I. Shrum, Scott, 1975- II. Title.
    HF1131.B68 2011
    650.071'173--dc23
                                                                2011027030

Dedication

Scott ▶

> *For my father, who taught me the value of laughing at myself every now and then.*

Omari ▶

> *For my parents, who showed me truth in God, power in education, and the burden of legacy.*

• • • • • • • • • • • • • •

Acknowledgments

It's safe to say that we hardly knew what we were getting into when we first decided to write a book about getting into business school back in 2002. Fortunately, the following people made the whole process much more bearable—for all three editions of the book—and the final product is much better because of their help. We are truly thankful for their assistance along the way:

John Abbamondi; Kirsten Beucler; Kavita Bouknight; Justin Crandall; Dawna Clarke; Jon Crawford; Kirsten Dalley; Nicole DeFelice; Brian Dukes; Buckethead Section, Kellogg Class of 2004; Stacey Farkas; Brigid Ganley; Willie Harbert; Anita Juneja; Shaan Kandawalla; Soojin Kwon Koh; Michael Lewis; Mark Lueking; Carolina Menezes; Markus Moberg; Campbell Murray; Matt Niksch; Kristen Parkes; Tom Pusic; Michael Pye; Sarah Richardson; Section A, HBS Class of 2004; Brian Schmidt; Adam Schwartz; Brendan Sheehan; Misha Simmonds; Gwen Smith; Gabe Solomon; Doug Stein; Christie St. John; Anita Thekdi; Chad Troutwine; Mike Williams; and Mike Worosz.

Also, this book probably wouldn't have happened if not for the supportive community of fellow business school applicants on the *Bloomberg Businessweek* online forums back in 2002. We'd like to thank everyone out there for putting up with our surveys and giving us great feedback as the first edition of this book took shape.

Finally, a few people have been particularly helpful, patient, and supportive in this process. Scott would like to especially thank his wife, Anita, for her support and expert proofreading. Omari would like to especially thank his wife, Kavita, for her continual support. These people believed in us and stuck with us the whole way through.

Contents

Preface

We've been humbled by the number of business school applicants whom we've helped to succeed since the first edition of this book was published in 2003. In less than a decade, what started out as a simple idea grew into a book, which grew into an online service helping applicants improve their application essays and resumes, which has since merged with one of the world's largest GMAT prep and admissions consulting services, Veritas Prep. Long before Facebook and Twitter became household names, applicants all over the world were spreading the word about *Your MBA Game Plan.*

What humbles us even more is how much more we have learned from our readers and other business school applicants. The MBA admissions game is constantly evolving, and by helping thousands of applicants sort through their own application strategies, we have learned far more than what we knew back in 2003: Our readers are savvier about the process, and they in turn have made us more insightful, which helps us assist new applicants even more. It's a virtuous cycle.

What's changed since 2003? For one, the MBA admissions game keeps getting more sophisticated. Thanks to books such as ours, other admissions consultants, online communities, and so on, the average applicant knows much more than the average applicant did eight years ago. And the mix of applicants has changed. Though bankers from New York are still a very common sighting among MBA applicants, more and more engineers and IT professionals from Asia are turning up in the applicant pool, making it ever harder for those applicants to stand out from the pack.

What else has changed? Admissions interviews continue to grow in importance. Many schools have radically redesigned their academic programs, throwing out the traditional core classes in favor of integrated curricula that put a great deal of emphasis on application-based learning and provide a solid dose of ethics. The economy went from ice cold at the start of the millennium to scorching in 2006 to teetering on the brink of a worldwide economic collapse in 2008, taking the job market on a wild ride with it. All the while, people kept taking the GMAT and applying to business school, mostly undeterred even when job-placement statistics looked grim.

But the more things change, the more they stay the same. Many applicants still miss the mark, focusing too much on their hard "stats" such as their GMAT score and GPA, and not enough on the story of who they are. They worry about having "enough" extracurricular activities in their applications, although just demonstrating a significant impact with one activity would serve them best. They ask their CEOs to write their letters of recommendation when a thoughtful, detailed letter from their immediate supervisor would help them far more. Or, perhaps worst of all, they choose which schools to apply to based on the rankings and nothing else, doing no more research than picking up a copy of *U.S. News & World Report.*

Since writing the first edition of this book, we've been in direct contact with hundreds more business school applicants. Many of them still fall short on at least one of the two goals that every applicant has: to show fit with an MBA program and to stand out versus the competition. The reason for these "misses" is usually *not* just the GMAT or some other application item that's easy to spot. The problem usually lies deeper in a person's application strategy, such as failing to show the admissions committee what makes that person unique or interesting, or failing to demonstrate sufficient enthusiasm for a given program. Unfortunately, many such applications are destined to fail before they're ever even submitted. Though the competition is tougher than ever, we believe that no one should be doomed to churning out applications that have zero chance of success.

So, we're back with the third edition of *Your MBA Game Plan.* Although the core MBA Game Plan message hasn't changed (you must always demonstrate fit with a school and stand out from the pack), we've built on the story and taken it even farther. We now profile more top-ranked business schools than ever before, including more programs outside of the United States, and have completely revised the other schools' profiles to include updated strategies. We've added even more MBA admissions essays, we have taken a closer look at certain applicant profiles in response to the rapidly evolving applicant pool, and, we've worked the countless other lessons we've learned during the past eight years into every other part of this book.

Our goal remains the same: to help you get into the business school of your dreams. We've been in your shoes, and hope to share with you what we've learned as we applied to business school in 2001 and in the years since then. (Wow, time flies!) We don't want to see you make any of the most common mistakes that applicants make every year.

If you can make it easy for admissions officers to see that you have a distinctive profile and would fit well with their schools' cultures, then you'll quickly get ahead of other candidates. And getting ahead is probably what you had in mind when you picked up this book in the first place.

Best of luck to you!

Scott and Omari

May 2011

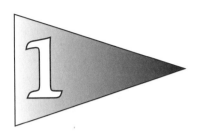

New Game, New Rules

To my relief, the cab slowed down and the driver waved me over. I had been on the verge of running for the last 30 minutes, trying to reach my interview with Harvard Business School on time. Sliding into the back seat of the taxi, I heavily exhaled directions to the admissions office, rejuvenated with confidence knowing that I would not arrive to the interview late. Now all I had to do was differentiate myself from the other 9,000 applicants and prove to the admissions committee that I embody HBS's culture and mission. Suddenly, it hit me: This would be no small task.

In many ways, the on-campus interview is a wake-up call. For many applicants, it is the first time that they interact directly with the competition and with their target schools. Stepping into the admissions office, my alarm went off as I began to discuss experiences, backgrounds, and objectives with other applicants who were waiting to interview. The conversations were enlightening, as gossip and advice on the application process were freely swapped. More so, however, these conversations were humbling. I spoke with a military pilot who had escorted the president around the country, a scientist in biotechnology who was working on a cancer-fighting antibody, and an Internet entrepreneur who had executed a multi-million-dollar initial public offering. What did I have to offer?

I no longer believed my family's frequent promises that I would be admitted. They obviously didn't understand what I was up against.

"Your interviewer is ready to see you now," the receptionist called out to me. Moments later, I was sitting across from an admissions officer. A 30-minute conversation ensued in which we discussed all aspects of my application, except for my GMAT score and GPA. Indeed, the interview was very similar to the several others in which I took part. Because most applicants to top business schools have the ability to succeed in the curricula, GPA and test scores are often ruled out as differentiating factors. So what remained to separate me from the thousands of other applicants?

The admissions officer asked questions about my story. What were my career goals, and how would attending business school play a role in meeting those goals? How would my professional and personal experiences enhance the classroom dynamic? In what ways had I acted as a leader to my peers?

Fortunately, I was ready. My responses were well crafted and were supported with specific details. These responses were all part of a strategic approach that I developed to target the schools to which I applied. The interview transformed into a platform on which I established my case. The admissions officer became my audience, measuring my storyline against other applicants' stories and against the school's sense of "fit."

By the end of the interview, I felt satisfied. I had covered each of my points and made a convincing case for why I belonged at HBS. Exiting the interview, I didn't concern myself with finding a taxi. I wanted to savor my victory. Thanks to my preparation, I was one step closer to being admitted.

The Increasing Popularity of Business School

Fueled by steadily rising post-MBA salaries and a burgeoning global economy that is sending ever more international business school students to American schools, the number of applications to top schools continues to climb. Despite a two-percent, year-over-year drop in applications to traditional two-year MBA programs reported by the Graduate Management Admission Council in 2010 (an almost inevitable decline after several years of strong growth during the last recession), the overall trend is undeniable. Admissions rates at top business schools continue to creep downward as more and more young professionals decide they want a top-tier MBA to bolster their career prospects.

Over the past decade, the rules of the business school application game have significantly changed. As a result of the overall increase in applications, the competition among applicants has intensified. All top-10 MBA programs (as ranked by *U.S. News & World Report* in 2010) have a mean GMAT score and GPA greater than 705 and 3.4, respectively, and these statistics continue to climb. Meanwhile, the number of seats at most schools is not climbing, and, in fact, some top schools have made fewer seats available to traditional full-time MBA applicants. The result is that schools are more closely examining all aspects of the MBA application beyond the basic statistics.

Many applicants, however, have responded to this increased competition by merely focusing on improving their GMAT scores and other "hard" stats. *U.S. News, Bloomberg Businessweek,* and other magazines prominently feature a school's average GMAT score next to its name, so it's only natural that applicants focus on this obvious component of the application. But while the GMAT may be the first challenge in the application process that must be navigated, high scores alone certainly won't win the business school application game.

MBA Application Strategy

Traditional strategic analysis examines the approach of a decision-maker given his environment and the tactics of other decision-makers who are in pursuit of similar objectives. As an applicant, you must succeed in an environment that demands differentiation against the competition and proper fit with the programs to which you apply. The ultimate questions that you as an applicant must answer are:

- ☒ How do I measure against the competition?
- ☒ How do I measure against my targeted business schools?

In our admittedly subjective estimation, after years of experience, we estimate that the probability of gaining acceptance to top business school programs looks something like this:

	Don't Fit Program	Fit Program
Differentiate From Competition	10%–20%	50%–70%
Don't Differentiate From Competition	0%–5%	10%–20%

The rest of this book focuses on developing answers to those two questions and getting you to the upper-right cell. It will do so in a functional and comprehensive manner, highlighting all aspects of the application process. You will learn how to position yourself based on your experiences and your target schools, how to write effective essays, and how to execute your application strategy.

Understanding the Competition

When Omari first started the business school application process, one of the first pieces of insight he was given dealt with the number of candidates applying with his professional profile: *If you want to gain admittance to a top program, you must first find a way to differentiate yourself from the thousands of other consultants who are applying.* This is good advice for any applicant, regardless of the profile. Therefore, it is helpful to get into the minds of admissions officers and of other business school candidates with the knowledge that these candidates will have strong applications that cross the officers' desks before and after your own application. At a high level, there are two aspects of your application that admissions officers will compare with other candidates' applications: your profile and your career goals.

Your Profile

The first aspect of differentiation that you must understand as a business school candidate is that all applicants have an Achilles' heel. We all have a weakness in our profile that will show up in our applications; it's just a matter of whether or not it is appropriately addressed. Whether the issue is number of years of work experience, lack of community service activities, low GPA, poor writing ability, low GMAT score, unconvincing interview skills, or overconfidence, all candidates have an aspect of their profiles that, unaddressed, could lead to the dreaded "ding," as rejections are commonly called.

Your profile consists of your academic background, professional experiences, and personal interests and activities. As much as possible, the components in your profile should be multifaceted and consistent with an overall theme:

Multifaceted

Admissions officers look for candidates who demonstrate multiple dimensions through various interests. A common question that is asked during business school interviews is: "Outside of your professional activities, what are your personal interests and endeavors?" Top business schools want to ensure that they do not merely admit workaholic drones, but rather candidates who lead interesting and inspiring lives.

Consistent

A while back, we spoke with Carrie, an applicant who was declined admittance to the Kellogg School of Management at Northwestern University. During her feedback session with an admissions officer, one of the messages that Carrie received was that she lacked community service experience. Actually, Carrie did have community service experience, but it wasn't *relevant* experience. It didn't fit with the overall message that she conveyed in her application. The community service activities in which Carrie took part appeared to be events in which she participated purely so that they could be posted on her resume. Admission committee members are savvy enough to detect when an applicant's attempts to enhance her profile are contrived, so you therefore need to weave the components of your profile into your story in a logical and consistent manner.

The second and third chapters of this book will assist you in differentiating your application story from the competition. Chapter 2 will outline the characteristics that admissions officers value, and show you how to demonstrate these characteristics in your own application. In highlighting those characteristics, you will ensure that your profile is multifaceted and consistent with a targeted story. This approach impresses top business schools, as they are searching for candidates who will add something unique to the classroom dynamic. Chapter 2 will also show you how to overcome certain weaknesses that your application may contain. Specific profiles will be covered in Chapter 3, which details each profile's typical strengths and weaknesses, and provides guidance on how to overcome the stereotypes that admissions officers tend to associate with each profile.

Your Career Goals

Where you are going is just as important as where you are coming from. Admissions officers often cite candidates' inability to articulate their post-graduation goals—and how the business school's curriculum will support those goals—as a contributing factor in a candidate's rejection.

As you communicate your career goals, you should convey an overall story that makes it easy for the admissions committee to see why an MBA makes sense for you. Typically, the career goal aspect of your story will either describe your motivation to make a career change or your intent to bolster your current career direction. Whichever career path you intend to pursue, the messages you communicate in the application should reflect innovation and an entrepreneurial spirit. That doesn't mean that all applicants should strive to start their own businesses, but rather that business schools are looking for candidates who want to contribute a fresh perspective and new insight to their chosen professions.

Use the application as a forum in which to display ambition and ingenuity as you discuss future objectives. Additionally, you should discuss the ways in which the targeted school's specific curriculum will aid you in achieving those objectives.

Chapter 4 will provide you with details on each component of the application process. Your story should be reflected in each of these components.

Understanding Your Business School Targets

Most business schools look for similar qualities in their applicants. They want students who demonstrate academic aptitude, leadership, an ability to work well with peers and subordinates, integrity, and ambition, just to name a few.

So, does this mean that the applications to your target schools should be the same? Of course it doesn't. Each school tends to emphasize certain traits over others, and looks for examples to support these traits. A quick look at the essay questions from a few business school applications tells you that each school asks about these qualities in different ways. Here's the irony: Each school claims to look for a unique type of candidate, yet it seems that every year there are some applicants who manage to get into all of the top programs. Do these candidates really have *every* trait that all of these schools are looking for?

Probably not. More likely, they understand the emphasis that each school places on specific traits, and they know how to highlight those traits in their application. Successful applicants know that MIT Sloan values analytical ability, and they therefore stress their methodical approaches to business problems. They know that Fuqua really does pride itself on its teamwork-oriented culture, and they highlight the success they've had while working in teams.

These may seem like obvious examples to an applicant who's done some basic school research, but this is an area in which many applicants stumble. They either don't give enough thought to highlighting the traits that each school looks for, or they "tack on" one trite example in a half-hearted attempt to meet the requirement. The result is almost always a rejection because the applicants failed to demonstrate proper fit with their target schools.

What Is "Fit"?

In short, "fitting" with a school means demonstrating that you have the ability to succeed there, you are someone the school would be glad to have as part of its community, and you will serve as an ambassador for the school after you graduate.

In order to convey proper fit with a school, you should demonstrate that:

- ▶ You understand what the school stands for and why it is important. When you say "Darden preaches leadership," you are able to give examples of what leadership means to you and explain why you want to further strengthen your own leadership abilities at Darden.

- ▶ You embody the traits that the school most wants to see in its students. You don't need to have climbed Mount Everest to have demonstrated accomplishment or aced the GMAT to demonstrate quantitative excellence. You do need to be able to illustrate how your everyday life is peppered with examples of the traits for which the school looks.

- ▶ You will become very involved in your business school, from contributing to class discussions to running student organizations to being an active alum 20 years from now. One great way to communicate this is by pointing to similar experiences with your undergraduate university.

- ▶ You are the kind of person with whom your classmates would want to work on a team project at 3 a.m. Exhibiting a penchant for working in teams and a sociable personality will establish the basis for this.

One other extremely important question that an admissions officer asks about every applicant is: "Would she actually attend this school if he were accepted?" Admissions officers assume that you're applying to multiple schools, and they know that their school may not be your first choice. But you need to convey enough knowledge and enthusiasm about the school to convince admissions officers that you would strongly consider attending their school if you were accepted. The history of the business school admissions game is littered with stories of people with stellar credentials who were rejected by "safety" schools. If you don't sound sincere about wanting to attend a given school, you can expect that school to return the favor by not wanting you.

Demonstrating "fit" in your application

Your entire application should spell out how well you fit with your target business school. Practically speaking, though, the parts of the application that will do this the most are your essays, recommendations, and interview. Think of these as your opportunities to talk about how your background and future direction correspond with what the school has to offer, and to discuss them in a way that lets your personality come through. Yes, you will answer different questions for each school, but admissions officers inevitably want to get to know what makes you tick, and they do it through the questions that they ask.

In essays, admissions officers most want to hear about actions that you have taken to solve a real problem or reach an actual goal, not what you would do in a hypothetical situation. They also want to hear what you learned from your experiences. Be as specific as possible in describing what you have accomplished and what you have learned in the process.

The same goes for recommendations. Almost everyone finds someone to write a positive recommendation for them, but a truly great recommendation will support your positioning by providing specific examples of how you demonstrated leadership, succeeded as part of a team, and so on. We can't emphasize this enough: *Be as specific as possible*! Doing so will help make it easier for an admissions officer to picture you making a positive impact at your target school and beyond.

Before you put together your applications, you should know exactly what you want them to communicate. Chapter 6 will help you build your game plan, which will bring out the messages that you want to convey to each of your target schools.

Selecting Your Schools

As important as it is to establish proper fit in your applications, you must first select the schools to which you will apply. The game is reversed, as you must decide which schools fit you rather than having the schools decide that you fit them.

Selecting schools should be an introspective process. You should be warned, however, that people who don't even know your name will have an opinion on where you should apply. Also remember that school rankings are just one piece of information to consider. Certainly rankings can be helpful tools in getting familiar with the schools' perceived strengths and weaknesses. Still, it's important that you do your own research. After all, no magazine or newspaper knows what really matters most to you.

Do not be enticed by prestige alone. Though it certainly may be a factor in making your selections, there are plenty of other criteria that should be considered. Some of the selection criteria that you may want to use in evaluating schools include:

- Curriculum emphases.
- Typical career paths of graduates.
- Teaching style.
- Student culture.
- Compensation upon graduation.
- Financial aid opportunities.
- International perspective and access.
- Geographical location.
- Facilities.
- Diversity.
- Cost of tuition and living.
- Class size.
- Use of technology.

Fortunately, there is an abundance of resources available to help you evaluate these criteria. Some of the steps you should undertake are:

- Visit business school Websites.
- Review curriculum information.
- Speak with current students and alumni.
- Speak with faculty.
- Attend business school forums.
- Visit the schools and sit in on classes.

We will discuss some of these resources and criteria in more detail later. We will also assist you in your evaluation of programs. Chapter 5 takes a look at the business school selection process and provides an overview of 35 top global business schools, with perspectives on how to gain admittance to them. Finally, we've compiled a list of frequently asked questions (FAQs), which you will find at the end of most chapters. These are questions that we've heard a number of applicants ask. The FAQs have been placed in different chapters depending on their topics.

The Business School Decision

The decision to apply to business school is likely to be one of the most important decisions you'll make in your career. For full-time students, the investment will likely be in excess of $150,000 before you even take opportunity costs (the salary you would have earned during those two years) into consideration. And with more than 70 percent of MBAs having to take out loans to pay for at least a portion of their education, it's clear that you shouldn't just wake up one morning and decide that you want to go to business school.

Interestingly, that seems to be exactly the way some business school applicants arrived at their decision. Others (read: investment bankers and consultants) scheduled "apply to business school" in their Outlook calendars four years ago as if it's as routine as scheduling a haircut. Regardless of how you arrived at this decision, you should really spend some time thinking about what you want to get out of the business school experience.

The bottom line is that you absolutely have to be passionate about attending business school before making the decision to apply. Sure, the thought of going $150,000 into debt is intimidating, but there are plenty of ways in which you can balance the costs of business school, including a large salary at the end of the rainbow. Perhaps the more daunting factor is the admissions process itself. Indeed, you must be passionate about earning an MBA, because the application process will deter anyone who isn't dedicated to getting in. Certainly, this book will help you with every step in that process, but we can't do much to instill the dedication that it takes to get in. That part is up to you.

Thankfully, business schools come in all sorts of shapes, sizes, and colors, so you should be able to select an MBA program that fits your needs. Here are some of your options:

▷ **Full-time:** As the title would suggest, full-time programs are the most involved option. Most MBA programs in the United States run for two years (although some one-year programs do exist), and require students to leave their professional positions. Many programs outside of the United States offer one-year programs, which are beginning to appeal to more and more students, given the reduced costs. Students like the full-time option, because it gives them full exposure to the business school experience. Certainly the opportunity costs are higher than with most other options, but the experience is richer, because of the amount of time spent with classmates, faculty, and speakers. Generally, full-time programs are seen as a good option for people who are considering some type of career transition, be it a new industry, function, or position. One of the benefits of full-time programs that allows this transition to occur is the summer internship. There is often heated debate over whether there is actually any financial benefit to attending a full-time program. Although there is no clear answer, our personal experiences have shown that in addition to making a career transition, there are great intangible benefits to being surrounded by intelligent, motivated people for two years. This book's focus, in terms of providing application strategy advice, will be on full-time programs. The application processes for part-time and distance-learning programs, however, are very similar. You can still benefit from the advice in this book should you decide not to apply to a full-time program.

▷ **Part-time:** If you are satisfied with your current career path and can't fathom the thought of breaking away from the workforce for one or two years, a part-time program might be what you're looking for. Part-time students generally follow the same curriculum as their full-time counterparts, but take all of their classes during the evenings and on weekends. Most part-time students take three to five years to finish their degrees. Many part-timers report that the class load combined with their normal work load can be intense at times, but they are happy not to have to take on the extra debt load or forgo their regular income.

▷ **Distance-learning:** These programs quickly rose in popularity as people became more comfortable with taking classes online. Typically, students will download course material and assignments from the business school Website and have access to faculty via the Internet. In some cases, students will occasionally meet in the classroom to discuss course material. Distance-learning programs are normally one to three years in length and feature curricula similar to that of full-time programs. The benefits are that you can continue your career in a location that isn't within close proximity of the program in which you're enrolled. More and more business schools recognize the value of this option, and more programs are offering online learning options every year. Be aware that a large trade-off you make in choosing a distance-learning program is that you will miss out on the opportunity to be surrounded by exceptional peers from all walks of life. If you are comfortable with this trade-off and are mostly interested in the hard skills that an MBA can deliver (especially if you want to move ahead in your current job, rather than find a new job), then a distance-learning option may be right for you. Just be aware that most online-only MBA programs don't carry anywhere near the cachet that their traditional counterparts do.

▷ **Executive MBA:** Executive MBA (EMBA) programs are similar to part-time programs in that they normally appeal to professionals who are further along in their careers than typical full-time applicants, and allow them to keep working full-time while earning their degrees. EMBA programs also sometimes resemble distance-learning programs in that they can give students multiple, flexible options for study. The main difference is that EMBA students are typically even further along in their careers than are students in the other program types. Also, the vast majority of EMBA students are sponsored by their companies. EMBA programs generally follow similar curricula as full-time programs and can take anywhere from two to five years to complete.

▷ **Other executive programs:** For those who are further along in their careers and have specific aspects of business they would like to learn more about, executive education programs might be the way to go. Executive education programs generally run for one or two weeks and provide established executives with the opportunity to improve their competency in one of a variety of business topics from mergers and acquisitions to leading change in an organization to supply chain management. Their short length allows executives to rapidly get educated in an area without infringing upon their work schedule. These programs are also a nice way to get up to speed on a business topic without enduring lectures on topics with which you are already familiar. Executive programs are, however, notoriously expensive. You can expect one these programs to set you or your company back anywhere from $3,000 to $35,000. Additionally, you won't receive any type of degree for your participation. At best, you can hope to receive some type of certification. Still, you will enjoy a fairly simple application process. Most applications request information on your professional background only (no GMAT, no essays, no interview, no recommendations, and so on) and can be accessed directly from business schools' Websites. Overall, executive education programs are much more interested in your ability to pay than your qualifications. So, if you're reading this book in order to develop a strategy to get into an executive education program, you can stop right now.

▷ **PhD:** If you are enamored at the thought of teaching business concepts, then you should consider going the PhD route. Business schools are always looking for fresh talent, knowing that faculty strength is a major differentiating factor in the eyes of applicants. PhD programs generally take four to five years to complete and, in many cases, require you to take some MBA coursework before specializing. Although you will be in school much longer than with a full-time MBA program, you will receive considerably more financial assistance. You should know, however, that PhD programs can be extremely difficult to gain admittance to, even more so than their MBA counterparts. Many PhD programs at top schools only take a handful of students per specialty each year. Additionally, landing your dream faculty position can be much more challenging than landing your dream business job because faculty spots at top schools are always limited.

Beyond thinking about what type of program you want to attend, you should also consider whether you want to apply for a dual degree program or a specialty program. Dual degree programs give you a chance to earn an MBA degree and another advanced degree in less time than it would take to complete both degrees separately. Unfortunately, there are rarely two-for-one deals on the price of pursuing a dual degree, but you may qualify for additional financial assistance. Some of the most popular degrees to combine with an MBA include:

> ▣ Law.
> ▣ Public policy.
> ▣ Education.
> ▣ International studies.
> ▣ Engineering.
> ▣ Medicine.
> ▣ Health administration.

If you decide to pursue a dual degree, you should make sure that you understand how the extra degree will be beneficial. Be wary of pursuing a dual degree merely for the prestige of getting additional letters after your name. In fact, some companies might be slow to consider you during recruiting, because of the fear that they'd have to compensate you more for both degrees, or the expectation that you're more likely to jump ship and chase other opportunities within a couple of years of being hired.

Also, know that a dual degree may actually provide you with less flexibility. If, for instance, you get a dual degree in business and medicine, then firms outside of healthcare will immediately ask why you're interested in them, given your background. With that said, if you have a firm understanding of how the additional degree fits in with your career goals, are willing to pay the extra tuition, and don't mind spending the additional time, then a dual degree may be worth pursuing. As you get older, start a family, and so forth, it will only get harder to step away from the workforce to gain yet another advanced degree. So, you may as well do it now if you're certain that's what you want.

Apart from dual degree programs, several schools offer specialization programs within their core business school curricula. These programs generally require you to take a few required MBA courses before following the specialization component of the curriculum. Examples of specialization programs include:

- Financial engineering.
- Systems engineering.
- Accounting.
- Healthcare.
- Manufacturing management.

Specialization programs are nice from the standpoint that they signal your dedication to a particular field. Recruiters from those areas tend to like that level of dedication, so if you're comfortable aligning yourself with a particular industry or function, you should consider specializing. Naturally, the flip side is that you are narrowing your business focus rather than broadening it. Also, specialization programs can sometimes be more difficult to gain acceptance to than their general management counterparts. Nonetheless, participants in these programs who have a clear career direction consistently speak highly about their experiences.

So there you have it: a whole world of opportunity from which you can select. It is of course a big decision to make. But once you make the decision to apply, we'll be with you the rest of the way.

FAQs

How specific should I be in discussing my career goals?

Simply espousing generalities with regard to your career goals will not win you the gold. Although you don't have to state what exact job title you expect to hold in five years, it is important that you convey a career direction in your application. Establishing a direction shows that you know what you want to get out of business school and aren't simply trying to boost your salary. As a general rule, you should be as specific as you feel comfortable discussing. In other words, don't discuss a career path in your application that you can't speak intelligently about. Overall, your career goals should make sense in the context of your application story and should be compelling, answering the question of why you want an MBA to pursue that career path. You should also be able to discuss how your career goals will have an impact on an industry, individuals, or society in general.

animation
mngment

What if I'm not sure what my career goals are?

Use the application preparation process to gain a better understanding of your talents and ambitions. Talk to your friends and family about what they see you doing and match that with your background. Refine your ideas as you investigate business school curricula until your application story takes shape. Odds are that by the end of the business school application process you will have a much clearer picture of what your career goals are. You just don't want the admissions committee to view you as an aimless vagabond. This is particularly true if you come from a less business-oriented background, in which case having a concrete story for why you need an MBA is even more critical than for a typical applicant.

If I apply to business school saying I want to pursue one career, but then pursue something else once I'm in, will that matter?

No one will care! Though MBA admissions officers do want to see a great deal of introspection and professional maturity in your application, they also know that you're still only a few to several years into a career that will last for decades. Whether or not it feels like it, you're still a mere pup in the grand scheme of things. Part of the value of attending business school—especially a two-year, full-time program—is the ability to explore new ideas and possible career paths. If you start out thinking you want to go into healthcare marketing and end up being a management consultant, that's completely fine. We're mainly concerned with discouraging you from saying you want to pursue a path in something such as social entrepreneurship simply because you think that's what admissions officers want to hear. Speak the truth when you apply, but know that, if you're admitted, you've also earned the right to shop around and consider as many career options as you please.

The Four Dimensions *of a* Perfect Applicant

Becoming the perfect business school candidate is as much an exercise in understanding and cultivating your relative strengths as it is in identifying and addressing your relative weaknesses. We all have strengths. The main challenge is to reveal your strengths in your applications and convince admissions officers that those strengths aren't outweighed by your weaknesses.

For every Superman there is a kryptonite. For every applicant there is a weakness. That's okay! This is the first reality that must be understood as you develop your position and become the "perfect applicant." Remember: A 780 on the GMAT does not blind admissions officers to generic career goals any more than a great stereo system makes up for a car that's missing an engine. To avoid this type of imbalance, you must express all four dimensions that every business school looks for:

1. Leadership	2. Innovation
3. Teamwork	4. Maturity

Leadership

Probably more than anything else, business schools want to be known as institutions that produce leaders in their fields. Admissions committees are therefore in search of applicants who display leadership ability in all facets of their lives. This doesn't mean that you need to have served as a captain in the Army or have started three new nonprofit organizations. Candidates who successfully demonstrate leadership in their applications exhibit how they have provided others with direction, shown initiative, and managed difficult situations in their professional, personal, and academic careers. And, above all, they need to show how they have made a positive impact on the organization and community around them.

It is not enough to merely state that you are a leader; you must provide examples of demonstrated leadership. Ultimately, the admissions committee should identify you as a high potential leader because of supporting details rather than overt statements. A good rule of thumb is "Show, don't tell."

Innovation

Innovation is a combination of traditional intellectual ability and creativity. Naturally, the former is reflected in the "hard" statistics such as your GMAT score and grade point average, but admissions committee members also look for the latter. Applicants who are visionaries are generally successful in establishing the trait of innovation. Innovation, in this case, can be as simple as finding a new solution to an everyday business problem. Past behavior is a terrific predictor of one's future behavior in similar settings, and admissions officers look for applicants they can envision doing bold, new things down the road. Stories that demonstrate this sort of professional creativity will help your cause here.

Teamwork

The success that Kellogg has had with integrating teamwork throughout its curriculum has spread through time to the other top business schools. Kellogg's success with a team-oriented curriculum has been supported by the way in which most companies now operate. Because companies utilize teams for virtually all of their functions, business schools are in search of applicants with strong team skills. A team-oriented attitude is now a baseline expectation of every applicant. This includes basic social skills and a willingness to share successes and take accountability for failures. Though top business schools are certainly known for being competitive environments, operating in teams has become an integral part of conducting business, and as such is a key aspect of the business school experience.

Maturity

Work experience has become a vital part of candidates' applications. On average, admitted applicants to the top business schools have almost five years of full-time work experience. Although some top programs have made a deliberate effort to admit more people right out of college during the past several years (most notably Harvard Business School, with its HBS 2+2 Program), this remains the exception and not the rule. More important than the length of one's work experience, however, is the quality and depth of that experience.

Top business schools are in search of candidates with multilayered experiences inside and outside of the workplace. An important aspect of the business school experience is that students teach one another based on their backgrounds. It is often said that everyone at business school, including faculty, is both a teacher and a student. Admissions committees therefore try to identify "mature" candidates who display professional maturity and integrity throughout their applications.

As an applicant, your goal should be to weave each of these dimensions throughout all of the application components. In general, application components consist of:

- Data sheets.
- Essays.
- Recommendations.
- Resume.
- Transcript.
- Interview.

In Chapter 4, we will step through each of these components in detail and show ways in which successful applicants have expressed the four dimensions.

To help you gauge how well your profile supports these dimensions, you should take an inventory of your activities and achievements. This will allow you to identify your strengths and weaknesses and address them accordingly.

Activities and achievements that typically support the four dimensions include the following:

Community Service

Through time, community service has evolved from a nice-to-have to a must-have on the application. During feedback sessions with rejected applicants, admissions committee members frequently mention that they wish they had seen more in the way of community involvement. It should be stressed, however, that this is a quality (not quantity) activity. You shouldn't merely write down every humanitarian act that you've ever performed. Nor should you try to join half a dozen community service organizations six months before applying to desperately demonstrate that you have a heart. Rather, it is important to show that you have aspirations of helping society as a whole and not just your personal bank account. Your goal should be to demonstrate deep impact through a few activities, not broad impact across many. Community service is a great way to express all four of the dimensions that you will need to demonstrate in your application, but it can especially be powerful in communicating maturity and leadership abilities.

GMAT Score

Although your GMAT score alone will never get you into a business school, it certainly can keep you out. As a general rule, if your score falls below a school's middle-80-percent range of scores, you will have to overcome long odds in order to be considered a contender. On the flip side, a GMAT score close to a school's mean indicates that you have the intellectual horsepower to excel in the business school classroom. Naturally, achieving a strong score on the GMAT gives you points in the innovation department. To avoid having to overcome a low score, you should review our section on the GMAT in Chapter 4. In that chapter we also answer the question of whether you should take the GMAT or the GRE, which many top MBA progams also now accept.

Hobbies and Extracurricular Activities

Any hobby that can support one of the dimensions or give the admissions committee insight into your personality is worth mentioning. At the end of the day, business schools are looking to admit people, not numbers, and discussing hobbies is a great way to differentiate yourself from the competition. These activities can also display your strengths in areas such as teamwork and innovation. As such, it isn't really important what the hobby is, but rather what the hobby says about you as an applicant. Do you like fly fishing? Great. Now tell the admissions committee why. Your target business schools are more interested in the reason than you might realize.

International and Cultural Exposure

As the trend of globalization continues and the world gets smaller, business schools want applicants who will have global impact. Use every part of the application as a platform to highlight your foreign language skills, multi-national experiences, and cultural awareness. Examples of this can be as grandiose as leading a business unit through a global merger across three continents, or as simple as working with a group of individuals with diverse professional and educational backgrounds. In general, including international or cultural experiences displays a willingness to operate outside of your comfort zone. In this way, it will help you to support the maturity and teamwork dimensions.

Professional Experience

For most applicants, professional experience will be the primary driver of the application. It is what admissions officers care about most of all (what better way to judge how successful you will be 20 years from now?), and it will permeate your essays, recommendations, interviews, and resumes. Because it has such wide-ranging usage, it should be utilized to support all four dimensions.

Undergraduate and Graduate Transcripts

Although your undergraduate and graduate transcripts can't be altered, you can emphasize different aspects of them to support your position. Perhaps you took myriad courses outside of your major during undergrad. You could use that multi-discipline approach to support your desire to attend a business school that focuses on general management. Naturally, a high grade point average (GPA) helps to support the innovation dimension and indicates your ability to succeed in a rigorous academic environment. A low GPA can be overcome, to a point, with a terrific GMAT score and successful post-college coursework.

Analyzing Your Strengths and Weaknesses

Odds are, you have some notable strengths that will make you a solid student and worthy contributor in business school, but you also have some weaknesses that might keep you out of your ideal school if they go unaddressed. That puts you in a pool that includes probably 99 percent of all business school applicants. This section will show you how to systematically identify and capitalize on your strengths while rooting out and neutralizing your weaknesses.

The Grid

Surprisingly, many applicants don't spend any time analyzing or even just writing down their strengths and weaknesses. This might seem like a trivial task—especially because you know yourself better than anyone—but remember that your goal is to sell yourself to someone whose only contact with you is through your application and possibly a 30-minute interview. Therefore, you need to organize your thoughts and make sure that you know exactly what traits you will emphasize for the admissions committee.

It helps to start by drawing out the four dimensions and activity/achievement categories in a grid, like the one here:

Activities/Achievements	Characteristics			
	Leadership	Innovation	Teamwork	Maturity
Community Service				
GMAT Score				
Hobbies and Extracurricular Activities				
International/Cultural Exposure				
Professional Experience				
Transcript(s)				

Figure 2.1

Next, list your activities and achievements, according to the categories, that bring out one or more of the dimensions. This process shouldn't happen in one 10-minute session. Rather, it will likely take a few minutes here and there as other activities and achievements come to mind. Ideally you can give yourself days or even weeks to make this happen. Some things to think about when you are looking into your past are:

- ◲ In what extracurricular activities did you participate while in college? For what did you volunteer? To what positions were you elected?

- ◲ How have you gotten involved in your community since graduating from college? What have you enjoyed about these experiences? What have you learned that you didn't learn in school or on the job?

- ◲ What do you like to do in your spare time? What do you enjoy about each of these things? How have they helped you gain a new perspective or exercise your creative side?

- ◲ Where have you traveled? What languages do you know? What have you learned from your friends of different backgrounds?

- ◲ What have you done on the job that might exhibit one or more of the four desired dimensions? Did you lead a team, identify a problem and find a creative solution, deal with a problematic coworker, and achieve a goal that no one thought was possible?

- ◲ What about your undergraduate academic experience might stand out? Did you study abroad or develop your own independent study? Did you dedicate yourself to one academic field, or did you pursue multiple interests? What awards did you receive?

Start by being fairly generous with yourself. Put everything that comes to mind in the grid. You can pare down the overlaps and the weaker examples later. Also, you may have participated in some activities that don't fit neatly into any of the previously mentioned categories. As long as they help bring out one of the four main dimensions that you want to demonstrate, include them. You can create a catch-all "other" category if needed.

When you are done, your grid may look like an expanded version of this:

Activities/Achievements	Characteristics			
	Leadership	Innovation	Teamwork	Maturity
Community Service				
Volunteer at a local soup kitchen				X
Founded a student group that assists the elderly	X	X		X
GMAT Score				
High quantitative score		X		
Hobbies and Extracurricular Activities				
Writing		X		X
Photography		X		X
Play keyboard for a small jazz band	X	X	X	X
International/Cultural Exposure				
Conversant in Spanish				X
Participant on a global project team			X	X
Professional Experience				
Developed a strategic plan to enter a new market	X	X		
Led a team in implementing a new technology	X		X	
Led internal training for new hires	X			X
Transcript(s)				
Difficult course load in quantitative areas		X		
Graduated with honors		X		

Figure 2.2

Note that you will likely have more Xs in some categories than in others. That's perfectly fine. The idea is not to have a completely full grid, but rather to use the grid as a tool for visualizing what your strengths and weaknesses are. Hopefully, your activities and achievements will complement each other and help fill in each column of the table to some degree, but don't worry if this doesn't happen when you first fill it out.

Also note that some activities may only demonstrate one dimension while others may demonstrate three or four of them. That doesn't mean that the former is less valuable than the latter. Keep in mind that the most important thing is to adequately demonstrate all four desired dimensions. An activity that provides your only strong example of leadership may end up being the most important piece of your application story, rather than an example that shows that you demonstrated all four dimensions moderately well.

After you are confident that you have covered everything in your background that is relevant to your application, start to trim the list if needed. If you have 10 examples that demonstrate teamwork, try to evaluate them through an admissions officer's eyes and rank them from most important to least important. The question you should ask yourself in order to rank them should be: "How effectively does this achievement or activity demonstrate what I am trying to show?" It's tempting to include glamorous examples over more common ones, but being one small part of a CEO's task force on cost-cutting may do less to show off your traits than having led the solution of a tough problem within your own department.

Also look for activities and achievements that overlap. If you have done four things that all demonstrate leadership and maturity, you won't need to mention all four of them in your application. Just one or two will do.

What to Do About Your Weaknesses

In the event that you look at one row or column of your grid and see a lot of white space, don't panic! Most applicants will encounter this challenge. Remember that the table isn't the end, but rather it is the means for identifying what you might need to work on while you build your application.

Following are some areas where applicants typically have some holes in their grids, and some ideas for bolstering your position in each.

Community Service

Not everyone has done a lot of community service, and it can be tempting to want to volunteer for five nonprofit organizations in the months leading up to your application deadline. Admissions committees can see right through this, however, so don't waste your time in a last-ditch attempt to look "involved."

If you simply do not have any community service activities to point to, look for other activities in your background that will demonstrate similar characteristics. Starting a volleyball club at the local gym won't solve world hunger, but it still shows that you like to get involved and can motivate others to do the same. If you find that your application still lacks the altruistic angle that a community service activity might demonstrate, then be sure to bring out your human side in other ways, such as more subtle examples of how you helped a family member or some-one on the job solve a problem. The bottom line is that you want to show that you like to get involved in the community around you, and that you are more than a GMAT score and fancy resume.

If you still have time before you begin the application process, be on the lookout for community service opportunities. Mentoring programs such as Big Brothers Big

Sisters are great ways to show your willingness to give back to the community. Just remember that the key is to make a strong impact in one or two areas, not to simply sign up for half a dozen activities. That single word—*impact*—should be your guiding light. Activities that give you the opportunity to say "That would not have happened if I hadn't been there" are the most powerful examples of all.

Another way to think of community service is as a powerful way to complement your work experience. If you haven't had many opportunities to lead a team at work, for example, then showing how you did so as part of a volunteer organization is a great way to demonstrate leadership abilities. MBA admissions officers know that most applicants are young and may still have somewhat limited work experience, so they're adept at scouring your entire background for evidence of high potential. This doesn't only apply to leadership examples; community involvement, though most often associated with leadership and a desire to make the world better, can give you opportunities to demonstrate all four of the key applicant dimensions.

GMAT Score

The good news about the GMAT (or GRE, for those schools that accept it) is that it is one of the few achievements that you can work on and improve in a short amount of time (compared to community service or an undergraduate transcript from five years ago). The bad news is that some applicants can spend months studying for it and still fall short of their goal. If your GMAT score makes you look weak in the quantitative or verbal departments, be sure to bring out other examples in your application that will counterbalance these weaknesses.

If your quantitative score is low, highlight any tough analytical courses that you took as an undergrad. Or show how you use your quantitative skills to unravel tough problems on the job, or even as part of a volunteer opportunity in which you participated. Remember that demonstrating an analytical skill set doesn't have to mean showing that you know calculus. There are practical, everyday activities that can help you demonstrate your ability to break down a problem or your comfort with using numbers to make decisions. The bottom line is that you just need to show that you won't be helpless two weeks into your first-year finance course.

If your verbal score is low, then you will need to work extra hard to highlight your communication skills. You can do this through your essays and your interviews. Keep in mind that admissions officers will be suspicious of someone with poorly written Analytical Writing Assessment (AWA) essays on the GMAT, but terrific application essays; that kind of application is often covered with fingerprints from a professional editor or admissions consultant. Remember that getting some help is okay, but the application you submit must be your own work.

You can also enlist support from your recommenders to address weaknesses in both the quantitative and/or verbal section. They may be able to provide examples that offset some of the concerns that your GMAT score raises. If your undergraduate transcript and your job don't help, consider enrolling in a statistics, finance, public speaking, or accounting course in a local community college. This shows a dedication to education and will impress the admissions committees. Many business schools are happy to suggest what kinds of courses they would consider as useful preparation for their programs.

Hobbies and Extracurricular Activities

This is usually the part of the application that gives applicants the least amount of trouble, as most of us have enough interests to keep us busy outside of school or work. Look at how your hobbies relate to your other activities, and they hopefully will provide a well-rounded picture of you as a person. If you already have the four desired dimensions covered reasonably well by your other activities and achievements, then use your hobbies as a way to provide a little extra depth and color to your application. Even seemingly silly or frivolous hobbies and interests can help in this way. If your hobbies truly don't add anything new, then de-emphasize them and let the other parts of your application stand on their own.

International and Cultural Exposure

For many people, this is a clear-cut, have-or-don't-have issue. If you haven't worked, studied, or traveled abroad, don't despair. Business schools like to see experience in this area, but realize that not everyone has had a chance to see the world. If this is the case for you, be sure to emphasize the success that you have had in working with people of various backgrounds or even different points of view from your own. Even two people from the same school who work for the same company have a lot of differences between them. Show how you have overcome these differences to build success, and, even more importantly, demonstrate that you value these opportunities to grow and push yourself outside of your normal comfort zone. The more easily admissions officers can envision you successfully working on a study team with four other people from four different countries, the better your chances will be. *Try working in HK/Taiwan. (intern)*

Professional Experience

People who worry about their professional experience are usually concerned with either the quality or quantity of the work that they have done. If you are worried about the amount of work experience that you have, take comfort in the fact that many business schools are actually pursuing younger applicants. They will still be interested in you as long as you have demonstrated success on the job, increasing responsibility in your assignments, and a true understanding of what an MBA can do for you. [If you are still an undergrad and are looking to go right into business school, your best chances of demonstrating leadership and maturity will be in your extracurricular activities and anything else where you took charge and made something happen outside of the classroom.]

Ultimately, though no applicant wants to hear "Wait till next year," the quantity problem can be solved by simply waiting another year or two before you apply. Or, if you apply and are rejected, you can apply again after gaining a couple of years' worth of terrific new experiences.

On the flip side, particularly as some top schools take an interest in younger applicants, there is such a thing as too much work experience. There's no cut-off in terms of years of experience, and every school will take great pains to point out that a couple of students in its entering class are pushing 40 years of age, but anyone with more than seven or eight years of work experience will invite questions along the lines of "Why are you only applying now? What took you so long to discover that this is what you want to do next in your career?" No school will judge you based solely on your age, but if you strike admissions officers as someone who's applying now just because his or her career is stagnating, then your chances of success will be low. Or, the school may decide that a part-time or executive MBA is ultimately a better fit for you.

Quality issues around work experience can be tough, but these can be overcome, at least in part, with your other application components. Do you feel as though your career is starting to plateau? Think about why this has happened and how an MBA will help you address the issue. Maybe your career progress has slowed because you lack important managerial skills that an MBA will give you. The important thing, in this case, is to demonstrate that your lack of upward mobility does not correspond to a lack of ambition or aptitude for success.

Does your work not seem interesting or exciting enough? Don't worry too much about this issue, as business schools love people from a variety of backgrounds. Being a foreman at a corrugated box factory may seem dull to you, but if you can highlight what you have learned about business on the job—and what you still have to learn—then you can make a strong case for yourself.

Some applicants have holes in their work records, as they took sabbaticals to travel, to care for a sick loved one, or to simply try new things. As long as you have a legitimate reason for such a hole and can convince the admissions committee that you are indeed ambitious and committed to studying business, they will appreciate the unique perspectives that these experiences will give you. It is always better to hit these holes head-on than to try to hide them and hope admissions officers don't notice them.

Undergraduate and Graduate Transcripts

If your transcript shows weakness, don't worry. Not all "weak" transcripts are equally bad, and there are some things you can do to help yourself.

A Stanford admissions officer once said about transcripts, "We're forgiving of slow starts, but not as forgiving of slow finishes." Most business schools have the same attitude. If you got off to a rough start your freshman year but showed steady improvement while in college, then you are probably in good shape. Admissions officers aren't itching to reject you because of a bad choice you made while you were still a teenager. They like to see that you got more serious about your work and were able to turn the academic tide.

If you were consistently poor or did worse as time went on, however, your challenge will be to convince the admissions committee that you're serious about academics and have the brainpower to succeed in business school. The former can be accomplished in your essays, where you will discuss what it is that you expect to get out of an MBA curriculum. The latter can be made up for by the GMAT or, if that is also weak, by earning strong grades in part-time courses at a local school.

Your transcript(s) may also be weak because you were simply too involved in extracurricular activities as an undergrad. Use this opportunity to turn a weakness into a strength by demonstrating your commitment and initiative at your undergraduate school, and making the case for why you will be equally involved in business school. You must balance that out, however, with a demonstrated understanding of the importance of academics in business school. In other words, you should try and convince the admissions counselors that you will get the school/activities mix right this time around.

Final Word on Strengths and Weaknesses

In general, a winning application strategy counteracts your perceived weaknesses with examples that show your strengths in those same (or similar) areas. The more that each part of your application can naturally complement and support the other pieces, the better off you will be. Some applicants will use the extra essay—which many schools provide as an option in their applications—to directly address a weakness such as a low GMAT score or undergraduate GPA. This is fine, but think of it as a last resort. One risk of devoting an entire essay to a weakness is that it highlights the very issue that you're trying to neutralize. There are times when the extra essay does help, however, and we will discuss these types of situations more in Chapter 4.

A Conversation With Soojin Kwon Koh

Soojin Kwon Koh is the Director of Admissions and Financial Aid at the University of Michigan Ross School of Business. Consistently ranked as one of the top-10 business schools in the United States, Ross is often acknowledged for its innovative curriculum and for turning out some of the most sought after business school graduates in the world. We checked in with Soojin to get her perspectives on the application process and advice on what applicants can do to improve their chances of gaining acceptance to the top business schools.

What's your take on the GMAT? Why is it important?

In general the application review process is all about adding dimension to what is an inherently two-dimensional evaluation. The GMAT is one of the primary factors we use to predict an applicant's propensity to perform well in the academic program. I don't think that it's necessarily a good predictor of how well an applicant will do in the career of her choosing, but in addition to the GPA, it does help to quantify intellectual capacity. It also allows many applicants to make up for less-than-stellar GPAs. Lastly, as a standardized measure, it puts applicants on similar footing, whereas GPAs come with a certain amount of bias depending on the undergraduate curriculum.

For applicants who have a relatively low GMAT, what do they have to do to at least be considered?

Strong work experience and undergraduate GPA help. Strong essays really make a difference. We also take a close look at the applicant's career goals and reasons for wanting to pursue an MBA. Does the applicant have clear reasons for wanting to get an MBA? Does she have a clear thought process? Has she demonstrated passion for pursuing an MBA at Ross? These three attributes can help put an applicant into the running. It does make the process a bit easier though when the applicant at least scores within the range of traditionally accepted applicants.

What does it mean to evaluate an applicant for fit?

Every school probably evaluates fit a little differently. We're looking to confirm that who the applicant is and aspires to be fits well with the Ross mission. In addition to having the appropriate level of intellectual capability, the applicant must exhibit attributes that are consistent with our culture, which is team-oriented and collaborative. If you're a person who prefers to work and excel on your own or generally just don't perform well in teams, then it's a major red flag for us. We also look for passion. That is a real desire to go out and make a difference. It's most impressive when an applicant communicates that she has the skills and motivation to pursue her dreams and she truly understands how Ross fits into that picture. So, it's important that the applicant truly understand what a school is all about and evaluate what role she might play in supporting that school's mission.

Would you encourage applicants to reach out to and spend time with current students so that they can get a better sense of a school's culture?

Absolutely. Students are the best reflection of what it's like to go to school here. Getting students' perspectives on the school's culture can definitely give applicants a good idea of what day-to-day life is like.

How do you evaluate recommendations? Aren't all recommendations glowing?

In recommendations we're looking to see whether the applicant truly is who she claims to be. We're looking for consistency. One thing we stress is for recommenders to provide specific examples. It's not enough for recommenders to simply say that an applicant performs at a high level. We want to know exactly what the applicant has done to merit such high praise. Anecdotes, tangible results, and specifics go a long way. It also helps to see how the applicant really goes above and beyond. It shows that the applicant is passionate about her work and is inclined to contribute a great deal in the future.

You would be surprised how many poor recommendations we receive. Some recommendations have maybe five lines and answer each question with one sentence. Obviously this type of recommendation does not send a positive signal with respect to the applicant's candidacy. Some recommendations might look positive at initial glance, but a closer read reveals veiled criticisms. It's interesting to me that that the applicant would not have picked up on the nature of the relationship before requesting a recommendation. That, in and of itself, is a signal.

How then would you recommend that applicants manage their recommenders?

We recommend that the applicant sit down with his recommender, explain that he is thinking about going to business school, explain why, and then discuss his intended career track and why. Moreover, the applicant can spend some time talking to the recommender about their working relationship and what he's accomplished through time. There is a fine line, however, as applicants have to be careful not to start coaching their recommenders and providing them with too many specifics. Because we require two recommendations, if both cite the same exact specifics then we question whether the recommenders have been coached on exactly what to say about the applicant.

What is one of the top mistakes that applicants tend to make?

One of the major mistakes is not clearly laying out what the applicant wants to do from a career standpoint and then laying out where the business school fits into the picture. A lot of applicants just apply to business school without taking the appropriate time to reflect on their career goals and on where we fit into the plan. For many, it just feels like the next natural step. Successful applicants tend to be much more reflective and consider the pursuit of an MBA as significant turning point in their lives. We want applicants to treat the application process with that level of significance. So we ask, "Why is an MBA from Ross necessary for this applicant?" We check to see whether the applicant has really researched us or whether she is simply applying to all of the top-ten schools and saying the same thing to all of them. If that's the case then we tend to discount the probability that you will really take advantage of all the different opportunities that we offer here. These opportunities would be wasted on someone who is looking to merely check the MBA off her list, so we tend to avoid box-checkers. We want applicants who are really going to come and embrace everything that is available.

So, what level of specificity is adequate when discussing career goals?

I would say as specific as is honest. We recognize that most students won't go on to do exactly what they discuss in their essays. What we're looking at is the applicant's thought process. We want to get into the applicant's head and heart to understand their motivations and what drives them. If the career goals are well thought out and make sense in the context of what we offer as a school, then the applicant is on the right track. We definitely don't want people to offer up career goals that simply sound good or are trendy. Rather, we want to see that they've spent some time researching their options, have made an initial choice and can defend it as a viable career objective. Certainly the more specifics the applicant can give, the more interesting an essay or discussion will likely result.

How would you recommend that applicants that come from traditional "feeder" industries (for example, consulting and investment banking) differentiate themselves?

In addition to academic and professional track record, we look at extracurricular activities. Extracurriculars such as community service, international experiences, entrepreneurial ventures, or activities related to sustainable development can be great indicators that the applicant would be a good match and we have evidence that the applicant would get involved with activities here on campus. Additionally, it provides us with some comfort that the applicant will be a good Ross alum even after they've graduated.

Are there major mistakes that you see among international applicants?

Oftentimes, we receive a number of applications that are virtually identical in terms of academic and professional experiences to international applicants. While it differs a bit from region to region, it's critical that the international applicant understand that the application process requires so much more than simply a high GMAT score or an impressive resume. At a certain point, you know the applicant is smart, but so are the next 200 applicants from their country, so you have to go beyond that to differentiate yourself. We're trying to achieve diversity here; not just in gender, ethnicity, geographical region and professional background, but also diversity in thinking. The last one is important, because we expect that each student will bring a slightly different perspective to the table. If an applicant sounds like hundreds of others, there isn't much of a reason to bring him in, even if his scores are off the chart. We know that diversity of thought can have a powerful impact on the ability to learn, so we are very careful to evaluate that and it's critical that applicants consider how they're different and what they will bring, as unique individuals, to the table.

What does it take for an undergraduate applicant to be successful?

In all of our applicants, we look for people who can make significant contributions to classroom discussions as well as to team-based assignments. As such, for an undergraduate applicant to obtain admission to Ross, he really needs to have outperformed his peers not only academically, but also in extracurriculars and hopefully also in business. The applicant may have started his own business or played a starring role in significant internships. No matter what it is, the applicant must be capable of significant contributions such that his classmates truly benefit from his presence on campus.

What makes for a great essay?

Great essays are the ones where you can see an applicant behind the words. After reading 500 words, if you feel as though you've really gotten to know the applicant a little bit better, then it's a successful essay. Whether there is heart, humor, or an experience that is different, a good essay is memorable and interesting. It doesn't need to be poetic or overly eloquent, but we do want to know that there's a human with interests and passions behind it.

How important is the interview?

It's another dimension that we use to characterize the applicant. The interview is a great opportunity to assess the enthusiasm of the applicant. It's relatively easy to assess characteristics such as energy level, body language, eye contact, and knowledge about the school. So, it definitely helps give us a sense of fit. It helps us to understand whether this is the kind of person who will work well on a team and think on her feet. But, it's not typically the aspect of the application that makes or breaks a person. We have non-admitted applicants call all the time requesting to re-interview, but it's rare that the interview is the only problem.

Any trends that you've seen among applicants that concern you?

Yes, it appears that there some applicants who are using essay consultants who actually write essays on behalf of applicants. And it's plainly obvious in many cases. With some international applicants, in particular, when you compare the GMAT writing samples to the essays, it's clear that they've crossed the line in terms of having someone else do the writing for them. I've seen essays on par with something that could be found in *The New Yorker* and it's such a red flag. I mean, I don't even think our staff could write as eloquently as some of these essays. We don't expect that essays read like Hemingway's work, but they should be authentic. It's almost refreshing to read essays from an international applicant that are flawed here or there, rather than some of the fake submissions that cross our path. We want to hear from applicants themselves and hear their voices.

Any other parting thoughts?

I'd love to get people to write so that we can really get to know them. When you're reading thousands of applications, it's refreshing to get the ones that come to life in your hands. You think, *wow it would be great to have this person here, because I can see that there is something about them that shows they would make a real contribution here and make great contributions after they leave.*

 FAQs

How important is the strength of your undergraduate/graduate school's brand to the admissions committee?

 Overall, what you did in college and what you've done since then are more important than what school you went to. Still, business schools do take your college's brand name into consideration, especially when considering your grades. Some schools are known to pay more attention to this than others. However, this should not be a major consideration when you apply. For every Princeton and Yale grad prowling the halls of top business schools, there is also a student from a lesser-known school. All schools love to brag about the number of undergraduate institutions that are represented by their classes (the numbers generally range from 80 to 200). You definitely shouldn't spend all of your time trying to sell your school if it is not a well-known one. You should, however, be able to explain why you decided to attend the schools listed on your transcripts and discuss their merits. Beyond that, however, keep the focus on you. At the same time, if you did go to a college with a great reputation, don't rest on your laurels and expect to gain admission based on reputation alone. It's an asset, but one that will quickly fall by the wayside if your other application components are mediocre.

What if I have been laid off from my job?

First of all, don't panic! Getting laid off does not squash your chances of getting into a top business school. There are several things that you need to do. Most importantly, you need to convince the admissions committee that you're not simply applying to business school because you're out of work and have no better option. If admissions officers sense that this is the case, then you *will* have squashed your chances. You can combat this perception by highlighting your career goals and how business school fits into the picture. Also, while you absolutely should not dwell on the fact that you were laid off, acknowledge that it happened and be prepared to explain why (hopefully it's something out of your control), and move on. Admissions officers understand that even great employees sometimes lose their jobs.

Also, you will need to work extra hard to weave professional success stories throughout your application, to make it clear that you are a "winner" who just happened to get caught up in bad circumstances. Recommendations are especially important here, particularly if they come from your ex-boss who regrettably had to let you go. Showing that you were a positive contributor and that you left on good terms will help a great deal. Finally, show that you've been productive in your time off. A Tuck admissions officer once commented that she couldn't believe how some laid-off applicants were content to do nothing for a year. Even things outside of your career such as pro-bono work or volunteering can show that you're not someone who's content to just sit back and take it when life deals you a bad hand.

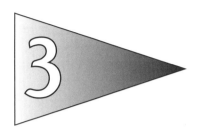

Applicant Profiles

What you communicate in your application will be largely dictated by who you are and where you want to go in your career. However, just as important in the eyes of business school admissions officers is where you have been. If you are an investment banker, for example, they will assume that you have more in common with other banking applicants than with military or nonprofit applicants. This means that, beyond what you tell admissions committees about yourself, they may assume that you have many of the traits (both positive and negative) that a typical banker has. [It is your responsibility to be aware of these commonly held stereotypes and to take advantage of the good ones while overcoming the bad ones.]

Although business schools rarely say so explicitly, it makes sense that your stiffest competition will come from those who are most like you. Schools don't necessarily operate off of hard quotas when admitting applicants with various professional backgrounds, but they can only take so many consultants—or so many accountants, scientists, international applicants, and so on—before their classes start to become homogenous. (So, you will be compared to other applicants with backgrounds similar to yours, and your job will be to stand apart from these other applicants. This is a core part of any winning application game plan.)

This chapter will help you achieve this goal. We will examine 11 of the most common applicant profiles, highlight some perceived strengths and weaknesses *or herself* / */zher-* for each, and discuss ways that an applicant with a given profile can set himself *self* apart from others with the same background. Naturally, much of the advice that applies to one applicant profile may apply to another. Also, there's a good chance that you don't fit explicitly into one of these profiles. For example, many people who studied engineering in college go into management consulting or investment banking. Those applicants may need to think through the pros and cons of more than one profile. Still, getting a sense of how admissions counselors think about various profiles will help you in creating your differentiated position. We recommend using this chapter in conjunction with your strengths/weaknesses analysis from Chapter 2 to develop your application strategy. Above all else, your application needs to reflect who you are. Beyond that, use the material presented here to separate yourself from the pack.

A special note for applicants from other countries, particularly those from Asia: During the past decade, the number of people in Asia (especially India and China) applying to top U.S. business schools has surged dramatically. This speaks volumes with respect to the growth in this part of the world and the important role that it will surely play in the coming decades. But, if you are one of these applicants, this means that the job of standing out from the pack has become much more difficult than it was just five years ago. We have expanded the "International" profile in this third edition of the book to address this important trend and to help applicants who fit this description. If you come from this part of the world, pay special attention to that particular section.

Finally, one of the hottest topics among MBA admissions experts in recent years has been business schools' growing affection for younger applicants. Though many admissions officers will vehemently deny that they're trying to "get younger" or that there's such a thing as an applicant who's "too old," the writing is on the wall at some top business schools. In this third edition of this book, we take a close look at the the root cause of this trend, and we discuss how you can use this to your advantage if you are still in college or you have only been working for one or two years.

1. Consulting

In many ways, consultants are made for business school. (Here we use the term *consultant* to refer not only to management consultants, but also those in other fields where their primary jobs involve project-based work for clients.) As a consultant, you most likely have a strong academic background, have had multiple experiences with myriad companies, and have finely tuned analytical and interpersonal skills. Additionally, you have direct access to a cadre of business school graduates through your firm, who serve as great advisors on the MBA admissions process and the life of a business school student.

Unfortunately, you will go up against thousands of other consultants who also are working hard to get into a top-ranked MBA program. As a result, it can be extremely difficult to differentiate yourself as a consultant. Consulting firms often have standardized analyst programs that "feed" business schools with applicants after they've had two or three years of experience. Through time, many business schools have become somewhat wary of these programs, because of their tendency to produce applicants who are simply looking to "get their ticket punched." They therefore look closely for clues that you really understand what business school is about and that you have good reasons for wanting to be there.

You can avoid the perception that you're just trying to get your ticket punched by being explicit about how you intend to utilize an MBA to reach your career goals. By the way, returning to consulting is certainly a valid career goal. But if you do go down that path, you need to be sure to discuss how you see yourself having an impact on the organization. Do you see an opportunity to increase your clients' revenues by implementing customer relationship management programs? Then discuss how you want to capitalize on this opportunity by studying the intersection of marketing and technology. Want to bring a more global viewpoint to your organization? Then show how international study opportunities at your target school will give you that viewpoint. The bottom line is that you have to provide tangible reasons for wanting to attend business school. In many ways, this is even more important for applicants who want to return to consulting than it is for those who plan on switching careers. Earning an MBA may very well be a logical next step for you, but your reasons for wanting one will need to go deeper than "All of the partners in my firm have an MBA."

One way to ensure that your message comes through clearly is by avoiding consultant jargon into your essays and interviews (and by encouraging your recommendation writers to do the same in the letters they write on your behalf). Many consultants have a tendency to write essays that are high-level and ambiguous. Admissions counselors comment that consultants often fail to adequately explain their specific actions on projects and the results of those actions. To the extent that you can quantify both, you will stand out from the pack. Take a close look at Chapter 4 for additional guidance on how to write and interview effectively.

The average number of years of work experience at top business schools is approximately five, even as some top schools make a push to pursue younger applicants. Consultants, however, tend to apply to schools after only two to four years of experience. If you fall into this group, then you should expect to be questioned about it and should find ways to emphasize your maturity. One way to do that is by discussing activities in which you are involved outside of consulting. Because of the long hours associated with their profession, many applicants from consulting are unable to talk about anything that is unrelated to work. To the extent that you are able to weave activities outside of the consulting world into your story, you will create opportunities for yourself to show off your leadership abilities and maturity. Though you may be tempted to say "I can't do any extracurricular activities because I'm so busy at work," keep in mind that (there are thousands of other consultants who do somehow manage to find the time to make a positive impact in their communities.)

2. Creative (me, sigh, "dumb" people)

If this header describes you, then you are what business schools and their students like to call a "poet." Whether you were previously a teacher, psychologist, musician, writer, chef, artist, or anything else that falls into this category, you bring something to the applicant pool that few others do. The trick will be to appear different enough to be interesting, but not so different that admissions officers will suspect that you can't hack it or fit in with your more business-minded peers.

First of all, don't let anyone tell you that you have no business applying. The fact that you want an MBA makes you qualified to apply. Whether or not you get in is up to the admissions officers who review your application, but the moves they've made in recent years—most notably, accepting the GRE General Test and introducing programs to try to sway more college seniors to consider business school—make it clear that they are very interested in working more creative types into their classes.

When you describe your past experiences, don't simply write or talk about what you did. Go a level deeper and talk about why you have done these things. For instance, a sculptor got into a top business school by describing the satisfaction he got from turning his ideas into something of substance. He then effectively tied it back to business, describing how he wanted to acquire the tools to do the same thing for business ideas. You don't need to be this explicit in tying your background to business (especially if it will end up sounding forced), but try to think in this way as you develop your application game plan. Admissions officers will value you for the unique perspective you can bring to the classroom, but it's up to you to show that you can connect the dots and apply your non-business experiences to business problems.

Most schools look for leadership skills more than anything else, and odds are that you've had a chance to display these skills at some point in your life. The more recent, the better, but don't be afraid to bring up examples of how you uniquely made a difference in a situation when you were younger. Don't worry if the story has nothing to do with business; leadership examples are universal, and your application will be much stronger for it. Your letters of recommendation can be especially helpful here, especially if you can get people with business backgrounds to vouch for your leadership skills and business potential.

Of course, business schools also look for a minimum level of quantitative skills, and this is one place where you won't get the benefit of the doubt. You absolutely must produce a GMAT (or GRE) score within range of your target schools' averages. Your best bet is to practice early and practice often, and give yourself enough time to take the exam more than once if needed. And plan on taking some pre-MBA courses in accounting and statistics before you apply. Doing so will demonstrate a sincere interest in earning an MBA, and answer questions in admissions officers' minds about you possibly applying to school as a dilettante who has nothing better to do. Taking these courses early will allow you to sell them in your application.

3. Engineering and Science

Engineers (here we will broadly use *engineers* to refer to anyone coming from a science, mathematics, or engineering background) typically have strong quantitative skills, and that is one reason why you will find a good number of engineers at any top business school. In fact, at least a third of most top business schools' students come from engineering backgrounds. Being an engineer, however, you will find that you need to sell your interpersonal skills, and prove that you understand the "big picture" when it comes to business.

Few engineers ever fail to make the cut in business school admissions because of their quantitative abilities. Even if you don't have an amazing GMAT score, you should be able to point to your undergraduate degree and recent work experience as evidence of these skills. Even better, you will hopefully be able to demonstrate strong problem-solving skills by virtue of the work you've done. Even if your past experiences seem ho-hum to you, an admissions officer will be interested to hear how you solved an important problem, and why you went about it in the way that you did. A good example can be as mundane as improving the flow rate through a valve by 2 percent, or contributing to a small enhancement in the efficacy of a new drug. Being explicit about the significance of the problem—and which of your skills helped you arrive at the solution—will go a long way toward selling these abilities.

Many business-minded engineers also enjoy the advantage of having a good overall story for why they want to earn an MBA. Whereas a consultant or an investment banker may have to spend a lot of time proving that she isn't just getting her ticket punched for a higher salary, you can craft a strong story about how you've mastered one discipline, and now you want to move on to achieve a broader view of how a business is run. Admissions officers will appreciate any evidence that you can provide that shows you understand the importance of the functions in a company outside of its research and development department.

The stereotype that you will most likely have to overcome is in regard to your interpersonal skills. An admissions committee will look critically for evidence that you can reach goals that require you to work with others. Any teamwork examples that you can provide will help you a great deal here, particularly stories that demonstrate your ability to understand others' motivations and to deal with them constructively. These examples of empathy will go a long way toward showing your ability to grow into the role of a leader.

You can also set yourself apart through extracurricular activities demonstrating your interests outside of the workplace. They can show your desire to actively seek out opportunities to make the world around you better, rather than simply waiting for an engineering problem to be handed to you. Examples of community service, volunteering at your church, or simply pursuing a creative or athletic passion outside of the office will help you distinguish yourself from the other engineers in the crowd.

4. Entrepreneurship

Few applicants can say that they've built their own business, giving entrepreneurs a leg up in the business school admissions process. If you are an entrepreneur, the key will be to drive home the strengths that admissions officers typically associate with people like you, while addressing the questions of why you want a degree now and how well you will fit into the business school culture. Here we use the term *entrepreneur* broadly. As such, our advice can apply to people who have set out to build organizations in a variety of fields, from technology to hospitality to nonprofit.

By definition, entrepreneurs are people who like to strike out on their own and make things happen. It doesn't take much imagination to see how you can spin a story rich in leadership, creativity, and ambition, no matter what your venture was. Whether you built a whole organization or simply created a new business opportunity within an existing company, you should have a lot of material to draw upon. When you discuss these experiences, be sure to not only talk about your accomplishments, but also about how you achieved them. Saying that you led your fledgling team to launch its first prototype on time is impressive, but it's more interesting to hear about how it happened. Stories about how you found the right people with whom to build your team, how you motivated them, how you managed personality conflicts among team members, and how you helped them overcome obstacles will all paint a great portrait of you as a leader.

The most obvious challenge you will face is that you already set out to build a business, and only now are you applying to business school. Admissions officers will undoubtedly ask, "If you thought you could make it on your own two years ago, how come you now feel like you need to sit in a classroom and learn again?" Your reasons will obviously depend on your own situation, but a stronger answer will emphasize your desire to learn and move toward new goals; a weaker one will focus on your desire to get away from the start-up scene.

The flipside of your perceived strengths is that an admissions committee may wonder if you have too much hubris for your own good. We know a successful entrepreneur who didn't get into Kellogg because he couldn't overcome the hubris question. The key is for you to communicate your appreciation for rigorous business training and to spell out exactly what skills you want to attain and why. Admissions officers don't like to see someone who's too much of a maverick to work well with others. You will need to demonstrate your penchant for teamwork, ideally through some of your past actions. *careful!*

So far, we have skirted the issue of whether or not your past ventures have been successful. Of course, it will be much easier to sell yourself if you have a long track record of success to point to, but you can also use failures to your advantage. The challenge will be to make sure that your business school application doesn't look like a "last resort" now that your entrepreneurial efforts haven't panned out. Not every start-up is a success, but ideally you'll have better reasons for wanting an MBA than "Well, my company didn't pan out and I need something to do." By emphasizing that you understand what went wrong and that you are now actively seeking learning opportunities in order to shore up your skills before you make another go at it, you have the potential pull together a unique application story.

5. Government

One of the better-known business school graduates of the previous 20 years—Peter Robinson, author of *Snapshots from Hell: The Making of an MBA*—was a White House speech writer before entering Stanford. In his book, Robinson describes being told that he and his non-business-background classmates were the ones who were added to the class to add some variety. It's to your advantage that you bring this variety to the table as it can help you a great deal if you are able to overcome what the top schools expect your weaknesses to be.

Whether you frequently dined on Air Force One (as one client of ours used to do!) or served as your town's dogcatcher, you can build your application story knowing that most other applicants will have far fewer unique stories to tell. You can start by emphasizing your strong principles and passion for making a difference. Business schools love people who are committed to making an impact wherever they go, and they know that people who have worked in government tend to exhibit this trait. No matter what specific field you worked in, or at what level, be sure that this passion and dedication are a central part of your application story.

You may also have excellent examples that demonstrate your interpersonal skills and communication abilities. To some degree, both will come through on their own in your essays and your interview, but be sure to explicitly sell these abilities at some point. Any examples of past successes where you put these skills to use will only help in winning over admissions officers.

One of the most common weaknesses of applicants coming from the public sector is a lack of quantitative skills. Many government-types have a reputation for being great with words but less so with numbers, and you will need to overcome this stereotype with supporting evidence. If your past jobs included any kind of work with numbers, such as fundraisers, budgeting, or research, then be sure to mention it. You should also show a minimum level of comfort with quantitative problem-solving through the other common tools (GMAT or GRE, undergraduate coursework, and/or pre-MBA courses). Similarly, you will need to answer questions about your business experience, or lack thereof. Admissions officers are often willing to accept a lack of business experience as long as you can communicate an understanding of the value of business training and how it will help you. By communicating both messages, you will be able to help set yourself apart from other government employees. Additionally, you should convey a clear vision for how an MBA will help you and why.

Also, emphasize your desire to innovate and make things happen. Many government applicants will have impressive stories to share about their past experiences, but government is rarely the environment in which someone can take big risks and pursue big opportunities. If you can build a convincing argument for how you want to shake up the status quo and why you need an MBA to do that, you will have an excellent chance of admission's success.

6. International

Obviously, the international applicant (that is, international from the perspective of U.S. schools) profile will overlap with at least one other profile covered in this book. Still, it is invaluable for international applicants to understand how they are viewed by admissions counselors, based on their geographical status alone.

First, we should state that business schools are eager to maintain or, in some cases, increase the percentage of their international students. Business schools and students find that having a large international presence is the best way to expand students' global perspectives. It's an amazing experience to sit in a classroom and hear voices from around the world weigh in on a variety of issues. This alone ensures that business schools will continue to enthusiastically pursue international applicants for the foreseeable future. Still, there remains a gap in access to information on the business school application process in terms of domestic versus international applicants. At a holistic level, our hope is that the third edition of this book contributes to minimizing that gap. At a more tactical level, however, it is important for international applicants to understand the stereotypical strengths and weaknesses with which they are commonly associated.

On the strengths side of the equation, a guaranteed plus is your cultural awareness. Interestingly, this tends to be a latent strength for international applicants on which they don't capitalize enough. As an international applicant, you're used to living in a truly global world and being exposed to various cultures, languages, and belief systems, so you accept this as a norm and don't emphasize these types of experiences as much as you should. Realize that the ability to speak several

or rip them off!

languages or dialects and expound on the social impacts of introducing economic liberalization policies is something most American applicants do not bring to the table. As such, demonstrate to the admissions committee your experiences in multicultural environments in order to show them how adding your voice to the classroom dialogue will appreciably improve the learning model.

Additionally, consider integrating your global perspective into your career goals. Your past experiences will often tie to career goals that extend beyond U.S. boundaries, a level of credibility that most American applicants will not be able to achieve. In terms of the ability to have a global impact, most international applicants have a natural advantage.

In terms of weaknesses, the biggest risk that many applicants face—especially those from India or China these days—is that they fail to stand out from the pack. As mentioned previously, the pool of international applicants is growing much faster than any other applicant group. In order to maintain diversity in the classroom, schools can only take so many applicants of any given type. As an international applicant, what this means is that your chances of getting in get a little tougher each year as the number of international applicants to U.S. schools keeps growing. That makes standing out from the crowd more critical than ever.

What makes many international applicants sound the same? Here are some of the most common things that we've seen:

▷ **Strong GMAT scores and academics, but not much else.** For the past decade, we have talked with countless applicants who have, at first, merely introduced themselves with the name of their university, their class rank, and their GMAT score. When it comes to extracurricular activities, hobbies, or anything else that can help admissions officers see them as real, interesting people, they often have very little to talk about. When trying to stand out versus thousands of applicants with 700+ GMAT scores and fancy degrees, you can't fight fire with fire. In other words, what will help you stand out is not an even higher GMAT score, but something else that helps tell the story of who you are, even if (especially if) it has nothing to do with your job or your academics. And keep in mind that admissions officers are not fooled by a half-hearted attempt to do just enough community service to be able to write about it in your business school application. You need to show passion for something and how you have made an impact. That will help set you apart.

▷ **Very similar-sounding career goals.** The growth of the markets in India and China has caused many applicants to come to the same conclusion about their career goals: "My goal is to earn my degree and then to return home to launch my own business (or run my family business)." To be clear, there is nothing wrong with this career goal. It's realistic and specific, which are both very important. But be aware that hundreds of other people from your country who are applying to the same school may have the same goal in mind, which will make it even harder for you to stand out. If this is truly your goal, then don't change it for the sake of being different—but realize that something else in your application will need to help set you apart from other applicants.

▷ **Unrealistic career goals.** For some international applicants, this is a function of not having enough information about graduate business school and the opportunities it can provide. For others, though, the problem is that they don't want to have common-sounding career goals, so they write things such as "My goal is to start a multinational telecommunications firm and conduct an initial public offering worth $1 billion within five years." An impressive goal, to be sure, but one that will make admissions officers wonder about how realistic or well-researched your career goals are, which, in turn, may make them wonder if you are a good fit for business school.

▷ **A background in technology.** Again, there is nothing wrong with this (see our "Engineering and Science" section on page 40). But be realistic about the fact that so many other applicants will have the same type of professional background. Why should admissions officers want you over 20 other similar-sounding engineers? (And don't answer that your GMAT score is higher!) One way to overcome this weakness is if you can demonstrate leadership abilities on the job. Maybe you haven't managed your own employees, but have you led a project or gone out of your way to make a positive impact on your organization? If so, be sure to emphasize that in your application. The key point: Admissions officers are much more interested in your leadership potential than in your technical proficiency. Remember that extracurricular experiences, community service, and hobbies can help you here, too.

To overcome the risk of not differentiating yourself from other international applicants, you should live and breathe Chapters 4 and 5. These chapters go through each of the application components in great detail and outline strategies for gaining acceptance to top business schools. Be sure to review each of the examples in order to gain an understanding of how admissions counselors will evaluate your application. Having a good understanding of how to assemble an application that tells a story (rather than an application that rattles off your achievements) is a great way to separate yourself from other international applicants who want to get into the same U.S. business schools.

Additionally, one of the questions that admissions counselors will ask themselves when reviewing applications from international candidates is whether they will take the initiative to share their perspectives with their classmates. There is a common understanding that as an international applicant you have a unique perspective, but in the admissions committee's eyes that perspective is worthless if it isn't shared. The best way to address this question is to provide examples of instances in which you've provided your perspective in a multicultural environment. Better yet, emphasize your desire to express your viewpoints during your time in business school, and your excitement for making a positive impact on your school. In addition to getting this point across in your essays, it is crucial that you emphasize it during your interviews. This may be your one point of direct contact with the admissions committee, and you definitely want them to envision you as a positive contributor to their school.

Finally, we cannot overstate the importance demonstrating proficiency with the English language. As much as the modern business world has become more global, a lack of English skills will be an almost certain application killer. Your TOEFL score (or PTE or IELTS score) will be critically important here, as will your overall GMAT score. And, of course, admissions officers will use your essays and interview to judge whether you'll be an asset or liability for your American-born peers when it comes to classroom participation and study teams.

7. Investment Banking and Finance

Business schools love bankers for their business training and analytical skills, and bankers love the schools because they often have no choice but to apply after a few years on the job. Your challenge will be to stand out from a sea of similar-looking applicants. You can do this by defeating the stereotypes that are most often associated with bankers and others coming from finance-related fields, including private equity and venture capital.

Let's start with the good news. As an investment banker, you will probably have to do very little selling of your business abilities. Schools will assume that you come with at least enough analytical skills to hack it in an MBA program. They will also expect that you are comfortable with big-picture business concepts and have enough polish to make yourself presentable to potential employers. Though you should at least provide some evidence of these skills, know that business schools will generally anticipate that you have these characteristics.

Of course, the hard part will be distinguishing yourself from the other gazillion bankers who also apply. You should, therefore, focus your story. Discuss not only what makes you a great banker, but on what makes you a *different* banker. To this end, any experiences in which you demonstrated leadership and truly made a difference in the outcome of a project will help a great deal. Admissions officers will look hard for examples of when you didn't simply follow your job description, but rather you went a step further and did something that few others would have done in order to succeed. This can sometimes be difficult in this industry, but that's exactly why business schools value these kinds of experiences so much.

Extracurricular activities can be even more powerful in setting you apart from the pack. Any way in which you can show a desire to get involved and make things happen will distinguish you. Again, schools are looking for examples of when you didn't merely do what was asked of you, but rather stepped outside of your comfort zone and made a difference. Yes, we know that you're normally too busy to have a social life, much less devote meaningful time to community service or other activities outside of work. However, remember that there are other bankers who do manage to find the time to flesh out their résumés beyond their day jobs, and that's your competition.

One stereotype that you will need to overcome is the one that paints most investment bankers as overly competitive and greedy sharks. (Financial melt-downs haven't helped with that image!) You most likely have had experiences during which you worked with others to execute a deal; don't overlook the importance of these experiences when describing your professional history. As much as an admissions committee looks for a track record of success, it will pay even more attention to how you accomplished those tasks, ensuring that you've done so with a measure of integrity. An applicant who knifed and clawed his way to the top isn't someone whom most schools will welcome with open arms. ⌐ her/zher

When it comes to your reasons for applying to business school, the story is often pretty straightforward. You know—and every school knows—that many bankers apply to business school because they have little choice. That won't be held against you. But you will really need to think about what you plan on doing with an MBA. Whether or not you plan on going back to banking, admissions officers will demand evidence that shows you really understand the value of an MBA, and that you're not simply out to get your ticket punched. Be prepared to discuss your strengths and weaknesses, and how an MBA will help you round out your personal traits and professional skills. To that end, explaining how an MBA will help you make a true difference is a great way to differentiate yourself from other bankers whose career objectives often come across as conventional.

Finally, recently there has been much chatter that some top MBA programs—and Harvard Business School in particular, now led by Dean Nitin Nohria—have developed a bit of an anti-banking bias after all of the bad press business schools have received since the economic meltdown of 2008. During the past year we have heard multiple stories from historically "shoo in" applicants that they were waitlisted or rejected by HBS when "everyone" told them they should have no problems getting in. This supposed anti-banker bias shouldn't come as too much of a surprise, because Dean Nohria has made multiple public statements about not wanting HBS to be seen as a school "that only turn(s) out MBAs who become consultants and investment bankers." (The evidence suggests that Harvard is serious: 25% of the HBS Class of 2013 comes from finance industries, versus 32% of the Class of 2012, according to a June 13, 2011, *Wall Street Journal* article by Joe Light ["Harvard Business School Changes Its Class Profile"].) HBS clearly wants to diversify its student pool and become less dependent on traditional feeder industries such as banking.

First, it's important to realize that, though this certainly doesn't sound like good news for you if you're a banker, the admissions committee isn't going to reject you solely on the basis of the title you present on your business card. Rather, when HBS says that it wants to continue to diversify its student pool, the school means that it doesn't want to merely add one more banker that appears to be the mirror image of the hundreds of others that are applying to the school. In other words, you must work even harder to set yourself apart, which is exactly what we've been espousing for years. Given this recent trend, however, you may need to work even harder to deliver differentiated messages in your applications, addressing the latent concerns that we've noted, while capitalizing on the anticipated strengths. This is an important theme for any school to which a banker applies, even if HBS has been more outspoken on this topic than others.

Second, we anticipate that market forces will slowly steer HBS back toward accepting more bankers again. After all, if investment banks, private equity shops, venture capital firms, and other employers who recruit at Harvard want job candidates who have strong financial experiences and acumen, the school would be remiss to turn its back on the industry. Overall, we believe that this trend has been to some degree overinflated, that if you can differentiate yourself you still have a decent shot, and of course remember that Harvard is just one fish in the sea (albeit a very big one). If you're a strong banking applicant who gets a no from HBS, you still may very well get a yes from Wharton, Columbia, or another top-tier MBA program.

8. Marketing

Marketing professionals usually have loads of relevant business experience to highlight in their applications. As a marketing professional, between previous schoolwork and your work experience, you should have ample evidence that shows you know how to get things done in a business setting. The challenge is to bring out the breadth of your business experience, especially when it comes to quantitative and leadership skills.

As a marketer, you will likely have little problem pointing to instances of innovation in your career. Most applicants with marketing backgrounds will have examples of creativity that they can draw upon, but you should think broadly and refer to examples of how you innovated in a variety of business scenarios, whether it was developing a creative new advertising campaign or finding a new solution to an old business problem. Choose broad examples instead of times when you simply developed a creative brochure or updated the look of your company's Website. Admissions officers will assume that, as a marketer, you have a good deal of creativity. It is up to you to demonstrate creativity in the broader, business-minded sense of the word.

Depending on what you did as a marketer, one challenge you might face is in presenting convincing evidence of your quantitative and analytical skills. Of course, many marketing jobs are quite quantitative, but admissions officers will look hard for proof of these skills. Naturally, the GMAT can go a long way toward making your case. If your GMAT score isn't as high as you would like, make a point of emphasizing the quantitative work that you've done on your job, whether it's analyzing market research data or budgeting for a project. No matter how mundane these experiences may seem, mentioning them can help a great deal. Also, if you didn't do much undergrad work in quantitative subjects, be prepared to take some courses in accounting or statistics before you attend school (or, ideally, before you apply).

Leadership will really help to set you apart from the pack. As someone coming from marketing, you probably spend much of your days working with other people. As a result, you will likely find that you have more teamwork examples to share in your application than many other applicants. Be sure to emphasize your teamwork dimension in discussing these stories. However, in relating your examples, make sure to be clear about what *you* did, rather than only on what the team accomplished. Don't make admissions officers search all day to figure out what you specifically did on a project in order to make it a success. To some extent, modesty can be your enemy here. You should get comfortable with the idea of using the word *I* instead of *we* a little more.

Also, the fact that you are already in business can actually present a challenge in terms of how you answer the "Why an MBA?" question. You won't necessarily have the obvious answer of wanting to change careers, and not every marketer ends up going to business school (unlike management consulting or banking, where leaving for business school is much more common). A skeptical admissions officer or interviewer may probe you on this. Valid reasons for pursuing an MBA can include the fact that you want to gain new, hard skills outside of what you already know, or that you want to bolster your leadership abilities. Whatever your reasons, be prepared to answer this question and be specific about the skills that you want to gain from an MBA.

9. Military

Applicants coming from the military are blessed with some of the best stories that anyone could possibly tell in a business school application. Tales of clearing a third-world playground of landmines and of whipping a motley platoon of new recruits into a well-oiled machine are the stuff of admissions officers' dreams. Unfortunately, nearly every other military applicant has similarly impressive experiences to draw upon, and not many of these stories explicitly spell out your potential for success at business school.

One of your best strengths as a military applicant will likely be your leadership experience. Any stories that you can relate about directing a group of men and women to achieve a tangible goal will speak volumes about your ability to lead, and most business schools value this trait above all else. You are also likely to have great examples of teamwork, which will further help an admissions committee picture you fitting into a classroom at its school. Don't be shy about sharing these stories, even if you think they've been told a thousand times before. Focus on these accomplishments in your essays and interview, and—more importantly—spell out what you learned as a result and how it will help you in your next career.

The most obvious challenges you could face are in cases when your great experiences have had little to do with business. As a military applicant, you need to show the admissions committee that your skills are directly transferable to the business world. More to the point, you need to show that you see how these skills will translate, and that you know what your own strengths and weaknesses are. You may not know accounting or marketing, but you understand why it is important that you have knowledge of them. Moreover, you can demonstrate your desire to bolster your knowledge in these areas by taking a pre-MBA course or two, particularly in accounting and finance. If you have taken any business-oriented courses that won't show up on your transcripts, be sure to let the admissions committee know about it. Admissions officers will understand that you're relatively new to the business world—in fact, they love nothing more than an applicant with loads of raw potential whom they can shape into a business leader—but they will look critically for evidence that you have the ability and motivation to learn business principles.

The other challenge you will face is in setting yourself apart from the rest of the military crowd. Most of your fellow military applicants will also have great stories about leadership, teamwork, and problem-solving, among others. You can stand out from the pack by demonstrating how you've gotten involved and contributed in situations outside of your military career. Just as a consultant needs to show how he has a life outside of his job, you will need to do the same. Also, many military applicants' leadership stories will be about "direct" leadership, in which there was a clear leader-subordinate hierarchy. Because the business world is often much murkier than this, providing examples of how you succeeded in a less-defined leadership role will further set you apart.

10. Nonprofit *ideal me!*

Some of the most unique members of every business school class tend to come from a nonprofit background. Admissions committees often adore these candidates, and they love to round out their incoming student bodies with students who have taken the road less traveled. In fact, over the past decade many top business schools have significantly invested in programs and departments that cater to students working toward social entrepreneurship and non-governmental organization (NGO) careers. As an applicant coming from this field, you can potentially fit this bill quite nicely. First, however, you will need to address the weaknesses that are most commonly associated with applicants coming from the nonprofit sector.

The good news is that you don't need to be shy about your nonprofit background. Just the contrary—even if you didn't gain a bit of "real" business experience during your career, your previous work will likely have given you a unique world perspective that few others can offer. And don't feel that you need to target only business schools that have big non-profit management programs. You were willing to take risks with your career in order to make someone else's situation better, and admissions officers at any school love to see passion and strong principles such as these. Odds are, you gained some very relevant experience, even if it was as dull as maintaining volunteers' schedules or procuring supplies. The trap that some applicants fall into is in simply stating what they have done, without going two more steps and spelling out what they learned, and how it will help them in their future career. This will be critical because admissions committees will expect a "non-traditional" applicant such as you to provide a vision for how you will get the most out of—and give the most to—their schools.

Another place where nonprofit applicants can fall short is in presenting a convincing case that they will be able to blend in and work with consultants, bankers, marketers, and so on. Although schools will value you for your unique perspective, they want to know that you have enough business sense to be able to contribute to group projects and help move along a class discussion. You can start by showing that you have the intellectual horsepower to stand up to the rigors of the more quantitative subjects. Your undergraduate GPA, GMAT/GRE score, or pre-MBA courses can help here. Also, you will need to show that you are able to think about broader business concepts, and that you understand their relevance to your career. You can touch upon this subject as you answer the "Why an MBA?" question. Admissions officers will appreciate the candidate who knows what she *or he/she* doesn't know and sees why these skills are important.

Some nonprofit applicants apply to business schools in order to change careers; others want MBAs to help them make greater impacts in their current fields. Your game plan won't vary significantly between these two scenarios. The main risk in the case of a career switcher will be in making sure that you have a good understanding of the field that you want to move into. If you plan on going back to the nonprofit sector, then your greatest challenge will be in convincingly spelling out what an MBA will allow you to do that you can't do today. Talking to current MBA students and recent graduates will help you a great deal here.

11. Recent Graduate   *me, possibly*

Throughout the 1990s, the trend was for business schools to accept applicants with more and more years of work experience. During the past decade, however, this trend has been reversed for certain schools, with the most notables being the Stanford Graduate School of Business, the Yale School of Management, and Harvard Business School. The rationale behind the reversal is that there are some exemplary undergraduate students and recent graduates who've had phenomenal experiences and, as such, shouldn't have to wait to attend business school.

Just to be clear: It is still very difficult to gain admittance directly from college or with less than two years of work experience. Besides, many students (and potential employers, whose opinions may ultimately matter more than anyone's) maintain the perspective that business school is most beneficial for students who have significant professional experience. Indeed, you can expect that most top MBA programs will keep their student population with less than two years of work experience in the 5- to 10-percent range. They will do so in order to preserve the classroom dynamic, in which all students are expected to take on the role of a teacher. Still, there is now a greater window of opportunity for the young and restless.

So why the change of heart? Why have programs like the HBS 2+2 Program (which encourages rising college seniors to apply for deferred admission after two years of work experience) and Yale Silver Scholars (which introduces a one-year internship in the middle of an otherwise-normal two-year MBA program for young applicants) grown over the past few years? Perhaps the biggest reason is that elite business schools actually see some of their stiffest competition coming not from other business schools, but from other types of graduate programs, such as law schools and public policy programs. These graduates accept most of their students directly out of college, and many top schools know that the next frontier in attracting dynamic, high-potential applicants is to lure more applicants away from those schools. Therefore, we see more business schools accepting some applicants right out of college, encouraging applicants to submit GRE scores, admitting students now so that they can matriculate in two years, and so forth. That the applicants are younger is a byproduct of this arms race between MBA programs and other elite graduate schools. It's a race to "get" the best and brightest before other schools do.

Another variable that plays into this trend is that the cost of pursuing a full-time MBA has increased dramatically, significantly outpacing the increase in post-MBA salaries. Luring older professionals who are established in their career, are already commanding substantial earning power, and have to justify much higher opportunity costs is proving to be more challenging, particularly compared to what it takes to lure younger applicants with the promise of a big-name graduate degree.

Similarly, schools that are interested in closing the gender gap that exists at most schools, find that they receive many more applications from women when they pursue younger applicants. Ultimately, schools are interested in casting the widest net possible to ensure they can produce the most compelling incoming classes possible. Pursuing elite younger candidates is one way of doing so, but it doesn't reflect a newly formed "ageist" mentality that signals a departure from desiring to have primarily experienced professionals in the classroom.

As a younger applicant, what you have going for you is clear. Admissions committees are consistently impressed with younger applicants' levels of innovation, creativity, enthusiasm, and pure intellectual horsepower. Additionally, younger applicants will often take the academic aspects of business school more seriously than their older counterparts because they're coming directly from academia. Therefore, a higher-than-average GPA and GMAT/GRE score are the minimum price of admission for you.

The challenge is also clear: You must emphasize your maturity, leadership, and teamwork dimensions to the hilt. For the most part, you'll know whether you can demonstrate your capabilities in these areas just by flipping through essay questions. If you struggle to come up with experiences to utilize in response to these questions, chances are you're not yet ready to attend business school. (Remember that admissions officers are looking for *truly exceptional* young applicants.) If you can recall applicable experiences, then your objective should be to discuss them in a way that shows you are multi-dimensional, take initiative, and have great interpersonal skills. These experiences could be related to an entrepreneurial venture that you started, an internship, a study abroad program, an academic achievement, a community service project, a student government position, or a club activity.

You must also be able to demonstrate career focus. The last thing an admissions committee wants to see are staid, shallow career objectives from a profile that it anticipates will produce dynamic, high-impact results. Admissions officers want to know that their young students will one day rock the world, or at least shake it a little bit. More than any other profile, you cannot afford to discuss your career objectives vaguely or without passion. You need to be clear about what skills you will gain from business school and how those skills will translate into a post–business school career.

Maybe even more importantly, you'll need to emphasize why right now is the perfect time for you to enter business school as opposed to sometime in the future. An example would be an idea that you have for an entrepreneurial venture that requires you to gain the skills provided by the target school and an urgency that requires you to get started immediately on the development of a business model.

Failing that, you can also make a case for why now is the perfect time for you to *apply* to business school, knowing that you need a couple of years of work experience before you matriculate. We recently helped a client gain deferred admission to Stanford GSB by helping him argue that he was preparing to take a big career risk as he graduated from college, and that pursuing an MBA in two or three years made sense. "Why not start laying the groundwork now, so that I can take a big risk now knowing that I'll be able to do more learning and growing at Stanford in two years?" was the gist of his argument, and it worked.

In a perfect world, your application would contain an assortment of experiences across the four dimensions. You want to push the admissions committee to the point where it has no reason to ding you other than the fact that you're younger than most applicants. At that point, your propensity to accomplish great things will outweigh what will suddenly appear to be a superficial statistic.

The Business School Classroom: A Diversity of Backgrounds

The sights and sounds of the business school classroom 50 years ago were much different from those of today. What was once a homogeneous student body in terms of professional experience, age, ethnicity, gender, and career goals, is now much more heterogeneous across every dimension. Today, the legacy of a homogeneous classroom still serves as a deterrent for many potential applicants who imagine that the business school experience consists of ex-consultants and investment bankers proselytizing the benefits of capitalism. This urban legend is decidedly false.

Although consultants and bankers still do tend to make up a significant portion of an incoming class (simply because so many of them apply to business school to begin with), they represent far less than 50 percent of the student body at nearly every top MBA program in the United States. Additionally, the business school classroom represents a multitude of perspectives from a variety of countries. (For U.S. schools, international students typically represent 25 to 40 percent of the class.)

For non-U.S. schools, the international population often surpasses 80 percent. Figure 3.1 and Figure 3.2 shown on page 54 display a typical business school class distribution of undergraduate majors and professional experience.

Not surprisingly, in order to maintain or increase the heterogeneity of each class, business schools are actively encouraging a diversity of backgrounds in the classroom. Students acknowledge that a variety of perspectives helps to create a dynamic learning environment in which duplication of opinions is rare. For an example of background variety, consider Omari's study group at Harvard Business School:

- A New Zealand physician.
- A Pakistani economic development analyst.
- A U.S. military intelligence officer.
- A Brazilian investment banker.
- A U.S. middle school teacher who taught in Nepal for two years.

So, how can these insights help you? First, if you're considering business school and have a non-traditional background, don't buy into the myth of homogeneity. If you have something to add to a school's learning environment, then there is a spot for you. Secondly, you should take some time to reflect on how you can differentiate yourself based on your background and your career goals. Fortunately for you, that's what this book is all about. Finally, once you get to business school, don't be afraid to share your unique experiences with your classmates. You'll be admitted largely because of your interesting background, so be sure to help those around you benefit from what you've learned along the way.

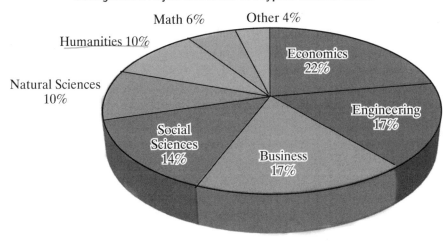

Figure 3.1

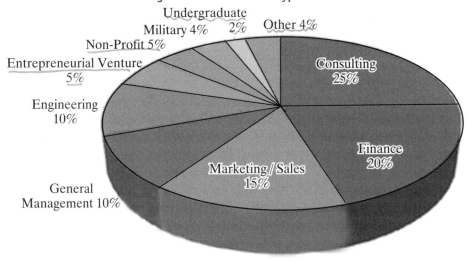

Figure 3.2

A Conversation With Dawna Clarke

Dartmouth's Tuck School of Business is known for innovation in management education, and Tuck's admissions office is known for innovation in MBA admissions, frequently reaching out to applicants and admissions experts to spread the word about Tuck. Much of the credit for this goes to Dawna Clarke, Tuck's Director of MBA Admissions. Dawna has worked in the field for more than two decades, also having served in the admissions office at Darden and Kenan-Flagler. We had a chance to talk with Dawna about how the MBA application process is viewed through an admissions director's eyes.

We hear admissions committee members talk about looking for fit when evaluating applicants. What does that mean to you? What do you look for to determine if an applicant is a good fit with Tuck?

Being a good "fit" is very important at Tuck because we have such a small class size. We look for people who have been involved and who have had an impact on either their company or their community in some way. We look at recommendation letters to see how they work in teams, and we read all the interview comments as well to get an idea of a person's interpersonal skills. Potential leadership qualities are important here because most of our events are student-led, but we don't mean by "leadership" that the applicants should have been heading up their company or their division. Leadership occurs in many ways: community service, leading new initiatives at work or in the community, helping others achieve their potential. However, it is impossible to describe the "perfect" Tuck candidate because there are no pigeon holes at Tuck. As a member of this community, each student's unique qualities are valued in classroom discussions, study group all-nighters, and teamwork negotiations. When we talk about diversity, we use the word in its widest sense: ethnicity, nationality, gender, and also educational and professional background.

What are some of the major mistakes that you see applicants make year after year?

The most common mistake is in choosing a school solely based on rankings. Most applicants, regardless of from where they come, tend to look at the rankings and really don't consider which school is best for their interests. And most of them really do not understand exactly what the rankings are measuring. We feel it is important for students to do a thorough job of researching the different programs, including talking to current students or alumni. By doing their "due diligence" they will find the school that will be the best option for their career goals.

How important is an applicant's enthusiasm for the program? Can you tell when an applicant is simply applying to Tuck along with every other top school?

Enthusiasm for Tuck is very important to us. We don't want people here who will not be able to adjust to the climate or the small-town atmosphere, because they will not be happy. We want everyone to be happy and satisfied with their experience, and I think we've done a good job through the years of attracting the sort of student who will thrive here. We realize it is not the right place for everyone and that is fine. Can we tell if they are just applying to a list of top schools? Sometimes yes, but we never ask where they are applying. That's not important to us. We just want to know why they applied to Tuck and if they don't know about the program and what we are all about, that tells us something. The best way to get to know more about Tuck is to talk with the people who know it best—our students, our alumni, our faculty, and our staff. We encourage applicants to take every opportunity to connect with us. We have a great campus visit program and the students love to show people around here. Once you have visited, then your essay about "why Tuck?" will be richer and more vibrant because you will have experienced it firsthand.

What advice do you have for less-traditional applicants, such as those coming from nonprofit organizations or more artistic career backgrounds?

We actually like non-traditional applicants. They bring a richness to the classroom because they tend to look at things from a totally different viewpoint. Every year we have students who come from teaching, law, and we are seeing more and more people from the nonprofit world. We have a rich tradition of community service and we work closely with nonprofits in our area through the Allwin Initiative for Corporate Citizenship. Often people who come in with a vague idea of doing something in nonprofit can find a very rewarding internship with one of our partner organizations.

What do you look for in trying to distinguish between applicants with very similar professional backgrounds?

This is probably the hardest part of the job. With two equally qualified candidates, how do you pick one? We rely on a number of things, but specifically on the letters of recommendation and the interview, and also the way the person has crafted the essay answers. I think the best way to differentiate yourself is to look outside of work and talk to us about what really interests you. This is what we are looking for—that spark of passion for something.

What is your take on the GMAT and its importance to an MBA application? For applicants with low GMAT scores, what else can they do to make up for this weakness?

The GMAT is one of those hurdles that everyone has to jump through and it is the one common denominator for every candidate. Based on research done by GMAC, we are convinced that the test is a good predictor of how someone will do in the first year of the program. We do look closely at the scores because our program is very demanding and rigorous in the first year, especially in the quantitative courses. But we do admit people with GMAT scores lower than our average when they have shown us a particular facet of their personality or their professional experience that tips the balance. Sometimes they can prove to us that they can handle the quantitative aspects by the work they do or by their undergraduate grades. I strongly recommend that people take the time to either follow a preparation course or study diligently at least two hours per day using free online or print materials.

What makes a really good essay? What makes a really bad one?

My main advice is to read the question and answer *what we are asking*. Don't cut and paste your essay written for another school into our application (or into any other schools' application either!). Each school looks for specific things. For instance, at Tuck, we are looking for leadership potential and we have a specific definition of what we mean by leadership, which does not necessarily mean "ordering other people around." We also want to know who the applicant is outside of work—do they have special interests that would enrich other students, what will they bring to Tuck? And finally, we look for a clear career path: What have they done? Why? And how will that get them where they want to go? The bad essays are those that skirt the question or that answer the question they wished we had asked but didn't!

What makes for a successful interview? How do you recommend applicants prepare for their interviews?

The interview is another facet of who the candidate is and an in-person interview is the best opportunity to really shine. We ask about their career choices in the past and their goals for the future, and we also ask random questions to find out more about their personality, how they work with others, what differentiates them from other candidates. We look for their level of comfort, and how they present themselves from a professional standpoint, too. We don't have a prepared list of questions. Like everything at Tuck, the interview is very personalized, so it is difficult to prepare for it in that sense. Of course, the candidates should be able to talk briefly about their career choices and why they want to come to Tuck, and the rest will follow from what is elicited from these responses.

Anything else you would like to share about Tuck or the MBA admissions process in general?

We realize that the applicants put a lot of time, thought, and energy into their essays and we treat each application with the respect it deserves. We read each application at least two times by two separate readers, and I personally read every single write-up before making a decision. Our decisions are generally by consensus, but, every now and then, we have some hot and heavy discussions! We want the best possible candidates who will leave a positive impact on Tuck, and we want to be sure that our program is the best for them.

 **FAQs**

What if the nature of my job makes it difficult for me to draw upon any useful leadership or teamwork examples?

This is a common question from people coming from a number of careers. If you feel like you can't come up with any pertinent examples from your experience, try broadening your definitions of leadership and teamwork. You may not have led a group to achieve a major breakthrough, but maybe you spotted and acted on a huge cost-savings opportunity that no one else bothered to tackle, even though you received no credit for it. This is a more subtle example of leadership, but one that business schools will still appreciate. Think of leadership as any instance when you had a positive impact on those around you, especially those instances that wouldn't have happened if you hadn't been there. Similarly, don't think of teamwork as just stories of you sitting in close quarters with a few of your peers, working all night to solve an impossible problem. A good teamwork example could be much broader, such as how you went out of your way to help someone in another department tackle a problem. Think about every person or group with which you've interacted, and consider using instances where you made a difference in helping someone else succeed. *managing UCBUGG short, extra hours outside of class*

If, in my previous job, I had a high-flying title, and now I'm applying to business school, won't that look weird?

It can certainly raise some eyebrows, but context is everything. This problem is most common during a recession, when some former vice presidents have to explain why they suddenly aspire to become junior consultants. If your fancy job title came from financial services, you don't have too much to worry about. Remember that admissions officers review thousands of applications from bankers every year, so they know the score. If your high-level position came because you were a founding member of a business, then in admissions officers' eyes you are an entrepreneur. This is good, although, as do all other entrepreneurs, you will need to present a convincing argument for why you want to go back to school now. Also, whether or not your business was a success, keep your application story focused on you. You will ideally have a good number of stories to tell about building a team or a product from scratch, so use them. Focus on your achievements and tie them together with where you want to go—and how business school will help you get there.

How much does my employer's brand name matter when applying to business school?

Having a well-known brand on your resume certainly helps, and business schools do tend to value two years' of experience at Goldman Sachs more than they do experience at an unknown investment firm. We won't try to convince you that these brand names mean nothing to admissions officers; they know that these companies have rigorous hiring standards, and coming from one of these firms is a signal that you're a strong performer. But the advice that we give regarding your undergraduate school's reputation applies here, too. If you come from a relatively unknown organization, spend enough time explaining what the company does, but then move on. You don't need to impress admissions officers with your company's five-year compound annual growth rate. Then, spend the vast majority of your time explaining what *you* did at the company, because that's what admissions officers really care about. Similarly, if you do come from a well-known company, don't plan on coasting on the company's reputation. In fact, if the company is known as a mill that turns out business school students, you will need to work hard to set yourself apart from the pack by selling your unique contributions. Two years "on the beach" at McKinsey isn't going to get you in anywhere, so focus on what you did that makes you different.

I've done something really unique. Do you think that will get me into business school?

The short answer is "not by itself." The fact that you did something unique, whether it was professional or personal, will certainly help in setting you apart from the crowd. But that alone will definitely not get you in. Think hard about what your unique achievement says about you, and how it fits into your overall application theme. Spending two years in South America helping locals build a farm is a great story, but it doesn't help you much if you can't relate it to the rest of your story. Also, just like every other experience that you draw upon, simply saying that you were involved in something is not enough. You need to show how you specifically contributed. Finally, a string of interesting experiences can actually hurt you if it is hard for admissions officers to see the connections between them. It is up to you to present your experiences in a way that makes sense to someone who only has your application (and hopefully an admissions interview, if you get to that point) as a way to get to know and fully understand the real you.

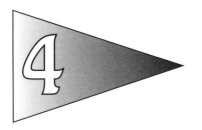

Understanding *the* Application Components

The Process

Now that you have a better understanding of your strengths and weaknesses, and are prepared to differentiate yourself according to your profile, it's time to examine the components of the business school application. So, what should you expect? Plan on spending an average of 30 to 50 hours on each application that you complete. Yes, your fourth application may take less time than your first, but be prepared to spend dozens of hours on each application, no matter how many you complete. You should also expect the application process to occupy your life the way an attention-starved newborn would. Along those lines, don't be surprised if you suffer from a form of "postpartum depression" once the process is completed; as odd as it sounds, spending a lot of time with your applicants and then never seeing them again can make for some sleepless nights as you worry about whether you left out any important details or missed a typo. If you follow some basic guidelines, however, you can save yourself some frustration and a lot of time.

The Tools

The Internet has drastically changed the way business school applications are completed. Imagine calling admissions departments to request applications, filling in data sheets by hand, or agonizing over essays while sitting behind a typewriter. Today, most schools won't even distribute, much less accept, paper applications. In general, you will find that business schools either utilize a service provider that hosts online applications from a number of schools simultaneously or contract with a developer that specializes in personalizing online application sites. Interestingly, despite their insistence on only accepting electronic applications, the first thing most admissions offices do with your application is print it out and review it on paper! Old habits die hard.

The Components

Business schools essentially all use the same framework in putting their applications together. These similarities allow you to approach each application in a similar manner. Still, don't fall into the trap of thinking that each school is looking for the same type of applicant. The differences in application strategy for 35 top global business schools are highlighted in Chapter 5.

In general, every business school will request the following information in its application:

- Data sheets (for your academic, professional, and personal information).
- Transcript.
- GMAT/GRE score.
- TOEFL score (for international applicants only).
- Interview.
- Essays.
- Recommendations.
- Resume.

The rest of the chapter will cover each of the application components in depth and provide you with strategies that you should integrate into your MBA game plan.

Data Sheets

Data sheets are pretty consistent from one application to the next. Each application's data sheets will typically ask for:

- Contact information.
- Basic biographical information.
- Education background.
- Employment history.
- Extracurricular activities.
- Awards.
- Achievements.

The bad news is that this component is often more time-consuming than you would think. One reason is that each school usually asks for something slightly different. For example, one school may ask for only one sentence to describe each job you have held, another may ask for a few bullet points, and yet another will ask for a paragraph of up to 150 words. So, be ready to devote some manual labor to writing up your background for each application.

The good news is that your work in Chapter 2 will almost directly translate to this section. The grid that you created will give you the opportunity to spell out everything that you have done, making it easy to pluck activities and enter them where needed. Also, the grid will help you think about what dimensions each activity highlights, which is important as you tailor your application for each school. For the most part, the information that you provide in the data sheets for each application will be the same.

Even in this apparently dry section, it is important to maintain your focus on demonstrating fit and uniqueness. As tempting as it will be to simply copy and paste, don't pass up an easy opportunity to set yourself apart. The data sheet is often the first thing that an admissions officer will review after picking up your application. Don't underestimate the importance of making a great first impression.

Data sheets often have very short word limits. In many online systems, you simply won't be allowed to go over the limit. Do yourself a huge favor and obey the limits given. Remember that your application will likely be read by a weary-eyed admissions officer who has to work his way through a shoulder-high stack of applications. Even though you will almost inevitably feel that you have more to say than what the application allows, be considerate and keep it concise. Your application reader will appreciate it.

One small, final tip: In your contact information, be sure to list your cell phone number in addition to your work phone number as the main point of contact. Chances are that the good news will be communicated in the middle of the day via a phone call, and you won't want to be at work wondering whether the phone is ringing at home.

Transcript

Naturally, there is not much that you can do about your undergraduate grades, assuming that you are already out of college. Still, there are a couple of things you should know regarding transcripts and how they affect your application.

First, on a logistical note, give yourself plenty of time to receive your transcript(s) from the school(s) you have previously attended. Even with today's efficient online systems, it can take anywhere from one week to a month to get a transcript back from a school (some offer rush processing), and you often need to have a transcript sent back to you in order to be able to send it off to your target business school. Start sending out requests as far in advance as possible. Also, it's fine to send multiple transcript requests to a school at one time, but make sure that you are clear about the directions for each business school. Some business schools require your college's registrar to not only sign a transcript but also to fill out a form; others ask for course descriptions to accompany a transcript. You can reduce the chance of error on your college's end by giving them enough time and letting them know exactly what to do for each MBA application.

Now, on to the contents of your transcript. Admissions committees look for evidence that you challenged yourself in a wide variety of academic areas—especially in quantitative ones—and came away with at least a 3.0 GPA, preferably higher. (Although there is no official required minimum, you may as well consider 3.0 the GPA under which you will have a tough time getting into a top-ranked MBA program.) Of course, if your undergraduate transcript is stellar, then most of your work is already done. Just be sure to highlight relevant coursework and emphasize your success in order to bring out your innovation dimension, as outlined in Chapter 2. If you can show that you were a dedicated, successful student in college, then it will be easy for admissions personnel to imagine you succeeding in their classrooms.

If your transcript isn't perfect, that's okay. You can usually make up for any apparent deficiencies in other ways. Review the transcript weaknesses section in Chapter 2 for tips on how to address poor grades. In general, poor grades can be addressed with a high GMAT, additional coursework (especially in quantitative areas), and perhaps an additional essay explaining your situation. We'll discuss appropriate usage of the additional essay in the essay section later in this chapter.

GMAT

There is probably no other aspect of the business school application process that strikes more fear into the hearts of applicants than the GMAT. For most, it is the first step toward applying and the key variable in determining which schools are "accessible." Pressure to perform well on the examination has increased as mean scores have spiked drastically over the past 20 years. Though we strongly believe that the GMAT score is only one component of the application and should not be emphasized at the expense of other parts of your candidacy, it certainly is a key factor in determining your success in applying. It is often said that a great GMAT score alone will never get you into a top business school, but a poor one can most certainly keep you out. We will take a look at the exam and then provide you with advice to help ensure that you don't fall into the latter scenario.

GMAT Background

Graduate business school programs use the Graduate Management Admission Test (GMAT) to help evaluate applicants' analytical writing, mathematical, and verbal abilities. Created and sponsored by the Graduate Management Admission Council (GMAC), the GMAT is purported to be the single best predictor of how well a student will perform in the business school classroom. In addition to sponsoring the GMAT, GMAC serves in its role as a nonprofit education association by disseminating information on graduate business education. In looking to augment your knowledge about the GMAT and graduate business school in general, check out GMAC's Website (*www.mba.com*). The Website provides several of the resources that are covered in the "How to Ace the GMAT" section in this chapter, in addition to sample problems and information on signing up for the GMAT.

The GMAT and your transcript(s) will be the major criteria used in assessing your academic ability. Business schools evaluate your GMAT score, in addition to your GPA, because it reflects applicants' capabilities in a standardized manner. GPA does not provide the same level of standardization given the large differences across college curricula. Thus, admissions officers use the GMAT as a way to compare "apples to apples" when evaluating candidates' academic aptitude.

The table following on page 63 displays the format and the content of the GMAT, effective June 2012, when GMAC will release the revised GMAT including the new Integrated Reasoning section.

Analytical Writing Assessment (AWA) Section

Whenever you hear people tossing around GMAT scores, chances are they are not referring to the Analytical Writing Assessment (AWA). For the most part, schools barely breathe a word about it, and many applicants don't even take the time to prepare for it. In fact, GMAC itself is downplaying the importance of the AWA, announcing plans to replace one of the two AWA essays with the new Integrated Reasoning section in June 2012. Nonetheless, you can't get through the exam without first getting through this often-neglected section.

Format and Content of the GMAT

	Questions	Timing
Analytical Writing Assessment	1	30 Min.
Integrated Reasoning	Multiple	30 Min. (est.)
Optional Break	–	8 Min.

Quantitative
  – Problem Solving
  – Data Sufficiency
	37	75 Min.

Optional Break	–	8 Min.

Verbal
  – Reading Comprehension
  – Critical Reasoning
  – Sentence Correction
	41	75 Min.

Total Time: 3 Hours 46 Minutes Score Range: 200–800		

Figure 4.1

The purpose of the AWA is to test your ability to present a coherent argument and to analyze an underdeveloped one. The section requires you to complete two 30-minute essays, which are divided into two categories: Analysis of an Issue, and Analysis of an Argument. (After June 2012, the AWA will feature just one essay: Analysis of Argument. So, if you own GMAT preparation materials that include Analysis of an Issue essays and you will take the GMAT in June 2012 or later, you can safely ignore those essays.)

Analysis of an Issue

This section begins with a statement and then asks you to analyze the issue represented by the statement and develop a short essay that takes a position on the issue. You will be evaluated based on your ability to:

> ▶ Dissect the issue and articulate/defend your position on it.

> ▶ Introduce relevant examples and facts.

> ▶ Write an essay that flows well organizationally and meets the standards of grammatically correct English.

Analysis of an Argument

This section is almost identical to Analysis of an Issue, but instead of an issue you will be presented with an argument. After reading the argument, which is generally only a few sentences in length, you will be asked to write an essay that evaluates the line of reasoning behind the argument, notes the explicit/implicit assumptions, provides ways in which the argument is weak, and cites evidence that would make the argument more compelling. You will be evaluated based on your ability to:

☑ Dissect the argument and articulate your analysis of its "rationality."

☑ Introduce evidence that could weaken and strengthen the argument.

☑ Write an essay that flows well organizationally and meets the standards of grammatically correct English.

Note that in both essays you will be evaluated on your ability to construct and dissect arguments, not on what arguments you actually make. So, don't worry about picking the "correct" side of an issue. Rather, pick a side of the issue that you can argue for most strongly, lay out your reasons in a clear and logical manner, and then move on. Also, no matter what position you take, keep in mind what facts could undermine your position, and demonstrate—at least in a sentence or two—that you have considered these possible weaknesses in your argument.

Integrated Reasoning Section

Starting in June 2012, the GMAT will feature a new section called Integrated Reasoning, which will represent the biggest change to the GMAT in more than a decade. Though students have taken the GMAT on computers since the 1990s, the test questions themselves haven't really changed from what they were on the old paper-based tests. Now, the GMAT will take advantage of the computer-based format and present data in a variety of formats, including spreadsheets, diagrams, charts, and short text passages. Test-takers will be asked to synthesize the data and answer questions about a business situation. For instance, a question might involve a small, sortable spreadsheet containing prices and sales results for a product, along with some additional charts and a short text passage about the company's promotional efforts. Test-takers will have 30 minutes to digest this information and answer a few questions about what kind of correlation exists between prices and sales, what promotions were most effective for the company, and what the company's managers should do to maximize profitability going forward.

Although many applicants have been spooked by the addition of spreadsheets to the GMAT, the exact format of the new question isn't what really matters. You don't need to be an Excel guru to answer these questions; rather, GMAC wants to see that you can take a small pile of information presented in a variety of formats, pick out what matters and what doesn't, and draw conclusions about what's going on. The addition of various new data formats means that the new Integrated Reasoning section should be even less vulnerable to tricks and shortcuts that sometimes are effective for more standardized question types. Now, you will really need to learn how to break down a situation and draw insights from the information provided, rather than using the process of elimination or applying a mnemonic by rote.

If you're intimidated by this sort of problem, you shouldn't be. (Or, you should learn to get over it!) This is exactly the kind of work that you will do in many MBA courses, and it's the skill that many employers look for in MBA grads. Management consulting firms, investment banks, consumer packaged goods companies, and other employers will challenge you with mini case questions that don't test your Excel abilities, but rather your ability to look at a somewhat-murky situation, pluck out the one or two things that really matter, and form an opinion on what to do next. This is a skill that you'll put to use many, many times in business school and beyond, so we recommend getting good at it now.

How can you do that? GMAC works hard to make the GMAT a test of *how you think* rather than *what you know,* and we expect that the Integrated Reasoning section will be the most effective question type yet for accomplishing this. Therefore, your focus should be less on burning through dozens of sample problems and trying to see how many you get right, and more on exercising the muscles that allow you to analyze business information in a way that helps you make effective decisions. As for "official" practice," as we write this, test preparation companies are only just beginning to create sample integrated reasoning questions, and GMAC itself has only released a handful of sample questions so far. This will change quickly as June 2012 approaches.

Once the new Integrated Reasoning section is live, we expect that it will be at least a couple of years before MBA admissions officers heavily rely on it to make decisions about candidates. The question type will be new for them, too, and it will be a while until they develop the type of shorthand intuition that allows them to say "720 GMAT score with a 44 in Verbal but only a 46 in Quant. Looks good but not amazing." Therefore, if you're among the first to take the GMAT with the new Integrated Reasoning section, don't fret too much. It's unlikely many (or any) applicants will be rejected because of their Integrated Reasoning scores for at least a little while.

Quantitative Section

The good news about the quantitative section of the GMAT is that it does not test advanced mathematical principles, such as multivariate calculus, differential equations, or multiple regression. The bad news is that the basic mathematical skills that the test does include (arithmetic, algebra, geometry, percentages, fractions, elementary statistics, combinations, and permutations) can appear to be quite complex if you are lacking a quantitative background.

During this section of the exam you will face 37 questions, which will be of two types: Problem Solving and Data Sufficiency.

Problem Solving

Problem Solving questions are generally straightforward in nature, to the extent that you are presented with a mathematical puzzle and are asked to provide an answer. The questions will be very similar to questions that many of us faced on the SAT and ACT. Although you most certainly need to spend time bulking up your knowledge of the quantitative concepts tested, very little additional time will need to be spent on understanding how these question types work.

Data Sufficiency

Data Sufficiency questions are a different story. Contrary to the popular belief that these types of questions were devised by a sadist, they are meant to test your ability to determine when there is enough information available to solve a problem. (This "Is there enough information available?" question also lies at the heart of many of the problems you will see in the Integrated Reasoning section.) The automatic temptation is to try to actually solve these problems when all that is required is for you to note whether there is sufficient data to solve them.

Each problem presents you with a question and two pieces of information, written as statements and labeled (1) and (2). Your task is to decide whether the statements provide enough information to allow you to solve the stated question. This produces an interesting dynamic in that all answers for this question type are the same. All Data Sufficiency responses look like the following:

A. Statement (1) ALONE is sufficient, but statement (2) alone is not sufficient to answer the question asked.

B. Statement (2) ALONE is sufficient, but statement (1) alone is not sufficient to answer the question asked.

C. BOTH statements (1) and (2) TOGETHER are sufficient to answer the question asked, but NEITHER statement ALONE is sufficient to answer the question asked.

D. EACH statement ALONE is sufficient to answer the question asked.

E. Statements (1) and (2) TOGETHER are NOT sufficient.

If this sounds at all confusing, don't worry, because it takes a while to get used to this type of question. With practice, though you will learn to like Data Sufficiency questions—or at least hate them a little less.

Verbal Section

The Verbal section is the last hurdle of the exam and is composed of 41 questions. By this point in the exam your eyes are blurry from staring at the screen for the last two hours, but it is important to focus because of the large amount of reading and analysis required by this section. In general, this section tests your ability to analyze and draw conclusions about written prose, identify and correct grammatical errors in English phrases, and assess arguments. It is *not* a test of how well you have memorized idioms or how fast you are at spotting typos. There are three Verbal question types: Reading Comprehension, Sentence Correction, and Critical Reasoning.

Reading Comprehension

This is another question type that will be familiar to those who have taken the SAT and ACT exams. The problems consist of passages, which can be as long as 350 words, and sets of questions that test your understanding of the passages. Passages are generally focused on natural sciences, politics/economics, and business topics. You can expect to see three or four such passages on an exam. You don't need to know anything about the topic at hand in order to answer these questions correctly; everything you need will be in each reading passage.

Sentence Correction

Each Sentence Correction question presents a statement or a phrase that is to be evaluated on its grammatical and stylistic elements. Part or all of the statement/ phrase will be underlined, highlighting the portion that you are to assess. You will have the option of selecting from four alternative phrases that would replace the underlined portion or to select the original as the correct phrase. Note that the first answer (answer A) will always be the underlined phrase included in the original statement/phrase.

When selecting the correct answer, you are to evaluate the possibilities based on the requirements of standard written English. In particular, you should consider grammar, sentence structure, redundancy, word selection, and effectiveness. Again, this question type goes deeper than testing your knowledge of idioms— your job here is to ensure that each statement succinctly conveys its intended meaning without any ambiguity.

Critical Reasoning

Critical Reasoning questions are similar to the Analysis of an Argument portion of the AWA section in that you will be tested on your ability to evaluate arguments. Naturally, the major difference between the two is that after you are presented with the Critical Reasoning argument, you must select a multiple-choice response to a question regarding that argument. Specifically, you will answer questions regarding the arguments' conclusions, assumptions, structure, rationale, and factors that could strengthen/weaken the argument.

The CAT

The Quantitative and Verbal sections of the GMAT both consist of multiple-choice questions that are presented as a Computer Adaptive Test (CAT). The CAT is designed to dynamically produce exam questions based on your performance on previous questions. These questions, which range in difficulty from low to high, are pulled from a question bank. The result is a unique exam for nearly every test-taker. The CAT begins by providing a question of moderate difficulty. About half of the test-takers are expected to get the question correct, and half are expected to get it wrong. If you get the question correct, then a more difficult question is supplied. If you get the question wrong, then an easier question is supplied. By the end of the test, the CAT finds your score based on the number of correct answers given to questions at different levels of difficulty. As one might imagine, there is a complex algorithm underlying this process, involving knowing how thousands of other test-takers have done on each of the problems you answered. The algorithm decides the appropriate level of difficulty for your next question, the value of that question, and eventually your score. Because your questions are generated based on previous responses, you may not skip a question and return to it, as is possible on some other standardized tests.

Over the years, we have seen many myths come (and sometimes go) with regard to how the GMAT's adaptive engine works. Perhaps the most pervasive one is the idea that, because the first few questions can cause a wide swing in the whether you receive harder or easier questions (based on whether you get them right or wrong), these questions are by far the most important ones in determining your final score. Many test-takers therefore spend far too much time on these questions, trying to ensure that they get every one right so that the computer puts them in the "smart" bucket, ensuring they will get a higher overall score at the end of the test.

The reality is that the GMAT holds so many data points on every one of the questions you will see that by the end of the test it will know your true level of ability, whether or not you get an early easy question wrong or an early hard question right. It's also flexible enough to account for "false negatives" and "false positives" (getting a question wrong when you really should have gotten it right, given your ability level, or vice versa). The people behind the test know, for example, that even if you make a pure guess, there's a 20-percent chance that you'll get a question right. They therefore know that every question helps in determining your final score, but that every question itself may be "wrong" in making that determination. So, they designed the scoring algorithm to stay flexible enough to withhold judgment on your true level until you've been presented with every question on the test.

Therefore, you're far more likely to impact your own score by finishing the exam or not. Spend too much time on these first 10 questions and you'll risk running out of time at the end of the section. No matter how well you did on the first 10 questions, not answering every question can knock your score down significantly. (GMAC itself has stated this publicly.) So, don't fool yourself into spending an extra 10 minutes on the first 10 questions; worry about finishing the test on time instead!

Your GMAT Score

So what's the bottom line? The bottom line will be revealed through four scores: Total, Quantitative, Verbal, and Analytical Writing Assessment (and your Integrated Reasoning score, starting in June 2012). The first three scores will be provided to you immediately after you complete the exam. Your AWA score will be sent to you a few weeks later. Here are the details on each score component.

Total Score

The Total score is the one that you'll hear thrown around the most. Total scores range from 200 to 800, with students at top schools averaging around 690. In addition to the score itself, schools will look at the percentile in which your score falls. The percentiles change on a year-to-year basis as scores go up, but the table (Figure 4.2) shown on page 69 should give you an idea of how competitive different scores are.

Quantitative Score

Quantitative scores are placed on a different scale than Total scores and range from 0 to 60. Given the quantitative rigor of business school curricula, most programs will place more of an emphasis on this score than Verbal, especially if you are lacking a quantitative background. The table (Figure 4.3) on page 69 provides information on Quantitative scores and their corresponding percentiles.

Verbal Score

Verbal scores are scaled in the same fashion as Quantitative scores. They, however, are not comparable, because examinee performance on each part of the test differs greatly. Obtaining a score of 40 on the Verbal section is much better

Approximation of Total Scores and
Percentiles of Examinees

Total Score	Percentage Below
760–800	99%
750	98%
740	97%
730	96%
720	94%
700	90%
680	85%
660	82%
640	75%
620	70%
600	64%
570	55%
550	49%
530	41%
500	34%

Figure 4.2
Source: Graduate Management
Admission Council Website (*MBA.com*)

Approximation of Quantitative Scores and
Percentiles of Examinees

Quantitative Score	Percentage Below
51	98%
50	93%
49	86%
48	82%
47	77%
46	75%
45	72%
44	68%
43	65%
42	61%
41	58%
40	56%
39	52%
38	50%
37	48%
36	43%

Figure 4.3
Source: Graduate Management
Admission Council Website (*MBA.com*)

than obtaining a score of 40 on the Quantitative section. These differences can be seen by comparing the Verbal score in Figure 4.4 on page 70 to the Quantitative score table (Figure 4.3).

Analytical Writing Assessment Score

Chances are that no one will ever ask you about your AWA score, because of business schools' heavy dependence on your responses to their own essays. Still, you should be familiar with how this portion of the exam is graded, because it is a criterion that schools consider (albeit to only a small extent). Your AWA score is an average of the scores you receive on the Analysis of an Issue and Analysis of an Argument portions, which are themselves averages of two independent scores. The result is a score that ranges from 0 to 6 in half-point increments, as opposed to one-point increments for the Quantitative/Verbal scores and 10-point increments for the Total score. The table (Figure 4.5) on page 70 shows how AWA scores and their percentiles match up. (This table was created using scores from the two-question AWA. As of June, 2012 the AWA will only contain one question.)

Approximation of Verbal Scores and
Percentiles of Examinees

Verbal Score	Percentage Below
46–51	99%
45	98%
44	97%
42	95%
41	92%
40	89%
39	87%
38	83%
37	80%
36	78%
35	73%
34	68%
33	66%
32	63%
31	58%
30	55%

Figure 4.4

Source: Graduate Management
Admission Council Website
(MBA.com)

Approximation of AWA Scores and
Percentiles of Examinees

Total Score	Percentage Below
6.0	91%
5.5	77%
5.0	56%
4.5	37%
4.0	21%
3.5	10%
3.0	5%
2.5	4%
0.5–2.0	3%

Figure 4.5

Source: Graduate Management
Admission Council Website
(MBA.com)

Note that, because the Integrated Reasoning section is so new, no scoring percentiles exist yet. Once enough people have taken the test with the new section, we expect that Integrated Reasoning percentiles will look very similar to those of the other sections on the GMAT.

Analyzing Your Score

Although it would be nice to score above or at the mean of your target schools, you shouldn't continuously take the exam until you hit that mark. In addition to mean scores, you should consider the 80-percent range of the schools. As mentioned in Chapter 2, it will be very difficult to get into your target schools if your score falls below that range. Indeed, this should be a consideration in selecting your target schools. When you take a look at the low end of the GMAT ranges of the top schools, you'll notice that they can roughly be divided into three categories:

greater than 650, between 620 and 650, and less than 620. The table (Figure 4.6) shown on page 72 displays these groupings, sorted by the low end of the range.

Note that these groupings are not meant to serve as some sort of ranking. They are not at all reflective of school quality and are merely one resource that you can use in deciding on your target schools.

Another consideration is your Quantitative/Verbal score split. You'll often hear that top schools look for students who have scored in the 80th percentile on both sections of the exam, which we consider to be a good rule of thumb. Though this isn't an official policy (not one that any school will publicly admit to, anyway), you should be cognizant of your background strengths, your score split, and the emphases of your target programs. Programs that are more quantitatively rigorous will naturally place more of an emphasis on your quantitative abilities. So, if your quantitative score is relatively low, then you will have to show your ability to succeed in that program through other parts of your application.

Submitting Your Scores

The score submission process occurs immediately after you complete the exam. As part of the $250 test-taking fee, you may submit your scores to up to five schools. Because you have to choose which schools you want to receive the scores before you see the results, you should make an initial selection of target schools before the exam. Naturally, that list can, and in many cases should, be revised after taking the exam. Once you submit your exam scores, you usually won't have to send any additional GMAT information to the selected schools, other than maybe entering your scores into the schools' application forms. The score report that the selected schools receive will include all of your GMAT scores from the past five years. (So, taking the GMAT over and over to try to "hide" a poor score won't work.)

Right after you finish the exam but before you see how you did, the computer will ask if you want to cancel your score. This gives you a "last-ditch" opportunity to erase the test if you just know that didn't go well (for example, if time ran out and you still have six questions to go on the Verbal section). If you're absolutely certain that you bombed the test, you can go this route, but know that there is absolutely no going back. If you click "Cancel" and then see 10 seconds later that you scored a 770, too bad! You will need to take the test again. Also, know that schools will be able to see the cancellation on later score reports that you submit; they won't see the score, but will see that you canceled a test sitting. So, it's not a perfectly clean slate even if you cancel your score.

We therefore recommend that you "let it ride" and accept your score unless you're absolutely certain that you bombed the test. Business schools really do care most about your highest GMAT score, and they know that many applicants take the exam two or three times before submitting their applications. You may as well accept your score; you just might be pleasantly surprised by how you did.

After the exam, you can send score reports to additional schools for an extra, nominal charge. The test-taking fee does not cover post-exam score submissions even if you don't select any schools on exam day.

Top Business Schools' Middle-80% GMAT Range

Business School	Middle 80% GMAT Range
Group 1	
Stanford University	680–770
Columbia Business School	680–760
UC Berkeley (Haas)	680–760
Harvard Business School	680–770*
University of Pennsylvania (Wharton)	680–760
Yale School of Management	680–760
UCLA (Anderson)	680–750
MIT (Sloan)	670–760
Dartmouth College (Tuck)	670–760
Northwestern University (Kellogg)	670–760
NYU (Stern)	660–760
University of Chicago (Booth)	660–760
Group 2	
INSEAD	650–750
University of Michigan (Ross)	650–750
University of Virginia (Darden)	650–740
IE Business School	640–760*
Duke University (Fuqua)	640–750
London Business School	640–750
U. of Southern California (Marshall)	640–740
University of Rochester (Simon)	630–710
Carnegie Mellon University (Tepper)	620–750
Emory University (Goizueta)	620–750
UNC (Kenan–Flagler)	620–750
Cornell University (Johnson)	620–740
IMD	620–730
University of Texas (McCombs)	620–730
Vanderbilt University (Owen)	620–720
Group 3	
ESADE Business School	600–770
U. of Western Ontario (Ivey)	600–740
University of Maryland (Smith)	600–730
Purdue University (Krannert)	596–710
Indiana University (Kelley)	590–730
Queen's University	590–730
University of Toronto (Rotman)	560–720
Michigan State University (Broad)	540–710

* Estimates

Figure 4.6

How to Ace the GMAT

Just like your approach to applications, you should have a strategy in approaching the GMAT that is well-thought-out and has some contingencies. A great GMAT score will help give you confidence as you begin to attack other aspects of the application. This section provides advice on how to tackle the exam and achieve results that broaden your school opportunities rather than limit them.

Start Early

There is nothing worse than having to complete applications while studying for the GMAT. Writing essays, managing recommenders, and completing data sheets are time-consuming enough, without the requisite hours of GMAT preparation. We suggest that you begin your preparation course or independent studying at least six months before you plan on starting your applications. This will give you ample time to retake the examination if need be. Trust us on this: The faster it's over, the happier you will be.

Once you have your strategy in place, take the next step and sign up for the exam. A lot of applicants don't sign up and lose their focus on studying as a result. If you are like most people, having an actual "D-day" set in stone will help intensify your focus and give you the motivation you need to get ready for the exam.

Know Your Strengths and Weaknesses

You've taken standardized tests before and are familiar with your performance. Additionally, you know your strengths in terms of quantitative skills and verbal dexterity. Finally, you know whether you need a highly structured environment and rigid schedule in order to study effectively, or whether you can be successful studying according to your own schedule. Given these considerations, come up with a plan that targets your weaknesses so that you can maximize your performance on exam day. If you historically perform poorly on standardized tests and have trouble calculating tips at restaurants, it probably isn't a good idea to go into the exam after only a couple weeks of preparation.

Despite what you might hear, it is definitely possible to improve your score through concentrated training, so don't get discouraged if you fall into the "can't calculate tips" category. In general, we will focus our GMAT advice to the average-to-poor test-taker, so make adjustments accordingly if you can score a 700 in your sleep.

Make a Decision About Whether to Take a Prep Course

Test preparation companies have become very popular with standardized test-takers across a variety of exams. Thousands of test-takers flock to test preparation companies each year, because of their ability to help applicants boost their scores. It's no different with the GMAT. Although very few people *need* to take a GMAT prep course, you should seriously consider taking one if:

> ☒ **You are a chronically poor standardized-test-taker.** Some people are gifted with the natural ability to perform well on standardized exams and don't need any assistance. For the rest of us, the very idea of taking

such an exam can cause sleepless nights. Enrolling in a GMAT preparation course can be a great way to build confidence and to get a handle on the challenges of the GMAT.

▶ **You need a structured approach.** A big plus of GMAT preparation courses is the fact that they place you on a standard schedule. It can be too easy to fall off the wagon in terms of studying, and taking a course can be a great way to ensure that you stay focused on preparation. Indeed, staying focused is probably the most important part of preparation.

▶ **You would like to maximize your access to resources.** Depending on which GMAT preparation course you select, you will gain access to a number of resources, including books, strategies, practice tests, question banks, and, of course, instructors.

▶ **You already took the GMAT and didn't do nearly as well as you had hoped.** We tell many applicants (especially those who start early) that they should build in enough time to take the GMAT more than once. If you've already taken it once and know that you're going to have a hard time even sniffing the high 600s on your own, then it may make more sense to pay for a course than to roll the dice, spend another couple of months studying, and risk getting a second score that you know won't get you into a top business school.

As the previous bullet suggested, all GMAT preparation courses are not created equal. Different courses provide different offerings in terms of teacher training, sample examinations, class size, and general preparation support. Here are the major players:

▶ **Kaplan:** Kaplan (*www.kaptest.com*) is the oldest player in the test-preparation market. In addition to the GMAT, it provides courses for all of the major standardized exams (SAT, ACT, GRE, MCAT, LSAT, and so on). As the first major entrant in the market, Kaplan has made a name for itself through its notoriously grueling exams. In terms of the GMAT, many students report that their actual GMAT scores greatly exceed the scores they received on Kaplan practice exams.

▶ **Knewton:** Knewton (*www.knewton.com*) is one of the newer breed of online-only test-prep companies to emerge over the past several years. The company was founded by a former Kaplan executive and boasts a pretty impressive roster of leaders who have been in the standardized test industry for years. All of Knewton's courses are delivered in a live, online setting, but the centerpiece of the company's offering is its adaptive learning engine, which Knewton promises will change the world of education, not just test prep. We have generally heard good feedback about the company's practice tests and prep materials, although it seems that do-it-yourself-type applicants tend to get more out of the course than those who need a more structured setting with individual guidance from an instructor.

⊠ **The Princeton Review:** The Princeton Review (*www.princetonreview. com*) made a dent in Kaplan's market share by offering smaller classes. The company also offers courses for each of the major standardized exams and provides admissions and K-through-12 services. Though the Princeton Review is no longer the test-prep juggernaut it once was, many MBA applicants still consider it for GMAT preparation because the company helped them do well on the SAT or ACT.

⊠ **Veritas Prep:** Over the last 10 years Veritas Prep (*www.veritasprep. com*) has grown to become the second-largest GMAT prep company in the world, after only Kaplan. The company focuses strictly on GMAT preparation and has grown quickly around the United States, Europe, and Asia. Our suggestion is that applicants interested in taking a GMAT preparation course consider Veritas Prep, given its instructors' credentials (all instructors have scored in the 99th percentile on the GMAT); extensive in-class training (42 hours for its most popular course); in-depth, online diagnostics to help students pinpoint weaknesses; and online and telephone instructor homework support. Additionally, the Veritas Prep–created exam questions closely replicate those you will see on an actual GMAT. **Full disclosure:** Since we published the first edition of *Your MBA Game Plan* (in which we independently recommended Veritas Prep), we have merged our own essay and resume evaluation services with Veritas Prep's MBA admissions consulting division, and Scott now serves as the company's Director of MBA Admissions Research. So, we're part of the Veritas Prep team now, but review the facts for yourself and see the extensive GMAT training that they offer. We still believe it to be the best in the industry.

Be aware that taking a prep course does not lift the burden of preparation from your shoulders. You are not paying for a higher GMAT score; you're paying for the resources and training that help you earn a higher score. In order to get the most out of your course, you will need to do at least as much work outside of the classroom as in it. Keep up with the course's brisk pace, and the payoff can be worth the time and money.

Should you decide to pass on taking a GMAT preparation course or decide to take on additional study outside of your GMAT preparation course (which many applicants decide to do), here are some suggestions that successful applicants have found to be helpful.

Become Familiar With Exam Strategy

One of the benefits of taking a GMAT preparation course is the strategies and exam shortcuts that are discussed. The courses do a good job of demonstrating how you should approach the exam. To learn about such strategies and just to get familiar with the exam in general, we suggest taking a look at an overall strategy-focused book such as *Cracking the GMAT* by The Princeton Review or *Kaplan GMAT 800.* These books, which include sample exams, are not too intimidating

⌐ getting your feet wet!

(caution!)

and provide solid, strategic advice that you will be able to readily apply. We have heard many complaints, however, with regard to the practice exams' ability to replicate a true GMAT in addition to the relative easiness of the questions. We therefore recommend these books as a starting point, only to be used to "get your feet wet."

If you want more specialized strategy for certain GMAT sections or question types, take a look at Veritas Prep's 15 GMAT books, each one targeting a specific topic on the GMAT. The company's *Combinatorics & Probability* and *Sentence Correction* guides have become very popular among GMAT students.

Online communities such as Beat the GMAT (*www.beatthegmat.com*) and GMAT Club (*www.gmatclub.com*) have become popular resources among applicants over the past decade. The two communities differ from each other in terms of feel—Beat the GMAT has lots of valuable material and is a little easier to get around, especially for new students, though some GMAT junkies prefer the more bare-bones way GMAT Club presents its extensive resources—but both provide enough GMAT strategy tips and practice resources that many applicants first try preparing for the test by mainly relying on these Websites. Even if you do enroll in a prep course or use other resources to prepare, both of these online communities are worth a look for GMAT prep tips and moral support from other applicants.

Practice on Real GMAT Questions

There is no substitute for practicing on actual GMAT questions. There is a certain logic that underlies the questions and their solutions that is uncovered by working on the questions over and over again. As such, we highly recommend The *Official Guide for GMAT Review* (or "The OG," as many test-taking fanatics refer to it), published by GMAC. The guide is comprehensive in that it provides hundreds of actual GMAT questions, which are accompanied by explanations of the answers. The guide also includes the entire bank of AWA questions, so you could theoretically prepare in advance for every AWA question you could possibly be asked on the day of the exam. We definitely don't recommend that approach, although reviewing a few of the AWA questions to get a feel for the essay topics is helpful. The next edition of the *Official Guide* will surely contain sample Integrated Reasoning problems, too.

The other integral part of your preparation should be GMAC's free GMATPrep test-preparation software. GMATPrep can be downloaded for free from *www. mba.com* and allows users to take two actual GMAT exams. Placing yourself under actual exam conditions can be extremely beneficial, as you get a feel for timing, how the algorithm works, and the overall length of the exam. Unfortunately, GMATPrep questions are drawn from the same bank as questions in *The Official Guide for GMAT Review* were drawn, so you may see some overlap. Nonetheless, applicants continuously state that these two resources were invaluable in their GMAT preparation.

One way you can approach the studying process is by labeling the various types of questions as you take them. For example, problem-solving problems can be labeled basic algebra, coordinate geometry, fraction, probability, and so on. In addition to providing them with a label, give them a difficulty ranking such as hard, moderate, or easy. By assigning labels and difficulty levels to questions, you can track your performance on different problem types and then identify the areas in which you are the weakest. Ideally, after going through enough questions, you will immediately recognize a question's type as soon as you see it, and know how you will approach it. It may seem that the GMAT has an infinite variety of questions, but after enough practice, you will start to see the same types of questions again and again.

Review Advanced Questions and Shore Up your Weaknesses

One common complaint about the resources offered by GMAC is that the questions provided are relatively easy when compared to the hardest parts of the GMAT. These complaints are especially directed at the quantitative questions contained in *The Official Guide for GMAT Review*. For additional assistance, consider picking up some of the topic-specific GMAT prep booklets that are offered by Veritas Prep (mentioned previously) and other GMAT prep companies. You can use these books as supplements to strengthen the areas in which you are the weakest. These guides, combined with the resources provided by GMAC, should give you ample material from which to prepare. In fact, many applicants will not need all of these resources to attain their target score. Your challenge is to understand the best preparation strategy for yourself, based on your needs, and utilize these materials and courses accordingly.

Don't Get Discouraged

It can be easy to get discouraged after reading your 15th science-based reading comprehension passage and getting all of the questions wrong. It can be even more discouraging to take the GMAT once or twice and not achieve the score for which you are aiming. It is important in those times to target the areas that are bringing down your score and attack them ferociously. Some applicants have found one-on-one GMAT tutoring to be helpful. Our suggestion is to make sure you've gained a strong understanding of how the exam works and are very familiar with the questions before looking for a tutor. If you don't understand the basic mechanics of the test, even the best GMAT tutor will only be able to help you so much.

If you remain dedicated to studying and follow these tips, you should be in great shape on exam day. Above all, remember that the GMAT isn't a test of your worth as a human being; it's just one part of the MBA admissions process, and you can beat it with enough work!

I will struggle w/ this!

A Conversation With Chad Troutwine

Chad Troutwine is co-founder and CEO of the Veritas Prep, a global GMAT preparation service. Prior to starting Veritas, Chad received his MBA from the Yale School of Management and his JD from the University of Missouri. Chad's position within Veritas makes him intimately familiar with the GMAT exam. We had the opportunity to sit down with Chad and get his perspectives on the examination that gives so many applicants sleepless nights.

What exactly is the GMAT supposed to measure?

Business schools seek the best students possible. In an effort to evaluate candidates from a global spectrum of undergraduate institutions, the Graduate Management Admissions Council (GMAC) created an objective measure of the verbal and quantitative abilities of their applicants. While many have roundly criticized the SAT for its racial and socioeconomic biases, the GMAT has remained relatively unscathed for more than 50 years. Contrary to popular belief, the GMAT has also proven to be a highly accurate predictor of a student's academic success in graduate business school. Still, the GMAT is not a valid proxy for the rest of the application process. Specifically, the GMAT is not particularly helpful in the ultimate task of any admissions committee—assessing an applicant's managerial prowess or leadership potential.

How much of this is innate, and how much can be learned?

Because the GMAT is a test of analytical skill, rather than a subject-based exam, a mythology developed that a test-taker could not dramatically improve her score. Kaplan, and other pioneers in the test preparation industry, exposed the myth—and Veritas has completely shattered it. Applicants who have a history of scoring well on standardized examinations will almost certainly do well on the GMAT. On the other hand, those who do not innately possess those skills can still acquire them. All standardized examinations have patterns. We have completely deconstructed the GMAT and created proven strategies to help our students exploit those archetypes.

What GMAT-related weaknesses do you most commonly see in applicants?

Applicants commonly design flawed preparation strategies. Specifically, we often see industrious students who are convinced that the secret to achieving a high score on the GMAT is simple: grind through as many practice questions as possible. They are misinformed. The ideal way to prepare for the GMAT is to learn a multifaceted and proven strategy *first*, then perfect that strategy with lots of sample questions. Students who jump right to the second part of the equation typically repeat the same errors, reinforcing their bad habits instead of correcting them.

What are some of the more correctable weaknesses for an average applicant who is preparing for the GMAT? What weaknesses tend to be harder for a typical applicant to correct?

me, most likely

Poor time management is prevalent, but easily corrected. Some students race ahead, leaving valuable minutes unused. Other students move too slowly, sacrificing precious time on early problems and leaving far too little time for later, often more difficult, questions. We offer several practice exams and pacing strategies to help alleviate both weaknesses.

Reading comprehension takes time to master. Students develop reading skills during a long period of time, particularly non-native English speakers. Other students struggle with esoteric rules of grammar. Still others have rusty (or non-existent) probability skills. The key for any student is to accurately diagnose weak areas and address them during the course of study.

UGH!

What's a reasonable level of improvement (from an initial diagnostic score to the actual GMAT) for which an applicant should shoot?

Improvement is a function of several different factors, so expectations should vary. If a student starts with a lower score (a 400, for instance), he could reasonably expect a 150 to 200 point increase. Conversely, if a student starts with a higher score (a 650, for example), she might be thrilled with a 60- to 100-point increase. A student who has previous exposure to the GMAT will likely begin with a higher diagnostic score, but may not have the same growth potential as her unexposed classmate.

Formal preparation should raise expectations, too. Students who prepare on their own suffer with stunted scores (when compared to those who take a full preparation course). Moreover, students who attend more comprehensive prep courses gain more insight, and typically earn higher scores, than those who settle for shorter programs. Nearly one-third of all Veritas students ultimately score a 700 (the 92nd percentile) or higher on test day.

Do you find that applicants who take the test more than once are able to significantly improve their scores?

GMAC statistics indicate that students do not improve much from one test to another. However, we are convinced that many of those repeating students do not take active steps to radically improve their prospects, and their results reflect that apathy. On the other hand, our repeaters are encouraged to adopt Veritas methods before retaking the test. As a result, our students (who previously took the GMAT) still average a nearly 100 point-increase, far more than the average for all test-takers.

It seems as though top schools' mean GMAT scores keep creeping up. What do you think that's all about?

We have three related theories. First, the pool of test-takers has improved. Raw quantitative scores have surged in the last decade, and the standardization of the GMAT has not kept pace. More students than ever are taking prep courses, so more arrive equipped to score well. Additionally, the number of international applicants has ballooned. According to GMAC, students in several international locales achieve higher average scores than their North American counterparts, particularly on the quantitative section. Tellingly, raw verbal scores have remained relatively flat for the same period. Second, GMAC has verified the predictive ability of the GMAT in several studies with many graduate business schools. Consequently, schools may be relying more and more on the GMAT, shading their means ever higher. Third, the scores began to climb steadily after GMAC switched the GMAT from a paper-and-pencil format to an exclusively computer-adaptive test in 1997 to 1998. Any test that consistently relies on reusing questions is vulnerable.

We've heard that GMAC has increased the number of combination and permutation problems featured on the GMAT through the years. What's your perspective?

We hear the same rumors, and they may well be true. Another plausible theory is that, as quantitative scores continue to rise, more students than ever are receiving difficult questions. "Perm/combo" questions typically come from the pool of very difficult questions, so they may be appearing more frequently because the relative skill of the test-takers is rising. We take no chances in our commitment to provide the best GMAT preparation available. Veritas is the only major GMAT preparation company to devote an entire lesson to perm/combo questions and other advanced statistics. Our dynamic instructors teach proven Veritas strategies, and our lesson booklets include hundreds of practice problems to help students hone their skills.

Some schools have begun to accept GRE scores in place of GMAT results. Do you believe that the GRE is an adequate surrogate? Do you think more schools will jump on the bandwagon?

The GMAT and GRE General Test are superficially identical: Each measures verbal and critical reasoning skills, quantitative ability, and analytical writing in a timed, computer-based format. The GRE is less expensive than the GMAT, so using it presumably increases the number of potential applicants, however slightly. In addition, applicants to other graduate programs that require the GRE will only need to take one test if they also apply to graduate business school. On the other hand, the primary argument for utilizing the GMAT as an evaluation tool is that it uniformly measures the aptitude of all applicants. This standardization creates a level playing field across all applicants. Accepting multiple test formats would jeopardize the one standardized aspect of the application. As such, I'm confident that admissions officers will continue to primarily use the GMAT to obtain an objective measure of quantitative and verbal abilities.

GRE General Test

We'd be remiss if we didn't at least mention the GRE General Test in this chapter. During the past few years Educational Testing Service (ETS), the organization that runs the GRE, has made impressive progress in getting top business schools to accept the GRE as well as the GMAT as the standardized entrance exam for applicants. Since 2005 Stanford, Harvard, Wharton, MIT, Dartmouth, and Duke (among others) have started to allow applicants to submit GRE scores in lieu of GMAT scores.

Much has been written in the press about the GRE's progress in the realm of top business schools, but few business school applicants have adopted it as a true GMAT alternative. In fact, for the 2010–2011 application season, every top business school that shared such data reported that the percentage of applicants submitting GRE scores was in the single digits. Although it's not a long shot to assume that this number will rise over time (especially with ETS rolling out a revised GRE in August 2011), it doesn't look like the GRE will displace the GMAT as *the* business school entrance exam any time soon.

How Does the GRE Differ From the GMAT?

At first glance, the two tests are quite similar. Each has a Verbal and a Quantitative section. Each has a writing section in which you submit two short essays. Both tests are computer-adaptive. Each test give you an overall score that can go as high as 800. Just knowing this, you'd be forgiven for thinking that the two tests are almost perfect substitutes for one another.

Where they differ most is in how they test each of the sections. Although the GMAT's verbal section features reading comprehension and critical reasoning, the GRE puts a great deal of emphasis on vocabulary, testing you on analogies and antonyms in addition to reading comprehension passages. In this way, the GRE looks a lot more like the standardized tests that you probably took to get into college.   SAT on steroids!

In the Quantitative section, though the GMAT's data sufficiency problems are legendary, the GRE has no exact counterpart. Instead, the GRE features two problem types of its own: Quantitative Comparison and Data Interpretation. These problems are rarely terribly difficult, but they do combine some of the "see what you can do with a limited amount of info" ideas that go into the GMAT's Data Sufficiency (and Integrated Reasoning) problems. The GRE's problem solving questions are similar to those that you will find on the GMAT, however, so if you're good at one you should be good at the other.

The most important practical point to be made here is that many test-takers consider the GRE to be much easier than the GMAT, particularly on the Quantitative side. In fact, a perfect score on the Quantitative section will get you in no higher than the 94th percentile, meaning that a perfect score only means that you're in the top six percent of all test takers. Make one mistake, and you'll drop down to the 89th percentile.

Though you may already be thinking, "Great! I'll take the GRE!" keep in mind that this actually could make your job harder, particularly if you're a terrific test-taker. Why? When everyone else does well, you need to be perfect in order to stand out from the pack. If you have an off day while taking the GRE, you (and admissions officers) may be disappointed by your percentile scores. At least right now, the GMAT is a more effective instrument in separating the great test-takers from the merely good ones.

Note that, as this third edition of *Your MBA Game Plan* goes to press, ETS is rolling out a new version the GRE General Test. We expect that the changes (which ETS hasn't described in great detail) will make the exam more similar to the GMAT. So, many of the differences here may go away. However, for the time being, we expect that the GMAT will continue to be the most commonly used test for business school admissions, by far.

Should I Take the GMAT or the GRE?

If many top business schools have started to accept the GRE General Test in the past few years, then there must be something wrong with the GMAT in admissions officers' eyes, right? We wondered about this, too, especially when GMAC embarked on a year-long project to interview MBA admissions officers from around the world and completely overhaul the GMAT (in response to the inroads the GRE was starting to make, no doubt). The result of this ambitious project? GMAC announced that it would replace one AWA question with the new Integrated Reasoning section, and everything else would stay the same.

Although GMAC never publicly shared the findings of its research, the feedback from admissions officers was pretty clear: "We kind of like the GMAT as it is now. Don't change it too much. If you really want to know, we don't rely on those AWA scores too much, so you can probably get rid of one of those. Is there any way you can simulate a mini case study, just like some management consulting firms give our students, in a standardized test setting? But that's about the only change we'd make to the test." We put a lot of words in admissions officers' mouths there, but we bet that this is pretty close to the feedback that GMAC received.

So, if they like the GMAT, why do business schools also now accept the GRE? This change has less to do with the two tests themselves and more to do with what kinds of applicants admissions officers are trying to attract. As we mentioned in Chapter 3, in the business schools' competition with one another to attract the absolute cream of the crop, top MBA programs are increasingly looking outside the traditional feeder industries of consulting and banking. They're trying to catch more young "rock stars" who might never have considered an MBA and already have GRE scores under their belts because of a passing interest in other graduate programs.

Are you an amazing college junior wondering what you want to do next? Why not give the HBS 2+2 Program a shot, or apply to Stanford GSB for deferred admission? As part of this push, business schools are trying to lower the barriers by accepting GRE scores. These kinds of applicants can absolutely apply with GMAT scores, but admissions officers are eager to tell them that they don't need to take the GMAT if they already have strong GRE scores.

What does this mean for other, more traditional applicants, such as bankers and consultants? Although they are also technically allowed to submit GRE scores to any schools that accept them, we urge those applicants to think about their overall application story. Admissions officers expect a GRE score to come from the recent college grad who has "high potential" written all over him, but is unsure of whether he wants to go into public service, or maybe get an MBA and go about his life's mission that way. If the banker who's been destined to apply to business school for the past four years submits a GRE score, on the other hand, admissions officers may ask, "What's going on here? You say you've been thinking about an MBA for years, but you never even took the GMAT? Are you serious about this, or aren't you?"

So, you can think of the GRE as the official exam of the exciting "different" candidate who's considering business school as an alternative to other graduate programs, though the GMAT is the test of choice for the young professional who's been planning his business school application for the past couple of years. If you fall into the former camp, have gotten some very positive signs from the admissions office about your chances and already have a great GRE score, then go with that. If you fall into the latter camp, as we expect most readers of this book do, then the GMAT will make the most sense for you.

Test of English as a Foreign Language (TOEFL)

If the GMAT is the mountain that applicants must conquer before receiving admittance into a business school program, then the TOEFL (which is run by ETS, the organization behind the GRE) is generally considered little more than a speed bump. That's not to say that the TOEFL is wholly insignificant, but an applicant who performs well on the verbal section of the GMAT shouldn't have to worry too much about the TOEFL.

As the title would suggest, the TOEFL's function is to measure the English proficiency of people whose native language is not English. If your native language is English, you can stop reading this section right now, as you will not be required to take the exam. Many schools will also allow applicants who studied in an English-only curriculum or worked extensively in an English-speaking country to waive the exam. Because business schools differ on the delineation of who is required to take the TOEFL and who is not, you should check the policies of your target schools.

One of the reasons the TOEFL is not as rigorous as the GMAT is because it is geared toward a wider audience. Indeed, the TOEFL is taken by aspiring students of multiple disciplines at multiple levels, in addition to people applying for scholarships, certifications, and government positions. As does the GMAT, however, the TOEFL takes place on the computer for most examinees. A paper-based exam is still available in some parts of the world, but here we will focus on the computer-based test, which ETS refers to as the Internet-based Test (or iBT) because the questions are actually served over the Internet, rather than coming from software that is installed on each individual computer. Note that, unlike the GMAT, the TOEFL is not adaptive; each test takers receives the same range of questions regardless of performance.

Format and Content

The TOEFL iBT consists of four sections:

1. **Listening:** Tests your ability to comprehend spoken English, as used in North America. You will hear a conversation, lecture, or classroom discussion and then be asked to answer a question about the conversation's meaning, implications, or supporting details. The content of this section is different from that of all the GMAT sections, so you shouldn't expect GMAT preparation to help you perform well on this part of the TOEFL. Note that you only get to hear each passage once, although you may take notes as you listen.

2. **Reading:** Tests your ability to comprehend written academic English. You will be asked to read three to five passages and then answer questions about each passage. Similar to the Listening section, questions focus on the meaning, implications, and details of the passages. ETS has gradually introduced new question formats to this section, going beyond the traditional multiple-choice question format to make it harder to get questions right simply through process of elimination and lucky guessing.

3. **Speaking:** Tests your ability to speak clearly and articulately about a topic with very little preparation. You speak your answers into a headset-based microphone. This section is actually new since the TOEFL moved to the iBT in 2005. For two questions you will be asked to speak spontaneously about topics for which you are familiar. Four other tasks involve reading short passages or listening to audio clips, and recording spoken responses to questions about what you just read or heard. Although it's a computer administers the test, at least three (and as many as six) ETS-trained graders will evaluate your recorded responses.

4. **Writing:** Tests your ability to write in English on an assigned topic. You will be asked to write a standard English essay that discusses a topic and provides supporting details. This section contains two essays: one in which you answer questions about something you have just read, and one in which you state and support an opinion on an issue.

The following is a summary of the TOEFL format and content:

Format and Content of the Internet-based TOEFL

Section	Time	No. of Questions	Types of Tasks
Listening	60–90 minutes	34–51	Listen to lectures and conversations, then answer questions about what you heard.
Reading	60–100 minutes	36–70	Read academic passages and answer questions about what you read.
Break	10 minutes	—	—
Speaking	20 minutes	6	Speak about a topic that you know well; speak based on audio and text passages given to you.
Writing	50 minutes	2	Read and listen to given information, then write persuasively about what you were given.

Figure 4.7

Scoring

You will receive a separate score for each of the four sections and a total TOEFL score. Individual scores for each of these three sections range from 0 to 30; total scores range from 0 to 120.

When you hear people talking about their "TOEFL score," they are generally referring to their total score out of 120. So what should you shoot for? Business schools sometimes are more explicit in stating what their TOEFL requirements are versus their GMAT requirements. Though they won't ever admit to having hard GMAT cut-offs, some do actually tell you to aim for a certain TOEFL score before applying. Although you should definitely find out what your target schools' TOEFL requirements are, top schools generally look for scores greater than 100, which would put you just above the 80th percentile. (This is similar to our rule of thumb for our GMAT Verbal and Quantitative scores.) The following figure provides the scores and percentiles of recent test-takers. You should also note that there is a separate scoring system for the paper exam.

Scores and Percentiles of TOEFL iBT Examinees

Scaled Score	Reading	Listening	Speaking	Writing	Total Scale Score	Percentile Rank
30	94	95	99	98	120	100
29	86	87	97	95	116	98
28	79	80	94	90	112	94
27	73	74	90	83	108	89
26	67	68	84	—	104	82
25	61	62	—	73	100	75
24	55	57	76	63	96	68
23	50	52	65	—	92	60
22	45	47	54	51	88	53
21	40	42	—	40	84	46

Figure 4.8
Source: ETS.org

TOEFL Preparation

Many applicants find it helpful to prepare for the TOEFL prior to preparing for the GMAT, as it is considered to be less difficult. Additionally, preparation for the TOEFL will help you practice for the verbal section of the GMAT.

Because test-takers' familiarity with English varies so greatly, it's difficult to suggest an appropriate amount of preparation time. On average, applicants generally find about two to three months of preparation to be enough. Similar to GMAT preparation, we suggest first gaining an understanding of exam strategy and then practicing on real TOEFL questions. For exam strategy and practice on real TOEFL questions, you should consider the resources that are offered on *www.toefl.org*. This site contains additional resources in which you might be interested, so check it out when you have a chance.

Performing well on the TOEFL is vital to international applicants' prospects of gaining acceptance to their target schools. By following these simple tips, you should be in great shape to do well on the exam.

TOEFL Alternatives: IELTS and PTE Academic

Just as a battle has broken out between GMAC and ETS over whether the GMAT or the GRE General Test will be the standardized test of choice for MBA admissions officers in the coming decades, a fight is simmering among ETS and two organizations that want to challenge the TOEFL's dominance as the test of English fluency.

The first challenger to throne, the International English Language Testing System (IELTS), has actually been around since 1989. It is run as a joint venture between British and Australian organizations, so it's no surprise that it's most commonly accepted by British and Australian schools, although more than 3,000 U.S. schools also now accept it. The IELTS is similar to the TOEFL in that it tests examinees' ability to read, write, speak, and listen to English, although it presents a variety of accents and phrase choices to try to wipe out the TOEFL's bias toward North American English. Your final IELTS score is on a nine-point scale, scored in half increments.

The other TOEFL challenger is endorsed by GMAC (yep, the same people behind the GMAT) and is called the Pearson Test of English Academic, or PTE Academic. It is run by Pearson VUE, the company that actually administers the GMAT for GMAC. The PTE Academic is also a computer-based exam and, as the IELTS does, presents examinees with English accents and phrases that test-takers might hear from anywhere in the world. Thanks to GMAC's relationships with top business schools, heavy hitters including Harvard, Stanford, London Business School, and INSEAD began accepting the PTE Academic almost immediately after its availability, although as of 2011 it was little more than a year old. It will be interesting to see how the GMAC/ETS battle plays out over the next decade.

We won't devote more space here to how to prepare for either exam, but free IELTS and PTE Academic prep resources are freely available from the organizations that run those exams. Just as we recommend with the TOEFL, we suggest that you first prepare for these exams (whichever one you choose to take) because they will likely be less difficult than the GMAT. If you find that these exams give you a very hard time, then you may want to take a step back before moving ahead with the overall MBA admissions process.

Interview

In one sense, your admissions interview will be the fastest part of your entire application process: just 30 to 60 minutes and you're done. Looked at another way, it will be the most stressful part: You need to come out from behind your computer and face a potential grilling. Neither view is exactly right. The work that you do on your interview will start weeks before it actually happens, as you craft your application (and can even start well before that). Ideally, by the time you sit down across from your interviewer, your extensive preparation will put you at relative ease. For the most part, your admissions interview will simply be another way in which you communicate the story that you have already constructed. As long as you have your game plan in place, your interview should only help you strengthen your story.

Why Interview?

Believe it or not, interviews are still a relatively new phenomenon in the world of business school admissions. Although many of the top programs conduct interviews "by invitation only," nearly all of them have a stated goal of interviewing all of the applicants whom they eventually admit. Other business schools make interviews optional, but highly recommend them. Finally, some business schools outright require interviews for all applicants. No matter what your target schools' policies are, there is a much greater chance that you will go through this ritual than if you had applied 20 years ago.

Why have interviews become a more important part of the admissions process? For one, business schools need more mechanisms to separate the great candidates from the good ones, as more and more people apply and the admissions process becomes more competitive. What better way to do that than to look an applicant in the eye and ask him why he wants to go to your school? Also, MBA programs have become more and more careful about building strong communities and cohesive student bodies. Because each class is a melting pot of personalities, schools want to personally inspect each one of those personalities before granting admission.

Every school looks for slightly different attributes in its applicants, but you can be sure that the admissions committee will be looking to answer a few key questions about you:

- ☒ Are you the person you say you are in your application?
- ☒ How are your communication skills?
- ☒ Are you someone your classmates would be glad to be around?
- ☒ Are you ready for business school?

The interview is often the best way to get at these answers. The purpose of an interview isn't to see how well you act under pressure or to try to trick you into revealing something terrible about yourself (although we do seem to hear a couple of horror stories about weird interviews every year). Think of it as a way to reinforce what you have already said about yourself in the rest of your application and to help the admissions committee put a face to the name and numbers in your application. Yes, your interviewer may probe around certain weaknesses in your application or resume, but this is your chance to attack those weaknesses head-on and put them to rest.

Types of Interviews

There are several different variables that determine exactly what the tone of your interview will be. These variables include: who interviews you, where and how the interview takes place, and how much the interviewer knows about you before your meeting.

Who could interview you:

▷ **Admissions officer:** These interviews tend to be the most formal, and the most specific in terms of what the interviewer is looking for. Admissions personnel will usually have a form from which they work, and will make an effort to cover each area before the interview is over. Beware, though, that if the admissions officer doesn't cover everything in the allotted time and some questions go unanswered, it will be considered your fault. Your main line of defense against this problem is <u>making sure that you don't ramble</u>. Later on, we will discuss how you can make sure to cover the most important parts of your story.

▷ **Student:** Some schools train their students to conduct interviews. These students will typically work off of the same forms that admissions officers use. Even though you may hit it off with some students and end up having an informal conversation, many students tend to conduct interviews "by the book" even more so than admissions officers. Schools tend to use the interview feedback they get from students in the same way as the feedback they get from admissions officers. So, you should treat an interview with a student the same as an interview with an admissions officer.

▷ **Alumni:** Alumni have a reputation for being a little more laid back in terms of how they conduct an interview. They will also have some guidelines for conducting the interview, but tend to be more willing to let it evolve into a natural conversation. Remember, though, that they are still evaluating you. Even more importantly, these are the interviews where you most risk not covering everything that you want to talk about. If there are certain messages that you want to convey and the interviewer just wants to talk about the Yankees, know that the onus is still on you to cover those messages. Also, keep in mind that alumni interviews tend to be the least restrictive in terms of time. Many alumni will let an interview stretch on for well over an hour, if you are both enjoying the conversation. Finally, be prepared for a little more variability in your experience. Although most applicants report having great interviews with alumni, there are more than a couple of horror stories of applicants being traumatized by weird, rude, or even harassing interviewers. These types of stories are rare, but know that experiences with alumni interviewers can be less consistent than with other interviewer types.

▷ **Faculty:** Though having a faculty member interview you is extremely uncommon, there are some schools that might have you interview with a professor. These interviews generally feel like a discussion with an admission officer, but tend to be more academic in nature. Therefore, you should go into the discussion having a good understanding of the academic choices you've made in addition to being able to articulate what you want to get out of the curriculum.

Where you could be interviewed:

▷ **On campus:** Most interviews with admissions personnel and students take place on campus. The bottom line is that you should try your best to get to campus to do your interview. It might seem minor, especially because many schools make off-campus interviews readily available, but visiting campus goes a long way in showing your interest in the school (especially if you live far away). Expect your on-campus interview to be conducted in the admissions office, usually in formal attire (although a few schools conduct business casual interviews). While you're on campus, take advantage of the chance to meet with current students, tour the grounds, and sit in on a class. Even if you've already done a visit, why not do it again? It helps you get to know the school and its student body better, and a more informed applicant is usually a more successful one.

▷ **Off campus:** Off-campus interviews are usually conducted by alumni, although some schools will do "tours" once or twice a year in which they visit major cities and interview a bunch of candidates at a hotel, or conduct interviews at a an MBA tour event (which is similar to a traveling job fair but for business schools). You can expect the format of these interviews to be the same as those conducted on campus. Interviews with alumni can take place anywhere, from coffee shops to restaurants to the alum's own office. We suggest picking a quiet place, but we advise that you try not to do the interview in the alum's office. Even the best-meaning alum can be easily distracted when surrounded by his co-workers and email. Also, you will probably feel more comfortable in a more "neutral" setting, so avoid the in-office interview if you can. If your alum suggests his office, reply that it might be nice to get out of the office, and be ready with a few alternatives to suggest. Most alumni will respond positively to this.

▷ **Phone/video conference:** Most schools prefer that you meet in person with an admissions representative. However, there are cases in which geographical, financial, or time constraints don't always allow that to happen. In those cases, your interview might be conducted over the phone or via video conference. These types of interviews are usually with admissions counselors and follow the same format as other interview types. They are given the same weight as other interview types, but, given the opportunity, we advocate trying to make it to campus.

How much your interviewer will know about you:

▷ **Resume-based interview:** Many schools' interviews are "blind," meaning that the interviewer has not seen your application before meeting with you. The most the interviewer will know about you is your resume, and some don't even see this before the interview. In these cases, you can expect a lot of general questions to start things off, such as, "Tell me about yourself," or "Walk me through your resume." Because the interviewer knows very little about you in these situations, and you usually have just 30 to 60 minutes to sell yourself, it is critical that you know what messages you want to communicate, and that you hit all of them before time is up.

▷ **Application-based interview:** A few schools have their interviewers read through your entire application before the interview. In this case, the interviewer is usually an admissions officer. After reading your application, the interviewer will develop a picture of you in her mind, and will come to the interview prepared with specific questions. Expect some probing of weaknesses and questions around your motivations for moves that you've made in the past, such as "Why did you decide to leave Morgan Stanley and go into venture capital?" You can help yourself most by knowing your story cold, anticipating weaknesses, and having reasons for why you've done the things that led you to apply to business school. You should also pay special attention to your career goals, because it is almost certain that you will be asked to expand on them.

Most of the preparation that you do for your interview will be the same no matter where you do it and who interviews you. The differences will mainly be nuances, such as how many specific questions the interviewer prepares ahead of time, how long the interview is, and how many questions you are able to ask. Now we'll dive into specific tips for acing the interview.

Interview Preparation

You are the best expert on you. You know why you've made the decisions that have led you to this point, what your strengths and weaknesses are, and (hopefully) where you want to go next in your career. The challenge is in figuring out how to best communicate all of this to your interviewer, and in being ready to tell various stories from your past that illustrate your abilities.

The questions you will get in an interview tend to fall into several broad categories: high-level questions about you, questions about why you want to go to business school (and where you want to go after that), and questions about specific experiences in your background. We will look at each of these question types in turn.

High-Level Questions About You

These are usually the most open-ended questions. An interviewer who asks these questions is giving you a chance to talk about your own history and traits, and to emphasize the parts of your background that are most important to your application story. Questions of this type include:

- ▣ "Tell me about yourself."
- ▣ "Walk me through your resume."
- ▣ "How would your friends/coworkers/supervisor describe you?"
- ▣ "What are your biggest weaknesses?"
- ▣ "What are your biggest strengths?"
- ▣ "How would you introduce yourself to your classmates?"

The first two questions are similar, and are often used to start off an interview. If an interviewer asks you to start this way, this is your chance to take control of the interview and explicitly state the two or three core messages that you want to emphasize. <u>Practice</u> is vitally important. Your goal is to develop an "elevator pitch" of approximately <u>three minutes</u> that describes your background, highlights your strengths, and provides a story above and beyond the simple facts on your resume. You don't want this introduction to come across as overly stiff or rehearsed, but we generally see applicants put too little preparation into the elevator pitch, rather than too much. The better prepared you are, the more natural you can make this introduction sound to the interviewer.

The following is a fictitious example of how someone might answer "Tell me about yourself." The answer to "Walk me through your resume" would be very similar, as you would still point out specific achievements and provide a context for your career path:

Growing up, I was always interested in cars, and I remember helping my dad change the oil in our car when I was as young as 6 years old. By the time I got to high school, I knew that I wanted to become an engineer, so I devoted most of my energy to studying math and science. I went on to attend Ellicot University, where I earned my mechanical engineering degree. I was also very involved in my fraternity, where I was treasurer, and I am proud to say that I started the Ellicot Racing Club, which is still going strong and has since grown to more than 30 members.

After graduating from Ellicot, I pursued my interest in cars by taking a job at Midwest Motor Company. I entered as an assistant design engineer. It was exactly what I dreamed of: I worked on projects that shaped the cars that millions of people drive. In my first year there, I made recommendations for a safer airbag system for Midwest Motor's small passenger cars that were ultimately implemented. We estimate that at least 500 lives are saved each year thanks to the new system. After my first year, I was promoted to design engineer, and I was placed in a team that was charged with redesigning the child safety restraints in Midwest Motor's minivans. It was a tough project because we were given a short deadline and very strict cost controls, and had government regulations to constantly think about, but we did a great job of finding creative solutions. I specifically found a way to use new materials that simultaneously increased the safety and reduced the cost of the restraint systems.

After two years, I asked to be moved into the safety engineering department, because the safety-related projects that I had worked on had really captured my imagination. The move also appealed to me because it represented my first opportunity to gain experience in managing others full-time. I moved into that group as a senior engineer, and was permanently put in charge of a team of four designers. We worked on a series of projects to improve the safety of Midwest Motor vehicles in small but important ways. The achievement I'm proudest of is leading my team to develop a new, safer design for fuel systems in SUVs, which I presented to senior management all the way up to the level of vice president of our division. The company is implementing the new design this year.

While I still enjoyed the engineering aspects of the job, what I found to be most rewarding was working with people from other functions, including production, finance, and even marketing. For the first time, I realized how much my decisions affected their jobs, and vice versa. It gave me a new appreciation for teamwork. I also learned how to work with people whom I didn't directly influence. Learning how to get things done by influencing others is something that I've been working on for the last year. I'm also working on applying this skill in the Great Lakes Foundation, a nonprofit group that I've been involved with for two years. I do fund-raising for the organization, and have gained a lot of experience in persuading people to donate their time and money to the cause of helping inner-city children find creative outlets for their talents.

Now that I've had a taste of how an entire organization works, I'm interested in one day building my own manufacturing business, particularly one that will help make transportation safer and more fuel-efficient. To do so, I would like to gain an even broader view of how to run a business. While I'll always be an engineer at heart, I now want to learn more about marketing, finance, and how to lead people. From my experience, I see these as the skills that make for the most effective managers. I then want to put these skills to use in running my own business. Given my experiences and my desire to gain new ones, I think now is the perfect time to pursue an MBA at the Ross School of Business.

Your own elevator pitch may be less involved than this one (and you may find that you don't even get all the way through yours if your interviewer hears something interesting and wants to dive right in), but this example gives you an idea of what you want to do. This applicant does a good job of:

- Communicating his high-level application themes, which are his passion for cars, his experience leading teams to results, and his specific reasons for wanting to go to school.

- Explicitly naming the results of what he worked on. Many applicants fail here; it not only matters what you did, but also what actually happened as a result of it.

- Highlighting what he specifically contributed as a member of a team. Applicants also tend to fail here by saying what "we" did, but never explicitly explaining what "I" did.

- Giving reasons for the moves that he made in his career, and making those reasons consistent with his overall story.

- Naming some of his extracurricular activities. Remember Business schools don't want someone who is married to his job!

- Tying together his past experiences into why he now wants to go to business school.

There is a balancing act here. You want to provide enough detail to make your story interesting, but you also don't want it to get too boring or bogged down in details. Develop your elevator pitch with what you feel is an adequate level of detail, and if you find that it's taking too long, then you can start to shave off details (you don't have to get *every* single detail out on the table in the first three minutes). Whatever you do, keep your high-level themes in there. After all, the main purpose of your elevator pitch is to get all of your main themes "out on the table."

The other questions are designed to see what you perceive your own strengths and weaknesses to be. Be honest when answering about your strengths and weaknesses. Your interviewer won't be impressed if you say that your biggest weakness is that you're a perfectionist who just plain insists on working too hard. Honest answers that reveal introspection and maturity usually impress the interviewer far more than you might think. This is why interviewers will sometimes give you what seem like curve balls—not to trick you or stress you out, but to get past the veneer and get a better feel for what truly makes you tick.

One thing you want to do in these answers, though, is focus on skills rather than personality traits when talking about your weaknesses. For example, saying "I need more experience managing teams and delegating authority" is better than answering with "I tend to be impatient with others." The former is something that you can clearly improve with time and practice; the latter is something that will likely never change. You will also win bonus points if you can briefly discuss ways in which you are trying to address your weaknesses. So, if you mention that you haven't had much experience managing teams, mention that you've requested to be placed on a project that would allow you to do so. This shows that you are aware of your growth opportunities and actively try to improve in those areas. Even better is to be able to point to a recent example where you already put some lessons to use and have made progress in improving yourself.

Questions About Why You Want to Go to Business School and Future Goals

These questions may include:

- ◪ "Why do you think now is the time for you to go back to school?"
- ◪ "What do you hope to learn in business school?"
- ◪ "What do you think you will contribute that will be unique among your classmates?"
- ◪ "Why do you want to come to this school?"
- ◪ "Where else are you applying?"
- ◪ "Where do you see yourself in 10 years?"

Some of these will overlap with the previous questions. Don't be surprised if you cover one of these areas in your elevator pitch, only to have your interviewer dig much deeper later in the interview. Most of these answers will come directly from your application. In your essays, you hopefully will do a good job of explaining your goals and why business school makes sense for you; now it is just a matter of verbalizing these reasons.

In order to answer the "Why do you want to come to this school?" question well, you obviously will need to have done your homework on the school. It's amazing that applicants still make the mistake of telling a Harvard that they want to go there because they like the case study method, without being able to answer any slightly more in-depth questions about how that method works. Be ready to list several reasons for wanting to attend the school, including both the tangible (curriculum offered, location) and intangible (culture, learning environment). You may be tempted to find the school's curriculum and to rattle off several names of classes in your interview, but be careful unless you can mention more about those courses, beyond their names. Interviewers know that anyone can find a few course names on a school's Website in a matter of minutes.

When answering the "Where else are you applying?" question, don't be afraid to be honest. The main thing is to have a reason for why each school appeals to you. You don't need to have the same reason for each school, and you may never even end up discussing your reasons, but it helps to have them ready. Admissions officers want to see if the schools you've selected have any commonalities, or if you're simply applying to the top five schools in the *U.S. News* rankings. If you're talking to an interviewer from a lower-ranked school and you rattle off a bunch of top 10 schools, the message can come through that you view the school as a safety. Don't waste your breath in an interview talking about other schools any more than you have to, but be prepared to answer the question if the interviewer presses you on this.

Questions About Specific Experiences in Your Background

Some schools will spend most of the interview on these kinds of questions. These types of questions are the ones that famously start with "Tell me about a time when you...." The idea here is to go deeper than your philosophy on how to manage others, how to prioritize projects, and so on, and to hear about how you actually handled these challenges in the past. Your job is to recall experiences from your background that will answer these questions, and to sum them up in tidy two- or three-minute stories that will help your interviewer see exactly what you did in a specific situation and what the result was.

There is a popular technique that successful applicants use to answer these kinds of questions. Most of your answers will ideally be broken down into the situation that you faced, the actions that you took, and the results of your actions. Not surprisingly, this technique is called "SAR," for Situation, Action, and Result. You can start your preparation by building a table that includes questions that you can expect along with your answers, broken down into the SAR format. After a short while, you will likely find that this technique feels very natural for telling your stories.

See Figure 4.9 on page 95 for a few sample questions, with fictitious answers entered into the SAR grid.

Each of your answers should take no more than two to three minutes. (You can actually tell a very in-depth story in this amount of time.) Of the SAR components, the situation is the least important. It's critical in that it sets up the next two parts, but don't spend too much time on it. You want to provide just enough background to make the interviewer understand the situation, and ideally to make her care. Err on the side of being brief, and the interviewer will stop you and ask for more depth if needed. For a three-minute answer, 30 seconds to one minute should be spent on the situation, a minute and a half to two minutes should be spent on the specific actions that you took, and the remainder on the results.

As mentioned previously, two places where applicants often fail are in not stating what the results were and in failing to mention what they specifically did to help reach a goal. Interviewers will be much more impressed if you can point to tangible results that came about as a direct result of what you did. Saying "We gained $5 million in business because of the ideas I implemented to make the product more reliable" is much more powerful than saying "We gained new business by making the product better." Be specific about what you did, and the results that you created.

This framework will work for nearly any question in which you're asked to describe a situation that you faced and how you resolved it. Ideally, you will be able to prepare for the questions that you are most likely to receive, and to outline an answer for each using the SAR framework. The great thing about SAR, though, is that it also helps you organize your verbal answers to questions that you didn't anticipate. If you find yourself faced with a question similar to this, take a deep breath, think about an example that could be used to answer the question, and start talking in the SAR format. If you find yourself still talking about the situation after a minute, move on and get to the meat of the story.

Question	Situation	Action	Result
Tell me about a time when you led a team to success despite opposition from others.	I was asked by my company's sales director to develop a version of our software for a new platform. I pulled together a team of developers to produce the product, but the VP of product management resisted, saying that it was a waste of time and effort.	I made a point of understanding why the VP was opposed to the project. I realized he was unhappy that the sales team came directly to the developers to make it happen. He was also dealing with flat sales on his existing products. I addressed each of these concerns, getting him involved in the process and showing him customer feedback that suggested that the new product could boost sales.	The VP gave his support to the project, and we rolled it out in under six months. The new product was a success, and now all of our products are being translated for the new platform. The sales director and product management VP both personally thanked me for making it happen.
Discuss a project that required the use of your analytical skills.	My boss asked me to identify and recommend some new potential sales targets for a product of ours that was facing slow sales. I knew little about the product or its market.	I met with one of our data analysts to identify the common traits among our current buyers. I then dug into market research data to find potential customers who exhibited similar traits. I recommended that we try a direct-mail campaign targeted toward a segment that we hadn't previously considered.	The direct-marketing test was a success, and we rolled out the campaign nationally. While sales had previously been declining 10 percent per year, this new campaign helped the product see its first double-digit sales gain since it was first launched.
Describe a time when you inspired someone to work harder.	I was running a civil engineering project that consisted of myself and two engineers. We were asked by a client to design a drainage system for its property. The unique landscape of the property meant we couldn't apply normal solutions to the problem. However, one member of my team was very busy with other projects and insisted on using a standard solution.	I knew that she was very busy, so I talked to her boss to free her up of some lower-priority projects that were consuming much of her time. Her boss agreed to do so after seeing how valuable this contract was. I then appealed to her creativity. I knew she took a great deal of pride in the work that she did, and I talked to her about how exciting it would be to design a solution that no one had developed before.	Once some of her time was freed up, she became passionate about the project and threw herself into it with the rest of the team. We ended on designing a new system that performed great and saved us and the client a total of $15 million. We couldn't have done it without her intelligence and energy. I made sure she was acknowledged for her hard work and we've had a great working relationship ever since.

Figure 4.9

With a decent amount of preparation, such surprises should be minimized. Still, it is impossible to prepare for every single question that you will be asked, so being prepared to think on your feet is as critical as preparing for specific questions. The following is a list of common questions that you might expect to get in a business school interview. Plug these into your own SAR grid and try to develop real-world stories from your own experiences:

Leadership

- ▣ "Discuss a time when you successfully supervised a diverse group of people toward a difficult goal."
- ▣ "Give an example of when you accomplished something significant that wouldn't have happened if you hadn't been there."
- ▣ "Tell me about a situation where you had to persuade someone to agree with your point of view."
- ▣ "Describe a time when you had to gain upper management's support for an idea/proposal."
- ▣ "Tell me about a time when you had to work with a difficult person in order to accomplish something that needed to be done."
- ▣ "Name a time when you had to convince someone who didn't report directly to you to do something he didn't want to do."
- ▣ "Describe a situation in which you identified key problems early on in a project and were able to avert a crisis."
- ▣ "Tell me about a time when you led a team to a goal even though the individual team members were skeptical that it could be accomplished."
- ▣ "Discuss a time when you had to make an unpopular decision."

Teamwork

- ▣ "Tell me about the toughest group that you ever worked in. What made it so tough, and how did you handle it?"
- ▣ "Describe a time when you had a conflict with another person in a corporate or school setting."
- ▣ "Tell me about a time when you worked with someone who didn't follow through. What did you do?"
- ▣ "What's the best team you've ever been on? What do you think made the team work so well?"
- ▣ "If you're building a new team to complete a project at work, what kinds of team members do you look for?"

Ethics

- ▣ "Describe an ethical dilemma that you faced in your career. How did you resolve it?"
- ▣ "Give me an example of when you pushed back against doing something."

▶ "What is the hardest decision you have ever had to make on the job? Outside of your job?"

Innovation

▶ "Name a time when you developed a unique and resourceful solution to a problem."

▶ "Describe a situation when you had to make an important decision without having all of the necessary information at hand."

▶ "Tell me about a time when you had to analyze facts quickly, identify the issues, and develop an action plan."

▶ "Give me an example of when you thought out of the box."

▶ "What was the hardest problem that you ever had to solve at work?"

▶ "Tell me about a time when you took a smart risk."

▶ "Have you ever had to bend a rule to get your work done more efficiently?"

Maturity

▶ "Tell me about your most spectacular failure. What happened? What did you learn?"

▶ "Describe one way in which your life so far hasn't turned out as you expected it would."

▶ "What is the worst professional decision you have ever made?"

▶ "Tell me about a time when you weren't very pleased with your performance."

▶ "Discuss a time when you didn't succeed on the first try."

▶ "Describe a situation in which you wish you had acted differently with someone in your group."

One note: For "failure" questions, don't be afraid to admit your failures. The most important thing that an interviewer is looking for with these kinds of questions is evidence that you learned from your past mistakes. Ideally, your answer will consist of what happened, what went wrong, what you learned, and how you applied that lesson in a later situation.

How to Carry Yourself in Interviews

In your admissions interview, you want to come across as personable, confident, interested, interesting, and sincere. For every one of these descriptors, think of the opposite. No one would want to be surrounded by arrogant, tentative, indifferent, dull, or phony people. In short, you want to convey that you are who you said you are in your application, and you want to show the interviewer that you're someone who would make a great classmate in business school. Yes, this may seem daunting, given the application themes that you already want to communicate. Most of these personality traits, though, should come through if you can relax and simply be yourself.

For the most part, your interviewer will set the tone of the discussion. As described earlier, some will be laid back and interested in getting to know you personally; others will want to drill you on specific parts of your resume or application. Obviously, how serious or informal you are will largely depend on the person across from you. Your job is to make adjustments accordingly, and to answer the questions that the interviewer asks.

No matter what the tone of the interview is, however, you absolutely must be sure that by the end of the interview you have covered the main themes that you came in with. For instance, you may have a laid-back, "get to know you" kind of interviewer who doesn't ask you the kinds of pointed questions that would allow you to talk about your strengths. If this is the case, it's perfectly appropriate to say "By the way, there are a couple of things that I think make me a good fit for this school. I'd like to talk about them and hear your thoughts" before the interview is over. (The "hear your thoughts" part is a particularly nice way to keep things in discussion mode rather than "I'm going to deliver a prepared monologue and will need five minutes of your attention" mode.) You don't want to be too transparent, but all but the most inept interviewer will appreciate the fact that there are certain ideas that you're trying to get across before the discussion is over.

If you have a stone-faced interviewer who won't laugh at your jokes, don't press the matter. Act professionally, answer the questions that are asked, and make sure to hit your main themes. In a way, these interviews can sometimes be easier because the interviewer's business-like questions will give you a better chance to strut your stuff and will minimize the risk that you'll miss something important. Many applicants who interview with HBS admissions officers report experiences that sound like this.

If you have a downright hostile interviewer (which happens from time to time), don't let yourself get flustered or goaded into an argument. Relax, think of it as the interviewer's half-baked way of testing your mettle, and answer the questions as they come. Don't be argumentative, but don't be afraid to be assertive, either. A hostile interviewer may be looking for poise and confidence more than anything else, so make sure to demonstrate these. Losing your cool won't get you in at any school, even if the interviewer *really* deserves a piece of your mind.

At the end of the interview, ask a couple of good questions. Good questions don't have answers that you could have gotten from the school's Website or brochure. If you are interviewing with an alum or a student, asking about her experience is always a good place to start. Similarly, if you are interviewing with an admissions counselor, ask what types of students she thinks get the most out of attending that school. If you interview with a faculty member, asking about the direction of the curriculum will usually generate an interesting response.

Also, keep in mind your audience as you ask these questions; don't ask a question of someone who realistically won't know the answer. For many applicants, a business school's admissions officers are the all-powerful deities who positively must know everything that's going on at the school (and everything that ever will happen). The reality is even the best, most "plugged in" admissions officers are so busy with managing the day-to-day and week-to-week processes of attracting and evaluating applicants that they don't necessarily know why the finance department's chair just stepped down, or how many students typically participate in the school's entrepreneurship boot camp in their second year. Admissions officers know a lot, but they especially know about the who's and what's and why's of putting together a terrific class. Questions that have to do more with personnel moves or grading policy details, though not off limits or inappropriate in any way, usually yield less useful responses than you might expect.

Interview Etiquette

It is appropriate to send your interviewer a short thank-you note after the interview. There is a small debate over whether that thank-you note should be e-mailed or handwritten. The benefit to e-mailing a thank-you note is that the interviewer is likely to receive it prior to submitting the evaluation report. A well-written note can reinforce your message and leave the interviewer with a positive feeling about your candidacy. In reality, odds are that the interviewer's mind is already made up, whether or not he's actually submitted his write-up. The hand-written note adds a personal touch that outweighs e-mail's "speed factor." The bottom line is that this is not a decision worth losing sleep over, as it won't have an impact on the school's decision to admit you. You should choose the method with which you feel most comfortable, although a handwritten note is what we'd recommend. Regardless of the communication method, keep it brief and try to echo one or two topics that were discussed during the interview. Don't bother trying to use it as a desperate attempt to get in a few final talking points.

We expect that interviewing will continue to become a more important application component with time. Schools consistently mention that it is a great way to differentiate applicants and, as more people apply to the world's top MBA programs year after year, admissions officers will need to keep working harder to separate out the best of the best. Although the interview is just one part of the admissions process, the most successful applicants will be the ones who go into their interviews with a clear, well-practiced plan of attack.

Essays

After GMAT preparation, writing your essays will likely be the most time-consuming part of the application process. Admissions directors often cite essays as the most important part of the application. The combination of these two factors means that you should dedicate a significant amount of time (15 to 25 hours per application, from initial concept brainstorming to final editing) to producing powerful and persuasive essays that are succinct in style.

Your essays should be the foundation upon which all other application components are built. You can think of your essays as a platform that can be used to tell your personal and professional story. There is no one official tone that you must use in these essays—these aren't official intra-company memos—so feel free to utilize a professional, informal, or humorous voice in establishing your story. The other components (recommendations, interview, resume, and data sheets) should substantiate that story. The more aligned your components are around common themes, the more positive the impact on your application. We will discuss putting together a game plan that links all of the components in Chapter 6.

As part of the story-telling process, you should try to augment your strengths and anticipate your perceived weaknesses. Use the analysis from Chapter 2 and the profiles in Chapter 3 in identifying and addressing both. In sum, your essays should effectively communicate your differentiated position, your embodiment of the four dimensions, and your fit with the school. As frustrating as the essay-writing process may seem, ultimately it helps crystallize your reasons for wanting to go to business school and some of your career objectives.

The rest of this section will review what admissions committees typically look for in essays, essay types that candidates predictably come across, samples of successful essays, and a prescription for how to approach the writing process.

What Are Admissions Committees Looking for in Essays?

There are three aspects of your essays that will be explicitly or implicitly evaluated by admissions officers:

▷ **Content:** In response to the question "What mistakes do applicants commonly make?" admissions officers often respond that many applicants fail to adequately address the essays' questions. Seems like a stupid mistake to make, but many applicants "copy and paste" an essay that doesn't quite fit, try to "shoehorn" responses that don't answer all of the questions' elements, or just completely miss the point of the essay. Regardless of the reason, not succinctly answering essay questions is an easy way to win your application a quick trip to the "ding" pile. Many other applicants are guilty of simply rehashing their resumes, offering nothing new in their essays that describes who they really are. In general, you need to answer the questions asked, and do it in a way that helps the admissions committee get to know you a little bit better as a person, not a GMAT score and a data sheet.

▷ **Clarity of communication:** It doesn't matter how strong your story is if your essays are hard to follow or are riddled with grammatical errors. Poor grammar dilutes essay responses and can ruin the best applicant's chances. You should focus on ensuring that you are using appropriate syntax, idioms, and sentence structure. Additionally, beware of run-on sentences, as they often lead admission counselors to confusion. Being concise and clear will always benefit your cause. Grammar is usually the area of essay-writing where having a second, third, and even fourth set of eyeballs can provide the most immediate help.

▷ **Structure:** Maintaining an organized structure and a logical flow of ideas will help increase the impact of your statements. Consider, especially for longer essays, using headers to help guide the reader. Another consideration in terms of structure is word usage. Though you certainly want to be descriptive in your writing, stay away from esoteric vocabulary. Your goal is to effectively communicate ideas, not to show off your knowledge of the English language. Finally, make sure that you observe word limits. As a rule, you shouldn't surpass word limits by more than 10 percent. Going beyond that can be an easy way to buy a "ding." Remember that admissions counselors are reviewing thousands of applications, so they can be very sensitive to applicants who don't respect word limits. Give them a break and use no more words than are needed to tell your story.

Essay Types

As you move from one application to another, you will encounter many essay questions that are similar in nature. We've found that there are basically 10 different types of essays that you will come across as you review various MBA programs' essays:

- ▶ Future goals and school fit.
- ▶ Leadership and initiative.
- ▶ Teamwork.
- ▶ Ethics.
- ▶ Personal philosophy.
- ▶ Personal evaluation.
- ▶ Hobbies.
- ▶ Diversity.
- ▶ Professional experience.
- ▶ Failure.

The types of essays that a school includes on its application are a reflection of that school's approach to learning and the sort of applicant for which it looks. Therefore, it is imperative for you to understand the implications that underlie the essay questions. Although we will cover the implications, it is important to note that essays don't always fall into one of these discrete buckets. For example, a question might ask about your approach to leading teams, which obviously touches upon both the teamwork and leadership themes. In fact, some of the example essays we use in the following pages can easily fit into two or three of these categories.

These sample essays express ways in which successful applicants have played on those themes. The applicants received admission to at least one of the schools reviewed in Chapter 5 and their backgrounds are diverse in terms of work experience, gender, academic background, ethnicity, nationality, GMAT scores, GPA, and so forth. For each essay, we provide some commentary on the applicant's perspective and highlight the attributes that resonated positively with the admission committee. Although no essay is necessarily perfect, these essays should help you in creating ideas for your own approach. And crafting your own approach is the key. This is *your* MBA game plan, after all.

In this third edition of the book, we've added new essays in Appendix A with commentary to provide even more insight on how to craft successful essays. The essays that follow come from successful applicants, and we've included a broader set of essays (both good and bad) in the Appendix, so you can get a better sense of what errors to avoid as you plan out your own admissions essays.

Future Goals and School Fit

This type of essay is almost universally used in applications. Nearly every one of the business schools profiled in this book includes this essay prompt in its application. This should give you an idea of how important fit is to schools.

For the most part, this question type is trying to drive at whether now is the best time for you to get your MBA. Additionally, the school wants to know how it fits into your long-term plans. Lastly, the school wants to know how you envision yourself having an impact, either in your career or, more broadly, on society. Practically speaking, business schools don't expect you to state an exact position in which you envision yourself a certain number of years from now, but rather where and how you see yourself making a difference. Many applicants fall short in this essay by providing a very generic response in terms of their future goals. Simply stating that you want to move into private wealth management is not enough. You must go a step beyond that, explain how you see yourself having an influence in that field, and explain how the school fits into the picture.

Many times this question type will ask for a summary of your professional background and then ask you to relate it to the school and your career goals. Be careful not to simply rehash your resume. Rather, provide some context as to why you've made the choices that have led you to where you are today; *that* is how this essay helps your overall application story. The three components (professional background, school, future goals) should be linked in a fluid manner. You should highlight your strengths, outline your future goals, and then underscore how the school will help you build additional strengths in order to achieve those goals.

Some examples of questions that fall into this type are:

- "Why is an MBA a critical next step toward your short- and long-term career goals? Why is Tuck the best MBA program for you?" (Dartmouth College—Tuck)

- "What is your career vision and why is this choice meaningful to you?" (Harvard Business School)

- "Describe your short-term and long-term career goals. What is your motivation for pursuing an MBA now and how will UCLA Anderson help you to achieve your goals?" (UCLA—Anderson)

- "What are your short-term and long-term post-MBA goals? How will Columbia Business School help you achieve these goals?" (Columbia Business School)

- "What are your career aspirations? What do you need to learn at Stanford to achieve them?" (Stanford Graduate School of Business)

Sample Essay ◄

Briefly assess your career progress to date. Elaborate on your future career plans and your motivation for pursuing an MBA. (Northwestern University—Kellogg School of Management)

Where I've been

I joined Withers Incorporated after graduating from Dawson University in order to experience numerous business practices across multiple functions. During my tenure at Withers, I have made substantial contributions on both a global and local level to our customers and internal initiatives. Operations and corporate finance are the primary areas in which I have practiced.

During the last year, I have narrowed my focus to financial cost analysis. As a leading contributor to a $32-million cost-reduction effort, I have expanded my knowledge of finance beyond the surface level. In order to expedite an assessment of the Firm's financial situation and gain an understanding of primary business drivers, I created financial models for four major business units whose yearly technology expenditures exceeded $400 million. I provided my expertise to more than 20 individual business and technology partners to validate cost reduction opportunities, and implement cost-reduction plans. By developing and honing cost reduction skills and understanding how to create strategies oriented towards reducing the bottom line of a company's budget, I have become a valuable asset to the Firm, even in an unstable economy.

> The applicant does a good job of quantifying the impact he had on the organization. By showing his ability to work in a numbers-oriented environment, he helped "make up" for a quantitative GMAT score that fell a little bit below Kellogg's mean score.

Exemplary results and the exhibition of strong management capabilities in Firm initiatives led to my appointment to the Global Finance Advisory Council (GFAC), a premier leadership group within the Firm. The primary function of the 10-member GFAC is to proactively shape and influence the direction of Withers' financial position from a macro level.

In an effort to provide consistency and standardize business units' approach to financing operations, I am leading an effort to create protocols for more than 2,000 managers globally. Developing standard protocols for the entire Firm has required me to adjust my communication style according to the business unit and geographical region.

> Clearly a demonstration of the leadership dimension. The applicant's strategy was to emphasize leadership in this essay, and the teamwork dimension in the interview and in a separate essay.

Where I'm going

As a result of working closely with multiple business units, I've gained a strong interest in initiating my own venture. This ambition drives me toward my professional goal: to redefine American fashion by developing an import business that specializes in a mélange of South American and North American clothing. In my travels and research, I have observed a growing interest in multi-ethnic clothing that uses fabrics, prints, and styles that are not indigenous to the U.S. Market studies have shown a strong demand on the West Coast for clothing and articles with South American motifs. Although these types of products exist in the United States, they are generally not marketed or distributed adequately, and are not tailored to the average American. I believe there

> Nice transition. Coupled with the header, it makes the direction of the essay clear.

is opportunity to promote a new line of fashion that fuses the cultures of the North and the South. Although at first glance this might appear to be a complete departure from my current career path, it will actually build upon the fundamental skills that I've acquired in the analysis of business models. Indeed, the ability to achieve operational efficiencies would be a key success driver in this mid- to low-margin business.

> Good discussion of future objectives. The applicant adds a nice touch by showing insight into the business and how his background could help him be successful.

The flexible Kellogg learning model would allow me to build upon these skills through its concentrations in entrepreneurship and marketing. Courses such as Entrepreneurship and New Venture Formulation, Managing Entrepreneurial Growth, Marketing Strategy, and Sales Promotion and Retailer Behavior would be vital assets in the development of my business model. During my visit to Kellogg, I was impressed by the way in which faculty actively show how theory works in practice. Being able to make that transition will also be vital to my success.

> Excellent work in terms of providing Kellogg specific information that would clearly be of benefit in achieving his career goal.

As a member of the Kellogg community, I would actively engage in the diverse range of global forums, club activities, and business plan competitions. All of these opportunities would bolster my efforts in becoming a successful entrepreneur.

> Providing one or two more Kellogg specifics in this section would have made this essay even stronger.

Leadership and Initiative

Business schools' increased emphasis on leadership is reflected in the large proliferation of this essay type. Many schools even have more than one question of this type on their applications. Questions will generally ask you to describe a situation in which you displayed leadership, initiative, and/or creativity. Schools are trying to gain an understanding of your approach to leadership and the style(s) you employ when the situation calls for it.

These are great questions for utilizing the "Situation, Action, Result" (SAR) framework, which we discussed in the "Interview" section. It is important that you cover each component of SAR in order to maximize the impact of your essays. We suggest, based on our experience studying essays and working with applicants, that you try and dedicate approximately 30 percent of the word limit to the situation, 50 percent to your actions, and 20 percent to the result. Although there is no hard and fast rule, this is just a guideline that can be helpful in evaluating whether you have dedicated enough time to each part. Business schools are most interested in your actions and the result of those actions, but setting the context of the situation is vital to understanding the other components. The takeaway is that, although you might write more for one component than another, they are all key to writing a solid leadership and initiative essay.

In many cases, schools will focus a portion of the question on teamwork, so don't think of the two as mutually exclusive. Indeed, showing that you have the ability to lead in a team environment is probably more important than showing your ability to lead on an individual level.

Some examples of questions that fall into this type are:

- *Describe an accomplishment that exhibits your leadership style. The description should include evidence of your leadership skills, the actions you took, and the impact you had on your organization.* (Yale School of Management)

- *Give us an example of a situation in which you displayed leadership.* (UC Berkeley—Haas School of Business)

- *Please describe a time when you took responsibility for achieving an objective.* (MIT—Sloan School of Management)

- *Discuss two examples that demonstrate your potential as a successful leader.* (University of Rochester—Simon School of Business)

SAMPLE ESSAY ◀

Tell us about a time when you built or developed a team whose performance exceeded expectations. (Stanford Graduate School of Business)

The thing I remember most about my first day as a Regional Manager at Global Rent-A-Car is that no one else wanted to be there. In fact, one of my new employees mentioned that he did not enjoy coming to work because he had nothing to show for it. I understood what he meant: The office was last in every category—profit numbers, customer service, and fleet growth. Even more interesting to me was when he mentioned that he did not trust the other employees in the office because he felt like no one wanted the office to be a success. I began to realize that the negative attitude in the office was not due completely to our poor performance, but to a lack of teamwork between the employees.

That day, I made it my mission to make the office a more desirable, fun place to work. I started by doing the least desirable activity myself—washing cars. By doing the job everyone liked least, I hoped the employees would begin to trust me. Indeed, my employees told me that when they saw me washing cars,

> Great details in here. Gives the reader the feeling that the applicant has his work cut out for him.

they realized that the goals of the office were more important to me than keeping my suit clean and that I had proved to them that the team took priority over the individual. To encourage them to get to know each other better, I started to take them out, as a group, every Thursday evening for drinks and appetizers at a nearby restaurant. Soon the employees were joking with each other and I could see that they were becoming closer.

As our team began to trust each other on a personal level, they began to trust each other on a professional one. I encouraged one employee who felt "trapped" in the office all day to take donuts to the corporate accounts in our area. At the end of the month we sat down and counted the number of referrals we had received from her sales calls. When she saw the increase in referrals from the month before, she began to realize that she was truly making a difference in our profits. She began to encourage the other employees to become involved in the marketing plan. Within six months we had increased our corporate business by almost 100

> Great discussion of the actions taken to resolve the issues the organization was facing.

percent, and it was directly attributable to the team marketing effort.

Under my leadership, we began to see our income and profit numbers skyrocket. I am now convinced that leadership cannot simply be an order from a supervisor; it must come from dedication to a vision that is greater than any individual. Our success was due, in part, to the fact that the employees began motivating each other. I now know that what makes work fulfilling is being part of something that you have helped create, and knowing that your efforts on the team are making a positive impact. My washing cars was a small price to pay for the kind of turnaround my team achieved in nine months and the dividends that accrued from working together.

> This is a strong finish. The applicant does a nice job of stating the results and then discussing what he learned.

Teamwork

Although many essays on leadership dedicate a portion of the question to teamwork, some focus purely on the interactions and relationships that you have with others. We consider these the "genuine" teamwork questions. The admission committee is looking to see how you communicate and cooperate in a group environment. Therefore, expressing your interpersonal skills is an essential part of answering these types of questions.

As leadership questions often do, teamwork essay prompts sometimes ask you to reflect on a situation. As such, using the SAR framework for these question types can be a great way to respond to them. Although SAR can be a great framework to use, don't feel chained to it. If you have a more creative and powerful way to get your points across, then go for it. Remember: SAR is just a framework to help you organize your thoughts.

It's interesting to note that there are now fewer overt teamwork questions in top business schools' applications than there were just a few years ago. Many of these questions have been replaced by "Diversity" questions, which we cover later in this chapter. Business schools have moved from asking about teamwork directly to sniffing for signs of a team-friendly attitude in your other essays and interview answers, as well as in your letters of recommendation. Don't think that schools don't value this dimensions any less; they're just evaluating it a bit differently than they used to.

Some examples of questions that fall into this type (taken from previous applications so you can see good examples are):

> ▸ *Using an example from your work experience, describe what factors contribute to a dysfunctional team experience. What steps can the individual or group take to help alleviate this situation and help develop a constructive team environment?* (Michigan State University—Broad)

> ▸ *Please give us an example of a difficult interaction you had with someone. Please describe the situation, what was difficult about it, and how you resolved it.* (MIT—Sloan School of Management)

SAMPLE ESSAY ◀

Describe an experience in which the relationships you developed enhanced the outcome of a team effort. (Columbia Business School)

A few years ago, I participated in a cross-continent choir that was composed of members from France and the United States. As a part of the American contingent, I traveled to Paris for vocal training and performances.

Arriving in Paris, we met our French counterparts for the first time and were immediately overwhelmed. Although we had considerable talent, and had performed several times together in the States, our French team members were well-known throughout the European continent. We felt additional pressure, as most of the songs we were to sing together were to be sung in French. For months prior to the trip we practiced the inflections and intonations that were to be used while singing the French compositions, but it became immediately apparent that we were far from meeting their standard.

Initially, the choir was fragmented based on citizenship. The cultural environment and the skills of the French team members intimidated us. In order to counteract the intimidation factor, I asked the choir director if each U.S. choir member could partner with a French choir member. The director agreed that having us pair off would be a good relationship builder and I was soon chatting it up with my partner, Serge.

> Nice description of why the team was initially fragmented.

I asked questions as they came to mind in an attempt to understand the French language, culture, and music. Serge often responded with his own questions and a dynamic dialogue ensued. Outside of the formal choir practices, Serge and I held sessions that focused on the proper pronunciation and delivery of the songs. In addition to learning more about the music, I began to learn more about the culture and the language.

During the next few weeks, Serge and I became inseparable. I learned that despite the initial surface differences that existed, we were very similar at the root. We both wanted respect, understanding, and the opportunity to succeed. Furthermore, I was amazed at the new perspectives and insights on life that I gained from him. The result was that I not only developed my vocal talents, but also realized a new appreciation for other cultures and the possibilities for improved communication across geographical borders.

> Terrific explanation of the actions taken to build the relationship.

My American compatriots had experiences similar to mine and we found that as a result of our newfound relationships, we performed on an entirely higher level. When we first practiced as a unit, one could easily distinguish our voices. Now we truly sounded like a single unit. The audiences were extremely receptive to our performances and unanimity. In fact, we went on to win first place in a regional competition.

This experience taught me the power of relationship building. No doubt our choir would still have been successful without partnering up. Still, I don't think our harmonies and melodies would have sounded as pure and I know that we wouldn't have had as much fun. Now, I always look to build an understanding with my

> The applicant does an excellent job of relaying the results of the actions and what she learned from the experience.

colleagues in order to enhance team dynamics.
. . . .

Ethics

Admissions officers have always looked for signs of strong ethics and integrity in applicants, but this facet has only grown in importance as many schools have added required ethics courses and modules to their curricula over the past few years. Odds are that, at least once during the application process, you will be asked for evidence that you're an upstanding citizen.

Many applicants struggle to come up with examples to use for essays addressing ethics. If you think about it long enough, however, you can certainly come up with an example in which your sense of ethics was tested. A relevant story doesn't need to be as intriguing as a corporate scandal. Many of the best ethics essays deal with subtle issues, such as deciding to do what's best for a group when you could have gotten away with less. For many questions, your response doesn't necessarily have to reflect on a professional situation.

Admissions committees are most interested in understanding your thought process in approaching ethical situations, so you should dedicate a good portion of your essay to that. Just as with other situation questions, you can use the SAR framework for most of these question types. Discussing your thought process generally would fall under the "Action" section.

Some examples of questions that fall into this type are:

> *Describe a time in which your ethics were challenged. How did you deal with the situation and what did you learn from it?* (Carnegie Mellon University—Tepper School of Business)

> *Describe a situation where your professional ethics were challenged.* (USC—Marshall School of Business)

> *In response to the recent financial crisis and the perception that many business leaders acted unethically, much attention has been given to various MBA Oaths. In what ways do you feel an MBA Oath will impact ethical behavior by MBA graduates? Would you take such an oath yourself? Why or why not?* (University of Notre Dame—Mendoza College of Business)

Sample Essay ◄

Describe an ethical dilemma that you faced in your professional career. How was it resolved and what did you learn from the experience? (Indiana University—Kelley School of Business)

It's funny how powerful the desire to receive accolades can be. As far back as I can remember, I've always sought approval from my superiors; whether they've been my parents, teachers, or managers. That's why it was so difficult for me to not fulfill my manager's request.

The request came two months after I started working for Ong Semiconductors as an economic analyst. My manager asked me to conduct a comprehensive market analysis for a new product we were planning to release in the next year.

Eager to prove myself, I dug right into the analysis. I estimated the €450 million market potential by hosting discussions with potential customers, analyzing research reports, and speaking with analysts. Working with engineers, I calculated the manufacturing costs at different production levels. Finally, I completed a competitive analysis that highlighted other companies' abilities to compete in the market. After working four 70-hour weeks, I submitted a draft of my analysis to my manager.

> Nice details in this paragraph. The applicant does a great job of providing the details of her hard work, highlighting her capabilities even in an "ethics" essay.

Apparently, it wasn't good enough. The competitive analysis didn't reach my manager's expectations. He began to press me to include more details, specifically details regarding my former employer. My manager requested that I include proprietary information on a potentially competing product on which my previous firm was working. The information request included: technical specifications, cost data, and the product launch date. It was clear that I was being asked to break a good-faith understanding I had with my old firm not to reveal proprietary information.

I could have easily provided all of the information and satisfied my manager's request. I probably would've received major accolades for the insights. Indeed, I'm confident that there wouldn't have been any direct ramifications for revealing the information. Still, based on my sense of ethics, I simply could not break the understanding I had reached with my old company. I did my best to explain this to my manager.

> The applicant effectively conveys the ethical dilemma and takes the reader through her thought process.

Needless to say, he wasn't pleased with my stance. A short time after our discussion, I was removed from the project. Through time, I discovered that the company had a history of conducting competitive analyses that bordered on corporate espionage. Three months after being removed from the project, I put in my notice and subsequently left the firm. A year later, several executives were investigated for illegal competitive practices.

> This paragraph shows that the applicant is willing to take action based on her convictions. She also subtly explains her five month stint with the firm; something that would otherwise be viewed negatively.

Reflecting on my experiences, I'm proud of the way I acted. While compliance would have allowed me to satisfy my manager's request, it would have also placed me on an ethical "slippery slope." I've reached the conclusion that, before I seek approval from my superiors, I must first seek approval from myself. This continues to be a personal rule that I actively observe.

> As all applicants should, she explains what she learned from the experience. The closing is also very effective in that it ties back to the introduction.

Personal Philosophy

Personal philosophy essays focus on your overall perspective on life. They often ask you to reveal "life-changing" experiences or to discuss something that is extremely important to you. Here, the admissions committee is really trying to get to know you and find out what drives you. A portion of the essay will often ask you to describe what you've learned from the experience. Responding to that is imperative because it provides insight into how you learn and what you value. This is important enough that, even if the question doesn't specifically ask you to describe what you learned, you need to cover it in your response.

You will run into at least one personal philosophy essay on most applications, so you should spend some time thinking about the message you want to send. (Increasingly, these questions are showing up as multimedia "essay" prompts, which we'll cover later in this chapter.) Once you've identified your message, it is important that you communicate it with passion. Although passion should be threaded throughout your entire application, it should ooze out of this essay.

Some examples of questions that fall into this type are:

- *What matters most to you, and why?* (Stanford)

- *We all experience significant events or "milestones" that influence the course of our lives. Briefly describe such an event and how it affected you.* (USC—Marshall)

- *What event or life experience has had the greatest influence in shaping your character and why?* (UCLA—Anderson School of Management)

- *What are you most passionate about and why?* (University of Michigan—Ross School of Business)

- *You are the author for the book of Your Life Story. Please write the Table of Contents for the book.* (Cornell University—Johnson School of Management)

SAMPLE ESSAY ◀

Please describe yourself to your MBA classmates. You may use almost any method to convey your message (e.g. words, illustrations). Feel free to be creative. (New York University—Stern School of Business)

My name

My middle name is Carlson. Carlson is a family name, passed on to me from my grandfather Michael Carlson Stevenson. It is a representation of the heritage and the legacy that I have been bestowed. It is also a reflection of the standard to which I will be held. In every facet of his life, Grandfather has been a visionary striving for excellence. He has extended his vision through education and servitude. Expanding the legacy of my grandfather is extremely important to me, because failing to do so would be to dishonor the very name that I bear.

> Interesting introduction, which speaks to the applicant's motivations. Although this essay prompt invites applicants to use any medium with which to express themselves, this applicant sticks to words, but keeps it interesting with a strong, revealing opening.

My grandfather

Grandfather has six sons, all of whom have either an M.D. or a Ph.D. Success in education was always emphasized in his household. Grandfather views education as a key that is necessary for achievement. If one is educated, Grandfather says, than he can effectively decide his own fate and help positively impact the fate of others. Grandfather himself holds a B.A. and an M.A. in education administration. After earning his degrees, Grandfather went on to start his own private school for pre-school to middle school students. He feels that if children are shown the value of education while they are young then they will not depart from that teaching as they grow older. As a result, he not only educated his own children, but also hundreds of children in his surrounding neighborhoods. He has provided education support through his own teachings, the establishment of scholarships, and career counseling.

> Family is clearly important to the applicant. The discussion of education provides some insight into his motivation for applying to business school.

As a public servant, Grandfather is well-known both domestically and internationally. In addition to his education initiatives, Grandfather has served his local community through the church that he pastors. Community service functions have included: Feeding and clothing the needy, and supplying financial support for area building projects. At an international level, Grandfather has provided support to initiatives in more than five nations, such as Haiti, Ghana, and Liberia. On several occasions, he has personally traveled to these emerging markets and directly assisted with the projects. The projects have ranged from the construction of schools, to the dispersion of food, to the building of churches.

My turn

I have found truth in Grandfather's beliefs on education and servitude. My successes have mainly been a result of effective preparation, which equates to proper education. Once knowledge has been obtained, I believe that it should be freely shared. As such, I am intrigued with the persuasive power inherent to speaking and writing. Whether it is delivering the commencement address to my graduating college class, writing editorials for the local newspaper, or leading a discussion on career success with indigent populations, I enjoy speaking and writing into the lives of others with candor and truth.

> This paragraph gives the admissions committee good examples of the applicant's commitment to education, communication, and community service. This essay really aligned well with the applicant's career objectives to start a nonprofit organization. The applicant also expressed an interest in starting a magazine that focuses on global community service opportunities. The closing is nicely linked back to the opening.

Communication contains the possibilities of inspiration, reconciliation, and illumination. To communicate well is to be understood. To communicate powerfully is to effect change. I will effect change. My middle name is Carlson.

· · · · · · · · · · · · · · ·

Personally, I think this essay is bland.

Personal Evaluation

This essay type calls for applicants to provide a perspective on themselves, most often as an evaluation of their own strengths, weaknesses, life experiences, and personal growth. The admissions committee wants to see evidence of maturity and self-awareness. Although you certainly don't want to cast yourself as inept, describing one or two areas in which you can to develop further is as important as depicting your strengths. It is important because the committee is interested to know how you can benefit from its learning model and its culture, so make sure you describe a connection between your growth areas and the school's strengths.

The most effective personal evaluation response supports your overall story in addition to displaying fit with what the school has to offer. It is also important that your response doesn't contradict what your recommenders write. For example, if you state that your interpersonal skills are some of your greatest assets and one of your recommenders writes that you need improvement in this area, then the rest of your evaluation might be called into question. This is just one more reason why creating a game plan for yourself and for your recommenders can be such an effective tool.

Finally, as mentioned in the interview section, the weaknesses that you present will ideally be skill-based, more than personality-based. After all, there is no MBA course that can change someone's personality. (For example, "I want to get better at connecting the big picture to the small details," is something where an eight-week MBA course can help; "I have a short temper" is not). Keep this in mind as you choose which weaknesses to discuss.

Some examples of questions that fall into this type are:

> *The best mistake I ever made was….* (Northwestern University—Kellogg School of Management)

> *What is the most difficult feedback you have received from another person or the most significant weakness you have perceived in yourself? What steps have you taken to address it and how will business school contribute to this process?* (Yale School of Management)

> *Tell us about a time in your professional experience when you were frustrated or disappointed.* (Harvard Business School)

> *What is the greatest challenge or hurdle you have overcome, either personally or professionally, and how did you manage to do so?* (Dartmouth College—Tuck School of Business)

> *Reflect on a time when you turned down an opportunity. What was the thought process behind your decision? Would you make the same decision today?* (University of Pennsylvania—The Wharton School)

SAMPLE ESSAY ◄

Give a candid description of yourself, stressing the personal characteristics you feel to be your strengths and weaknesses and the main factors, which have influenced your personal development, giving examples when necessary. (INSEAD)

Kaizen

The Japanese have a concept known as "kaizen," which roughly translated means continuous improvement. In recent history, this term has become most closely associated with the improvement of manufacturing operations and adopted as a mantra by several companies. However, the original meaning of the word kaizen carries an even more noble intent than business success—its intent is a successful life. A person adopting the philosophy of kaizen

> This section sets up a nice context for why the applicant is strong in certain areas and how she is able to identify the areas in which she needs to improve.

✓ intro could be shorter

knows that human perfection is unattainable, yet strives to achieve it every day. Following this philosophy means always acting in a manner that increases knowledge and leads to personal development. Having always been a highly motivated person, this concept struck a chord with me and I adopted the philosophy of kaizen, making self-improvement a daily goal.

Through time, the adoption of this principle has allowed me to build strengths in several areas. While I realize I still have several areas in which I can grow, I know my belief in kaizen will help to address those areas.

Strengths

My leadership skills, broad educational and professional experiences, analytical abilities, and strong personal presence are all strengths on which I continually rely.

> Rather than stating that leadership is a strength, the applicant goes a step further and provides nice examples of how she displayed leadership.

The leadership skills I first developed playing team sports have allowed me to become a leader in my educational and professional endeavors. At Carella College, I was a founding member of the Investment Club and delivered presentations at most club meetings. While working for Amariglio Financials, I supervised a 35-employee department of mostly first- and second-generation Americans. With Taverna Holdings, I led client training sessions for more than 50 employees, and have also served as a mentor to newly hired Taverna Associates.

My broad educational and professional experiences developed my unique perspectives into business. Having examined companies from both an external shareholder view as a securities analyst and from an internal management perspective, I have insight into both the challenges faced by companies in developing and implementing strategic direction and the

> The applicant clearly understands how much INSEAD values global professional experience and displays fit by highlighting her exposure to international business.

shareholder perception of strategy's value—something every executive should evaluate. My global experience, resulting from work experiences in the United Kingdom, Germany, France, South Korea, and Canada, have provided insights into the unique challenges of competing internationally and of growing a company through international acquisitions.

Some of my strengths are inherent. My ability to read and comprehend information at a rapid pace began when I first started reading the newspaper's sports section at age 3. My calm demeanor has also been a constant in my life, allowing me to remain composed and positive in challenging situations. This translates into a strong personal presence, often noted by managers as making me seem older than my years.

Weaknesses

Well-handled

I also recognize my development needs. In pursuing the goal of owning a successful large venture capital firm, my prior focus on large corporations has limited my knowledge of how to start and manage a small business. By pursuing an MBA at INSEAD, I hope to increase my knowledge of small business financing and development.

From a skills perspective, I need to work on reigning in my strong perspectives. While being willing to debate a position is an attribute, at times I defend my point so strongly that I may miss the value in my opposition's argument. One of INSEAD's appeals is the opportunity to debate viewpoints with a group of incredibly intelligent people, learning from their experiences while sharing my own.

> The stated weaknesses align well with INSEAD's strengths.

I hope to be able to build upon my strengths and address my weaknesses during the next year at INSEAD, as I continue to live by the kaizen philosophy.

> Nice job of connecting the closing back to the opening.

Hobbies

Another way that business schools sometimes try to find out more about you is by explicitly asking about activities in which you're involved outside of work. These questions provide you with a great opportunity to convey your interests outside the professional environment. You can use the opportunity to express one of the dimensions that wasn't as strongly articulated in other parts of your application.

Don't be afraid to have a little fun with these essays. Admissions officers read so many dry resumes—and essays that are nothing more than rehashed resumes—that they welcome a chance to learn something about you that may be a little unusual or even offbeat. Of course, you need to keep it appropriate, and the hobby you describe should ultimately fit in with your overall application story, but here's one place in your application where you can really let your personality shine through.

Finally, not many schools specifically ask questions about your hobbies, but rest assured that they all want to know about you beyond your GMAT score and transcripts. Every application has room for you to work in your passions outside of work, whether it's in your personal philosophy or failure essays, the optional essays that most schools' applications offer, or the admissions interview. Don't feel that you need to keep these stories bottled up unless you're explicitly asked for them.

Some examples of questions that fall into this type are:

▷ *One thing people would be surprised to know about me is....* (Carnegie Mellon University—Tepper School of Business)

▷ *Please tell us about yourself and your personal interests. The goal of this essay is to get a sense of who you are rather than what you have achieved professionally.* (Columbia Business School)

▷ *What motivates you to continue contributing to the community?* (Georgetown University—McDonough School of Business)

SAMPLE ESSAY ◂

People may be surprised to learn that I.... (Northwestern University—Kellogg School of Management)

People may be surprised to learn that I enjoy acting as a dance choreographer. I have found cultural dance to be an outlet that allows me to utilize innovation and imagination through graceful moves, balanced by synchronized music.

During the last 10 years, I have choreographed numerous folk dances for audiences of more than 5,000 people. Each performance is significantly different. Two years ago, I choreographed a dance for 16 women. Each of us carried candles throughout the performance, adding effervescence to execution. The following year, I modified a traditional Swedish dance that manipulates pieces of ribbon on a central pole. As part of a grand finale act, I, along with 11 other participants, performed the ribbon dance in a manner that reflected a classic Norwegian drama.

> Shows a combination of creativity and dedication.

In addition to the energy and creativity that is required by choreography, I also enjoy the teaching aspects. Teaching participants how to move with harmony and style are key to the successful implementation of any dance. It is satisfying to be able to not only see the participants learn the components of the dances, but also to watch them as they add their own personality to the movements. I will continue to choreograph dances, because it provides me with an avenue through which I can celebrate my culture, spirit, and life.

> The applicant's interest in teaching certainly would benefit Kellogg's team-based learning approach. The applicant successfully raised that point during her interview.

Diversity

Diversity essays can be similar to personal philosophy essays in that they are asked in an attempt to find out how you are unique. However, diversity essays differ in that they will frequently ask how your uniqueness will contribute to the classroom.

It is important to understand that admissions committees have a broad definition of diversity, and that isn't limited to culture or ethnicity. Diversity is defined as unique experiences or background, so it applies to professional roles that you've played, perspectives that you have, hobbies in which you participate, topics that you've studied, and so on. Regardless of how you are unique, be sure to bring it out in response to this type of question in order to show that you have something different to bring to the classroom dynamic.

Since we published the first edition of *Your MBA Game Plan,* no essay type has been added to more top business schools' applications than this one. This suggests that admissions officers are increasingly as worried about how you'll fit in with the whole as they are with your own individual achievements. Keep this in mind not only as you answer this essay prompt, but also as you develop your overall application story.

Some examples of questions that fall into this type are:

> ▶ *How will your background, values, and non-work activities enhance the experience of other Duke MBA students and add value to Fuqua's diverse culture?* (Duke University—Fuqua School of Business)

> ▶ *We expect that Ross MBAs will not only be effective leaders, but also effective teachers. How will you contribute to the learning experience of your peers at Ross?* (University of Michigan—Ross School of Business)

> ⊵ *The Darden MBA program expects students to actively participate in learning teams, the classroom, and the broader community. Please share one or two examples from your past experience that best illustrate(s) how you will contribute to this highly engaging and hands-on learning environment.* (University of Virginia—Darden School of Business)

> ⊵ *Describe a situation in which you had to work with a diverse group of people (those with backgrounds or opinions different from your own) to accomplish something. What conflicts arose and how did you resolve these conflicts? What did you learn about yourself and accomplishing work as a group that you can bring to Krannert?* (Purdue University—Krannert School of Management)

> ⊵ *At the McCombs School of Business, you will be part of an active and diverse community. How will you use your personal strengths and unique experiences to enrich the McCombs community during your two years in the program?* (UT Austin—McCombs School of Business)

SAMPLE ESSAY ◀

Tuck seeks candidates of various backgrounds who can bring new perspectives to our community. How will your unique personal history, values, and/or life experiences contribute to the culture at Tuck? (Dartmouth College—Tuck School of Business)

Diversity of talents on the court

During the course of my basketball-playing career, I have captained my high school and college varsity basketball teams, represented the state of California in a national invitational, and led the country in free-throw shooting accuracy. These individual successes came as a result of hard work, personal sacrifice, and commitment. However, as I matured as a person and leader, I recognized that these individual accomplishments meant nothing when compared to team victories and championships. I learned an early lesson in teamwork, and the potential for team success when a group of uniquely skilled individuals was well-managed and integrated appropriately. In looking back at our team successes, I realize our victories and championships could not have been accomplished without the collaborative efforts and diverse talents of those around me.

> The applicant does a nice job of setting the context of the essay by discussing his previous experience with the power of diversity and teamwork. He also is able to discuss some past accomplishments that might not have otherwise come out.

Diversity of talents off the court

Since beginning work, my lesson in diversity has logically translated to my life in the business world. Early in my career, I worked on a project with an information systems expert from mainland China and a business major from a small Midwest town. Although we made up a relatively small project team, each of us had very unique backgrounds and project experiences. These backgrounds and experiences contributed to individual strengths, as each of us led the portions of the project that most accurately aligned with these strengths. Additionally, due to the size of the team, we actively participated in all engagement stages, ultimately learning a great deal from each other. The project was an eventual success, and it helped to equip me better for future engagements in which I could maintain larger management responsibilities.

My current project team also exemplifies the value of diversity. From a cultural standpoint, my team has members from nine different countries. Because each practitioner has gone through different educational and cultural experiences, they are able to bring a unique perspective in attacking project issues and creating business solutions. In a professional sense, my team is made up of practitioners with backgrounds in technology implementations, Oracle database design, business process, system testing, and user training. The complex technology and business aspects of the project require a constant interaction among these different professionals. There is no doubt that this effective integration of individual contributions has directly led to our successful project completion.

> These two paragraphs transition nicely into how diversity can be an asset in the professional environment.

In each of these engagements, my challenge as a leader and team member was to evaluate and capitalize on the diverse abilities within my team. I have benefited from these challenges, as I have been able to cultivate new functional expertise and business perspectives. However, in a much larger sense, these engagements were successful due to the diversity of talent that we maintained as a team. Although the merging of talent is sometimes challenging, the benefits achieved in effectively doing so can be as substantial as winning a team championship.

Looking ahead toward future growth

As I grow through personal and professional experiences, I have come to realize that diversity can be an extremely valuable part of a successful team. I look forward to the learning opportunities that will come with interacting with the energetic, tight-knit community at Tuck, and will enjoy the challenge of merging our diverse perspectives as we grow into business leaders of the future.

> Nice closing. The admissions committee gets the sense that the applicant understands the value of diversity and that he personally would have a lot to add to the diversity of Tuck.

Professional Experience

With the large emphasis that business schools place on work experience, it isn't surprising that a number of them have essays dedicated to discussing a professional accomplishment or experience. Admissions committees are interested in seeing how you perform in a professional environment and how you learn from work experiences. This is your opportunity to display innovation, leadership, and teamwork abilities (in fact, many of these essay prompts overlap with questions in other buckets), so take advantage of it.

Some examples of questions that fall into this type are:

> ▶ *Please give us a full description of your career since graduating from university. If you were to remain with your present employer, what would be your next step in terms of position?* (INSEAD)

> ▶ *Share one of your most significant professional accomplishments. Describe your precise role in this activity and how it has helped to shape your management skills.* (Emory University—Goizueta Business School)

> ▶ *Describe your greatest professional achievement and how you added value to your organization.* (Cornell University—Johnson School of Management)

> ⊠ *Tell us about a time when you went beyond what was defined, established, or expected.* (Stanford Graduate School of Business)

> ⊠ *Please describe a time when you took responsibility for achieving an objective.* (MIT—Sloan School of Management)

SAMPLE ESSAY ◄

Briefly assess your career progress to date. Elaborate on your future career plans and your motivation for pursuing an MBA. (Northwestern University—Kellogg School of Management)

After graduating from Coggins University with a bachelor's degree in business, I took a job with Gardner Technologies, a company that sells data analysis tools for large businesses. All new Gardner employees must pass an intensive six week database "boot camp," and I came away from my training with a deep understanding of database technology and an appreciation for how it can be used in business. My specific interest was in the intersection of technology and marketing, and in my first year at the company, I further familiarized myself with database technology while I served in a corporate marketing role.

> Succinct statement of professional interests. Shows the rationale behind decisions that the applicant makes later on in his career.

I developed and executed marketing campaigns with the company's partners and represented the company at industry events. Through time, I took a greater interest in how the company was marketing its individual products, and I was able to pursue this interest by working with the product management team to develop a marketing plan for each of the company's four main product lines.

During this time, I reported to the vice president of marketing. After my first year, he asked me to join a newly formed group, Technology Marketing Solutions (TMS). TMS's goal was to develop deep expertise in each industry that Gardner served, including Healthcare, Telecommunications, and Finance. The group's role quickly turned into a strict business development function as we pursued large e-commerce deals with a handful of prospective partners. It was an exciting opportunity for a 23-year-old because we were negotiating deals worth more than $10 million each. However, I found that I was drifting away from the application of technology in marketing, and I wanted to reverse that trend.

> Nice example that shows the reader that the applicant had a significant level of responsibility even in the early period of his career.

That's when the opportunity at The Source presented itself. The Source operates one of the most popular personal finance and investing sites on the Internet (FinSource.com). Most of the Website was free when I joined in 2007, but the company did sell some products on the site, mainly investing books and stock research reports. I was hired into the product management group to improve how we marketed our products to our users and to turn more of them into paying customers. It was a great opportunity in that the company's large database of users allowed me to put my database skills to use.

> The last sentence of this paragraph shows that the applicant searches for background fit in making career decisions. This is subtle, but important to the admissions committee.

In my first year, my team had some great successes, including improving our promotion conversion rates by 50 percent through the use of new database targeting techniques. We also introduced a successful new line of online seminars that teach paying customers about a range of personal finance topics. My most satisfying personal accomplishment was leading the market research for and launch of a new investment newsletter, which is now our most profitable premium service.

> Great details provided in these two paragraphs.

Earlier this year, I was promoted to the role of senior marketing manager, and I now report to the company's vice president of marketing. With the title have come new responsibilities, including the goal of generating $2.3 million in revenue for our existing products, and leading the marketing launch of a new financial advisory service that is expected to generate $5 million in its first year. I am currently the only person in the company without an MBA who has revenue-generating responsibility.

It's a challenging role, especially because we are like many other startups and have had to figure out how to reach our goals with a reduced staff. Even more importantly, I don't have any direct reports and must therefore manage people in other departments through indirect influence. During the last two years, I have learned how to influence and cooperate with others to get things done, learning a great deal about leadership and teamwork in the process. I have found this aspect of my professional development to be most rewarding, and I plan on further developing these skills at Kellogg and in my future career.

> The last paragraph serves as a nice summary. The applicant does an excellent job of relating his professional experience to Kellogg's strengths.

· · · · · · · · · · · · · ·

Failure

Similar to essays on ethics, many applicants struggle in coming up with responses to these types of questions. Failure essays will typically ask you to describe a situation in which you did not meet an objective or you made a mistake. Applicants often wonder if they should actually write about a true lapse in judgment, or simply disguise an accomplishment and call it a "failure."

What admissions committees are really looking for here is how you learn from your mistakes. They want to hear about a situation in which you truly did fail, not a cloaked accomplishment. This is another essay type that lends itself to the "Situation, Action, Result" (SAR) framework. The difference here is that you should focus a majority of the essay on the "Results" section, telling the admissions committee how this experience has impacted your outlook. To a certain extent, the greater the failure, the more learning you can discuss. That's not to say that you should reveal some sort of fatal flaw, such as a tendency toward criminal behavior, but admissions counselors know that we've all "messed up big time." This essay is really one in which you should discuss such an event, and, more importantly, discuss what you learned and the steps you've taken to ensure that it won't happen again.

Some examples of questions that fall into this type are:

> ◨ *Describe a failure that you have experienced. What role did you play, and what did you learn about yourself? How did this experience help to create your definition of failure?* (University of Pennsylvania—The Wharton School)

> ▣ *What have you learned from a mistake?* (Harvard Business School)
> ▣ *Describe a time in your career when you were frustrated or disappointed. What did you learn from that experience?* (University of Michigan— Ross School of Business)

SAMPLE ESSAY ◄

Describe a situation taken from school, business, civil, or military life, where you did not meet your personal objectives, and discuss briefly the effect. (INSEAD)

It's one thing to fail to meet your objectives in the business world, but quite another to fail to meet them while serving in the military. In the business world not meeting personal objectives could mean revenue goals are not met, a transaction falls through, or, in a worst-case scenario, colleagues lose their jobs. In the military, however, not meeting personal objectives could mean that people lose their lives. The magnitude of that difference translated into a powerful learning from an unfortunate experience.

> This opening paragraph sets the tone for the situation and certainly makes the reader realize that the discussions that follow will not be trivial.

When a military coup ousted an inspection team to prevent the discovery of weapons of mass destruction, I went to Eastern Europe to plan subsequent air strikes. Despite my personal objectives to exceed the expectations of my senior officers, I made a colossal mistake on my first assignment.

> Very succinct explanation of the situation, which allows the applicant to quickly get to the other parts of the essay.

I was charged with investigating the appropriate approach to taking out a bunker that housed some of the illegal weaponry uncovered by the inspection team. Eager to prove myself in a new environment and uncomfortable asking for assistance, I went to work. Using modeling software, I created a blast pattern to depict the strikes' destructive radius. Simply following the step-by-step training that I received, I did not acknowledge the fact that this pattern partially covered a nearby building. This was a glaring error that became evident later that night.

Standing before tense pilots, my briefing lasted 30 seconds before whispers grew into an agitated roar. The senior officer leading the strike proceeded to "dress me down," pointing out that the structure alongside the bunker was housing for the coup's families. The strike approach that I chose would have easily damaged this building, injuring or even killing civilians in the process. Because my training had never accounted for this sort of risk, I never considered threats to non-military structures. My inexperience and narrow reliance on procedure almost cost innocent lives. Because our jets were about to launch, the assault on the bunk was eliminated.

> The imagery in this paragraph is very effective.

I was relegated to observer status for my remaining week on site, making the lesson stick, and turning me into a better officer and person. I learned that computers and procedures are simply

> The applicant does a nice job in these two paragraphs of covering what he learned as a result of the experience. Additionally, he touches upon how he's focused on building skills for which the admissions committee looks. Finally, his closing is very effective in that it ties back to the first paragraph.

tools, but teamwork and interpersonal communication lead to real understanding. By performing my analysis alone rather than engaging the experts around me, I hampered the mission. Furthermore, I learned that, by asking questions of the people around me, I can gain access to a wealth of information that otherwise remains underutilized. Six months later, when I ran my own team in Bosnia, I turned these realizations into meaningful action by instituting information sharing in a formalized manner.

Ironically enough, despite the magnitude of difference in impact, these are all lessons that easily translate back into the business environment and that I certainly intend to employ as I switch careers.

. . . .

Additional Information

In addition to the 10 main types of essays, most schools also allow applicants to respond to an optional "catchall" essay that basically asks whether there is any additional information that the applicant would like to share with the admissions committee. Most applicants who respond to this essay abuse it by either pasting in an essay written for another school or by highlighting weaknesses in their applications without adequately putting those concerns to rest. Neither of these approaches matches this essay's purpose.

That purpose is to allow applicants to discuss any evaluation criterion for which they might appear to be an outlier. This essay lets an applicant attack glaring weaknesses head-on and provide additional information as to why it really isn't a weakness, or what the applicant has done to overcome it. Good reasons for using this essay include addressing a GMAT score that falls below the school's 80-percent mark, pointing out that you worked 30 hours a week to pay for your undergrad tuition (which negatively affected your GPA), accounting for gaps in your employment history, or explaining some other extraordinary circumstance.

When addressing one of these weaknesses, our advice is to acknowledge it, explain what happened or why the weakness exists *without appearing to whine or make excuses,* and then move on. No need to dwell on it or list a litany of excuses. You just want to let the application reader know that you understand that the issue at hand is a weakness, and that you have a good argument as to why it won't negatively impact you in the business school classroom or beyond. No need to do any more than that, and trying to do any more will just draw undue attention to the issue.

If, however, there is no exceptional aspect of your candidacy that hasn't already been addressed in some other aspect of the application, then it would be in your best interest to skip this essay. Although it might seem that the longer you can keep an admissions officer's eyes on your file, the better, it's far more effective to make your case in as few words (and as few essays) as possible. Admissions officers will appreciate the fact that you made them read only what was needed, and nothing more.

Some examples of questions that fall into this type are:

▶ *If you feel there are extenuating circumstances of which the Admissions Committee should be aware, please explain them here (for example, unexplained gaps in work, choice of recommenders, inconsistent or questionable academic performance, significant weakness in your application).* (Duke University—Fuqua School of Business)

⊠ *Are there any extenuating circumstances in your profile about which the Admissions Committee should be aware?* (UCLA—Anderson School of Management)

SAMPLE ESSAY ◀

Is there anything else that you think we should know as we evaluate your application? If you believe your credentials and essays represent you fairly, you shouldn't feel obligated to answer this question. (Indiana University—Kelley)

The failure of regression analysis

My favorite aspect of regression analysis has always been the "outliers." These anomalies defy logic by refusing to conform to their destiny, outlined by defined variables.

Through the years, standardized tests have been touted for their ability to predict academic and career success. Several econometric analyses have been created to support these contentions. For every one of these models, however, there are a few instances in which the predicted result of low standardized test scores deviates from the line. I am the deviation.

> This applicant takes an unconventional approach to this essay type by referencing an analytical tool. In doing so, he's able to show off his strength in an area of perceived weakness and also subtly present a potent argument for looking past what otherwise would have been a "game-breaking" GMAT score. It turned out to be a "game-winning" approach.

The GMAT experience

The disappointment I felt when I pressed the "enter" button and saw my 550 GMAT score flash across the screen is indescribable. How could I receive such a low score after months and months of tireless study? The fact that it was my third attempt at the exam made the failure all the more painful.

Still, my experience with the GMAT exam is reflective of my history with standardized tests. Throughout high school and college, I have always underperformed on these exams. I have learned that my "standardized test anxiety" does not have to limit my academic or career success; rather I use these "failures" as motivating factors to succeed inside and outside the classroom.

> The applicant is very effective in setting the stage for a deeper argument as to why his GMAT score does not accurately reflect his abilities.

The experience of an outlier

Throughout my undergraduate career, I was able to balance a rigorous course load in the business engineering (BE) program and multiple extracurricular activities. Earning a 3.87 GPA in the BE program allowed me to gain a strong foundation in business operations, procurement, and logistics. The BE program at Kuziev University was recently ranked as the second best program in the nation and focuses on the student's ability to apply quantitative analysis to business case scenarios.

Early success in quantitative courses such as Economics and Applied Calculus allowed me to serve as a tutor for three of my four years. As a tutor, I trained students in fundamental mathematic and economic concepts, through review sessions and challenging practice examinations. Building upon my tutoring experience, I developed a new academic coaching program within the College of Engineering. The coaching program allowed me to assist more than 70 students through resume and networking workshops, test-taking strategy sessions, and time management analysis. In recognition of stellar academic performance and my representation of the College of Business, I was named as Kuziev University's "Most Outstanding Business Student" for the graduating class of 1998.

> The applicant shows that he clearly has the academic background and quantitative ability to succeed in an MBA program.

These victories did not, however, preclude my attempts to succeed on the GMAT examination. In fact, I modified my approach to the exam several times, dedicated more than a year to studying, and even worked with a tutor for a four-month period. Taking more than 20 practice exams and mastering more than 4,000 practice problems, I tried to push beyond my standardized test anxiety and surpass my historical performances. I certainly feel that I have a good grasp of the exam material, as I consistently score in the high 600s on practice exams.

> This paragraph demonstrates that the applicant has given the GMAT his all and that he didn't merely take the GMAT one time without preparing.

Although I fell short in this area, my "failure" only further motivates me to prove that I am the exception to the rule. I continue to manage these "failures," because I refuse to be defined by them. Indeed, I succeed in spite of them, as I am an aberration. I am the outlier.

> Great closing. The last sentence connects well with the introduction.

Nice!

The New Breed of Multimedia "Essays"

During the past four years a handful of top MBA programs—including Chicago Booth and UCLA Anderson—have made waves by introducing new forms of "essays" to their applications, including recorded audio responses, short video clips, and PowerPoint slides. At least one school (NYU Stern) even invites applicants to send in *anything,* as long as it's not perishable! Still others have announced that they've made the entire application review process electronic, making it easier for these schools to adopt multimedia application components in the near future. (Imagine an admissions officer scanning your resume on an iPad and then clicking on an icon to see you give a 60-second video response to a question. Some business schools already have that capability.)

The fact that admissions officers introduced these big changes suggests that they're no longer getting what they need purely from written essays. A great essay helps admissions officers get to know applicants better and—most importantly when it comes to the admissions process—separate the great applicants from the merely good ones. Over time, however, as applicants have read MBA admissions guides (such as this one, perhaps?), scanned online forums, and subscribed to blogs about the admissions process, the less-savvy ones have started to sound more and more similar to one another in some of their written responses. The result is that admissions officers feel a need to introduce new formats that they hope can help them identify which applicants really have what they're looking for.

However, whether you're writing a 500-word essay, filming a short video clip, or preparing a four-page PowerPoint document, the rules are very much the same. Just as an essay that doesn't fit with the rest of your application can hurt you, a video response that doesn't fit will do the same thing. A dull audio clip will help you no more than a dry esssay will. And just as rehashing your resume in your essays will hurt your cause, rehashing your resume in a PowerPoint file will produce the same result. The format has evolved, but the rules definitely have not.

One final piece of advice: Though style definitely matters, admissions officers still care far more about substance, even in the case of video and PowerPoint responses. You do want to present a polished final product, but you're not being measured on how well you can work special effects into a video or animate text in a PowerPoint slide. Just as an overly polished essay can, an overly produced multimedia response can make admissions officers wonder if they're getting to know the real you. The same advice still applies: Reveal at least a little bit of the real you, don't get too cute with gimmicks, and make sure your response adds something meaningful to your overall application story.

Final Thoughts on Essays

There's no doubt that your essays can be your greatest point of differentiation from the rest of the applicant pool. It's incredibly important, therefore, that you are able to write your story in the most effective manner possible. Again, Chapter 6 will help with the assembly of the full game plan package.

Here are a few last tips that should help you put together the best essays possible:

- ⊠ **Make edits to your essays in several rounds.** You will constantly make revisions to your essays as you find better ways to express yourself and different methods for highlighting your attributes. As such, you should look at essay writing as a repetitive process that ultimately results in a masterpiece. You should never submit an essay with which you are unsatisfied.

- ⊠ **When you are done with your essays, set them aside for a couple of days before submitting them.** Sometimes applicants get caught up in the writing and editing process and simply want to get the essays out the door as soon as possible so that they can check that task off the list. This mentality is certainly understandable, but can be detrimental as, in many cases, it leads to essays that have been rushed. By leaving completed essays alone for a couple of days, you will be able to read them with a fresh perspective, and will most likely be able to evaluate them better. Even just waiting 24 hours can give you a surprisingly fresh pair of eyes when reviewing your own work.

- ⊠ **If possible, provide your recommenders with a sample essay.** In addition to providing your game plan to your recommenders, consider giving them a sample essay that discusses your career goals. This will bring out some details of your story that they are less likely to have a handle on, and will help create an application with messages that are fully aligned.

Recommendations

If your essays are the most important embodiment of the core messages that you want to communicate, then your recommendations are a close second. There is no more powerful way to reinforce the image that you're trying to present than by having a former supervisor or coworker corroborate it. Think of each recommender as a character witness who is ready to illustrate your strengths with unique examples from your past. Just as in a court case, you can't afford to have a witness who is lukewarm. Your recommenders need to exude passion about you as a person, confidence about your career potential, and belief in your ability to succeed at business school.

Most schools ask for two or three recommendations, with a few asking for just one. Some leave open the option of submitting an additional recommendation. Consider this extra recommendation *only* if it would add something new to your application story. If your first two recommenders tell the admissions committee that you're a great team player, then you don't need a third person telling them that, too. If you do have one recommender in mind who has seen strengths of yours that no one else has seen, though, then adding that extra letter to your application can certainly help.

Who Should Write Your Recommendations?

More than anything, your recommenders need to know you well. You may be able to get a letter from your executive vice president and CEO, but if she hasn't worked with you much, it will be very apparent in your recommendations. Admissions officers evaluate a recommendation based on its content much more than on the name signed at the bottom of the letter, so keep that in mind.

The only exception to this rule is if the potential recommender is someone of *significant* influence at the school—that is, he or she is a significant donor or has some other way to affect the school's decisions. If you know someone who has a building named after him or who has a close relationship the president at Harvard, then that's probably a favor worth calling in. Otherwise, the admissions committee will probably be less impressed by your recommender's status than you are. And don't assume that choosing an alum of your target school will impress the admissions committee; knowing an alum doesn't mean you're "in the club" in admissions officers' eyes.

Also, in an attempt to provide variety, choose recommenders who can give examples covering a wide range of work experiences. If your boss will be most able to cite examples of your leadership abilities, then get your second recommendation from a coworker who has seen how well you work in teams. Ideally, each recommendation that you submit will present a well-rounded picture of you. But it is acceptable to have recommendations that each emphasize a particular dimension, if each of your recommenders has mostly seen you perform in certain types of situations.

Most schools want at least one of your recommendations to come from your immediate supervisor. This person should know you best in terms of your working style, your ambitions, and your strengths and weaknesses. If your current supervisor doesn't know you particularly well (perhaps you've just moved into your current role), then be sure to also get a recommendation from the person who knows you and your capabilities best. If this means going to a past supervisor who has managed you relatively recently, that's okay.

Of course, you may not want your boss to know that you are applying to business school. This is quite common, especially in disciplines outside of the traditional "feeder" industries of consulting and investment banking. Schools understand this, and most have a provision stating, "If you cannot get a recommendation from your supervisor, please attach a note explaining why." In this case, consider approaching a former boss (within your company or in a past job) or someone else with whom you have worked closely. Admissions officers prefer to hear from someone who supervised you or someone who was above you on the organizational chart, so start with those people first. The recommender needs to be more than a buddy, but a colleague who has seen you in a variety of situations can still write a good recommendation if he can provide strong examples of your leadership abilities, teamwork skills, and so on.

A few schools also ask for a recommendation from a professor or advisor from your undergraduate school. In general, unless a school asks for a recommendation from an academic source, concentrate on just professional recommendations. As with everything, there are a couple exceptions. The first is if you had an exceptional achievement in college that will bolster one of your application dimensions (something more than great grades or run-of-the-mill lab work). The second is if you are just graduating or a very recent graduate. If either is the case, a recommendation from this source may be worth the effort, particularly if it can emphasize any leadership traits or maturity that you haven't been able to demonstrate as much in the office. Otherwise, we strongly recommend that you stick with recommenders who can discuss your post-college accomplishments.

What Should They Say?

Your recommendations should support the position you establish for yourself in your other application components. They should add depth to this position by citing examples that go beyond what you cover in your own essays.

Start with the grid that you built for yourself in Chapter 2. Odds are that you covered many of the Xs in your essays and data sheet, but not all of them. Your recommenders can help cover more of these examples, most often the ones pertaining to professional experience. Each example that they bring up will ideally complement what you have said about yourself in the rest of the application. A little bit of redundancy can actually help to reinforce your key messages, but you need to make sure that your recommendations aren't simply rehashing what you have already said about yourself.

As for how they deliver the message, the advice that applies to your essays applies here as well. As the old writer's adage goes, "Show, don't tell." It is far more powerful for a recommendation to illustrate your abilities by describing concrete examples than to simply say that you are a good leader, strong analytical thinker, and so on. The stories of what you did in specific situations are what admissions officers are looking for. Next, we will discuss how you can arm your recommenders with the stories they can use as support for their opinions of you.

How Can You Be Sure They're Saying the Right Things?

Ah yes, the time-honored question. How much coaching is too much, and what do you do if you're afraid that your manager can't write an effective recommendation? It depends on several issues.

First, the ethics of the matter. Everyone would agree (we hope) that you shouldn't write your own recommendations. Outside of the ethical reason not to write your own recommendation, chances are that you'll struggle to write a letter as well as a good recommender would. We've found that recommenders can come up with examples that we've long since forgotten. Also, avoiding the self-written recommendation allows you to steer clear of the "how positive sounds too positive?" dilemma. Just as it's an uncomfortable experience to stand in front of a group and extoll your own virtues, writing about how great you are can be very awkward, and you will tend to downplay your own strengths and accomplishments. It's just human nature. So, be sure the letter of recommendation is in your recommender's own words.

But what if your boss says, "I'm too busy. You can go ahead and put it together and I'll be happy to sign it," leaving you to write it on your own? One option is to simply find another recommender, but odds are that you picked that person for a reason. Your other option is to try to make the process as easy as possible, and you can do that by providing the recommender with substantial background information, which we will show you how to do.

Next, it's a question of how comfortable you are coaching your recommenders. Again, it needs to be written in their words, but you can help your chances a lot by at least suggesting some stories from your work history that can illustrate your key application dimensions. Even better, create a game plan, as shown in Chapter 6, and share that with your recommenders. Also, try to provide them with a sample essay or two that provides additional details on your career goals. Review the plan with them and discuss how important the recommendation process is. In those discussions you will inevitably end up doing a lot of self-promotion, so take some time now to get comfortable with the fact that you will be tooting your own horn, or at least asking others to toot it for you! It can also be helpful to provide your recommenders with a sample recommendation, such as the one shown on page 128, to give them an idea of the level of quality that you are expecting.

You can decide for yourself how much detail you want to include in the game plan you share with your recommenders. The idea is to give each recommender enough information so that she can make a statement about you and then back it up with a short, illustrative story. Ideally, you will give each recommender a different set of stories, so that you don't have three people all writing about the same things. This requires some extra coordination on your part, but is an important step to ensure that each recommendation adds something new (and that they don't all sound like they were written from the same template). Fortunately, once you do this exercise for one school's application, it's not too difficult to replicate for your other applications.

Of course, if you find that you can't provide multiple types of stories to each recommender, that's okay. As mentioned previously, not every recommendation needs to sell 100 percent of your skills; it is most important that your recommendations all work together to present a complete picture of you as a well-rounded applicant. So, if one really stresses your teamwork skills and one puts more emphasis on your leadership skills, that's fine. In fact, it's ideal in that it helps keep your letters of recommendation from all sounding the same as one another. Of course, you may never see what each of your recommenders writes, but you can definitely influence their output by carefully controlling the inputs that you give them.

Sample Recommendation

The following is a sample recommendation that includes typical questions found on numerous applications. Note the recommender's style, as she illustrates the applicant's strengths and doesn't merely state them. We've highlighted the aspects of this recommendation that we feel are especially strong.

Top Business School Recommendation

Dear Members of the Admissions Committee:

I have had the pleasure of working with Shannan on several projects during the last 20 months, both directly as a Project Manager, and indirectly as a member of Kramer-Dover Consulting's Outsourcing Business Unit. I have had the opportunity to get to know Shannan professionally and personally, and I believe that I can fully evaluate and recommend Shannan for enrollment at Top Business School.

I am a Project Manager in the San Francisco office of Kramer-Dover, having worked here for 12 years. I have seen many professionals in that time frame, and Shannan is clearly one of the best I have ever seen. This is no small accomplishment, as Kramer-Dover hires only the best and brightest people, and Shannan is consistently in the top 15 percent of that group of people in terms of professional capabilities. In addition, she rounds out her professional expertise with many personal activities and pursuits. Consequently, the phrase that comes to mind when I think of Shannan is "Renaissance Woman."

Shannan would be a great asset to Top Business School and any future employer. Specific answers to your standard questions are included below.

Sincerely,

Cindy D. Peterson
Project Manager
Kramer-Dover Consulting

The introduction letter to the recommendation adds a professional touch and allows the recommender to summarize her thoughts before answering the specific questions. Note how she explicitly states here that Shannan is among the best she's ever worked with. This is a strong signal to the admissions committee that Shannan is worth a closer look.

1. **Define your relationship to the applicant and describe the circumstances under which you have known him or her.**

I first met Shannan on a project we worked on together at a telecommunications client approximately 20 months ago. As a firm, we had just begun to develop a new Outsourcing Business Unit. The first project that Shannan and I completed was the first engagement of its kind for our firm, and we believe one of the first of its kind for anyone in the industry.

I was the Project Manager on this engagement, responsible for the success and deliverables to the client for the project. Shannan was a lead consultant, reporting directly to a manager who reported to me. This engagement lasted approximately four months. During this time, Shannan and I had daily interaction in developing the methodology and deliverables associated with this new Business Unit. Because of the complexity and uncertainty of determining how this methodology applied to our client, there were numerous late-night meetings and discussions that we used to refine our approach and thought process.

During the next eight months, as I moved on to another client, my interaction with Shannan was less frequent. Our contact was mainly during meetings when our Business Unit professionals met to further our thinking and better develop our deliverables that we used at our clients. Shannan took a lead role in helping develop many of our tools, which I subsequently used for other clients. At one time, I had Shannan come to my client site for a few weeks to help "kick-start" our engagement by training other consultants on our tools. The client was so impressed by Shannan's expertise that he begged me to place her on the project. Shannan continued to play an advisory role and we completed the project in record time. The client was able to reduce operational costs by more than $100 million, due in large part to Shannan.

For the past eight months, Shannan has been reporting directly to me in another Outsourcing engagement at another large telecommunications client. We interact several times a day due to the complexity and sensitivity of the client and Shannan's key leadership role on the team.

2. **What do you consider the applicant's primary talents or strengths?**

I believe that Shannan has several significant strengths that enable her to be successful as a consultant. A few of her exceptional strengths include:

- **Leadership:** Shannan has the unique quality of commanding respect from her peers, clients, and leaders. Although Shannan would be considered a junior member of the team in her current assignment based on age or years of experience, she became the leader of the team. This was due to her grasp of the details, with the foresight of being able to articulate the activities required to complete the project successfully.

- **Client Relationship:** Our current engagement started as a small assignment with a minimal span of influence. Largely due to the development of solid relationships with our client, we were able to create a significant role with the client in one of its key strategic areas. Shannan played a major role in developing that relationship. There was actually a time when I was telling the client to hire a less

> The recommender does a good job of giving a specific example of how Shannan's relationship with the client played a crucial role in the success of the project.

expensive consulting firm, and they refused because they trusted and believed in our consultants, namely Shannan.

- **Teamwork**: Shannan is everyone's favorite consultant to ask questions of. Many consultants and clients refer to her on a wide range of issues including finance, industry information, regulatory interpretation, and consulting tools. Everyone feels comfortable going to her, because she is very approachable, friendly, articulate, knowledgeable, and goes out of her way to help.

> These bullet points really highlight Shannan's strengths and position her as a leader who is great to work with and for.

3. What do you consider the applicant's weaknesses or developmental needs?

Shannan's development needs revolve around gaining more high-level experience in the consulting profession. These types of experiences include:

- Conducting formal performance reviews and career development discussions with subordinates within the firm.
- Having a significant role in the selling of our professional services to our clients.
- Developing a broad base of client roles, relationships, and engagement experiences.
- Presenting in more formal settings to high-level client or firm leadership.

4. What did you like best about working side-by-side with the candidate?

Shannan is a very well-rounded individual, professionally and personally, which makes working with her enjoyable. She is not one-dimensional, and always has some insight or anecdote to share with a team. She epitomizes Kramer-Dover's core attributes of integrity, teamwork, flexibility, leadership, reliability, and professionalism.

Outside of her demonstrated professional capabilities, one aspect of Shannan's character that greatly impresses me is how she is just all-around a great person—a "Renaissance Woman." On top of her professional talent (and related time commitment), Shannan still finds time to be a Big Sister through the Big Brothers Big Sisters Program. This is a relationship that she has developed over several years, not a "try it and see if I like it" kind of relationship. Shannan is also active in fund-raising and recruiting at her undergraduate alma mater.

> This section demonstrates Shannan's desire to get involved with the community and her initiative. The school's takeaway is that Shannan is multi-dimensional.

5. Comment on the applicant's personal integrity.

I rate a person's integrity and behavior based on how their peers and clients perceive them. Shannan has an enormous amount of respect. People enjoy being around her. They can "bank" on her answers to their questions as being accurate. Shannan conducts herself in a very professional manner under very stressful conditions. She is a role model for new

> Understandably, admissions officers will view anything less than "This candidate has impeccable integrity" with a wary eye. Don't even consider a recommender if you don't think he will give you high marks in this area!

consultants in our firm. I trust Shannan to perform with the utmost integrity and accountability in all aspects of her profession.

6. Please discuss observations you have made concerning the applicant's leadership abilities, team, and/or group skills.

I believe the largest change in Shannan over the past 20 months is the growth she has exhibited in the leadership area. When I first worked with Shannan, she was very effective at doing what she was told. Now, she clearly goes beyond performing tasks and seeks out ways to increase the performance of the entire team, not only her own work. Shannan is the leader of the team, and also shows an active interest in several of the other teams by inserting herself in areas that she can help to resolve issues, answer questions, and overall contribute to their progress.

7. What impact has this person had on the organization in which he or she works?

Shannan has had a major impact on Kramer-Dover. On an individual level she has been responsible for generating more than $25 million for the firm. From a client perspective, she has been directly responsible for improving profitability by almost $250 million. When you take into consideration how much she has trained internal employees and external staff in addition to the benefits of having her in a team environment, Shannan is responsible for having an even much greater impact.

Additionally, Shannan has helped create a lot of internal interest for the telecommunications industry in general and specifically our Outsourcing Business Unit. Although I am not part of her region, it is my sense that Shannan is very popular within her peer group. I receive many phone calls from consultants in her region who would love to be part of our projects. We have been able to staff some of those consultants in large part due to Shannan's influence. Her presence is a signal to others that it must be interesting to work on our engagements. This impact has resulted in large growth in terms of the number of projects we sell in addition to the number of consultants we have been able to staff.

> The idea of looking for applicants who positively impact those around them has grown among MBA admissions officers in recent years. Be sure that each of your recommenders can name at least one or two things you have done that no one else could have quite achieved in the same way.

8. What will this individual be doing in 10 years? Why?

I'm not even sure what I'll be doing in 10 years, but my guess is that Shannan will be a successful partner in our firm. She has indicated to me that she would like to come back to our firm post-graduation and practice in our growing Mergers and Acquisitions Business Unit, focusing on the telecommunications industry. She enjoys the challenge that consulting brings, and possesses all of the major attributes required to be successful. I'm convinced that she will not only be a partner, but a global leader within our firm. I'm convinced of this because Shannan has been successful in everything she has been determined to do.

> The game plan that Shannan provided to her recommenders helped make sure that this message aligned with her essays on career goals.

9. If you have additional comments that you think would assist the Admissions Committee in making this decision, please add them here.

Shannan is the best all-around consultant with whom I've had the opportunity to work. She has become an invaluable resource to numerous employees in our firm, and to our clients. She has managed to do outstanding work in our difficult working environment through the use of her leadership, teamwork, analytical, personal, social, and all-around consulting skills. She has managed to meet the ultimate professional challenge—earn respect through outstanding professional effort and achieve outstanding results. She has also become a personal friend whom I trust and hold in high regard. I believe Shannan would become a welcome addition to Top Business School.

> Strong closing that again touches upon Shannan's main strengths. Again, notice how she is unequivocal about how Shannan is one of the best employees she's ever managed. Don't underestimate the importance of this.

. . . .

Logistics

The best piece of advice we can ever give you is simple: Give your recommenders enough time to do their thing! You should plan on giving each recommender at least two months to go from start to a finished recommendation. Right about now you may be asking: "But what if I don't have two months?" If that's the case, then start immediately, but realize that you may already be making tradeoffs in terms of recommendation quality. Just like essays, very few great recommendations are written overnight. Even if you're particularly close with someone and think that you can get a week's turnaround from him, you still risk getting a rushed recommendation. Unfortunately, the admissions committee will likely translate this into either you being disorganized or your recommender not particularly caring about whether or not you get in (which also reflects badly on you). Ideally, your recommender will have enough time to digest your game plan, write her piece, let it sit for at least a few days, then revisit it and make improvements where needed—again, very similar to the essay-writing process.

Also, make sure that you know what your recommenders need to do once they're done writing their letters. If you think the submission process is confusing as an applicant, know that as an outside recommender it may be even more so, particularly in today's world of online form submissions, password resets, and so on. As such, build enough time into your planning to account for this "back-end" part of the process. If a recommender fails to get her letter to the school in time, the admissions committee will consider it to be your fault, period.

Some of your recommenders may want to write a single letter that you can use for multiple schools. Although most schools' recommendation forms are quite similar, there are enough subtle differences that you should try to avoid this as much as possible. Some schools expressly discourage this practice. If a really valuable recommender insists that she can't write you multiple recommendations, make sure to start by getting a recommendation for your most selective school, and then weigh the benefits of recycling that recommendation for another school versus getting an entirely new letter for a different school. Again, you should think about your recommendations in totality. So, if you already have a strong, specific recommendation for a particular school, then having a second one that is somewhat recycled is more acceptable.

This is another reason to limit the number of schools that you target. Naturally, as this number grows it becomes more difficult to receive a letter that is written specifically for each school. In general, you should avoid asking a potential recommender to complete more than three recommendations. Or, at least spread the recommendation requests out between rounds, so that the recommender doesn't face six deadlines that are all back-to-back. This will help ensure that you receive specific responses for each recommendation.

Overall, we advise erring on the side of choosing recommendations that were written specifically for a given school. But this isn't always feasible, so you can afford to get some mileage out of an existing recommendation if you feel that it still adds something to your application that your other recommendations don't, and that it actually answers the questions that the admissions committee asks (which is obviously important!). If you can't get specific recommendations written, ask your recommenders to write a single recommendation that covers all of the questions for which your target schools ask.

Resume

In many ways, preparing a resume or curriculum vitae for your business school applications seems redundant. After all, you are already required to report your employment history in the data sheets and describe your professional experiences and career goals in great detail in your essays. So what's the point of requiring the resume? For one, the resume summarizes your background in one page. This allows the admissions committee to get a high-level understanding of where you're coming from and what you've accomplished. The resume is often what makes a first impression on admissions officers, so you'll want to put your best foot forward. Secondly, your resume will often be the only reference point that your admissions interviewer has on you. For those two reasons, it's important that you prepare a resume that reflects your story from both a background and a career goals standpoint.

Format

We suggest that you follow the standard one-page, reverse-chronological order format. Producing a resume that is longer than one page shows an inability to state concisely the important aspects of your background. Given the fact that admissions representatives probably won't spend much more than two minutes reviewing your resume, your goal should be to make your points succinct yet effective. Writing your resume in reverse chronological order allows you to display your progress over time. Additionally, the admissions representative will probably spend the majority of her time concentrating on the top of your resume, so you want your best stuff to come across first.

One way that you can make sure that your format fits well with your target schools is by using your target schools' formats in creating your resume. Many business schools have standard formats that their students are required to follow during their own job hunting. Using those formats can be a simple way to show that you've done some due diligence on the school and ensure that your format works. You should be able to gain access to a school's format through a friend, a colleague, or a quick Google or LinkedIn search. Going with a business school's standard format gives you the added benefit of having a pre-formatted baseline resume from which you can work once you start classes.

In general, though, your resume should consist of three sections: education, experience, and additional. The commonly followed rule is that if you are coming out of school, you should place the education section first, but in other cases, the experience section should be placed first. The placement of one in front of the other is supposed to reflect their level of relative importance based on where you are in your career. In terms of business school admissions, your academic background is just as important as your professional background, so you have some flexibility here in terms of placement. If you follow a business school's format, then the education section will almost certainly come first.

Content

It's easy to get wrapped up in figuring out what format you want to use for the resume, but don't let that overshadow the more important task of creating your resume's content. As much as possible, you should try to make sure that your resume reflects the four dimensions: innovation, maturity, leadership, and teamwork. You should also make sure that progression in responsibility and achievements are highlighted. Finally, it should be clear that your career goals are achievable in light of your background, and that the target school is a good place for you to develop the skills you need to achieve those goals. This means emphasizing the experiences that are relevant to your career goals and de-emphasizing those that are not.

In covering your experiences, you should focus on your actions and their results, not on your job descriptions. Provide tangible figures as much as possible. This is probably the biggest mistake that applicants make in regard to the resume. They make subjective statements, such as "Interfaced with Sales and Marketing in order to evaluate product potential." This statement is of little value to the resume reviewer and basically just takes up space. Your focus should be on providing the reviewer with hard numbers, so that she can see how your actions translate into success. Remember: Admissions officers care about the impact you've had on the organizations around you, not just what you've done.

Let's take another look at how this statement could be phrased: "Worked with seven members of Sales and Marketing in evaluating a new product with $125 million revenue potential. Evaluation led to eventual launch and 35-percent market share." Certainly this approach takes up more room, but it is more effective than wasting space with esoteric statements about your contributions.

To serve as an example, consider the case of a fictitious applicant named Stephen Pearson. Stephen's career goal is to work for a venture capital firm, focusing on high-tech investments. Take a look at Stephen's resume and pay particular attention to how he focuses on actions and results. His resume certainly isn't perfect, but it does do a nice job of touching on each of the four dimensions while showing fit with his career goals. We've added some commentary to stress the aspects of the resume that we feel are truly solid.

SAMPLE RESUME ◄

STEPHEN PEARSON

2220 Tenth Street, Apt. 320

New York, NY 10027

(212) 555-1234

spearson@coldmail.com

EDUCATION

Carella University   **Washington, D.C.**

Bachelor of Arts degree in Mathematics and Economics, Honors   May 1999

- Honors thesis in Economics.
- Elected Economics Student Association Representative.
- Co-Founder of student investment fund.
- Co-Chaired Big Brother/Big Sister Program.

> Stephen immediately comes across as someone who is intelligent, well-liked, and willing to get involved, and who takes initiative.

Chartered Financial Analyst (candidate)

Passed all three levels of CFA exam and completed 18 of 36 months investment-related work experience.

> Don't hesitate to show accomplishments that are in progress. For example, if you are learning a new language, taking a statistics course, or participating in a public speaking class, try and mention it somewhere.

PROFESSIONAL EXPERIENCE

Eisenberg Wexler-Mergers & acquisitions Group   **New York, NY**

Associate   **2001–2003**

Constructed more than 100 financial models including discounted cash flow, comparable company and accretion/dilution analyses. Evaluated more than $4.5 billion potential transactions including leveraged buyouts, acquisitions, and spin-offs. Worked with more than 10 advisory teams composed of company executives, attorneys, investment bankers, and accountants. Received highest rating among the associate class.

> Nice summary. Shows Stephen's ability to stand out even in a highly-competitive environment.

- Led associate in the $145 million leveraged buyout of Stapleton International, manufacturer of semiconductors.
- Structured the $900 million sale of Seeber Trust, software development company. Conducted benchmark, competitor, and valuation analyses, assisted in bid evaluation, and oversaw auction processes. Led due diligence process, which included more than 75 hours of dedicated company analysis.
- Researched more than 40 companies in the high-technology sector to identify potential clients whose combined market capitalization was

> Displays deep industry knowledge that certainly would be used in his desired career.

over $70 billion. Led more than 20 meetings with clients to discuss financing needs and strategic objectives.

- Assisted in business development efforts, including the hosting of M&A seminars that more than 150 executives attended and resulted in more than $75 million in business.
- Created financing strategy and raised more than $70 million for Schudmak Incorporated through debt and equity offerings.
- Developed training materials and oversaw training of 35 new analysts and summer MBA associates.

> Shows willingness to perform "extracurricular" activities and an ability to work with others.

Sanni Mutual funds   **San Francisco, CA**

High-Yield Bond Analyst   **1999–2001**

- Researched high-tech and aerospace industries to determine trends and develop outlook on industry opportunities and threats.
- Made buy/hold/sell recommendations to portfolio managers for $150 million in industry holdings based on industry outlook and analysis of the underlying companies' financial information and business strategies.
- Analyzed Japanese economy, specifically banking industry, and recommended the sale of $30 million of Japanese bank preferred shares 10 months prior to Japanese sovereign credit downgrade by rating services.

Management Trainee

- Supervised a diverse department of 35 employees, mostly 1st- and 2nd-generation Americans from 7 countries.

Waller Securities   **Washington, D.C.**

Brokerage Intern   **Summer 1998**

- Created a database that segmented 45 brokers' accounts according to sales potential.
- Completed the Series 7 exam and received license to buy and sell financial securities.

> Displays fit with future career goals and profession from here to the point he achieves CFA status.

ADDITIONAL INFORMATION

- Languages: Conversant in Spanish, working toward fluency.

> Language capabilities are always an added bonus.

- Community: Teach economics through Junior Achievement to a 27-student class and helped establish two new Junior Achievement programs in the local community.

> Nice job of showing community involvement. He doesn't simply list community service activities.

- Hobbies: Traveling, personal investing, golf, chess, deep sea diving.

> Shows he has a life outside of work.

We've placed additional resume examples in Appendix B along with critical commentary, so you can get a better sense of how to develop a compelling resume for your application.

The Admissions Consultant Question

It's a question that many business school applicants ask at some point in the process: "Should I invest in an admissions consulting service?" No matter how excellent your experiences are or how sharp your story is, the intimidating odds of getting into the top schools means that this question will likely cross your mind somewhere along the way.

First, let's look at what an admission consultant can do for you. Typical service offerings provided by admissions consultants include:

> ▣ An end-to-end service that starts with an in-depth interview, where the consultant will get to know you and learn about your experiences, your goals, and your strengths and weaknesses. The consultant will then help you develop a compelling application story (this is usually the most valuable part of the consultant's offering), and work with you to weave it through every part of your application, especially your essays and your recommendations. The consultant will also coach you on how to handle the interview. Admissions consultants tend to know the top business schools quite well, and they will give you a professional second opinion on which schools you should consider based on your profile.

> ▣ A more limited offering that covers certain parts of your application, most often your essays. These services appeal to applicants who are confident that their application stories are sound, and want some help in fine-tuning their message. Some consulting services, such as Veritas Prep (the company with which Scott and Omari are affiliated), offer "a la carte" services in addition to end-to-end services; others strictly offer essay editing services.

Naturally, the more a consultant does for you, the more you will pay. Some will charge you a flat fee for their services, whereas others will charge you on a per-application or a per-essay basis.

Once you hire a consultant for the "full-service" treatment, he will first take an in-depth inventory of your career up until this point. He will quiz you on:

> ▣ What extracurriculars you did in college.

> ▣ Why you chose your major.

> ▣ Your grades in college.

> ▣ Why you chose your current employer.

> ▣ Evidence of success in your job.

> ▣ Your extracurriculars outside of the workplace.

> ▣ Your future career goals.

> ▣ Your GMAT scores (if you have taken the exam).

> ▣ What you're looking for in a business school.

> ▣ Which business schools you are targeting.

> ▣ Why you're interested in those schools and not others.

He may also ask for writing samples, including any application essays that you have already written. All of these questions will help him answer the question of "How good are this applicant's chances?" He will evaluate you using the same criteria that admissions committees use, and will be pretty frank about your chances at each of your target schools, possibly suggesting that you narrow or broaden your scope.

Once your admissions consultant knows you better, he will work with you to develop an overall application story. This will be the high-level "Here's who I am, and this is where I want to go" theme, similar to the story that this book helps you create. Once that is in place, he will work with you on each of the application components. Most consultants will spend the majority of their time on your essays, followed by your recommendations and your interview. If your GMAT score is too low, an admissions consultant can help point you to the right resources or recommend ways in which you can compensate for it.

The most value that admissions consultants provide is usually in helping you present your story in a coherent package, providing you with candid feedback and supplying you with third-party insight. They usually have a good idea of what each school is looking for and are usually on top of the trends in business school admissions. Some even offer post-admissions advice, such as which courses to take once you get to school, although most applicants mainly pay for the chance to improve their admissions odds.

So, overall, admissions consultants do tend to help people get in. They are similar to GMAT prep courses in that they certainly increase applicants' probability of being accepted. They're usually very skilled essay editors, and the best ones are able to evaluate your essays just as an admissions officer would. But know that no admissions consultant—at least not any scrupulous one—will write your essays for you. He will push you, stretch your thinking, and help you remember accomplishments that you didn't think would matter in your application, but he will not simply take your resume and spin it into a golden application. The bottom line is that only you can write your own story. Admissions consultants can help you discover it, but you'll have to tell it.

Once you decide to work with an admissions consultant, make sure that you only select a firm that strictly adheres to schools' policies with respect to completing applications. Schools rightly require that students have written every aspect of their application (except recommendations, of course). As consultancies have gained popularity, admissions counselors note that they regularly see essays, in particular, that clearly have not been written by the applicant. Besides the obvious ethical reasons not to pursue a consultant who offers to rewrite your essays, you also risk having your application thrown out, because it has obviously been doctored by a professional. Remember: You are the best expert on you. Your application doesn't need to read like Hemingway to gain admission. It need only represent your passions, motivations, capabilities and fit with the target school. A consultancy can certainly help you get there, but at the end of the day the work must be yours and yours alone.

Perhaps the best way to be safe is to only consider consultants who are members of the Association of International Graduate Admissions Consultants (AIGAC), a non-profit organization dedicated to maintaining the highest ethical standards among admissions consultants around the world. Member consultants are subject to rigorous screening and re-certification to ensure that they only provide consulting services that are professional, fair, and ethical. Doing so will help ensure that you're not only getting an experienced consultant, but also one who won't steer you down the wrong path and actually end up hurting your chances in the long run.

There are definitely situations in which a business school candidate would benefit from an admissions consultant, more than the average applicant would:

- ◙ **No business experience:** We discussed these kinds of applicants in Chapter 3. They absolutely can get into business school, but they may have an unclear understanding of how to communicate their experiences in a way that admissions officers will respond to. Also, unlike bankers or consultants, they likely know far fewer people who can give them advice throughout the process. Thus, admissions consultants can often add insight (about the admissions process and about individual schools) to which they might not otherwise have access.

- ◙ **A glaring weakness:** Some people will never get above a 600 on the GMAT, no matter how hard they try. In instances such as these, an admissions consultant can help applicants bolster their perceived analytical abilities (often by encouraging them to do the things that we advise in this book) and help them overcome weaknesses with an application that shines in every other way. More generally, consultants can sometimes help an applicant rise above a shortcoming that would otherwise keep him out of his target school.

- ◙ **International applicants:** Similar to the "no business experience" crowd, some international applicants may have a harder time getting their hands on sound application advice and information on their target schools, in which case admissions consultants can help. Also, consultants can help them with simple language barrier issues that could keep them from gaining admission.

Lastly, some applicants enroll the help of an admissions consultant because they simply lack the confidence that they can get in on their own. If you've read this book, have evaluated your own background, and still feel that you don't stand a chance, then it's perfectly fine to hire a consultant. But don't fool yourself into thinking that the competition walks on water and that the only way you stand a chance of getting in is by hiring a professional. It's easy to get caught up in an imaginary arms race in which everyone else is taking GMAT prep courses and buying books on how to get in, so you need to do them one better by hiring a full-blown admissions consulting service. The reality is that most other applicants are just like you: They have some good experiences, are bright, can communicate pretty well, but also have a weakness or two. Some have GMAT scores higher than yours, and some have more impressive professional experiences, but none of them is any more entitled to a top-tier MBA than you are. So relax and let your personality and your strengths come through in every part of your application. Using this book will help you do exactly that.

FAQs

Does it matter which round I apply in?

The old adage is "The earlier you apply, the better." Generally, admissions officers state that there is very little difference between the first and second rounds. They know that more applicants tend to apply in Round 2, and they plan accordingly. Beyond Round 2, however, many schools fill just a handful of remaining seats, so your odds of getting in can start to drop significantly, especially if your target school received more applicants than expected in the earlier rounds. We recommend not even considering applying after Round 2—or, more generally, the January deadline, if your school has more than four rounds or is on a rolling admissions basis—unless you find yourself in an extreme circumstance such as needing to dramatically improve your GMAT score before applying.

If you forced us to choose, we would recommend Round 1 over Round 2 for a couple of reasons. First, more applicants apply in round two than in any other round, meaning that you may have a better chance of standing out in round one, although we believe this advantage to be very slight. More importantly, applying early helps to communicate your interest in the school and signal that you're an applicant who's really put a lot of time and thought into the process, which certainly will help you. Finally, applying in the first round means that you will receive responses from your schools by mid-January—or even mid-December at a growing number of schools—giving you time to react and pull together more applications if Round 1 doesn't go as planned.

If you are confident that waiting to apply in the second round will give you time to take your application from good to great, then you should *definitely* wait and apply in Round 2. You want to make sure to put your best foot forward, even if that means waiting a round. A great Round 2 application will beat a good Round 1 application every single time.

Note that some schools offer "early action rounds," which are meant for applicants who know that a given school is their first choice. The deadlines are typically offered early enough that, if you don't obtain admission, you can still apply to other schools in the second round. If your top selection offers an early action round, it's probably worthwhile to participate. It shows the school that you are serious about attending and there tends to be a lower number of applications submitted during this round. Just remember that schools expect you to attend if you submit during this round and are subsequently admitted.

As an international applicant to U.S. business schools, how do I translate my GPA?

For the most part, you shouldn't need to translate your GPA. In general, international applicants (defined as an applicant who is neither a U.S. citizen nor a U.S. permanent resident) are required to submit their official academic records in their original language along with literal English translations prepared by the academic institutions. Most schools will also accept translations from the consulate, embassy, or other such organizations of the institutions' country. Business schools are very familiar with the various grading policies across countries and are very aware that the 4.0 scale used in the United States is not universal. For that reason, U.S. business schools take a close look at your academic standing relative to your classmates in assessing your performance. You should follow up with your target schools in order to understand their specific policies.

Do my AWA scores really matter?

In comparison to the base and individual GMAT scores, the AWA has very little impact on your chances. The Graduate Management Admission Council has essentially acknowledged this by eliminating one of the AWA essays in favor of the new Integrated Reasoning section on the GMAT coming in June 2012. In judging applicants' writing ability, schools tend to emphasize their own essays much more than the AWA and pretty much glance at the score as a quick double-check of your ability to communicate in writing.

With that said, you shouldn't totally blow off the AWA. There are some cases in which the school will take a closer look at the score; most notably in a situation where admissions officers suspect someone else other than the applicant responded to application essays. That alarm can be triggered when the applicant comes from a highly technical or international background, has the essays of a literary genius and an AWA score of less than 4.0. Therefore, you should become familiar with this portion of the exam and attempt a few sample essays, but you shouldn't spend nearly as much time preparing for it as you do preparing for the main sections of the GMAT.

Is it possible to increase my GMAT score more than a few points?

As a business school applicant, you will most likely run into some people who will insist that the GMAT exam is similar to an IQ test in that you can't improve your score. This is definitely not the case. Although you may never be able to hit 800, you can definitely improve your score by a significant amount. Visit any online community and you will find a number of applicants who were able to increase their score by well more than 100 points with a lot of work. The key is to remain diligent in preparation and to change what you're doing if your preparation so far hasn't earned you the score you want.

What do schools do if I retake the GMAT?

Schools almost universally take your highest total score into consideration if you retake the GMAT. This is in the school's best interest because it allows the school to report higher average GMAT scores to magazines for their rankings. In fact, many applicants take the exam two or three times, and admissions officers know this. You shouldn't, however, take the examination over and over again indiscriminately. Schools that see such behavior will question whether you understand what the purpose of applying is. Taking the exam more than three times may raise some eyebrows, so you should put your best foot forward on each attempt.

How early in the process should I interview?

As with everything else in the application process, scheduling an interview earlier rather than later should only help your chances (when it is actually up to you to schedule the interview). From a logistics perspective, scheduling early is beneficial because spots are taken very quickly. Friday interviews can be especially difficult to lock down. We recommend spending a great deal of time on your application, getting it done early, and then doing your interview shortly thereafter.

Should I always do an interview, even if it's optional?

Yes, you should make every effort to interview with your target schools. It will demonstrate your interest and help the admissions committee put a face to a name. If it's difficult for you to arrange an interview (such as for geographic reasons), then going through the process of setting one up is all the more impressive. If you can't do one in person, try to at least arrange a telephone interview, which is better than nothing. If it seems like too much effort, remember that there are thousands of other applicants who will somehow find the time to make it happen.

What should I do if the interviewer is rude or late?

If your interviewer is considerably late, but it doesn't affect the amount of time that you have for the interview, let it go. Focus on being positive and getting your main points across once the interview begins. If your interviewer's late arrival does cut into the amount of time that you have, then consider requesting a follow-up interview. Few interviewers will put you in this situation (the ones that do are typically harried alums), but if they do, be positive and polite, but firm.

If your interviewer is just plain rude (again, this tends to happen with alumni more than with admissions personnel), keep your cool. They may very well be testing you, so the worst thing you can do is try to fight fire with fire. Stay calm and confidently answer the questions that they ask. Remember: It's up to you to emphasize your main points. It's not up to the interviewer to get you to bring them out. If you are asked an inappropriate question (it's been known to happen), know that you don't have to answer it. Stay positive and professional, but let the interviewer know that you won't get sucked in.

After the interview, if you feel that the interviewer behaved unprofessionally and that you weren't able to make your case because of it, consider contacting someone in the admissions office to request a new interview. Again, keep it as positive as possible and remember that the goal is to get yourself into business school, not to get back at your interviewer. Presenting the news as "You'll probably want to know about this to keep it from happening again" is far more effective than "Hey, this wasn't fair and I'm mad about it!"

Some candidates are tempted to contact the admissions office after they have a bad interview, even if the interviewer did nothing wrong. Don't do this. It will sound whiny, and will most likely only hurt your chances. Also, a lot of applicants feel that they bombed their interview when they actually get a positive evaluation. In that case, calling undue attention to the interview can only hurt your cause. Only contact the admissions committee if the interviewer behaved rudely or unprofessionally in some way.

What if I freeze up?

If your interviewer asks you a question and your mind goes blank, it's entirely okay to take a moment to collect your thoughts. In fact, most interviewers appreciate it when an applicant says something along the lines of "Let me think about that for a moment" or "That's a good question." Silence is okay. In fact, silence is considered to be one of the most effective communication tools there is, so learn to get comfortable with it. Pausing shows that you're giving a question a lot of thought, which is good.

Whatever you do, don't just start talking and hope for something good to come out. Many applicants do this, but rambling always ends up doing more harm than good. If you are at a loss, simply take a deep breath and take a few moments to gather your thoughts before speaking. It will only help you.

If I intend to return to my present company after graduation, what message should I convey?

This is an area where many applicants fail miserably. Uninspired by the fact that they will return to their present employer after business school, applicants who fall into this category tend to write about their MBA plans in a dull way, making it sound very much like a ticket that they need to get punched, and nothing more. If you intend to return to your current company, then say so. It's fine to acknowledge the fact that it's the career path you would like to follow. If your company and your supervisor support you in this plan (even if not financially), even better, because it demonstrates that they think you're worth the investment.

However, you need to be very specific in demonstrating how an MBA will help improve your skills. Additionally, you need to demonstrate how you intend to have an impact on the future direction of the company. This doesn't mean listing the titles you hope to achieve, but rather stating the problems you want to address and some form of innovation that you would like to use in addressing them. Simply highlighting the fact that you intend to return to XYZ consulting firm will make you sound just like hundreds of your direct competitors. Go the extra step, and be explicit about what you will do that you can't do without an MBA.

Who should I have review my essays?

Ideally, among the people who review your essays will be a good writer/editor, one person who knows you really well, and someone who does *not* know you well but is familiar with the business school application process (such as a current student, alum, or fellow applicant). You obviously want a good writer to read your essay to check for grammatical errors and ways in which you can improve the structure of your essays. You would also like someone who knows you well enough to read them, as a sort of litmus test to make sure that the essays actually sound like they came from you. After all, your own voice should come through in your essays. Finally, someone who has navigated the admissions process will be able to provide other insights as to how well your essays help your overall application story. One person may very well fit all three of these descriptions, in which case you don't need too many people reading your essays.

Showing your essays to at least one person who doesn't know you too well can help, because that person is better able to flag areas that are confusing to someone who isn't familiar with your background. You may be an amazing candidate, but if a stranger reads your essays and can't tell that you have the makings of a future CEO, then admissions officers may not be able to tell, either. Plus, having an extra set of eyeballs to catch typos is always a good thing. If you're at a loss here, a friend of a friend is usually a good place to start.

One note: It is possible to get too much feedback. Some applicants try to incorporate so much feedback into their essays that the final product sounds nothing like what they started with. As a result, the application no longer sounds as though it were written by the applicant. Remember that you have the final say on everything that goes into your essays. Don't feel obligated to include every last bit of advice that you receive.

How many recommenders should I recruit?

You may only need two or three recommenders total, but it depends on how many schools you apply to, and on how busy your recommenders are. Start by recruiting your immediate supervisor or, if this isn't possible, another coworker who knows you well and can comment on your professional abilities. You'll then want to add one more colleague from your work, and perhaps someone who can comment on your abilities in another light, such as someone whom you know from a community service organization.

You can reasonably expect each person to complete at most three or four recommendations for one admissions round. More is possible, but you'll risk spreading each recommender too thin. So, be ready to recruit more recommenders as needed, assuming that each additional recommender is also qualified to comment on your strengths and weaknesses. Ideally, though, your immediate supervisor will complete a recommendation for every one of your target schools. Because most schools ask that one of your recommendations come from your supervisor, do everything in your power to make it easy for her to complete a recommendation for each one of your applications.

My supervisor's writing is horrendous. What should I do?

This can be a delicate situation, depending on how close you are with your supervisor, but there are ways to deal with it. If you know ahead of time that your supervisor's writing isn't strong, but don't feel comfortable reviewing her recommendation, then consider recruiting a capable third party to serve as an editor. Ask your boss: "Would you mind having Jane give it a read-through before you submit it?" Most bosses will respond positively, or they may even suggest that you review it yourself, but few will balk at the suggestion. After all, they want to help you get in (unless they hate you, in which case you should ask someone else for a recommendation!).

Once you or someone else is able to review it and make changes, pick your spots carefully. Don't obsess over every word or punctuation mark (although you want to catch all obvious typos), but rather focus on making sure that the recommendation is readable, is well-organized, and makes the points that you want emphasized. Don't be afraid to suggest the changes that need to be made. When you go back to your boss with the revisions, keep everything very positive and give reasons for your suggestions. Most supervisors will appreciate the help. If yours doesn't, and you know that the final product is destined to be terrible, then start looking for a Plan B. (This is another reason why you should start early and give yourself plenty of time.) After all, how intelligent your recommenders come across in their written work will reflect upon you, too.

How do schools use the evaluation grid that recommenders are required to fill out?

Admissions officers know that most recommenders feel that they need to give "Outstanding" ratings for each trait in the evaluation grid, lest they hurt their applicant's chances. They therefore don't place too much emphasis on the grid, and instead spend most of their time reading the recommendation letter. Still, the grid communicates a good amount of information very quickly, and application readers will scan it to get an idea of what your strengths and weaknesses are.

If your recommender gives you the absolute best rating in each category, then that actually doesn't give the admissions committee much to go on (other than the fact that you're amazing, which the rest of your recommendation had better support). If you receive "Outstanding" ratings for four categories and receive "Very Good" for the other two, then the admissions committee will think about those two a bit more, and see what your recommender has to say about those traits elsewhere in the recommendation. In any case, what the grid says is less important than the supporting evidence that is presented in the written recommendation. Nonetheless, you probably don't want your recommender giving you anything lower than the second rating. Anything less than that will likely catch an application reader's eye and cause him to dig deeper.

Your main focus should be on arming your recommenders with examples that illustrate each of the traits in the grid will help you the most. Fortunately, you know what the grid is because you can see the form that each recommender receives. For each category, be sure to give your recommenders at least one or two examples of things you've done so that they can easily select "Outstanding."

What is an appropriate gift to get my recommenders for their assistance?

Writing recommendations is a difficult job, especially when you consider the busy schedules of those who are often asked to do it. After it's all said and done, your recommenders definitely deserve some recognition for their efforts.

Giving each recommender a token of your appreciation is the least that you can do as an applicant. Depending on how well you know your recommenders, there are a number of great gifts with which you can provide them. Common examples include: a gift certificate to a nice restaurant, fresh flowers, or wine. Some applicants wait until they receive their admittances and then give their recommenders a memento from their chosen school, such as a shirt, sweatshirt, or coffee mug. Naturally, this strategy can backfire if you don't get admitted.

Regardless, there is only one simple rule that you should follow: Don't be cheap! In addition to a thoughtful gift, a handwritten thank-you card is also always a nice gesture. Outside of common courtesy, showing your gratitude is a good idea, because you never know whether you might have to call on your recommenders again to serve as your champions (for job references, and so forth). Making them glad that they helped you now will only make it easier for you to ask for their help again in the future.

How should I structure my resume if I'm a recent college graduate or have no professional work experience?

As mentioned in Chapter 3, if you're in this situation, you should try to emphasize your leadership, maturity, and teamwork dimensions. Because you don't have much professional experience, the education section should come first. Here you should discuss as many extracurricular activities as possible that display those dimensions. Additionally, this is a case in which you should include your GMAT score and your GPA, assuming that they're high, to show your intellectual capacity. If you have any work experience, including internships or entrepreneurial ventures, make sure to include them.

Developing Strategies
for the Top Programs

By now, you have completed the first half of your own MBA Game Plan, which is differentiating yourself from the competition. You've demonstrated your strengths and bolstered your weaknesses. You have multiple examples that demonstrate your leadership and problem-solving ability. Your abilities will leap off the page as the admissions committee pores over your application.

Great. You're halfway there. Now comes the other—equally important—part: demonstrating how you and your skills are a good fit for each of your target schools. Applicants sometimes forget about this part of the process. After all, plenty of schools' essay questions seem pretty similar. No harm in just copying and pasting, changing the name of the school, tweaking a few lines, and moving on, right? In reality, doing this means possibly missing out on providing what each school is really looking for.

Researching Schools

So how exactly do you determine what a school wants in its applicants? You can learn plenty from the usual sources:

▷ **The school's Website:** This is the starting point for most applicants. Here you can get high-level info on the school, learn about its curriculum and faculty, evaluate the various programs that it offers, and start to get a sense for what it's known for (or, what it wants to be known for, which is sometimes even more important).

▷ **Third-party Websites:** For a different perspective and the occasional reality check, you can always refer to third-party Websites such as *Businessweek*, Poets & Quants, and About.com's Guide to Business Majors.

▷ **Brochure and application:** These are readily accessible on any school's Website. It can be painful to look at brochure after brochure of what seems to be the same material, but really spend some time with these. Think about how long each admissions officer will spend getting to know your application, and spend at least twice as much time with the school's material. More than many applicants realize, schools are fairly explicit about what they are looking for, and these materials will often put this information front and center. Don't ignore it.

▷ **Rankings:** Business school rankings are notoriously overused, but they can give you a good high-level flavor for each school. Although the brochures may tell you what the schools want to be known for, the rankings are sometimes another good reality check that let you know what a school is actually good at. See our "Understanding the Rankings" section for more advice on how to (and how not to) use them.

▷ **Campus visit:** Whether or not you interview on campus, you should plan to visit each school in which you are truly interested. Walk around, meet some current students, sit in on a class, and at least visit the admissions office to let them know you came. The administrator on duty may blow you off, but it's worth a shot. Whether or not you get any good face time with an admissions officer, make sure to mention your visit somewhere in your application to demonstrate your sincere interest in the school. Remember that actions always speak louder than words.

▷ **Current students:** Students are probably the most underutilized resource. Even if you don't visit the campus, it's easy to find business school students' contact info on the Web. Many schools now have student ambassadors who are there to speak with interested applicants. Try to find a student with whom you have something in common and drop her an e-mail. Some students are just too busy to have a real heart-to-heart with you, but odds are that you'll easily find someone who's willing to give you the skinny on the school. Think of a few things you want to know about life at the school and fire away. This is a safe way to ask "dumb" questions about the school (although there are no dumb ones...).

▷ **Alumni:** Alumni are especially helpful in helping to answer questions about what life will be like after business school. Also, ask them about their experiences in school, but schools evolve over time, so realize that someone who graduated 15 years ago probably had a pretty different experience from what you would face.

Understanding the Rankings

The periodic ranking of top business schools has become one of the most visible aspects of the business school selection and application process. Since 1988, when *BusinessWeek* (now *Bloomberg Businessweek*) released its first biennial ranking, multiple media outlets have also taken a cut at evaluating business schools including: *U.S. News and World Report, Financial Times,* and, for a relatively short period, *The Wall Street Journal.* Of course, each outlet claims to have the most precise, and therefore applicable, ranking methodology and has sold thousands of magazines or newspapers as a result of their claims. Indeed, the rankings are generally the first place aspiring applicants look when deciding whether and where to apply. No doubt you will evaluate the ranking that rates your favorite school the highest as the most "fair."

Not many people would have expected it 20 years ago, but the rankings now have gained a lot of power in influencing both applicants and schools themselves. Here is a quick look at what some of the major issues surrounding the rankings are.

Impact

Rankings have had a powerful effect on the business school world. Recruiters, admissions directors, faculty, students, and applicants all keep a close eye on them. With time, most schools have made positive changes to their facilities, curricula, and recruiting processes as a result of issues that the media outlets have uncovered. If a business school makes a jump in the rankings, then the dean will most likely trumpet the success. Should a business school slip, however, then crisis-management techniques often kick in. It is not unheard of for members of the business school community to be fired over a poor ranking.

Controversy

The power of the rankings has also become the center of controversy. The main goal of media outlets is to sell newspapers, magazines, and books. Their core competency is probably not to provide suggestions for business school improvements. Nonetheless, this is often the result of their insights. Many would argue that the rankings' ability to affect business school change has become too great and needs to be curtailed. Your own challenge is to understand the rankings and their methodologies so that their impact on your decision-making is not overstated.

Methodologies

Bloomberg Businessweek

The oldest and perhaps the most publicized modern ranking of business schools comes from *Bloomberg Businessweek*. Its ranking methodology focuses on three components: student evaluations, recruiter evaluations, and the schools' intellectual capital. *Bloomberg Businessweek*'s perspective is that customer evaluation (in this case, students and recruiters) is what matters most in evaluating a business school's abilities. The rankings are mainly based on responses to surveys taken by recent business-school graduates and a majority of the recruiters who hire them. Because of the survey format, *Bloomberg Businessweek*'s rankings are always accompanied by detailed anecdotal information.

The *Bloomberg Businessweek* rankings are often criticized, however, for their high degree of subjectivity. Using recent graduates' perspectives as a heavily weighted component of the rankings is the aspect of this subjectivity that is most often denounced. These criticisms definitely carry some validity, as it seems a bit contradictory to create a relative ranking using input from students who have only attended one business school. That contradiction is compounded by alumni's incentive to inflate the scores that they use in evaluating their schools. Why would an alumna give her school a low evaluation when she has such a vested interest in the school's status? Another apparent weakness of the *Bloomberg Businessweek* rankings is the time at which the students are evaluated. Because they have only recently graduated, it is difficult to imagine that they have more than a limited view of the value of their MBA.

Financial Times

The rankings released by *Financial Times* are undisputedly based on the most complex methodology of all of the media outlets. First released in 1999, in response to *Businessweek* and *U.S. News and World Report*'s omission of international programs, *Financial Times* uses 20 criteria in its evaluation of business schools. These criteria can be segmented into three groups:

1. **Employment:** Salary increase during a three-year period, return on business school investment, career progress, achievement of post-MBA goals, job employment success, and recruiter recommendations.

2. **Diversity and International:** Women faculty, students, and board members; international faculty, students, and board members; international mobility and curriculum.

3. **Faculty and Research:** Faculty with doctorates, number of doctoral graduates, and faculty publications.

The *Financial Times* differentiates itself from the others by taking into account graduate performance a few years after graduation and by evaluating the schools' international and research foci. However, only 2 percent of the weighting in the ranking takes the recruiters' perspectives into account, and there is no formal evaluation of curricula outside of the international and research components.

U.S. News and World Report

U.S. News and World Report releases an annual ranking of the top business schools along with rankings for advanced degree programs in education, engineering, law, and medicine. Its rankings first appeared on the scene in 1990, using a mixture of subjective and objective criteria for its evaluations. This mixture creates a straightforward balance that is absent in the other rankings. The methodology is composed of seven criteria: dean and program director evaluation, recruiter evaluation, starting compensation, job placement, GMAT score, undergraduate GPA, and percentage of application rejections.

Many would argue, however, that the methodology has contributed to selection bias. By heavily weighting the GMAT score and undergraduate GPA, *U.S. News* may encourage admissions committees to turn away applicants who might cause them to slip in the rankings. The academic peer evaluations have also raised eyebrows, as deans and program directors have an incentive to discount other business schools in their ratings.

Usage

So the big question remains: *How should I view the rankings?* The rankings should be viewed as another source of information, but definitely not as the be all, end all. If you decide to apply to the schools ranked 15–20, based on the assigned number alone, then you are probably making a bad choice. The high variation of where schools fall in the different rankings alone indicates that different schools will be better for you based on what you value. As such, rankings are a good starting point for researching schools, but shouldn't be the focal point.

If you find yourself obsessing over the rankings (most of us do at some point), use your gut. Ask yourself: *Is there really a huge difference between the 10th-ranked school and the 15th-ranked school?* Probably not. There are differences, but they will be in the details, which you will uncover through your own research.

The question you should really ask yourself is: *What school(s) can meet my academic, professional, social, geographic, and financial needs?* Naturally, the answer to this question will be different for every person. That is why no single set of rankings really works for everyone. It is a question that you must answer based on all the information available. No methodology will simply produce it for you.

The rankings of the three media outlets are listed on pages 152–153.

Differences Across Schools

As you explore potential target schools, you will notice that many of the brochures look and sound the same. Indeed, there are several business school trends that have pushed schools to adopt similar learning models. Once you visit the schools, however, and dig a little deeper, you will begin to notice that there are larger differences across schools then you initially thought. Three differences across schools that you should pay special attention to are the learning model, typical career paths of graduates, and the culture.

The Learning Model

Most business school curricula are composed of a combination of three pedagogical methods:

▷ **Case study:** The case study method is an integral part of many students' business school experience. Cases are two- to 50-page documents that focus on real-world management situations and generally place the reader in the shoes of a decision-maker. Each case generally focuses on a single topic within a course and can be written for any class from marketing to finance. Class discussions based on the case method are consistently dynamic and rarely conclude in a single solution. The professor generally begins class with a dreaded "cold-call." A cold-call is a business school tradition, whereby an unsuspecting student is asked to introduce the case and provide his perspectives on how the decision-maker (referred to as the case protagonist) in the case should respond to the challenges described by the case. After the student has provided his perspectives, the professor invites other students to participate, and a dialogue ensues. Generally, students speak for more than 80 percent of the class with the professor directing the conversation flow. Sometimes, the case protagonist is even present and provides concluding comments on the class's dialogue.

▷ **Lecture:** We're all familiar with this teaching method. Most schools use the lecture format to teach the more technical aspects of their curricula.

▷ **Experiential:** Experiential teaching methods, which include business simulations, consulting projects, business plan development, and group activities, have become quite popular among business schools. Many students enjoy the opportunity to put the knowledge that they've gained in the classroom to work. As global business perspectives become increasingly important, more schools are adding study-abroad programs and international tours in which students get to interact with business leaders from around the globe. Some schools have even made such trips a mandatory part of the MBA curriculum.

Businessweek 2010 US Business School Rankings		Businessweek 2010 Non-U.S. Business School Rankings	
School	**Rank**	**School**	**Rank**
University of Chicago (Booth)	1	INSEAD	1
Harvard Business School	2	Queen's University	2
University of Pennsylvania (Wharton)	3	IE Business School	3
Northwestern University (Kellogg)	4	ESADE	4
Stanford University	5	London Business School	5
Duke University (Fuqua)	6	University of Western Ontario (Ivey)	6
University of Michigan (Ross)	7	IMD	7
University of California - Berkeley (Haas)	8	University of Toronto (Rotman)	8
Columbia Business School	9	York University (Schulich)	9
Massachusetts Institute of Technology (Sloan)	10	University of Cambridge (Judge)	10
University of Virginia (Darden)	11		
Southern Methodist University (Cox)	12		
Cornell University (Johnson)	13		
Dartmouth College (Tuck)	14		
Carnegie Mellon University (Tepper)	15		
University of North Carolina (Kenan-Flagler)	16		
University of California - Los Angeles (Anderson)	17		
New York University (Stern)	18		
Indiana University (Kelley)	19		
Michigan State University (Broad)	20		
Yale School of Management	21		
Emory University (Goizueta)	22		
Georgia Institute of Technology	23		
University of Notre Dame (Mendoza)	24		
University of Texas - Austin (McCombs)	25		
University of Southern California (Marshall)	26		
Brigham Young University (Marriott)	27		
University of Minnesota (Carlson)	28		
Rice University (Jones)	29		
Texas A&M University (Mays)	30		

Financial Times 2011 Business School Rankings	
School	**Rank**
London Business School	1
University of Pennsylvania (Wharton)	1
Harvard Business School	3
INSEAD	4
Stanford University	4
Hong Kong UST Business School	6
Columbia Business School	7
IE Business School	8
IESE Business School	9
Massachusetts Institute of Technology (Sloan)	9
Indian Institute of Management, Ahmedabad	11
University of Chicago (Booth)	12
Indian School of Business	13
IMD	14
New York University (Stern)	15
Yale School of Management	15
CEIBS	17
Dartmouth College (Tuck)	18
HEC Paris	18
Duke University (Fuqua)	20
ESADE Business School	21
Northwestern University (Kellogg)	21
National University of Singapore School of Business	23
University of Michigan (Ross)	24
University of California - Berkeley (Haas)	25
University of Cambridge (Judge)	26
University of Oxford (Saïd)	27
SDA Bocconi	28
Manchester Business School	29
Cornell University (Johnson)	30

U.S. News 2010 Business School Rankings	
School	**Rank**
Harvard Business School	1
Stanford University	1
Massachusetts Institute of Technology (Sloan)	3
Northwestern University (Kellogg)	4
University of Chicago (Booth)	5
University of Pennsylvania (Wharton)	5
Dartmouth College (Tuck)	7
University of California - Berkeley (Haas)	7
Columbia Business School	9
New York University (Stern)	9
Yale School of Management	11
University of Michigan (Ross)	12
University of Virginia (Darden)	13
Duke University (Fuqua)	14
University of California - Los Angeles (Anderson)	15
Carnegie Mellon University (Tepper)	16
University of Texas (McCombs)	16
Cornell University (Johnson)	18
Washington University (Olin)	19
University of Southern California (Marshall)	20
Ohio State University (Fisher)	21
University of North Carolina (Kenan-Flagler)	21
Indiana University (Kelley)	23
Georgetown University (McDonough)	24
University of Minnesota (Carlson)	24
Georgia Institute of Technology	26
Arizona State University (Carey)	27
Emory University (Goizueta)	27
University of Rochester (Simon)	27
University of Wisconsin	27

As you research schools, you will discover that they all place different emphases on these three approaches. When reviewing the learning models, consider the type of academic environment from which you will benefit most. Also, know that business schools differ in terms of the amount of work (inside and outside of class) that students typically must complete. You should be able to get a decent feel of a school's workload by speaking with students and reviewing curriculum requirements. Beware, however, of asking students to compare the workload at their school to that of other schools, as students are notorious for exaggerating cross-school differences.

Typical Career Paths of Graduates

Business schools probably focus on recruiting more than any other type of graduate school program. As soon as students begin classes, there is a strong emphasis placed on career selection and development. Most business school graduates evaluate their alma maters, to a large degree, based on the schools' ability to help them meet their career objectives. It makes sense, therefore, to examine the career opportunities that different business schools provide. What you will find is that different companies recruit at different schools generally because of geography or skill and experience requirements. Many students find themselves in a situation where they decide to attend a school only to find out that many of the companies in which they are interested do not recruit from that school.

Most programs release an annual career guide that provides a wealth of recruiting information, which should give you an idea as to whether that program aligns well with your career goals. Keep in mind, however, that schools can sometimes be generous when they list who their "recruiting partners" are. They often lump all companies who hired any graduates—whether the company came on campus and hired a dozen people or hired just one person who got the job on her own—into one list in their brochures. So, pay attention and make sure that the companies in which you are really interested actually have a presence on campus (because landing a job with one of these companies is typically much easier than pounding the pavement and seeking out opportunities at a firm that doesn't normally recruit at your school). One good measure is learning how many alumni from your school are at a given company. Additionally, you should consider speaking with current students and alumni to see if your career goals fit well with the recruiting support that the school provides. Finally, consider the overall level of support that the career center provides students and what its relationship with recruiters is like. Career centers can differ drastically in terms of their performance and you certainly want to be at a school that offers a broad level of support and that maintains close relationships with recruiters.

The Culture

Although the learning model and recruiting opportunities may be the most obvious areas to research prior to selecting your target schools, examining schools' cultures is just as important. The best way to get a feel for a school's culture is to visit the campus, chat with students, and check out a class. Each school has its own mission, values, and norms. This has a powerful effect on the student experience, and you should take the time to gain an understanding of the type of culture with which you best fit prior to deciding on your target schools. Also, don't forget that any school's culture is the sum of the individual personalities at the school. When you visit, make sure to meet students and ask yourself: *Do these seem like the kind of people I'd want to study with at 2 a.m.?*

Application Strategies for 35 Top Global Business Schools

Now that you have an idea of how to approach the school selection process, we will delve deeper and provide specific strategies on how to get into 35 top global schools. Though we provide insights for each of these schools, the techniques we've outlined in previous chapters are applicable to all business schools. There are dozens of other good schools that we don't cover here.

Also, note that business schools are constantly evolving. Although we revise the school profiles for each edition of *Your MBA Game Plan,* be aware that your target school may have recently overhauled its core curriculum once again or introduced a new program in which you would be interested. As always, there's no better source of current information than your own legwork, although we intend for each edition to give you a solid head start and help you start to narrow down your school choices. More importantly, the strategies we outline are time-tested and have applicability over a very long period of time.

The purpose here is to apply the dimension framework described in Chapter 2 to 35 top global MBA programs and to give you some school-specific information that you can utilize in developing application strategies for your target schools. These 35 business school application strategies provide application requirements, school background information, and advice on how to approach the school's application. The application strategies also feature a section called "insider information," which highlights a trend that you can leverage in your application or a key insight that insiders say should be featured in your approach. This represents some of the most valuable information we've uncovered while helping applicants through our work with MBA Game Plan and Veritas Prep. Finally, for each school we've called out up to four other schools that call for a similar application strategy. Please note that this is not to say that the schools are exactly alike, or that you should automatically apply to one because you're applying to the other. Rather, this means that applicants have been successful in employing similar strategies across those schools.

Don't read too much into the 35 schools we selected. This list by no means represents "Scott and Omari's List of the 35 Best Business Schools in the World." We reviewed substantial amounts of data on nearly 100 MBA programs and picked 35 schools globally that we believe make-up a compelling cross-section of the world's best programs. In this way, we hope that we've covered at least a few schools that every applicant is interested in investigating in more detail. Please keep in mind that these strategies have wide applicability, so even if your number-one school isn't included in the list, the tips we provide will still likely apply.

Without further ado, here are individual application strategies for 35 of the top business schools in the world, presented in alphabetical order by university name:

Carnegie Mellon University—Tepper School of Business
Pittsburgh, PA
www.tepper.cmu.edu

Application at a Glance
Application due dates (1st, 2nd, 3rd, 4th round):
Oct. 25, Jan. 3, March 7 (final international deadline), April 25

Requirements
Essays: Three two-page essays

Interview: By invitation only; school has a preference for on-campus interviews, but off-campus and phone interviews are also conducted

Recommendations: Two, with one preferably coming from a supervisor

Application Fee: $100

School at a Glance

Dean (start of tenure):	Mark S. Kamlet, Acting Dean (2011)
Admissions Director:	Laurie Stewart
Program Size:	404 full-time
Acceptance Rate:	28%
Yield:	49%
Mean undergraduate GPA:	3.4
Mean GMAT:	696
Middle–80% GMAT:	620–750
Average years of work experience:	4.6
International:	30%
Women:	29%
Minority:	27%

Your Carnegie Mellon Application Strategy

Carnegie Mellon's Tepper School of Business has academic credentials that few other schools can match. The school has produced eight Nobel laureates, which puts it in league with the University of Chicago's Booth School of Business. Tepper is highly analytical, with a great deal of quantitative rigor integrated throughout the entire curriculum. The school's former name—Carnegie Mellon Graduate School of Industrial Administration—invokes images of a program turning out leaders for the manufacturing sector. But this sells the school short, as the school is also well known in finance circles, where Tepper grads' quantitative skills are also highly prized.

Although many schools have a minimum math requirement for applicants, Tepper expects its applicants to have at least completed one college-level calculus course along with another course in calculus, statistics, or linear algebra. Don't worry: These courses are not required at the time of application, and you can take these courses part-time before enrolling. Nonetheless, realize that analytical skills are something that will have to come through in your application no matter what discipline you want to pursue. More than half of each full-time class holds an undergraduate degree in a technical major, so you have to prove that you're capable of keeping up with applicants that have computer science and engineering backgrounds (if you don't have one yourself). These capabilities will mostly be represented in your GMAT score, your undergraduate studies, and your previous work experience.

The school's emphasis on analytical abilities is apparent in its core curriculum. Required courses in probability, statistics, and operations management have the usual dose of quantitative lessons. But classes such as financial accounting and managerial economics also have a stronger analytical bent than you might find at other top schools. One unique feature of the program is its mini-semester system. Students have four mini-semesters in each of their two years at Tepper, instead of the normal two-semester system. Starting in the spring semester of their first year, students can begin taking electives, including ones in Tepper's other schools, which provide a great opportunity to tap into the university's other top-ranked departments.

Tepper students can earn a General Management MBA, or specialize in one of six MBA Tracks: Financial Engineering, Investment Strategy, Management of Innovation and Product Development, Technology Leadership, Global Enterprise Management, and Entrepreneurship in Organizations. Approximately 25 percent of students elect to pursue an MBA Track, which often calls for close collaboration with with other departments within Carnegie Mellon. These MBA Tracks can be ideal for students who truly know what they want out of business school and want to focus their MBA education on a specific career.

Tepper also touts its practical, hands-on approach to learning, exemplified by its Management Game, first introduced in 1958. The game has evolved into a highly involved computer simulation that students tackle in their second year. Student teams each run their own simulated business, making decisions affecting operations, finance, marketing, and labor relations. Tepper students don't just compete against each other, but against students at other top business schools around the world. Adding a level of realism to the game is the fact that each team is assigned a real-life board of directors, made up of local business leaders. Teams also practice contract negotiations with local labor leaders and consult with third-year law students at the University of Pittsburgh.

Industries that graduates pursue are relatively evenly divided across financial services, manufacturing, consulting, and technology. Not surprisingly, many Tepper alumni are active entrepreneurs, and the school looks for entrepreneurship traits in its applicants. If you have entrepreneurial aspirations, be sure to discuss them in your essays and during your interview as part of the innovation dimension, discussed in Chapter 2.

Insider Information

Community is a big part of the Tepper experience. Tepper has always been one of the smallest of the top business schools, and the benefits of the small size are an extremely close-knit community and a student-to-faculty ratio of just 5:1. As you would expect in such a small community, students get to know each other very well, and word quickly gets around about who is or isn't a team player. Be sure to emphasize the teamwork dimension in your application, and also make clear to the admissions committee that you appreciate the value of such an intimate learning environment.

Schools That Call for a Similar Approach

- ▣ MIT (Sloan)
- ▣ Purdue (Krannert)
- ▣ University of Chicago
- ▣ University of Rochester (Simon)

Columbia Business School
New York, NY   *www.gsb.columbia.edu*

Application at a Glance

Application due dates (early decision, regular decision): Oct. 6, April 13

Requirements

Essays: Two (one of 750 words, one of 500 words)

Interview: By invitation only

Recommendations: Two letters of recommendation

Application Fee: $250

School at a Glance

Dean (start of tenure):	R. Glenn Hubbard (2004)
Admissions Director:	Linda Meehan
Program Size:	1,293 full-time
Acceptance Rate:	15%
Yield:	72%
Mean undergraduate GPA:	3.5
Mean GMAT:	713
Middle–80% GMAT:	680–760
Average years of work experience:	4.6
International:	40%
Women:	34%
Minority:	18%

Your Columbia Application Strategy

Perhaps more than any other school, Columbia is nearly synonymous with finance and banking. Students rave about the school's finance faculty and the access that they have to top Wall Street executives. With more than half of a typical Columbia graduating class going into banking, it's no surprise that nearly every Wall Street firm is stacked with Columbia alumni.

Accordingly, most finance-minded applicants—especially those on the East Coast—consider applying to Columbia. If you are one of them, you will need to especially focus on differentiating yourself from a large pool of similar-sounding applicants. Therefore, start thinking now about what makes you different from the rest of the investment bankers (and aspiring bankers) who apply to Columbia.

Although Columbia's core curriculum remains heavy in finance and related courses, it has recently been refined to allow students greater flexibility. Referred to as the "flexible core," first-year students may now select courses that best align with their professional aspirations while still achieving an educational foundation that is rooted in classical general management. Even with this added curriculum flexibility, be aware that much of your time will be spent on finance-related topics. Of course, you will also need to demonstrate an ability to handle a quantitative workload, ideally through your GMAT score and relevant work experience.

Beyond finance, Columbia also places a great deal of emphasis on entrepreneurship. The subject is studied both inside and outside of the classroom, with the Eugene M. Lang Center serving as the hub of much of this activity. Launched in 1996, the Lang Entrepreneurial Initiative Fund provides seed capital to worthy business plans crafted by Columbia students. The Fund acts less like a traditional business plan competition and more like a venture capital firm, taking an equity stake in any Columbia start-up with promise. The Lang Center also sponsors the Entrepreneurial Greenhouse Program, a semester-long course that students take in the spring term of their second year. More than just a seminar in entrepreneurship, the Greenhouse Program provides mentorship and even limited funding to helps students cover typical start-up business costs. Students must submit a business plan to be considered for the program, and just 15 to 20 students are accepted into the program each year.

Another notable program—the Global Social Venture Competition, which grew out of a partnership between Columbia and Haas—keeps growing in stature. It has taken on multiple partner schools around the globe, and now welcomes submissions from MBA students at any school. One student-run initiative at Columbia is the A. Lorne Weil Outrageous Business Plan Competition. As the name suggests, the competition awards students for business plans outlining ideas that are big and ambitious enough to be deemed "outrageous." Obviously, if you have an entrepreneurial itch, research these programs and be sure to highlight this interest in your application.

One more recent development at Columbia is the creation of the Program on Social Intelligence (PSI). This program helps students sharpen their ability to read and understand the behaviors of others and in doing so to understand their own effect on other people—in other words, it helps students increase their "social intelligence." Though other schools have started similar programs, what's most notable about PSI is the extent to which the school is working it into the whole student experience. PSI starts with exercises during Columbia's orientation for first-year students, but goes beyond that with integration into the core curriculum, career services, study groups, end even student clubs. The importance of the PSI program provides insight into how Columbia views leadership development. Take note of this as you think about what stories to highlight in your admissions essays.

Insider Information

Don't plan on waltzing your way into Columbia if you're an overly competitive shark. Although they acknowledge that their peers are competitive, most students and grads consider Columbia to be a competitive but helpful community. Students spend their entire first year in the same "cluster" of 60 students, taking their core classes together. Like other schools, Columbia encourages cooperation and trust within these clusters. As such, you will need to demonstrate the ability to get along with your peers. Also, as do other schools in big cities, Columbia wants its students to spend more time on campus with each other. Demonstrating your enthusiasm for the program and a willingness to get involved in extracurricular activities will help show your fit with Columbia.

Schools That Call for a Similar Approach

- ▶ NYU (Stern)
- ▶ University of Pennsylvania (Wharton)
- ▶ University of Chicago
- ▶ University of London (LBS)

Cornell University—Johnson Graduate School of Management
Ithaca, NY   *www.johnson.cornell.edu*

Application at a Glance

Two Year Program application due dates (1st, 2nd, 3rd, 4th round):
Oct. 5, Nov. 9, Jan. 4, March 22

Requirements

Essays: Three (400 words each)

Interview: By invitation only

Recommendations: Two; both should come from people who are familiar with your professional capabilities and at least one from a direct supervisor

Resume

Application fee: $200

School at a Glance

Dean (start of tenure):	L. Joseph Thomas (2007)
Admissions Director:	Randall Sawyer
Program size:	548 full-time
Acceptance rate:	22%
Yield:	54%
Mean undergraduate GPA:	3.3
Mean GMAT:	700
Middle–80% GMAT:	620–740
Average years of work experience:	4.5
International:	32%
Women:	37%
Minority:	22 %

Your Johnson Application Strategy

Johnson is a quintessential small MBA program. With less than 300 members in each class, students receive a high degree of attention from faculty and from the dean. Perhaps no other top business school program emphasizes professor accessibility as much as Johnson does. Professors at Johnson literally open their homes to students and go the extra mile to ensure that opportunities to learn course concepts extend beyond the classroom. Indeed, joining the Johnson program is more like joining the Johnson family. Your application should echo that sentiment in addition to reflecting the core values upon which the Johnson program has built its reputation.

The values that are central to the Johnson program include a dedication to analytical rigor, an action-oriented approach to learning, and a collaborative learning environment. Your application should highlight your ability to think in an analytical manner. This could manifest itself through a discussion of how you focus on developing solutions, your approach to analyzing problems, or an analytically driven business idea that you have. Analytical in this sense doesn't purely mean numbers-oriented (although Johnson will take a close look at your quantitative GMAT score), but rather it means based on rational and in-depth thought and examination. Examples you can provide along those lines will help you establish fit with the analytical strength Johnson values in addition to its application-focused learning model. As a member of the Johnson family, you will be expected to contribute to your classmates' learning and to the school as a whole. Said in another way, Johnson is looking for applicants who are team players. Though you definitely shouldn't shy away from publicizing your accomplishments, be careful not to come across as arrogant in tone, and be sure that your recommenders reflect positively upon your teamwork skills.

Although Johnson is a general management program, it does offer optional concentrations in the second year of the program. These concentrations are divided into two categories: breadth and depth. Breadth concentrations include consulting, entrepreneurship, leadership, global management, and sustainable global enterprise. Depth concentrations are featured in the areas of corporate finance, financial investing, financial analysis, marketing analytics, marketing management, private equity, and strategy. As implied in the types of depth concentrations, Johnson has great strength in its finance curriculum. Johnson even offers a financial engineering program that focuses on subjects such as derivatives, portfolio analysis, stochastic processes, and computer-based modeling. Another alternative for those who are interested in technical training is the Twelve Month Option MBA program. This program requires an advanced scientific or technical degree and is perfect for those applicants who don't want to be out of the workforce for two years.

As do many other MBA programs, Johnson has jumped on the "leadership bandwagon." However, leadership potential is not merely a criterion listed in brochure material; it is one of the most important applicant characteristics by which you will be evaluated. In fact, Johnson offers up to 25 two-year, full-tuition scholarships to students who have demonstrated exemplary performance in the area of leadership. The admissions committee will look to see whether you take initiative on a regular basis and will specifically assess how you have an impact on your professional and personal environments. Writing about leadership roles that you've taken on and how those roles have progressively increased in level of responsibility is a great way to implicitly state your further leadership potential. Your interview is another proving ground on which leadership will be discussed. You should anticipate that you will receive several questions on leadership, especially questions asking you to provide examples of displayed leadership. You should also anticipate being asked a question on current business events, so make sure you have a decent understanding of what's going on in the business world before your interview. Respond to "Situation" questions using the SAR interview framework discussed in Chapter 4. Chapter 4 also contains a comprehensive set of interview questions on leadership that will serve as great preparation.

The emphasis of your application should be on the leadership and innovation dimensions. Your ability to establish fit along these lines will help grant you entry into the Johnson family.

Insider Information

The Immersion Learning curriculum is probably the best example of Johnson's action-oriented approach to learning. Immersion Learning, also referred to as "the semester in reality," is an experiential method that allows students to take a hands-on approach to functions such as capital markets and asset management, managerial finance, entrepreneurship, strategic operations, strategic marketing, and sustainable global enterprise. Students visit companies, work on actual business challenges, and are evaluated based on the solutions that they develop in response to those challenges. Discussion of Immersion Learning can be a great way to display your knowledge of the Johnson learning model.

Schools That Call for a Similar Approach

- ☒ Dartmouth College (Tuck)
- ☒ University of Michigan (Ross)
- ☒ University of North Carolina at Chapel Hill (Kenan-Flagler)
- ☒ University of Virginia (Darden)

Dartmouth College—Tuck School of Business
Hanover, NH   *www.tuck.dartmouth.edu*

Application at a Glance

Application due dates (Early action, 1st, 2nd, 3rd round):
Oct. 13, Nov. 10, Jan. 3, April 1

Requirements

Essays: Four essays of approximately 500 words each

Interview: Strongly recommended

Recommendations: Two "Confidential Statements of Qualifications"

Application Fee: $225

School at a Glance

Dean (start of tenure):	Paul Danos (1995)
Admissions Director:	Dawna Clarke
Program Size:	510 full-time
Acceptance Rate:	19%

Yield:	49%
Mean undergraduate GPA:	3.5
Mean GMAT:	712
Middle–80% GMAT:	670–760
Average years of work experience:	5.3
International:	33%
Women:	33%
Minority:	18%

Your Tuck Application Strategy

Dartmouth's Tuck School of Business is a small but highly respected MBA program. The country's first graduate school of management offers one of the smallest programs among top schools, with about 250 students in each class. The small class size—coupled with the school's location in rural Hanover, New Hampshire—results in a close-knit community in which everyone knows everyone else. Many Tuck students even live together in on-campus housing in their first year, and the school recently completed a "living and learning" complex to keep students nearby.

Academically, Tuck's MBA program focuses on turning out strong general managers. Most of the first-year curriculum consists of mandatory core courses in the main management disciplines, with students taking two elective courses and completing a first-year project in the spring term. The second year is open for electives, although no specific majors are offered. First-year students complete most of their coursework in study groups, which Tuck emphasizes as a way for students to grow closer and to develop their teamwork skills. More than the average top program, Tuck is looking for students who demonstrate strong teamwork skills, so be sure that this is a main theme in your Tuck application.

Tuck also takes leadership seriously. The Cohen Leadership Development Program is a highly personalized extension of the first-year curriculum. It relies on team coursework, peer assessments, and one-on-one coaching to help students develop their own leadership development plans. The Cohen program also extends into students' second year, with a series of summits and speaking engagements featuring successful executives.

Tuck's close-knit community extends well beyond Hanover, New Hampshire. The school's alumni are known for their fierce loyalty to the school and to each other, and Tuck touts its alumni's annual giving rate of more than 65 percent as evidence of this dedication. Although the school may not have an alum at every company or in every industry, Tuck students are known to get good results from the alumni they do call on. In your own application make sure that you can provide convincing proof that you too will be an active alum, preferably by demonstrating loyalty to your undergraduate school.

Tuck's remote location means that it's not for everyone. Some applicants, especially those with spouses, often find it difficult to relocate to Hanover. To its credit, Tuck goes out of its way to make the transition a smooth one, often providing spouses and partners with full-time work around campus. Still, some applicants who visit the school ultimately decide that it's not for them. This means two things for you: (1) Make sure that you really want to attend Tuck before you apply. It's a great school, but its size and location sometimes turn people off. Save yourself a lot of time if you think these aspects of the program will be a problem for you. (2) Even more importantly, you really need to demonstrate why Tuck is for you. Tuck's students tend to be passionate about their school, and you need to demonstrate this same passion in your application. Visiting the school—especially for your interview—can go a long way toward helping you make your case. Also, think about applying in Tuck's Early Action round (with applications due by mid-October) if you are sure that Tuck is where you want to be.

Insider Information

Tuck may not be the household name that Stanford and Harvard are, but its general management program is regarded as one the best in the country. Tuck graduates have strong reputations in consulting and financial services, particularly on the East Coast, where nearly two-thirds of its graduates live after school. If you are considering a career in general management, or are interested in consulting or banking, don't overlook Tuck. If you can demonstrate that the school's environment is right for you, and make a case for why the general management approach is what you want out of business school, then Tuck will give your application strong consideration.

Schools That Call for a Similar Approach

- ▶ Harvard Business School
- ▶ University of Virginia (Darden)
- ▶ University of Western Ontario (Ivey)

Duke University—Fuqua School of Business
Durham, NC

www.fuqua.duke.edu

Application at a Glance

Application due dates (Early action, 1st, 2nd, 3rd round):
Sept. 30, Nov. 1, Jan. 5, March 8

Requirements

Essays: Three two-page essays

Interview: Strongly recommended

Recommendations: Two letters of recommendation

Application Fee: $200

School at a Glance

Dean (start of tenure):	Blair Sheppard (2007)
Admissions Director:	Liz Riley Hargrove
Program Size:	885 full-time
Acceptance Rate:	30%
Yield:	51%

Mean undergraduate GPA:	3.4
Mean GMAT:	687
Middle–80% GMAT:	640–750
Average years of work experience:	5.6
International:	39%
Women:	39%
Minority:	20%

Your Fuqua Application Strategy

No school has come as far as Fuqua (pronounced "FEW-kwa") has in the past four decades. Duke enrolled its first class of MBA students in 1970, but things really started to happen after the school took Atlanta industrialist John Brooks Fuqua's name (and his money) in 1980. What was once a well-regarded school with mostly regional appeal has grown into one of the top MBA programs in the world.

Fuqua initially used its small size as an advantage over the business school competition, employing an innovative curriculum that allows for breadth and flexibility. The program has grown in size over time, but innovation remains a central theme of the curriculum. Students have four terms (of six weeks each) per year, meaning that they get a taste of many more subjects than students at most other schools. They also complete at least five electives by the end of their first year, which some Fuqua students have credited as a competitive advantage heading into summer internships.

Fuqua's academic emphasis has traditionally been on general management, although students can earn concentrations in two areas, ranging from typical subjects such as finance and marketing to broader topical areas such as social entrepreneurship and international business. One program that has become a signature for Fuqua is its Health Sector Management (HSM) program, which is the largest program of its kind at any top business school. If you are interested in biotech, pharmaceuticals, medical devices, or healthcare management, then take a close look at this program, which draws a wide range of recruiters to Fuqua every year.

Another theme that is prevalent at Fuqua is teamwork. Work in most classes is done in teams, and Fuqua's graduates have gained a strong team-oriented reputation among recruiters. Students often refer to themselves as "Team Fuqua," and they mean it. This atmosphere is reinforced by faculty and administration who go out of their way to make Fuqua an intimate environment. When you apply to Fuqua, make it clear that you understand what it means to be part of a close-knit community, and spell out why it appeals to you. Along those lines, Fuqua students are heavily involved in everything going on at the school. If you are applying to Duke, make sure that this is what you want out of your business school experience. More importantly, make sure to emphasize this in your application through multiple examples of teamwork and involvement.

Admissions interviews are usually conducted by alumni or second-year students. It is, therefore, important to position yourself as a prospect that your interviewer would like to have as a classmate. This means you should provide examples of professional excellence, but do so in a non-arrogant tone. In the back of his mind, your interviewer will be evaluating you as a potential team member in addition to evaluating you as an applicant overall. Also, if you have three years professional experience (or less), you should expect to receive questions on your ability to contribute in the classroom. Have a response prepared as to why now is a good time for you to attend Fuqua.

Another way to show your fit with Fuqua is to demonstrate your sincere interest in the program. Even though Fuqua is still a highly competitive school that's tough to get into, its yield (percentage of accepted students who enroll) is somewhat low compared to that of other top schools. The school therefore wants to be sure that if it accepts you, you will enroll. Within the last few years, Fuqua has introduced an early action round that targets applicants who know that the school is their first choice. This should help boost its yield percentage. The bottom line is if you can demonstrate that you truly want to attend Fuqua—and explain why this is so—you will greatly improve your chances of admission.

Insider Information

As do many other top schools, Fuqua has been placing increasing emphasis on the importance of global business. The school replaced its pre-term course for first-year students (formerly called Integrated Leadership Experience) with a new three-week program called the Global Institute. The program puts students in learning teams that study issues related to leadership and ethics in the context of a global business climate. It's a nice warm-up for incoming students, and a clear indication of how important international business is to the Fuqua administration. Though a background—or even a strong interest—in international business is definitely not a prerequisite, keep this in mind as you craft your Fuqua application strategy.

Schools That Call for a Similar Approach
- ≥ Northwestern (Kellogg)
- ≥ Dartmouth (Tuck)
- ≥ University of Michigan (Ross)
- ≥ UC Berkeley (Haas)

Emory University—Goizueta Business School
Atlanta, GA   *goizueta.emory.edu*

Application at a Glance
Application due dates (1st, 2nd, 3rd, 4th round):
Nov. 1, Dec. 1 (recommended international deadline), Feb. 1, March 1

Requirements
Essays: Four essays (two of 1,000 words each and two of 500 words each)

Interview: Strongly recommended

Recommendations: Two letters of recommendation

Application Fee: $150

School at a Glance

Dean (start of tenure):	Lawrence M. Benveniste (2005)
Admissions Director:	Julie Barefoot
Program Size:	340 full-time
Acceptance Rate:	34%
Yield:	42%
Mean undergraduate GPA:	3.3
Mean GMAT:	676
Middle–80% GMAT:	620–750
Average years of work experience:	5.1
International:	33%
Women:	32%
Minority:	19%

Your Goizueta Application Strategy

Emory University's Goizueta (pronounced "goy-SWET-uh") Business School is one of the smallest of the world's top programs, with just 150 entering the school's traditional two-year MBA program each year. One big benefit of this small size is Goizueta's 5:1 student-to-faculty ratio, which very few other schools can offer. And, like other small programs, Goizueta is noted for its close-knit culture and high student involvement in every aspect of the school. Students have a strong voice in many of the school's departments, including admissions, curriculum development, marketing, and facilities planning. Not surprisingly, the school expects that each of its students will get involved in at least one opportunity to leave a mark on the school.

Goizueta promotes its own flavor of leadership training, which it calls "Leadership in Action." The school believes that effective leadership requires seven important traits—courage, integrity, accountability, rigor, diversity, team, and community—which it introduced as its "Core Values" in 2002. Goizueta students are immediately introduced to the school's Core Values during their orientation week, with one activity devoted to each of the traits the school has identified. Students participate in ropes courses and skydiving to learn courage, perform service projects to gain a sense of community, and so forth. In other words, the school expects each student to embrace its Core Values, and you should be prepared to explain what these values mean to you.

Perhaps Goizueta's most important espoused Core Value is courage, which the school defines as a willingness to take risks and push yourself out of your comfort zone. The school believes that this is an important component of leadership, and you can therefore expect the Goizueta admissions committee to look for examples of this trait in your application. The school is most interested in the applicant who takes the road less traveled and who is willing to take some risks. Any way you can demonstrate this trait in your own past—and what you learned from it—will help the admissions committee see how you fit in at Goizueta. Think about how you can weave these stories into your entire application, particularly in Goizueta's essay questions.

Before the start of each semester, Goizueta students take part in a pre-term course called LEAD Week, an intense program that gives them exposure to real-world business issues. Before the start of the first-year fall term, students study critical leadership and presentation skills through a series of case studies devoted to a particular company. To start the second year, student teams come together to compete in a business plan competition, with each team preparing a business plan from scratch and implementing it. LEAD Week programs also give students the opportunity to study abroad.

Additionally, Goizueta Plus is a series of seminars that students take their first year, giving students the opportunity to develop their own "brand" as leaders and to hone their presentation and interviewing skills. These programs are constantly evolving, but they remain a centerpiece of the Goizueta program, and expressing an understanding of how they embody the school's Core Values will help strengthen your application.

Although most schools prefer students with some amount of work experience, Goizueta explicitly states that students need at least some post-college, full-time work experience in order to apply. Certainly all schools look for maturity in their applicants, but Goizueta is explicit about the importance of this dimension of your application. It is therefore important to choose essay and interview stories that emphasize your own professional maturity.

Insider Information

Further demonstrating the school's commitment to leadership, the Goizueta Advanced Leadership Academy gives students a chance to receive even more personalized leadership training. Students must apply to the program, which matches participants with professional executive coaches who help them create their own leadership development plans. Students in the academy also take part in group activities such as hiking the Appalachian Trail, sailing to the British Virgin Islands, and participating in an improvisation workshop. If you're particularly interested in using your two years in business school to bolster your leadership skills, keep Goizueta and the Advanced Leadership Academy in mind.

Schools That Call for a Similar Approach

- ▶ Cornell University (Johnson)
- ▶ Dartmouth College (Tuck)
- ▶ UNC (Kenan-Flagler)
- ▶ USC (Marshall)

ESADE Business School
Barcelona, Spain
www.esade.edu/mba

Application at a Glance

Application due dates (1st, 2nd, 3rd, 4th, 5th, 6th, 7th round):
Oct. 15, Dec. 10, Feb. 11, March 18, April 15, May 20, July 8

Requirements

Essays: Four essays (approximately 320 words each)
Interview: By invitation only

Recommendations: Two letters of recommendation

Application Fee: €130

School at a Glance

Dean (start of tenure):	Alfons Sauquet (2008)
Admissions Director:	Camila de Wit
Program Size:	334 full-time
Acceptance Rate:	46%
Yield:	57%
Mean undergraduate GPA:	N/A
Mean GMAT:	670
Middle–80% GMAT:	600–770
Average years of work experience:	5.8
International:	84%
Women:	30%
Minority:	N/A

Your ESADE Application Strategy

Based in Barcelona, ESADE is one of Spain's two powerhouse business schools (the other is IE Business School in Madrid). Armed with an extremely flexible, full-time program and core strengths in the areas of leadership development, entrepreneurship, and international business, ESADE has a tremendous amount to offer aspiring MBAs. The school is in search of applicants that will take full advantage of its competencies, demonstrate impressive leadership capabilities, and display a penchant for innovation.

The ESADE full-time track allows students to select from three different program time durations: 12, 15, or 18 months. With this level of flexibility a student can tailor her MBA program according to her individual personal and professional needs. All students participate in a pre-term and three terms of the core curriculum. Beyond the core curriculum all students also take at least eight electives. The differences among the three programs relate to the student's desire to pursue a corporate internship and/or participate in an exchange program. All students start the program at the same time and do not have to finalize their program pathways until the end of the second term.

The ESADE program places a great deal of emphasis on leadership training, which is represented in the curriculum by the Leadership Assessment and Development (LEAD) Programme. The objective of LEAD is to heighten participants' emotional intelligence, which in turn is believed to maximize leadership capabilities. The program starts with a series of exercises and surveys to uncover baseline predispositions with respect to personality and perspective. This initial diagnostic also highlights areas on which participants would like to focus for personal and professional improvement.

Two integral aspects of LEAD are feedback and coaching. Each participant is assigned to a learning team and also receives a personal coach. Both sources collect behavioral observations, which are delivered to participants as part of a

360-degree assessment. This part of the process is designed to bring potential personal development obstacles to the forefront and ultimately leads to an individualized learning plan that provides a customized road map for improving specific aspects of a participant's emotional intelligence. With such a strong emphasis on the leadership development process, ESADE is in search of applicants that have demonstrated raw leadership capabilities and more importantly, are motivated to evolve their leadership approaches and perspectives as maturing business leaders. Simultaneously, the school would like to see strong teamwork capabilities, given the importance of the learning teams in LEAD and an underlying belief that the best leaders also make for great team members.

Entrepreneurship is a big deal at ESADE and probably the primary way in which it seeks to make a name for itself. Entrepreneurship's high level of importance is reflected in the depth to which it is integrated into the core curriculum. Core entrepreneurial coursework covers the basic frameworks for evaluating new ventures, a feasibility study during which students analyze the viability of actual business ideas, and, lastly, the opportunity to develop business plans with support from ESADE's Entrepreneurship Centre (CINEM). After business plans have been developed, students may participate in business plan competitions, presenting to venture capital and angel investors. ESADE keeps close tabs on the progress of its alumni's start-up businesses and believes that those with innovation inherent in their business model are the most likely to succeed. To the extent that entrepreneurship appeals to you and you have an innate streak of innovation, be sure to bring it out in your application.

As a business school based in a hub of European economic activity, ESADE rightly articulates a global vision throughout its program. To assist in furthering this vision, each class contains an impressive degree of international diversity with the proportion of students from outside of Spain typically standing at more than 80 percent and representing more than 55 nationalities. Although courses are taught predominantly in English, there is a bilingual (Spanish and English) track, and all students are expected to have a mastery of both languages by graduation. The school also offers courses in German and French for those who believe that merely being bilingual is not global enough. To pull the international experience together, ESADE offers both one term exchange programs as well as shorter "study tours," consisting of a week-long dedicated immersion in a region of the student's choice. Given the great deal of flexibility that the curriculum and its international programs afford, it will be important to consider what your path would be as you complete your ESADE application.

Insider Information

As with many programs that offer a curriculum that is shorter than 24 months, ESADE is looking for mature applicants with significant professional experience to help offset the shorter duration of the program. Indeed, applicants with less than two years of post-undergraduate experience do not even qualify for the program, and the average student enters the program with nearly six years of professional experience. Although the program does offset the shorter duration with an advanced suite of customized career-services capabilities, the school will still take a very close look at how you express your maturity dimension. Therefore, it is very important that you take extra time evaluating where ESADE fits into your career goals and ensure that you express fit with the capabilities that the school offers based on your past experiences and future aspirations.

Schools That Call for a Similar Approach

- ➤ IE Business School
- ➤ University of Southern California (Marshall)
- ➤ MIT (Sloan)

Harvard Business School
Boston, MA   *www.hbs.edu*

Application at a Glance
Application due dates (1st, 2nd, 3rd round): Oct. 1, Jan. 11, March 31

Requirements
Essays: Four (three of 400 words, one of 600 words)

Interview: By invitation only

Recommendations: Three, with one preferably from your direct supervisor

Resume

Application fee: $250

School at a Glance

Dean (start of tenure):	Nitin Nohria (2010)
Admissions director:	Deirdre Leopold
Program size:	1,874 full-time
Acceptance rate:	12%
Yield:	84%
Mean undergraduate GPA:	3.7
Mean GMAT:	719
Middle–80% GMAT:	680–770 (estimate)
Average years of work experience:	3.4
International:	36%
Women:	35%
Minority:	22%

Your Harvard Application Strategy

Leadership is unquestionably the most emphasized dimension at Harvard Business School (HBS). The school's mission is to "develop outstanding business leaders who contribute to the well-being of society." This mission, along with the school's community standards, can be found posted in every classroom on campus. Candidates' potential as leaders should therefore permeate every aspect of the HBS application. Leadership should be projected on multiple levels; professional experience, academic experience, extracurricular activities, hobbies, and community service can all be used to highlight leadership capabilities. Good examples demonstrate your ability to have positive influence over the actions of others. A focus on leadership should also play a role in describing your career goals. More than most schools, HBS will closely evaluate your career goals based on their level of impact on society. Finally, remember to describe your leadership style and how it has changed over time. The admissions committee is really interested in what you have learned along the way and will be impressed with reflections on your "leadership evolution."

HBS is known as the quintessential general management program. In line with the mission of the school, students' decision-making ability across multiple business disciplines is the constant focal point. Students do not formally specialize in a particular aspect of business, as they do at most schools, and take the first year required curriculum in sections of 80 to 90 students. Although the case study method is the central method of teaching at HBS, a new experiential-based pedagogical approach was added to the curriculum in 2011. First-year students now participate in a year-long course entitled Field Immersion Experiences for Leadership Development (FIELD). FIELD employs application-focused methods, placing students into small teams and offering them the opportunity to get hands-on leadership experiences in dealing with global challenges. This refinement to the HBS curriculum marks a substantial evolution in its approach to business education and is worth exploring as you assemble background information for your application.

The section experience is one of the defining aspects of the HBS learning model, as each student is expected to take on the responsibility of teaching her classmates. Students constantly draw from their own background and experiences, creating a dynamic atmosphere that is supplemented by the faculty's insights. To ensure that classrooms are filled with numerous perspectives, students' backgrounds are extremely diverse in nature. It is not uncommon for most sections to contain lawyers, teachers, investment bankers, doctors, consultants, brand managers, professional athletes, military officers, and entrepreneurs. Taught in two full terms, the first year of required curriculum is followed by an entirely elective curriculum in the second year, which is conducted in four modular half terms. Students utilize this year to further hone their decision-making abilities in areas that they believe will be the most beneficial for their careers.

Applicants should be aware that their undergraduate school's reputation will be factored into the selection process at HBS. The undergraduate schools that are most densely represented are Harvard University, University of Pennsylvania, and Stanford University. This, however, should definitely *not* be a deterrent to applicants from lesser-known schools. Indeed, more than 250 undergraduate institutions are represented in a typical HBS class. Nonetheless, applicants who graduated from schools with less brand strength than most should make a concerted effort to highlight the strengths of their school and their accomplishments at the school. One way to do this is through the recommendation process.

HBS is one of the few business schools that doesn't mind recommendations from former professors. Though your recommendation approach should primarily focus on your professional experience, a recommendation that highlights your academic prowess can help augment your position as an applicant. The professor's recommendation can add credibility to your school's reputation, thereby granting credibility to your entire application. Should you go down this path, however, make sure that the professor is in a position to comment on your leadership capabilities and on your professional goals. If the professor isn't that familiar with you and your story, then it's best to seek a recommendation from a different source.

Being part of the HBS community is a lifelong commitment. This is highlighted by the fact that the alumni network is often one of the first points that is raised when discussing HBS's differentiating factors. It is therefore to your advantage to show ways in which you have been a champion for your alma mater. The admissions committee isn't just concerned about what you will bring to the table during your time in the classroom, but also how you will remain involved with and support the school in the future.

Insider Information

Despite having added field study to the curriculum, the case study method remains the lifeblood of the HBS learning model. This cannot be stressed enough. By graduation, students can expect to have conquered more than 500 cases in addition to textbooks, notes, and articles that provide conceptual depth to the case scenarios. Each case addresses a class topic and provides a "real-world" example on how the topic is applicable. New cases are constantly produced by professors, and students will often receive a freshly written case hot off the press less than a week before discussing it. Second-year students are even granted the opportunity to assist in the case writing process by participating in a field study. Producing cases has become such a core part of HBS that a majority of business schools purchase their case studies from it.

Displaying a grasp of the case method and how it is utilized at HBS is an excellent way to differentiate yourself from other applicants. You should emphasize your ability to engage in open discussions and your desire to learn based on real-world business applications. Both of these components are central to the way case studies are taught at HBS and are also believed to play a significant role in making the FIELD curriculum a success. Discussing your learning style and how you would benefit from case studies will help demonstrate your understanding of the learning model.

Schools That Call for a Similar Approach

- ⊠ INSEAD
- ⊠ University of Virginia (Darden)
- ⊠ University of Western Ontario (Ivey)
- ⊠ Yale School of Management

IE Business School
Madrid, Spain
www.imba.ie.edu

Application at a Glance

Application due dates: Rolling admissions

Requirements

Essays: Three (500 words each)

Interview: By invitation only

Recommendations: Two

Resume

Application fee: €250

School at a Glance

Dean (start of tenure):	Santiago Iñiguez (2004)
Admissions director:	Julián Trigo
Program size:	440 full-time
Acceptance rate:	33%
Yield:	51%
Mean undergraduate GPA:	N/A
Mean GMAT:	680
Middle–80% GMAT:	640–760 (estimate)
Average years of work experience:	5.0
International:	90%
Women:	32%
Minority:	N/A

Your IE Business School Application Strategy

For entrepreneurs, by entrepreneurs. The Instituto de Empressa (IE) Business School was initiated based on that dictum in 1973 and quickly became established as one of the leading international graduate business programs. Whereas many business schools have been accused of being mired in tradition and falling behind in terms of reflecting the needs of a dynamic business community, IE has leveraged its relative youth by deploying an innovative one-year program that remains committed to the spirit of the entrepreneur and the ideals of global business.

The core of the innovation aura that surrounds IE is its curriculum. The program starts off with a module called "launch," which focuses on building soft skills, such as communication, negotiation, team building, coaching, and leadership. To engage students in a productive dialogue, IE utilizes workshops during this launch segment. These workshops continue throughout the core curriculum as part of IE's ACCELERATE program. After the launch module, the curriculum divides the traditional management disciplines into three core periods: business fundamentals, core management, and concept integration. In between each of the periods there are two smaller modules that focus on helping IE students become change agents with the skill sets to become successful entrepreneurs. After the third core period and a short break, students begin the elective portion of the curriculum, which includes a broad assortment of courses from which students can choose.

If curriculum is the core of IE innovation, then the Venture Lab is one of its primary engines. The goal of the Venture Lab is to help seed the creation of business ventures initiated by IE students and alumni. Students must navigate a systematic selection process before gaining entry into the Venture Lab, based on IE's desire to provide investors with high-quality "deal flow." A selection committee composed of investors and entrepreneurs evaluate students' applications to the Venture Lab based on their disruptive potential, the size of the potential market, value proposition, and team members. Once accepted into the Venture Lab, student teams are assigned a mentor with industry-specific experience to help assist with challenging the business model and pushing the team to maximize the venture's prospects for success.

The Venture Day represents the culmination of the process. A biannual event in which the top five projects are presented to interested investors, the Venture Day represents the close linkage between the academic and professional spheres that IE maintains. Even though many student teams are not selected to participate in the Venture Day, most assign a high value to the process of evaluation, business model development, and in-depth feedback. Indeed, IE has even established a Venture Academy that actively works with alumni start-ups, so that entrepreneurial engagement can continue even after graduation.

Although it's obvious that any entrepreneurial inclinations that you might have should be expressed in your application to IE, it is important to note that the school views entrepreneurship as a state of mind, not necessarily as a state of being. As such, the applicant who positions herself as an innovative change agent within a corporate environment will certainly be viewed as more entrepreneurial (and more aligned with IE values) than the applicant who works for a start-up but never challenges the status quo. It is critical, therefore, that you reflect on your entrepreneurial state of mind in whatever capacity that you operate in.

Based in Madrid, IE pursues a truly global mission, as reflected in its student body, faculty members, and global partnerships. Applicants from outside of Spain make up more than 80 percent of the student body, with nearly 70 nationalities represented. Courses may be taken in either English or Spanish, with about 30 percent of the class pursuing the Spanish track. The school even offers intensive Spanish courses, so that students can develop and refine their language skills and acclimate to the local environment. Approximately half of the faculty hail from outside of Spain, with more than 20 nationalities represented. The faculty maintain close relationships with the professional world, so that they can infuse an application-based approach into their teaching.

The flexible learning model incorporates a multitude of international opportunities into its practicum, including a unique partnership with the Wharton School, traditional exchange programs at 40 business schools around the globe, and "short" exchange program opportunities that typically consist of a week-long focused study abroad. IE is certainly in search of applicants that are looking to expand their worldview and simultaneously share the perspectives of their unique country-specific experiences.

Insider Information

Maturity is a key dimension that IE looks for in its students. Work experience is a prized asset, to the point that the school states that a minimum of three years of professional post-graduate work experience is required. Though the school does make exceptions, IE clearly values work experience and expects its students to contribute a great deal to the classroom environment based on previous experiences. This expectation aligns closely with the "can do" attitude and entrepreneurial ambition that IE looks for in its applicants.

Schools That Call for a Similar Approach

- ▶ ESADE Business School
- ▶ University of Southern California (Marshall)
- ▶ MIT (Sloan)

IMD

Lausanne, Switzerland

www.imd.ch/mba

Application at a Glance

Application due dates (1st, 2nd, 3rd, 4th, 5th round):
Feb. 1, April 1, June 1, Aug. 1, Sept. 1

Requirements

Essays: Eleven essays (approximately 200 to 400 words each)

Interview: By invitation only

Recommendations: Three

Resume

Application fee: CHF 350

School at a Glance

Dean (start of tenure):	Dominque V. Turpin (2010)
Admissions director:	Lisa Piguet
Program size:	90 full-time
Acceptance rate:	22%
Yield:	83%
Mean undergraduate GPA:	N/A
Mean GMAT:	670
Middle–80% GMAT:	620–730
Average years of work experience:	6.8
International:	99%
Women:	23%
Minority:	N/A%

Your IMD Application Strategy

To call IMD an exclusive business school would be a substantial understatement. The one-year full-time program only allows 90 hand-picked applicants into the program each year. The acceptance rate is a mere 22 percent, the school boasts a yield of more than 80 percent, and students have an average of nearly seven years of work experience (the school requires a minimum of three years to be accepted). These remarkable statistics are underscored by one of the most in-depth and rigorous applications of any business school, featuring eleven essays, three recommendations, and an intense interview (if you make it that far). Thankfully, beyond the intimidating application and general IMD mystique is an impressive program with an incredible amount to offer those who do successfully navigate the application.

Located on Lake Geneva in picturesque Lausanne, Switzerland, IMD is the quintessential intimate international business school program. With a student to faculty ratio of only 2:1, classes are kept very small and learning is highly individualized. The smaller size is also beneficial when it comes to recruiting, as there are 1.5 students for every recruiter who visits campus, which IMD proudly notes is the lowest ratio of students to recruiters of any business school. The low ratio also reflects the strength of the IMD brand with the corporate community.

The intimacy also speaks to the importance of strong interpersonal skills, as admitting a few lone sharks into the program could easily damage curriculum dynamics that rely heavily on team activities. Understandably, the admissions committee is hypersensitive about weeding out individuals who likely would not succeed in an environment that requires this level of teamwork and therefore will review your application closely in that context.

The central aspects of the IMD curriculum have historically been a commitment to learning the business fundamentals, leadership training, and contextual learning. Although that commitment remains, in 2011 IMD announced an evolution in its program to include a new "action learning" approach. In essence, action learning is an application-based approach that provides students with experiential learning opportunities such that they can more readily apply what they learn in the classroom to the real-world professional environment. This evolution in approach is now directly embedded in the curriculum via company projects that are conducted in parallel with academic learning. Broken into five separate projects, which align with the five academic learning modules, students lead different assignments for companies that are at a variety of stages in the business lifecycle, from pure start-ups to large multinational companies.

Leadership development is held paramount at IMD. There is an entire five-module initiative that focuses on leadership training and spans the traditional classroom curricula. The objective of the five modules: understand yourself, work in teams, lead in difficult environments, influence organizations, and personal reflection is to produce insightful, dynamic professionals that are responsible in the way they lead teams and organizations. To complete this transformative process, students must dedicate hundreds of hours to the process of introspection and putting new leadership skills into practice.

The initiative begins with the development of an in-depth autobiography, referred to as a personal and professional identity narrative (PPIN) that is maintained throughout the year and serves as a central resource for the leadership development process. Individual and team coaching are also an important part of the initiative and are coupled with peer reviews and in-depth self-analysis, bringing a highly customized feel to the program. Learning is then actualized through leadership and team-building exercises that replicate high-pressure environments, putting new leadership capabilities to the test. This aspect of the program benefits greatly from the broader IMD action learning approach.

Ultimately, IMD expects its alumni to have major positive impact in the world. Because it turns out so few graduates each year, the school has an unstated commitment to ensuring that each accepted applicant offers maximal opportunity to extend the IMD brand and reach. As such, to gain successful entry, demonstrated leadership experiences must be woven throughout your application. Beyond experience, a capacity and desire for further leadership development is greatly appreciated by IMD. Given that its students will have to undergo such a rigorous process of introspection and development, the admissions committee wants to ensure that admitted students are motivated to participate and willing to devote their time and energy to ensuring that the program works for them.

Contextual learning in "IMD speak" refers to the need for business leaders to adapt their style, perspectives, and actions based on their business environment. IMD translates this philosophy into its curriculum by incorporating different business types into its projects and by infusing a diverse and rich international flavor. Despite a class size of only 90 students, more than 40 countries are typically represented and each student is required to speak at least one language in addition to English. (Most students have a reasonable command of three or more.) The result is a school that mirrors its native Switzerland: small and intimate, but with a diversity of languages and perspectives.

Students are able to deploy their contextual learning by participating in international consulting projects as well as an initiative called Discovery Expedition. Discovery Expedition is a two-week program during which students travel to an emerging market and work directly with local businesses in an effort to learn about the challenges faced in that business environment and transfer some of the knowledge gained during the IMD program. The admissions committee will evaluate your application closely, assessing your global mindset and ability to succeed in and benefit from a program such as Discovery Expedition. Presenting yourself as a capable global leader is therefore imperative to your application's success.

Insider Information

Entrepreneurship has rapidly become one of the major themes emphasized within the IMD program. Although new ventures are often the focus of the entrepreneurial dialogue, the school firmly believes that the skill set of an entrepreneur is just as important to the success of larger organizations, given their innovation and growth requirements. IMD students are also often called upon to play advisory roles within start-ups. More than half of leading technology start-ups have worked with IMD full-time or Executive MBAs. You can certainly improve your chances of success by detailing your entrepreneurial mindset, particularly in the context of leadership.

Schools That Call for a Similar Approach
- ◪ INSEAD
- ◪ University of London (London Business School)
- ◪ Harvard Business School

Indiana University—Kelley School of Business
Bloomington, IN
www.kelley.iu.edu/mba

Application at a Glance

Application due dates (1st, 2nd, 3rd, 4th round):
Nov. 1, Jan. 5, March 1, April 15

Requirements

Essays: Three essays (two pages each)

Interview: Recommended

Recommendations: Two; both should come from people who are familiar with your professional capabilities

Resume

Application fee: $75

School at a Glance

Dean (start of tenure):	Daniel C. Smith (2005)
Admissions director:	James Holmen
Program size:	454 full-time
Acceptance rate:	31%
Yield:	49%
Mean undergraduate GPA:	3.3
Mean GMAT:	664
Middle–80% GMAT:	590–730
Average years of work experience:	4.9
International:	26%
Women:	30%
Minority:	22%

Your Kelley Application Strategy

Curriculum innovation is one of the strongest assets of the Kelley learning model. The curriculum often receives accolades for its integrated, cross-functional approach to teaching. The basis of the approach is that real-world business challenges are not discretely segmented into functions and therefore business school should be taught in an integrated manner. The admissions committee is looking for applicants with leadership potential who view business issues in a cross-functional way and are interested in participating in a learning model that is taught in an equally integrated and flexible fashion.

Faculty members are trained to lead courses utilizing a "team-teach" approach, allowing for cross-discipline perspectives as they apply to myriad business challenges. This means that you might find yourself at the center of a holistic discussion that requires consideration of economics, marketing, and operations all at once. Because there are faculty members present from each of the disciplines in the room simultaneously, this can make for a very rich dialogue. The first semester, referred to as the "Integrated Core," is taught by eight faculty members and combines eight business disciplines: business analytics, corporate finance, critical thinking and ethics, economic foundations, financial accounting, marketing, operations strategy, and strategic management. The goal of the Integrated Core is to provide students with tools and intuition that will be invaluable in making management decisions. One way for you to display an appreciation for the Kelley approach is to discuss how the results of actions you've taken in a business environment have been beneficial to multiple functions and not just the one to which you belong.

Outside of the core curriculum, students select majors from a set of six options: entrepreneurship and corporate innovation, finance, management, marketing, strategic analysis of accounting information, and supply chain operations. If none of the options suits their needs, students can design their own majors that fit with their career interests. To supplement their specialized study, students can apply to participate in an "Academy." Academies are industry-focused and allow students to take part in career-focused course work and professional development activities such as discussions with professionals in the industry, a speaker series, and trips to relevant companies. There are Academies for Consumer Marketing, Entrepreneurial Management, Corporate Finance, Business Marketing, Consulting, Investment Banking, Investment Management, and Supply Chain and Global Management. In addition to one of the Academies, you might consider the PLUS Life Sciences option, which is available as a complement to any of the Academies. PLUS is closely associated with the Kelley Center for the Business of Life Sciences, which serves as a strong basis for life sciences–oriented research and conferences. Discussing these learning opportunities and how they would benefit you in achieving your career goals is a great way to establish fit with Kelley.

Technology is viewed as a powerful enabler of many of the strategies discussed in the classroom, and Kelley strives to be recognized as a front-runner in the usage of technology. As is the case with most other top business schools, Kelley would like to be known as an institution that produces leaders and has established its Leadership Development Institute to help support that objective. From an international perspective, Kelley has gradually increased its curriculum's emphasis on globalization and has also added several study abroad opportunities. If you have the background or the direction to capitalize on any of these trends, make sure to spell them out in your application.

If the curriculum is the heart of the Kelley learning model, then the faculty is the lifeblood. The faculty receives high praise for accessibility, commitment, and expertise. The strong commitment of the faculty has helped create a collegial environment in which teamwork is a strong norm. The admissions committee will be very interested to hear ways in which you can contribute to this environment. Loners and gunners need not apply.

Insider Information

Although interviewing with Kelley is not required, it is encouraged. The interview is an excellent opportunity for you to establish fit with the program as well as to display a true desire to attend the school. Your initiative will be duly noted by an admissions committee that is looking to increase its yield percentage.

Schools That Call for a Similar Approach
- Michigan State University (Broad)
- Purdue University (Krannert)
- University of Maryland (Smith)
- University of Texas at Austin (McCombs)

INSEAD
Fontainebleau, France, and Singapore   *mba.insead.edu*

Application at a Glance

Application due dates: Sept. 29, Dec. 1, March 9 (September Intake); March 30, June 15, Aug. 3 (January Intake)

Requirements

Essays: Five (200 to 500 words each)

Interview: By invitation only

Recommendations: Two; both should come from people who are familiar with your professional capabilities

Application fee: €200

School at a Glance

Dean (start of tenure):	Dipak Jain (2011)
Admissions director:	Caroline Diarte Edwards
Program size:	994 full-time
Acceptance rate:	25% (estimated)
Yield:	75% (estimated)
Mean undergraduate GPA:	N/A
Mean GMAT:	703
Middle–80% GMAT:	650–750
Average years of work experience:	5.5
International:	92%
Women:	33%
Minority:	N/A

Your INSEAD Application Strategy

Spanning two continents and with a major presence on a third, INSEAD is considered to be a preeminent international MBA. The one-year general management program operates on campuses in France and Singapore, and maintains an alliance with the Wharton School. INSEAD also maintains a campus in Abu Dhabi that offers a handful of open-enrollment programs outside of the full-time MBA program. Given its international emphasis, INSEAD is in search of applicants who bring significant international exposure, academic excellence, and a solid professional background to the table.

The curriculum itself is general management in nature and lasts for 10 months. There are two different start dates, one that begins in September and another that begins in January. After receiving admittance into INSEAD, students may state their preference for either the Fontainebleau or Singapore campus. In either case, the program structure is the same, and students have opportunities to visit the campus to which they are not assigned. The curriculum is divided into five eight-week periods and calls for students to take 14 required courses and 11 electives. Electives consist of advanced topics in finance, accounting, general management, marketing, entrepreneurship, international business, ethics, and running family businesses. Members of the January intake participate in a summer internship between periods three and four.

As far as international diversity goes, you would be hard-pressed to find another business school that rivals INSEAD. No one nationality represents more than 10 percent of the student body, and less than half come from Western countries, meaning that the "international student" concept is essentially nonexistent. Students are quick to acknowledge this level of diversity as a differentiating factor, as the learning model gives credence to multiple cultural perspectives without showing bias to any. INSEAD also demonstrates its commitment to a global mindset through language requirements. Students must be proficient in at least two languages by matriculation and three by graduation. To establish fit, you should incorporate an international perspective in both your background and in your future goals. The admissions committee will closely evaluate your ability to have an impact on global business, so make sure that your story is not entirely nation-centric.

INSEAD views itself as an academic business institution. This is revealed through the large amount of general research that the school produces in addition to the writing of specific cases. Based on this perspective, INSEAD conducts a thorough assessment of your academic background. Specifically, the admissions committee will look at the reputation of your alma mater(s), your performance in the classroom, and your ability to handle quantitatively rigorous courses. If you don't have a numbers-intensive background or have not fared well in such classes, consider taking a statistics or finance course at a community college.

Due in part to the abbreviated duration of the program, INSEAD tends to accept applicants with at least several years of work experience (more than 50 percent have more than five years). The school believes that students with more professional experience are better able to adapt to the one-year curriculum and leverage it in their career development. Indeed, INSEAD takes career development very seriously, as each student is matched up with a mentor to assist with the process. The school even has teleconferencing equipment readily available so that students can interview with firms that are unable to make the trip to campus. Your challenge is to present your professional experiences in a way that highlights your success in the workplace and your ability to contribute to the classroom.

Despite INSEAD's tendency to accept more experienced applicants, you may still want to consider applying if you are younger, as the school does accept a small number of less-experienced applicants each year (about 10 percent of students have three years or less). If you fall into this category, it is even more important that you emphasize the maturity dimension and discuss an array of experiences that are academic, professional, and personal in nature.

Teamwork is an essential part of the INSEAD learning model. The school's strength in diversity would be pointless if no cross-cultural learning was involved. As such, students are assigned to study groups of five to seven in order to heighten the learning experience. Groups are diverse across multiple dimensions, including nationality, professional experience, gender, age, and education. Team members work closely together on class assignments and in some cases even exams. Any cross-cultural team-based experiences that you can discuss will go a long way in establishing fit with the INSEAD mission.

Insider Information

Although INSEAD has won international acclaim for its advances in business education, it is not resting on its laurels. INSEAD is actively seeking to expand the size of its program, especially the Singapore campus. INSEAD has room to expand its program in part due to its high yield (approximately 75 percent), which should allow for more opportunities among applicants. With expansion on the way, potential applicants should consider INSEAD even if they are not linguistic savants. If you have a true desire to pursue a global career and are willing to put in work to develop your foreign language abilities, then INSEAD might be the business school for you.

Schools That Call for a Similar Approach

- ▶ IMD
- ▶ Harvard Business School
- ▶ University of London (London Business School)

Massachusetts Institute of Technology—MIT Sloan School of Management
Cambridge, MA   *mitsloan.mit.edu*

Application at a Glance

Application due dates (1st, 2nd round): Oct. 26, Jan. 4

Requirements

Essays: Three (500 words each)

Interview: By invitation only

Recommendations: Two letters of recommendation

Application Fee: $250

School at a Glance

Dean (start of tenure):	David Schmittlein (2007)
Admissions Director:	Rod Garcia
Program Size:	800 full-time
Acceptance Rate:	14%
Yield:	68%
Mean undergraduate GPA:	3.6
Mean GMAT:	711
Middle–80% GMAT:	670–760
Average years of work experience:	5.0

International:	42%
Women:	36%
Minority:	27%

Your Sloan Application Strategy

MIT's Sloan School of Management has combined the quantitative strengths of its parent school with a focus on entrepreneurship to establish itself as one of the most highly regarded MBA programs in the world. The school is also well-regarded on Wall Street, where Sloan grads are prized for their analytical skills.

As expected, the school's curriculum emphasizes the quantitative side of business. Courses such as *Data, Models, and Decisions* and *Economic Analysis for Business Decisions* will test your quantitative abilities, but Sloan also encourages students to apply the skills that they learn in these classes to nearly all of their coursework. Graduates speak highly of the hard skills that they learned at Sloan, so make sure that this is what you want out of your MBA experience. Also, be sure to demonstrate that you are comfortable being surrounded by numbers, through your GMAT score, previous coursework, or job experience.

Sloan's curriculum provides a lot of flexibility and control for the individual student. After completing the standard first-semester core courses, students are free to chart their own course for the rest of their time at Sloan. One especially unique aspect of the curriculum is the school's Sloan Innovation Period, a break during each semester in which students can take week-long seminars and hands-on workshops in a variety of subject areas, including leadership, management communications, achieving work-life balance, and entrepreneurship.

Speaking of entrepreneurship, it's a big deal at Sloan, as characterized by students' participation in MIT's annual "$100K" entrepreneurship competition. The competition, which started as the "$10K" competition back in 1990, allows Sloan students the chance to develop a business plan and compete against students from other MIT programs for cash and start-up business assistance. Many companies founded in the competition go on to be successful, and Sloan touts the fact that these companies now have a combined market capitalization of more than $15 billion.

Sloan students who really want to focus their MBA education on entrepreneurship can enroll in the school's Entrepreneurship and Innovation program (E&I). Students who are accepted into the E&I program are placed into their own cohort and take their core classes together, plus an additional class on technological entrepreneurship, concluding in a group trip to Silicon Valley after the first semester. They continue to take additional entrepreneurship-oriented electives, and finish their two years at Sloan with an MBA as well as an additional certificate in entrepreneurship and innovation. If you are serious about entrepreneurship, then consider applying to this program, which requires no more than checking a box on your Sloan application.

Another important program at MIT Sloan is its Leaders for Global Operations (LGO) program, a two-year dual-degree program offered in conjunction with MIT's School of Engineering. Participants receive two degrees in two years: an MBA and a Master of Science from one of seven participating School of Engineering departments. Coursework includes engineering, change management, information technology, and operations management through a variety of in-class and on-the-job experiences. Students spend more than six months on-site as an intern with a sponsor company, culminating in a thesis. The best part of the program is that students receive substantial fellowships, thanks to sponsor companies including Amazon, Boeing, Cisco Systems, Dell, Genzyme, Intel, Nokia, and Novartis. The bad news is that the program is very exclusive—just 45 to 50 students participate each year—but give it a look if you want to work in a technical field after business school.

Insider Information

MIT Sloan says that its mission is "to develop principled, innovative leaders who improve the world and to generate ideas that advance management practice." Note the words *innovative* and *leaders*; the admissions office will look for both of these dimensions in your application. To that end, Sloan typically asks applicants to discuss leadership and innovation in their essay questions. The questions will ask you to describe specific situations in which you had a positive impact on a group, had to put an idea into action, or advocated a certain position. The school is clearly looking for dimensions beyond basic quantitative skills, and the essays are where they will look for them.

Schools That Call for a Similar Approach

- ◪ Carnegie Mellon (Tepper)
- ◪ Stanford University
- ◪ University of Chicago
- ◪ University of Pennsylvania (Wharton)

Michigan State University—Eli Broad Graduate School of Management
East Lansing, MI   *broad.msu.edu/mba*

Application at a Glance

Application due dates (1st, 2nd, 3rd, 4th, final round):
Nov. 1, Jan. 10, March 1, April 15 (final international deadline), June 1

Requirements

Essays: Three (one two-page essay, two one-page essays)

Interview: By invitation only

Recommendations: Two, both preferably from people who are familiar with your professional capabilities

Resume

Application fee: $85

School at a Glance

Dean (start of tenure):	Stefanie Lenway (2010)
Admissions director:	Jeff McNish
Program size:	200 full-time
Acceptance rate:	28%
Yield:	54%

Mean undergraduate GPA:	3.2
Mean GMAT:	640
Middle–80% GMAT:	540–710
Average years of work experience:	4.4
International:	37%
Women:	27%
Minority:	22%

Your Broad Application Strategy

Over the last two decades, Broad (rhymes with "road") has expanded its brand beyond "regional MBA" status. This expansion can be attributed to a quick rise in the business school rankings and Broad's strength in practical specializations. Students can select from four primary concentrations (Supply Chain Management, Marketing, Human Resource Management, and Finance). The Supply Chain Management (SCM) specialization has especially helped place Broad on the map. SCM, which focuses on manufacturing operations, logistics, and purchasing, continues to draw recruiters from across the nation who are looking to optimize their product and information flows. Referencing your concentration interests and explaining how a background in those areas could support your career goals should be key components of your application strategy.

Another large asset of the program is its career services function, which consistently ranks among the nation's top five. Broad's career services group has made extensive efforts to attract a bevy of innovative companies to campus. As a result, Broad students now enjoy an average rate of job offers that is greater than that of many other top programs. Some of the major recruiters include Apple, Deloitte Consulting, General Motors, Intel, Johnson and Johnson, IBM, Proctor & Gamble, and Motorola. Broad's success on the career services front is one of the reasons why the school ranks so highly in terms of return on investment among two-year programs. You should take note, however that there is relatively little investment bank presence on campus. Along those lines, be sure that your career goals align well with Broad's strengths.

Broad students rave about the school's small size and the access to professors. They enjoy the intimate environment and the close relationships that are developed within the program. Unlike at most other MBA programs, chances are that you will leave Broad knowing all of your classmates' names. In your application be sure to emphasize your teamwork capabilities, because the admissions committee routinely weeds out those who would not succeed in a close-knit community environment.

Broad has also made a name for itself through case competitions. Held around the globe, case competitions allow teams of three to six students to display their analytical, public speaking, and persuasion skills. Broad actively encourages students to participate in these competitions and assists in students' preparation for them. The results speak for themselves, as Broad students have come away with high placements in a number of these competitions. If you have any interest in participating in case competitions, bring them up as a great discussion point.

Broad's application is fairly compact in comparison to the applications of other top programs. With three short essays, the Broad application makes it more difficult for candidates to differentiate themselves from each other. As such, it is important that your baseline statistics (GMAT and GPA) are close to those of the current MBA class. This importance has been compounded as Broad looks to improve its baseline statistics in order to continue its movement up the rankings. Therefore, you should utilize the optional essay to address weaknesses in baseline statistics that are 10 percent below the means.

Overall, Broad is looking for bright candidates who aren't afraid to get their hands dirty while working to solve managerial issues. If you can position yourself as such and hit the mark in terms of GMAT and GPA, your application will resonate positively with the admissions committee.

Insider Information

Broad offers an integrated core curriculum and offers a range of team-building exercises as part of its learning model. A large portion of class assignments are completed in teams and, from the moment orientation begins, students are placed on project teams and students' skills are continuously enhanced through team-building workshops and activities. As part of the core curriculum, students are required to take the course *Leadership & Teamwork*. This course provides students with an experiential learning opportunity through which they can work in teams under different simulated conditions. The bottom line is that you should present yourself to the admissions committee as a team player who is open to further examination of your team skills.

Schools That Call for a Similar Approach

▶ Indiana University (Kelley)

▶ Purdue University (Krannert)

▶ University of Maryland (Smith)

New York University—Leonard N. Stern School of Business
New York, NY   *www.stern.nyu.edu*

Application at a Glance

Application due dates (1st, 2nd, 3rd round): Nov. 15, Jan. 15, March 15

Requirements

Essays: Three essays: (one of 750 words, two of 500 words)

Interview: By invitation only

Recommendations: Two letters of recommendation

Application Fee: $215

School at a Glance

Dean (start of tenure):	Peter B. Henry (2010)
Admissions Director:	Anika Davis Pratt
Program Size:	807 full-time
Acceptance Rate:	15%
Yield:	50%

Mean undergraduate GPA:	3.5
Mean GMAT:	717
Middle 80% GMAT:	660–760
Average years of work experience:	4.7
International:	38%
Women:	35%
Minority:	24%

Your Stern Application Strategy

Though NYU's Stern School has many things going for it, the selling point that comes up most often is its location. Stern sits right in New York City's Greenwich Village, between Manhattan's Midtown and Financial District. Students and grads rave about the school's location, and the administration smartly plays up its ties to New York when promoting Stern.

Given Stern's location, it is not surprising that roughly 40 percent of grads go into investment banking, where the Stern name and alumni network are strongest. Taking into account other finance- and investment-related jobs, this number climbs to more than 50 percent. Although Stern's overall academic reputation is strong, most people consider its finance department to be by far the school's greatest strength. If you are interested in work outside of finance, don't rule out Stern, but know that finance is where most of the action has historically been. The good news is that the school is aware of this perceived inequity and has worked hard to boost its other academic departments.

Although Stern is best known for finance, its approach to management education is mostly a general one. First-year students go through a complete required curriculum of courses in all of the business fundamentals, with the bulk of elective coursework coming in the second year. Stern grads earn either a general management MBA or pursue up to three specializations in areas including finance, marketing, strategy, product management, and entertainment.

Stern's New York ties are also very apparent in its faculty makeup. The school boasts dozens of adjunct professors, many of whom are highly regarded veterans of the New York business community. The school prides itself on giving its students lessons with real-world applications, and part of this is letting students hear lessons straight from these veterans' mouths.

Stern heavily promotes the strong spirit of community among its students. Students and grads sometimes comment that they were pleasantly surprised to find that the culture is more cooperative than they expected. If you apply to Stern, don't discount the importance of teamwork in your message. The school is less impressed by individual achievers than it is in well-grounded people who have excelled in their past jobs by working with others. This is underscored by a consistent Stern message that its students are just as strong in terms of emotional intelligence as intellectual intelligence. Also, know that the other key ingredient in Stern's community is student involvement, from its Stern Student Corporation (Stern's version of student government) to its many student-run clubs and conferences. Stern is looking for people who like to get involved, so be sure to bring this out in your application.

The school is also serious about entrepreneurship, and offers students a number of ways to pursue the subject while at Stern. The Berkley Center for Entrepreneurial Studies serves as the hub for this activity, running conferences and facilitating a mentoring program for budding Stern entrepreneurs. Stern's annual business plan competition is one of the most popular of its kind, offering a traditional business plan track, a social entrepreneurship track, and most recently a technology venture track, with prizes of up to $75,000. This is an area of the program that the school continues to emphasize. If you consider yourself to be an entrepreneur, or you want to be one, be sure to let the Stern admissions committee know about it.

Insider Information

With an admitted student yield of about 50 percent, Stern gets stiff competition for finance-minded students. It's an outstanding program, but one that happens to have another top-ranked finance-oriented school (Columbia) just uptown and another within driving distance in Philadelphia (Wharton). Showing the admissions committee that Stern really is where you want to be—and having convincing reasons for why this is the case—is important. In your Stern application, take particular note that the essays specifically ask you to describe what interactions you have had with the "Stern community" and what you have done to learn more about the program. It's a great question, and a strong cue that you need to really do your homework about Stern. If you do, you can greatly improve your odds of success.

Schools That Call for a Similar Approach

- ▣ Columbia
- ▣ University of Pennsylvania (Wharton)

Northwestern University—Kellogg School of Management
Evanston, IL   *www.kellogg.northwestern.edu*

Application at a Glance

Application due dates (1st, 2nd, 3rd round): Oct. 14, Jan. 11, April 7

Requirements

Essays: Four (three of 600 words each and one of 400 words)

Interview: Required

Recommendations: Two, with one preferably coming from a supervisor

Application Fee: $250

School at a Glance

Dean (start of tenure):	Sally Blount (2010)
Admissions Director:	Beth Flye
Program Size:	1,260 full-time
Acceptance Rate:	20%
Yield:	59%
Mean undergraduate GPA:	3.5
Mean GMAT:	706

Middle–80% GMAT:	670–760
Average years of work experience:	5.3
International:	33%
Women:	30%
Minority:	16%

Your Kellogg Application Strategy

Decades ago Kellogg made its mark in the management education world by emphasizing teamwork in the classroom and in the workplace. Although Donald Jacobs—who led Kellogg for 26 years and oversaw its rise to prominence—stepped down as dean more than 10 years ago, the culture of teamwork that he helped create is still very apparent. Most homework assignments and projects are done in teams, and the school employs a peer-review system in which students can rate each other's strengths and weaknesses as teammates.

Marketing is the school's other best-known strength, and much of the credit for that goes to Philip Kotler, who has written some of the best-known marketing textbooks in the world. The rest of the marketing faculty includes many other heavy-hitters who have distinguished themselves in their own right. All of this leads to heavy recruiting from companies looking for marketing experts and brand managers.

Although Kellogg is best known for marketing, the school's curriculum is considered to be more general management in nature, with students typically concentrating in two or three subject areas through electives. The most popular subject isn't even marketing, with more Kellogg students studying finance than any other major. And as is the case with many other top schools, consulting and banking are the most popular fields that Kellogg grads go into. McKinsey, Boston Consulting Group, Goldman Sachs, and the other blue-chip usual suspects do more hiring at Kellogg than the biggest marketing-related firms.

As you would expect, Kellogg's admissions office looks for teamwork-oriented people. "Sharks" or hot shots need not apply. This doesn't mean that Kellogg only looks for touch-feely people; rather, it looks for people who know how to get things done when working with others. However, the school isn't only looking for team players. Kellogg is very much in search of leaders with the ability to succeed in a team environment. The school utilizes its 360-Degree Leadership Assessment to help first-year students identify strengths and weaknesses in their leadership styles and even offers an elective course through which a development plan is created in conjunction with a personal leadership coach. With this in mind, think of personal examples of how you've led teams toward a goal in the past. Most applicants will just think about teamwork in terms of how they helped others accomplish a goal, but show the admissions committee how you led a team to success and you'll be in great shape.

Kellogg also looks for people who will get involved at the school. A distinguishing characteristic of Kellogg is that pretty much everything is run by its students, from clubs to international study trips ("Global Initiatives in Management") to an almost endless series of professional conferences that the school hosts. A current student will probably even interview you if you conduct your interview on campus. It's not uncommon for a student to get involved in five or six different clubs and activities over the course of his two years at Kellogg.

What this means for you is that you need to demonstrate that you will *get involved.* The best way to do this is by showing what you've done in the past to get involved in your profession, school, and community. Less can be more: Instead of listing seven clubs or organizations that you have marginally participated in, focus on the one or two things that you're really passionate about, and show exactly how you got involved in those things *and made a difference.* The grid from Chapter 2 should help strengthen this important part of your application story.

Insider Information

As part of its increasing emphasis on leadership, Kellogg has put a lot more focus on ethics in its curriculum. The school's pre-term CIM (Complete Immersion in Management) program for first-year students presents them with business challenges dealing with issues of leadership and ethics. The core of this pre-term is Kellogg's Leadership in Organizations that delves deeply into these topics. Going even further, the school offers a required pre-term course for all second-year students (and one-year students) called *Values, Ethics, and Strategic Crisis Management,* in which students tackle ethics case studies and crisis simulations. Accordingly, the admissions office looks for applicants with strong principles and past examples of when they did the right thing in a tough or murky situation. Keep this in mind as you craft your overall application strategy for Kellogg.

Schools That Call for a Similar Approach
- Duke (Fuqua)
- Dartmouth (Tuck)
- UC Berkeley (Haas)
- University of Michigan (Ross)

Purdue University—Krannert Graduate School of Management
West Lafayette, IN   *www.krannert.purdue.edu*

Application at a Glance

U.S. citizen and permanent resident application due dates (1st, 2nd, 3rd, 4th round):

Nov. 1, Jan. 10, March 1, May 1

International student application due dates (1st, 2nd round): Nov. 1, Feb. 1

Requirements

Essays: Three 500-word essays

Interview: By invitation only

Recommendations: Two, with one preferably coming from a direct supervisor

Resume

Application fee: $55

School at a Glance

Dean (start of tenure):	Jerry Lynch, Intermin Dean (2010)
Admissions director:	Brenda Knebel
Program size:	230 full-time
Acceptance rate:	36%
Yield:	39%
Mean undergraduate GPA:	3.3
Mean GMAT:	643
Middle–80% GMAT:	596–710
Average years of work experience:	3.7
International:	50%
Women:	25%
Minority:	14%

Your Krannert Application Strategy

Originally positioned as a graduate program in operations, Krannert changed its degree title from Master of Science in Management to MBA in 2001. The label made official the expansion of the program, which occurred over the next decade. Today Krannert is recognized as an MBA program with strengths in technology, manufacturing, and other analytical functions. The school is looking for applicants who can thrive within a quantitatively intense environment, support its traditional strengths, and also continue building its brand in other aspects of business. At heart, Krannert is still a quantitatively centered program, so you should display some proficiency in this area through your GMAT score, transcript(s), or professional experiences.

It's not surprising to hear Krannert MBAs refer to their alma mater as "Techno MBA," as the program regularly utilizes technology to support its hands-on learning philosophy. Many students choose to specialize in Management Information Systems, one of seven functional specializations the school offers. The others are Accounting, Finance, Marketing, Operations, Organizational Behavior and Human Resources, and Strategic Management. In addition to functional specializations, the school offers interdisciplinary concentrations in Analytical Consulting, Global Supply Chain Management, International Management, Technology Innovation & Entrepreneurship, and Manufacturing & Technology Management. Discussion of your goals should include a small blurb on where you see one or two of these specializations coming into play.

Technology is used to simulate e-commerce transactions, the power of enterprise application integration, financial trading, and database architecture. In addition to these examples, Krannert provides numerous opportunities for its students to translate theory into application. The Student-Managed Investment Fund (SMIF) provides students with the opportunity to help manage a six-figure financial portfolio and distribute a portion of the gains to Krannert and other graduate programs. During the Digital Information Industry Simulation, students act as the CEO of a large technology company, making decisions that have an impact on the results of the company. Krannert also offers MarkStrat3, another computer simulation that allows student teams to compete against one another, trying to win market share and increase profits in the high- tech industry. Providing an example in which you took an abstract idea and implemented it is a powerful way to highlight your fit with Krannert's philosophy on translating theory into application.

Given Krannert's strong technology focus, it is important that you display familiarity and comfort with technology. This doesn't mean that you have to come across as a techno wiz, but to the extent that you are at ease with discussing the benefits of technology and sharing ideas of technological innovation, you should do so. Keep in mind, however, that Krannert is also trying to expand its brand beyond just technology and operations, so don't shy away from bringing up interests in other aspects of business. Telling a story about how you would like to apply tech-savvy business principles to industries outside of traditional technology can also help your application stand out.

Krannert provides all of the benefits that come along with most small MBA programs, including accessible faculty, a close-knit student community, and an emphasis on teamwork. Immediately after beginning the program, you will be assigned to a four- or five-person team. Students within a team come from diverse professional backgrounds and spend time working on group assignments for the first eight weeks of class. Having strong team skills is important to succeeding in these groups, and is therefore something upon which the admission committee will rate you. Use the essays to discuss your ability to contribute to a team.

Insider Information

One of the areas that Krannert is actively looking to expand in is its global presence. The program already receives a large number of applications from international candidates (70 to 80 percent of all applications) and maintains a large number of international students (almost half of students). Krannert is looking to leverage its popularity among international candidates and offer more opportunities abroad. One international program the school is actively promoting is the German International Graduate School of Management and Administration (GISMA) program. This program features an eight-week module in Hannover, Germany, during which students take classes taught by Krannert faculty and visit German companies. To the extent that you have global aspirations, be sure to highlight them in your application. Doing so should underscore your fit with the school.

Schools That Call for a Similar Approach

- ▶ Carnegie Mellon University
- ▶ Michigan State University (Broad)
- ▶ Indiana University (Kelley)

Queen's University—Queen's School of Business
Kingston, Canada   *www.queensmba.com*

Application at a Glance

Application due dates (1st, 2nd, 3rd round): Nov. 19, Feb. 4, March 18

Requirements

Essays: Three 500-word essays

Interview: Required

Recommendations: Three letters of reference

Resume

Application fee: None

School at a Glance

Dean (start of tenure):	David Saunders (2003)
Admissions Director:	Lori Garnier
Program size:	119 full-time
Acceptance rate:	unkown
Yield:	unkown
Mean undergraduate GPA:	N/A
Mean GMAT:	652
Middle–80% GMAT:	590–730
Average years of work experience:	4.5
International:	40%
Women:	32%
Minority:	N/A

Your Queen's Application Strategy

Frequently noted as one of the top international business schools, Queen's offers a one-year full-time MBA program that has taken the often cited business school initiatives of personalized coaching and teamwork into uncharted territory. Based in Kingston Ontario, the university sits neatly adjacent to the vast St. Lawrence River. The business school, which prides itself on remaining true to its rich tradition while maintaining a dynamic curriculum, considers its "coaching culture" to be one of its key program differentiators. Each student has the opportunity to leverage the perspectives of a personal coach, a career coach, a team coach, and even a fitness coach. Students truly enjoy this level of individualized attention and benefit from both the guidance and support aspects of the initiative.

The Queen's philosophy is that by having experts walk students through the process of introspection that they can maximize their own understanding of their strengths and opportunities to grow. It is important the admissions committee see that you are open to the process of introspection and that you would benefit from the school's customized coaching approach.

As a smaller program, Queen's takes advantage of its intimate, quaint environment by emphasizing a team-based learning culture. Whereas many programs make claim to a focus on teamwork, Queen's has made it such an integral part of the program that it essentially defines the Queen's MBA experience. In essence, Queen's tries to mirror the professional environment that requires strong team skills in its program. Students are assigned to a learning team of six or seven for the entire core curriculum and a significant component of students' grades is based on performance in a team environment. Dedicated team rooms and a team coach help solidify the tactical and support requirements that help produce teams with individuals who are dedicated to working collectively for group success. To that end, Queen's is very interested in only admitting applicants who will flourish in its diverse team environment. The admissions committee is very much aware that even one outlier can contradict all of the positives that a team-based approach can produce. As such, it will take a keen interest in how you have previously performed in team environments.

Given a pragmatic view of teamwork, it's not surprising that Queen's offers a curriculum that also tries to mirror the "real world" professional environment rather than stopping with standard academic pedagogy. In addition to case studies, Queen's students participate in experiential opportunities such as simulations and project-based consulting work. These experiential experiences extend to the international arena. Approximately 50 percent of Queen's students hail from outside of Canada, and the school boasts a globally trained faculty. To capitalize on these assets, Queen's has established strong relationships with 20 international business schools, enabling a variety of international exchanges and ultimately a cross-cultural learning environment that rivals the best international programs.

Similar to other one-year programs, Queen's is in search of applicants who express a significant amount of maturity. The core curriculum, which runs from May to December, consists of five themes: leading the organization, managing financial resources, strategic leadership, the human dimension, and sustaining innovation. Within each of these themes, students take an assortment of courses as supported by customized coaching. From January to April students pursue one of five electives, which include consulting, marketing, finance, innovation and entrepreneurship, and general management. To ensure success in this highly focused environment, the admissions committee looks for applicants who are mature enough to truly understand their career objectives and make substantial contributions to their teams. Make sure that you express your maturity dimension in ways that show you would succeed in the Queen's curriculum.

Insider Information

The broader Queen's university is renowned for its strengths in research, science, and technology. This has significant implications for the MBA program, as nearly 30 percent of students pursue careers in the technology sector. Queen's is looking to further capitalize on its strengths in technology through entrepreneurship and innovation. The school offers an entrepreneurial-focused internship called "dare to dream" that allows participants to work closely with faculty members and other contacts through Queen's Centre for Business Venturing in developing business concepts. If you have any entrepreneurial aspirations, be sure to bring them out in your application, as Queen's interest in innovation will likely only increase with time.

Schools That Call for a Similar Approach
- ▷ IE Business School
- ▷ University of Michigan (Ross)
- ▷ University of Southern California (Marshall)
- ▷ University of North Carolina (Kenan-Flagler)

Stanford University—Graduate School of Business
Stanford, CA   *www.gsb.stanford.edu*

Application at a Glance

Application due dates (1st, 2nd, 3rd round): Oct. 6, Jan. 6, April 6

Requirements

Essays: Three (all essays combined should not exceed 1,800 words total)

Interview: By invitation only

Recommendations: Three. Two should come from people who are familiar with your professional capabilities and at least one of which from a direct supervisor. One letter from a peer with whom you have worked on a team or a project (can be professional, extracurricular, charitable, or otherwise). Academic recommendations are discouraged.

Resume

Application fee: $265

School at a Glance

Dean (start of tenure):	Garth Saloner (2009)
Admissions Director:	Derrick Bolton
Program size:	765 full-time
Acceptance rate:	7%
Yield:	78%
Mean undergraduate GPA:	3.7
Mean GMAT:	726
Middle–80% GMAT:	680–770
Average years of work experience:	3.9
International:	37%
Women:	35%
Minority:	22%

Your Stanford Application Strategy

The instructions to Stanford's application indicate that it evaluates candidates based on three high-level criteria: intellectual vitality, demonstrated leadership potential, and your personal qualities and contributions. Sounds simple enough, right? The difficulty with navigating the Stanford application is the degree to which these three criteria must be emphasized. In demonstrating your fit with these three criteria your emphasis should primarily be on the innovation and leadership dimensions.

The most obvious example of Stanford's alignment with innovation is its strength in entrepreneurship. Closely linked with Silicon Valley, Stanford has achieved an entrepreneurship branding that other schools dream of. Although Stanford is a general management program to its core (students do not select majors), electives based on entrepreneurship are in abundance. Courses that focus on areas such as venture capital, business model development, private equity, and entrepreneurial strategy are the backbone of Stanford's entrepreneurial strength.

Discussing your entrepreneurial inclination can be a great way to unite the innovation and leadership dimensions, but it should not be done to simply appear as though you fit with Stanford's values. Recognize that a large percentage of applicants who apply to Stanford will discuss entrepreneurship in their application. Therefore, should you go down this path, include vivid details about your ideas and also be sure to discuss their potential impact on society. This will help separate you from the pack.

Recommendations should be viewed as an extremely important aspect of your Stanford application. The admission committee will take a close look at your recommendations in evaluating your leadership potential and your teamwork capabilities. If there is one application in which you should avoid submitting generic recommendations at all costs, this is it. Be sure to follow the instructions closely and submit two professional recommendations and one peer recommendation.

Academic aptitude is a criterion that Stanford evaluates more rigorously than most other top business schools. Because the curriculum is quantitatively heavy, the admissions committee will look closely for measures that indicate that you will be able to succeed within the learning model. Therefore, your GMAT score (Stanford also accepts GRE scores) will be looked at closely in addition to your transcript(s). If your scores don't reflect a high standard of analytical background, you will need to express it through your professional experiences and/or additional coursework. You should also be aware that, though those accepted by Stanford come from a multitude of undergraduate institutions, a large majority attended "high prestige" universities. If you are not among this group, you should discuss your school's strengths and your reasons for attending it.

Although Stanford's emphasis on teamwork may not be as strong as it is at Fuqua, Kellogg, or Tuck, it is definitely an important part of the learning model. During their first quarter at Stanford, students are assigned to study groups of four to five people and work together on a daily basis. You can display a penchant for working with others by discussing previous professional and extracurricular team involvement.

The essay portion of the application is your opportunity to demonstrate your ability to contribute to the diversity of the Stanford community. Because the Stanford essays collectively have a longer word limit, you should really focus on telling your unique story, but doing so in a logical, flowing manner. Include headings in your essays so that your readers can follow your framework easily. Consider writing your Stanford essays after you've completed other applications. This will allow your story to be more polished. And don't even bother trying to shoehorn an essay from another application into your Stanford application. Ultimately, your essays should reveal your passions, both professional and personal, and highlight your distinctiveness. You probably haven't scaled Mt. Everest or won a marathon, but don't let that keep you from positioning yourself as unique in some way.

One applicant we spoke with, who was denied admission after her interview, mentioned that the alumnus with whom she interviewed suggested that her lack of distinctiveness contributed to her ultimate denial. "He complimented my competitive profile, but stated that I had no point of differentiation in my perspective, which weakened an otherwise strong profile." This is fairly typical feedback for rejected applicants.

You can assert a distinct passion for Stanford by visiting the school, checking out a class, and chatting with current students (yes, this goes for those of you on the East Coast, too). Make sure that this visit finds its way into your essays in your discussion of "why Stanford?" Your enthusiasm for Stanford will resonate positively with the admissions committee as it strives to maintain a high yield percentage.

Insider Information

The Stanford learning model doesn't offer majors, but it does offer certificates in public management and global management. The Public Management Program (PMP) prepares students for positions in the social sector and the Global Management Program (GMP) prepares students for opportunities at a global level. Both certificates are supported by a large number of electives, programs, and career resources. More than one third of the student body pursues certificates in PMP or GMP, and Stanford is actively looking for ways in which it can augment these programs. Discussing how you would utilize the resources offered by these programs in conjunction with your career objectives is a great way to display fit with Stanford.

Schools That Call for a Similar Approach

- ▶ MIT (Sloan)
- ▶ UCLA (Anderson)

University of California at Berkeley—Haas School of Business
Berkeley, CA   *www.haas.berkeley.edu*

Application at a Glance
Application due dates (1st, 2nd, 3rd, 4th round):
Oct. 13, Dec. 2, Jan. 20, March 16

Requirements
Essays: Six (four short essays, one of 500 words, one of 1,000 words)

Interview: By invitation only

Recommendations: Two, both from people familiar with your professional capabilities

Resume

Application fee: $200

School at a Glance

Dean (start of tenure):	Richard Lyons (2008)
Admissions director:	Stephanie Fujii
Program size:	480 full-time
Acceptance rate:	11%
Yield:	54%

Mean undergraduate GPA:	3.5
Mean GMAT:	718
Middle–80% GMAT:	680–760
Average years of work experience:	5.0
International:	38%
Women:	29%
Minority:	18%

Your Haas Application Strategy

In a world filled with business schools, Haas maintains a high degree of distinction. That distinction can be seen just by reading through the Haas essays, which at times seem more like questions from a psychologist rather than from an admissions committee. Indeed, the essay questions are indicative of a school that is serious about admitting applicants who can maintain almost paradoxical balances—applicants who are committed to traditional business learning, but display a bit of personal panache. Applicants who would be willing to stand alone based on personal conviction, but are willing to unite in the name of teamwork. Applicants who are looking to make waves in the marketplace, but remain cognizant of social and ethical responsibilities. This balance is summarized through Haas' four key principles: question the status quo (bold ideas), confidence without attitude (evidenced-based decisions), student always (community), and beyond yourself (integrity). If you can paint a picture of yourself that reflects these traits, in addition to satisfying the more common admissions requirements, then you stand a good chance of being accepted into the Haas family.

For the last several years, Haas has benefited from a symbiotic relationship with nearby Silicon Valley. This has resulted, not surprisingly, in an intensified focus on entrepreneurship. Haas now boasts multiple opportunities for students to cultivate and test their business ideas as well as to interact with mentors and experts. The Lester Center for Entrepreneurship and Innovation, founded in 1991, supports a variety of activities, such as the Berkeley Business Incubator, UC Berkeley Entrepreneurs Forum, and entrepreneurship fellowships and internships.

Technology has also been a natural outgrowth of Haas's geographical location. The Management of Technology (MOT) Program is one of the central Haas offerings that focuses on technological advances and their relationship to business. As an interdisciplinary certificate program, MOT represents the joint efforts of Haas and the Berkeley College of Engineering. As part of the MOT program, students may pursue paid opportunities through fellowships created specifically for participants in the program.

An emphasis on international business is highlighted in Haas's course offerings, in addition to the International Business Development (IBD) and International Exchange programs. IBD offers students the opportunity to participate in a global consulting project with a team composed entirely of Haas students. In terms of exchange programs, Haas offers several in locations such as London, Barcelona, and Hong Kong.

In addition to offering certificates in each of these areas (entrepreneurship, technology, and international management), Haas also offers certificates in real estate and health management. Although the Haas learning model is rooted in general management precepts, displaying an understanding of one of these certificates might apply to you and your professional aspirations should be a critical part of your application.

Demonstrating the teamwork dimension is also important, as Haas admissions counselors are actively looking for applicants who display team spirit. The learning model promotes a cooperative, intimate environment in which students participate in multiple group assignments and interact closely with faculty. To demonstrate fit with these characteristics, you should display a pattern of getting involved and a sense of community.

The Haas learning model has a strong bent toward applying abstract theories to real-world situations. This approach begins with the faculty, a majority of whom have significant experience within the marketplace, and extends to the students, who boast an average of five years of work experience. The maturity dimension is highly valued at Haas and gaining acceptance with less than three years of work experience can be challenging. As an applicant, you should try to display a diversity of experience and insight into how complex issues such as globalization, ethics, environmentalism, and politics impact business operations.

Insider Information

As other business schools scramble to revamp their programs in order to promote a new focus on ethics and social responsibility, Haas will benefit from its reputation as a pioneer in the field. With a required course in ethics, and numerous electives, programs, and events focused on the topic, Haas gives full treatment to the interaction of business, ethics, and social responsibility. The Social Venture Business Plan Competition is a hallmark of that interaction, as business schools across the country compete for a total of $100,000 by presenting plans that outline business propositions that have a societal or environmental component. Although a majority of Haas grads pursue careers in the traditional areas of consulting and finance, they all are all influenced by Haas's incorporation of social issues within the learning model. As you present your profile, make sure that you reflect a cognizance of societal and ethical issues that extend from business issues.

Schools That Call for a Similar Approach

- ▷ Duke University (Fuqua)
- ▷ UCLA (Anderson)
- ▷ USC (Marshall)
- ▷ Yale School of Management

University of California at Los Angeles—Anderson Graduate School of Management

Los Angeles, CA *www.anderson.ucla.edu*

Application at a Glance

Application due dates (1st, 2nd, 3rd round): Oct. 20, Jan. 5, April 13

Requirements

Essays: Two (750 words each)

Interview: Recommended

Recommendations: Two, both from people familiar with your professional capabilities and one preferably from your direct supervisor

Resume

Application fee: $200

School at a Glance

Dean (start of tenure):	Judy D. Olian (2006)
Admissions Director:	Mae Jennifer Shores
Program size:	710 full-time
Acceptance rate:	25%
Yield:	47%
Mean undergraduate GPA:	3.5
Mean GMAT:	711
Middle–80% GMAT:	680–750
Average years of work experience:	4.8
International:	31%
Women:	34%
Minority:	30%

Your Anderson Application Strategy

Sun, beach, entertainment management program—though Anderson definitely has these assets that few other MBA programs can match, it also excels in the traditional areas that are valued by applicants. The Anderson program offers a general management curriculum that allows students to select from specializations in 14 areas or even create their own specialization. The specializations cover a wide range of topics including Finance, Marketing, Entrepreneurial Studies, Technology Management, Venture Capital & Private Equity, and Brand Management. In support of its flexible general management learning model, Anderson is in search of candidates who display a unique balance of leadership and teamwork capabilities.

Anderson views leadership in three basic ways. First, it recognizes leaders for their ability to convey strategic direction and vision to others. Vision allows for the unification of the group behind a common goal. Second, Anderson views leaders as problem-solvers who apply their analytical and communication skills to overcome challenges. Finally, Anderson defines leaders as people who cultivate the first two capabilities in others. Anderson does not view leadership and teamwork in separate spheres, and therefore notes that the best leaders are also the best team players. The Anderson learning model provides students with opportunities to improve their balance of leadership and teamwork skills through team simulations, team-building exercises, analytical models, and projects. Your challenge is to display fit with Anderson's definition of leadership. One of the best places to do that is in answering the essay questions. Try to provide an example that shows your leadership skills along the lines of the three definitions.

Anderson's entrepreneurship program has served, in many ways, as the model for many other business schools. The program offers a blend of coursework, entrepreneurial resources, and "hands-on" opportunities. At the core of Anderson's entrepreneurship program is the Price Center. The Price Center provides support for the development of course materials, research, and experiential opportunities. One such opportunity, the Knapp Venture Competition, is a traditional business plan contest, through which participants can win venture capital funding. The Venture Fellows Program and the Student Investment Fund—two competitive programs that students must apply for—expose participants to venture capital and investment management activities. Students can also gain exposure to new ventures through the Wolfen Award, which calls for selected students to complete a feasibility study on a start-up as part of an internship. Because of Anderson's strength in entrepreneurship, discussing your own entrepreneurial inclination can be a great way to display fit with the school and to differentiate yourself based on your unique ideas.

In addition to the Price Center, Anderson has cultivated five other academic centers with an objective of establishing strong research capabilities and industry relationships across a spectrum of disciplines. These five academic centers focus on the areas of economics (The UCLA Anderson Forecast), entertainment (The Center for Management of Enterprise in Media, Entertainment, and Sports), finance (The Laurence and Lori Fink Center for Finance and Investments), real estate (The Richard S. Ziman Center for Real Estate), and international business (The Center for International Business Education and Research).

Despite Anderson's low acceptance rate and its great reputation, the school has a relatively low yield percentage. The school is looking for improvement in that area and will evaluate applicants closely to see if they are really committed to Anderson or are just applying to diversify risk. Along those lines, establishing fit is extremely important. You are given an explicit opportunity to show that Anderson is your top pick in its essays. Be sure to capitalize on that opportunity by displaying intimate knowledge of the program and then go the extra step by explaining how you would get involved in school activities to further bolster Anderson's reputation.

Insider Information

A unique aspect of the Anderson learning model is the Applied Management Research Project. This six-month project is the last requirement of the MBA program and follows in line with Anderson's perspective on leadership, teamwork, and applied learning. The projects are completed in teams of three to five, and generally consist of a strategic consulting assignment or the development of a business venture idea. In either case, students are able to apply their entire Anderson toolkit in a comprehensive manner. Discussing your interest in this project—and more generally, in the hands-on learning opportunities that Anderson offers— during your interview or in your application is another good way to show fit.

Schools That Call for a Similar Approach

- ▣ Stanford University
- ▣ University of California at Berkeley (Haas)
- ▣ USC (Marshall)

University of Chicago Booth School of Business
Chicago, IL
www.chicagobooth.edu

Application at a Glance

Application due dates (1st, 2nd, 3rd round): Oct. 13, Jan. 5, April 13

Requirements

Essays: Three (one of 900 words, one of 750 words, and one of four pages)

Interview: By invitation only

Recommendations: Two letters of recommendation

Application Fee: $200

School at a Glance

Dean (start of tenure):	Sunil Kumar (2011)
Admissions Director:	Kurt Ahlm
Program Size:	1,100 full-time
Acceptance Rate:	25%
Yield:	62%
Mean undergraduate GPA:	3.5
Mean GMAT:	714
Middle–80% GMAT:	660–760
Average years of work experience:	4.8
International:	36%
Women:	35%
Minority:	25%

Your Booth Application Strategy

The University of Chicago Booth School of Business (Booth) enjoyed perhaps the most noticeable renaissance of any top MBA program over the past decade, thanks in large part to Edward Snyder, who assumed the Dean's position in 2001 and stepped down in 2010. Snyder and his administration worked hard to promote the Booth's strengths while addressing some perceived weaknesses. More recently, alumnus David Booth furthered the renaissance by giving $300 million to the business school in 2008. The donation, which stands as the largest ever given to a business school, will be used to attract and retain star faculty and further the school's research interests. The school renamed itself in 2009 in honor of Booth.

Booth's strengths are impressive, including a roster of Nobel laureate faculty members—six as of last count, more than any other business school—its high number of well-placed alumni, its strong international brand name, and its top-flight reputation with recruiters. As for weaknesses, for decades the school had a reputation as a leading MBA program, but one that tended to turn out grads who were quantitative-heavy and not as well-rounded as grads from Booth's peer schools. The school has also faced a perception that Booth students are somewhat less involved in the school than those at other top programs, partly a result of the school having to compete with all that the city of Chicago has to offer.

The school has improved its reputation on all fronts, partly through curriculum changes and partly because of its cutting-edge facilities. A grade-nondisclosure policy has taken the edge off of grade competition. Leadership Effectiveness and Development (LEAD), a mandatory course for first-year students, helps students develop their leadership, teamwork, and communication skills in an experiential environment. The school has also branched out well beyond finance, developing impressive strength in marketing and general management programs, among other areas.

The school's Charles Harper Center is the center of the school's full-time MBA program. Booth has done a lot of work to encourage its students to stay on campus and get involved with school-related activities. Students rave about the facilities, which include a number of public spaces and group meeting rooms. The school realizes that facilities only go so far, however, and that the most important ingredient for a cohesive student body is the students themselves. Given that, the admissions office will continue looking for applicants who demonstrate a willingness to get involved with meaningful extracurricular activities. This is something to consider if you are looking closely at Booth.

One part of the school's reputation that is unlikely to change is its rigorous academic program. No matter what type of student Booth tries to attract, it will not lessen its emphasis on hard finance and quantitative skills. Finance is still the most popular area of concentration out of the 14 offered. One noteworthy aspect of the school's curriculum is its flexibility. LEAD is the only required course in the entire program, with students choosing from a menu of courses to satisfy their core curriculum needs. This level of flexibility truly sets Booth apart from other business school learning models. Keep this flexibility in mind as you think about how you might fit with the Booth program.

One area that has received greater academic emphasis in recent years is entrepreneurship. Started in 1996, the school's New Venture Challenge (NVC) has grown to become an annual tradition. Booth loves to promote that, since its inception, NVC has helped launch more than 60 companies that have raised more than $125 million. Teams of student entrepreneurs work on business plans over a six-month period and three rounds, with the entrants also taking classes and workshops on the subject of new venture development. The winning team is granted $25,000, as well as one year of support in ARCH Venture Partners' business incubator. If you are interested in entrepreneurship, the NVC is a great chance to get hands-on experience as well as extensive coaching.

Insider Information

As Booth has climbed to the top of business school rankings again, it has attracted a broader applicant pool, some of whom may not be a great fit with the school. The obvious benefit is that the Booth admissions office can choose from an even stronger, more diverse pool of applicants. But the school's challenge is to figure out who really belongs at Booth, as well as who really wants to attend. This is evident in at least one of the school's essay questions, which explicitly asks applicants about how Booth fits into their future goals and plans. Don't take this question lightly. First, be honest with the admissions committee (and with yourself) about why you are considering Booth. Then, be sure to demonstrate your fit with the program and how you will contribute to the school's community.

Schools That Call for a Similar Approach
- Carnegie Mellon (Tepper)
- Columbia Business School
- MIT (Sloan)
- University of Rochester (Simon)

University of London—London Business School
London, UK   *www.london.edu*

Application at a Glance
Application due dates (1st, 2nd, 3rd, 4th round):
Oct. 6, Jan. 5, March 2, April 20

Requirements
Essays: Five (one of 750 words, four of 300 words each)

Interview: By invitation only

Recommendations: Two, both from people who are in a position to comment on your suitability for the LBS program. LBS values both professional and educational references.

Resume

Application fee: £160

School at a Glance

Dean (start of tenure):	Sir Andrew Likierman (2009)
Admissions Director:	David Simpson
Program size:	802 full-time
Acceptance rate:	13%
Yield:	68%
Mean undergraduate GPA:	N/A
Mean GMAT:	701
Middle–80% GMAT:	640–750
Average years of work experience:	5.3
International:	89% (foreign nationals)
Women:	28%
Minority:	N/A

Your London Business School Application Strategy
Looking for a truly international MBA experience? Most other business schools' international immersion claims pale in comparison to what London

Business School (LBS) offers. Incoming students can expect that nearly 90 percent of their classmates will hail from countries outside of the UK. That representation tallies up to 80 nations in total. Combine that with a language proficiency requirement that calls for students to have a reasonable fluency in at least two languages (including English) and exchange programs with more than 30 business schools abroad, and you have the makings of an environment that encourages a fluid multicultural dialogue. Indeed, "becoming an international citizen" is one of four themes that LBS's program expresses. The admissions committee will be looking closely to see what type of international citizen you will be, so be prepared to discuss your international and cross-cultural experiences. You can expect a good portion of your interview to be dedicated to this subject.

In addition to demonstrating that you have the ability to be an international citizen, you should also make sure to display fit with the other three LBS learning themes: becoming a leader, becoming an independent thinker, and making things happen. These themes should not be viewed in disparate silos, but rather as intertwined objectives. LBS views leadership in three different ways: being competent and confident across a wide range of functions, being creative and flexible in your leadership style, and achieving results. Think of professional and personal examples that display these leadership characteristics and try to integrate as many of them as you can into your essays.

One of the ways that LBS believes your leadership abilities will be enhanced during the MBA program is through team opportunities. Immediately after beginning the program you will be assigned to a study group of six to seven classmates, in which you will tackle a multitude of group assignments. The emphasis on teamwork is so strong that these group projects are worth approximately 50 percent of students' overall first-year grade. In addition to participating in a study group there is an expectation that students will also play leading roles in at least one of LBS's 50 club opportunities. In sum, these experiences allow students to enhance the three LBS leadership characteristics, while cultivating their team skills. To show your willingness to get involved, you might want to pick a couple club opportunities that interest you and mention them in your essays.

Becoming an independent thinker highlights LBS's desire to develop not only business leaders but also, to a certain extent, thought leaders. This is underscored by the fact that LBS is one of the only business schools that has its faculty conduct a majority of interviews. Given this type of interview, it is to your advantage to acquaint yourself even more than usual with the curriculum. LBS is also one of the few business schools that values recommendations that are written by professors. The interactive LBS learning model benefits most when students have a high regard for the classroom dynamic and for academic preparation. Discussing your view of academics and how it has played a role in your outlook is a great way to display your stance as an "independent thinker." Ultimately, LBS expects its students to take the academic theories learned in the classroom and "make things happen."

The "making things happen" theme, a mixture of innovation and implementation, is often expressed through entrepreneurial ventures. The combination of the Foundation for Entrepreneurial Management, Sussex Place Investment

Management, and the Centre for Creative Business serve as a business incubator and a capital fund from which students can access valuable capital and resources. Students can also opt to participate in the school's Entrepreneurship Summer School, which allows participants to develop and test business plans through their early stages. At the end of the experience, students present the results of feasibility studies to expert panels for feedback. Participants are then encouraged to further hone their business plans throughout their second year. If you have entrepreneurial ambitions, make sure to bring it out in your application.

Insider Information

One of the centerpieces of the LBS learning model is its Second Year Project. A team-based experiential exercise, the Second Year Project takes place toward the end of the LBS program, calling on students to leverage all of the education and tools they garnered over their course of study. As part of the project, students assemble teams of two or three, and are assigned to businesses to help them tackle meaningful strategic and operational challenges. Teams also shadow a manager for a week and are required to observe that manager's approach to leadership, challenges, and colleague interaction. At the end of the project, students record their observations and reflect on the implications those observations have on their professional development.

This reflective nature is something that LBS looks closely for in its applicants; the thought being that reflection produces maturity. Indeed, the LBS learning model suggests that the four themes cannot be achieved without reflection. It is therefore imperative that you demonstrate a thoughtful nature in discussing your past experiences. Describing personal discoveries that you gathered from activities and events is a good way to do so.

Schools That Call for a Similar Approach

- ▶ Columbia Business School
- ▶ INSEAD
- ▶ IMD
- ▶ University of Pennsylvania (Wharton)

University of Maryland—Robert H. Smith School of Business
College Park, MD   *www.rhsmith.umd.edu*

Application at a Glance

Application due dates (1st, 2nd, 3rd, 4th, 5th round):
Nov. 1, Dec. 15, Jan. 15, March 1, April 30

Requirements

Essays: Two two-page essays

Recommendations: Two required

Application Fee: $75

School at a Glance

Dean (start of tenure):	G. "Anand" Anandalingam (2008)
Admissions Director:	LeAnne Dagnall

Program Size:	278 full-time
Acceptance Rate:	35%
Yield:	36%
Mean undergraduate GPA:	3.3
Mean GMAT:	658
Middle–80% GMAT:	600–720
Average years of work experience:	4.6
International:	39%
Women:	33%
Minority:	21%

Your Smith Application Strategy

Smith initially made a name for itself among business schools for its emphasis on technology throughout its MBA program. With the bursting of the dot-com bubble, the school began to push beyond this emphasis and now boasts well-regarded tracts in entrepreneurship and international business. The school remains dedicated to advancing the field of technology management, however, and the school's core curriculum weaves tech-related commentary into most of its classes. Students can tailor their general management education to concentrate in topics including electronic commerce, e-service, information systems, and supply chain management.

One tangible example of the school's technology focus is its Netcentricity Laboratory, or "Net Lab," which Smith has built as a proving ground and learning environment for applications including e-commerce and supply chain management. Students use models and simulations to learn the nuances of these systems in a series of e-business lab courses. The Net Lab also contains a Financial Markets Laboratory—modeled after a Wall Street trading floor—which gives students a chance to apply what they learn in the classroom to real-time financial decisions. Naturally, the more you can speak with a passion about the importance of technology in your career path, the better fit you will demonstrate in your Smith application.

Speaking of Wall Street, the school also has a real-money portfolio called the Mayer Fund, which is run by a dozen second-year Smith students. Founded in 1993, the fund gives students a chance to manage a portfolio currently worth more than $2 million. The fund is a great chance for aspiring money managers to get their feet wet and gain exposure to the top executives who make up the fund's external board of directors. If you are interested in finance, consider discussing your interest in the Financial Markets Lab or the Mayer Fund in your application.

Another example of hands-on learning at Smith is its MBA Consulting Program. Teams of four to six second-year students earn credit toward their MBA while consulting for major corporations and government agencies. Even if you're not interested in consulting as a post-MBA career, make sure that you demonstrate enthusiasm for the real-world lessons that this program provides. In fact, if you're not a consultant, emphasizing the appeal of this program may help your application stand out even more, as long as it's consistent with the rest of your story.

Smith students and grads describe the school's culture as being a very cooperative one. Teamwork figures into a lot of what students do, both in traditional classes and in programs such as the MBA Case Competition, in which all second-year students compete. Accordingly, be sure to frame your past successes as instances of team success wherever possible in order to demonstrate a fit with the program. And though leadership isn't talked about as much at Smith as at other schools, any examples you can provide to bolster your leadership dimension will help you stand out from the pack.

As are other schools that compete with the top programs for candidates, Smith is careful about selecting candidates who are truly interested in its program. Demonstrating your knowledge of the school, and especially your enthusiasm for its focus technology, global focus, and entrepreneurship, will help you make your case that Smith is where you want to be.

Insider Information

Smith is very committed to entrepreneurship, and its Dingman Center for Entrepreneurship is a major hub for start-up activity in the Washington, D.C., region, giving entrepreneurs access to experienced mentors and potential investors. If you are serious about entrepreneurship, look closely at the school's Dingman and Lamone Scholarships. Students are selected based on their entrepreneurial experience, their desire to start a business after business school, and their start-up ideas. They receive personal mentoring and business plan advice from experienced entrepreneurs in the Dingman Center. In exchange, Dingman and Lamone Scholars volunteer at the center, offering their own advice to others and running educational seminars in entrepreneurship and networking. Think about this program if you plan on starting your own business, especially on the East Coast, where Dingman's reputation is strongest.

Schools That Call for a Similar Approach

- ◪ Indiana University (Kelley)
- ◪ Michigan State University (Broad)
- ◪ Vanderbilt University (Owen)

University of Michigan—Stephen M. Ross School of Business
Ann Arbor, MI   *www.bus.umich.edu*

Application at a Glance

Application due dates (1st, 2nd, 3rd round): Oct. 11, Jan. 5, March 1

Requirements

Essays: Four (one of 100 words, one of 300 words, two of 500 words each)

Interview: By invitation only

Recommendations: Two; suggest that both come from a direct supervisor, employer, or someone who is familiar with your professional capabilities

Resume

Application fee: $200

School at a Glance

Dean (start of tenure):	Alison Davis-Blake (2011)
Admissions Director:	Soojin Kwon Koh
Program size:	910 full-time
Acceptance rate:	23%
Yield:	79%
Mean undergraduate GPA:	3.4
Mean GMAT:	701
Middle–80% GMAT:	640–760
Average years of work experience:	5.2
International:	28%
Women:	34%
Minority:	24%

Your Ross Application Strategy

The key to getting accepted into Ross is to demonstrate balance across the four dimensions (leadership, innovation, teamwork, maturity) throughout your application. Regardless of the application component(s) in which you emphasize these dimensions, they should each make a couple of appearances. It is imperative, therefore, that you take time to analyze your strengths and weaknesses for each of the dimensions before beginning the Ross application.

Ross is consistently recognized for its innovation and its focus on applying business principles to real-world scenarios. Both of these attributes are integrated in the learning model along with a solid dose of general management courses. A good example of this combination is Ross's Multidisciplinary Action Project (MAP). Students are required to work on teams in completing a seven-week project for companies pre-selected by Ross. The projects are highly analytical and allow students to apply the skills they learned in the classroom to a variety of companies. For those who have inclinations that are more international or entrepreneurial in nature, Ross offers its IMAP and EMAP programs. Another example of Ross's application-based learning is the Tozzi Center. The Tozzi Electronic Business and Finance Center features a trading floor, an elliptical classroom, and a computer laboratory. The trading floor allows for dedicated, real-time access to the global markets. It is used for a multitude of financial class exercises and student projects. Having and displaying knowledge of these types of programs should be a major component of your Ross application process.

Demonstrating the ability to apply business principles in a rational manner is especially important. Recruiters repeatedly complement Ross grads on their practical approach, which has been a large reason for Ross's success in the business school rankings. One applicant who was recently accepted displayed a practical approach by explaining how she identified a neglected growth opportunity within her business segment. The applicant took initiative by creating a marketing plan that focused on the opportunity and was able to see her idea through to implementation. These are the types of applicants Ross seeks.

Given Ross's focus on professional excellence, it is not surprising to see that accepted students have an average of five years of work experience. This should not discourage applicants with less professional work experience, but recognize that Ross will especially want to know how you can contribute to the program if you have less than three years of work experience. You should anticipate being questioned on this point during your interview.

Almost all activities at Ross are team-based, so check your ego before beginning the application. Providing one or two examples of your teamwork capabilities should go a long way toward establishing fit with the program.

Overall, if you meet the baseline criteria, express the four dimensions, display knowledge about the learning model, and exhibit passion for the school, you should be in a much better position to receive an acceptance letter from Ross.

Insider Information

Through time, entrepreneurship has received greater attention at Ross and it is now a major aspect of the learning model. The school has vast resources for aspiring entrepreneurs, such as the Samuel Zell-Robert H. Lurie Institute for Entrepreneurial Studies, which supports students as they explore their own business plans and start-up ideas. Ross will continue to expand its support of entrepreneurial activities because it produces a virtuous cycle. Successful ventures led by students reflect positively on the curriculum, thereby attracting more potential students.

The Ross application process allows for ample opportunity to discuss innovative entrepreneurial ideas and those opportunities should be capitalized on. That is not to say that all applicants should be aspiring entrepreneurs, but to the extent that you can display entrepreneurial spirit, do so. That spirit can be expressed through an idea for a new business or through an idea for your current company. The admissions committee will certainly take notice of your penchant for entrepreneurship and hopefully recognize your ability to augment the Ross brand. Being recognized as a potential brand builder is a great way to move your application into the yes pile.

Schools That Call for a Similar Approach
- Cornell University (Johnson)
- Duke University (Fuqua)
- Northwestern University (Kellogg)
- USC (Marshall)

University of North Carolina at Chapel Hill—Kenan-Flagler Business School
Chapel Hill, NC   *www.kenan-flagler.unc.edu*

Application at a Glance
Application due dates (1st, 2nd, 3rd, 4th round):
Oct. 22, Dec. 3, Jan. 7, March 18

Requirements
Essays: Three of 500 words each
Interview: By invitation only

Recommendations: Two, at least one from a direct supervisor

Resume

Application fee: $140

School at a Glance

Dean (start of tenure):	James W. Dean Jr. (2008)
Admissions director:	Sherrylyn Ford Wallace
Program size:	577 full-time
Acceptance rate:	35%
Yield:	45%
Mean undergraduate GPA:	3.3
Mean GMAT:	677
Middle–80% GMAT:	620–750
Average years of work experience:	5.3
International:	26%
Women:	30%
Minority:	16%

Your Kenan-Flagler Application Strategy

Through the last two decades, Kenan-Flagler has made great strides in establishing its name among the top business schools. With an intense focus on analytics, leadership, and teamwork, as well as a small-program culture, Kenan-Flagler has grown in popularity among applicants and recruiters. The learning model features an integrated general management curriculum that is broken into four eight-week modules that encompass its core curriculum. At the beginning of the third module, students participate in an integrative exercise that pulls together all of the tools and functional areas mastered during the first semester into a hands-on opportunity to apply them to tangible business scenarios.

During the second year, students can select from eight "career and enrichment concentrations" (Corporate Finance, Marketing, Entrepreneurship, Investment Management, Global Supply-Chain Management, Management Consulting, Real Estate, and Sustainable Enterprise). As the names indicate, these concentrations are more oriented toward career development than traditional functions. This is indicative of a learning model that prides itself on having close ties to industry development. Those close ties are supported by having a corporate advisory board, comprised of experts from top companies, that provides guidance on the concentrations' curricula. In addition to serving on the board, these experts also provide students with career advice and job opportunities. To fit well with its focus on career development, Kenan-Flagler looks for applicants who are strong in the maturity dimension. The school discourages those with less than two years work experience from applying and takes a close look at applicants' professional records in search of tangible achievements.

Analytics plays a large role in the Kenan-Flagler learning model and therefore in the applicant selection process. The program is known for its quantitative rigor, so if you have a relatively low quantitative GMAT score and a weak quantitative background, you should consider taking a couple extra courses in economics, statistics, or financial accounting. As do many other schools, Kenan-Flagler has an analytical workshop that students can attend before classes start, but taking initiative to shore up your quantitative skills will show the admissions committee that you will be able to succeed in its numbers-driven environment.

The Kenan-Flagler culture strongly emphasizes both leadership and teamwork, but the admissions committee will more actively evaluate your leadership potential. To bolster that potential, first-year students take a course called *Leading and Managing* during the first module. Students begin the course by reviewing leadership evaluations filled out by their former colleagues. These evaluations pinpoint leadership growth opportunities that students focus on throughout the course. Each student ultimately produces a leadership plan that details the areas in which she would like to improve. There should be at least three aspects of your leadership capabilities that you emphasize in your application: use of analytical skills to assess situations, ability to leverage resources (both people and tools) in developing solutions, and success in implementing solutions. Discussion of these leadership traits will help you establish fit with Kenan-Flagler's mission.

If you are considering an entrepreneurial career path, discussing it in your application is a great way to get your application a second look. We're not talking about merely mentioning that entrepreneurship is an interest, but rather actually discussing the innovation you would like to bring to the market. The latter will get you further, because Kenan-Flagler is interested in students who are serious about entrepreneurship. It has spent the last several years augmenting its entrepreneurial program and is hoping to become a household name in the area. Under the direction of the school's Center for Entrepreneurial Studies, students can now select from a suite of electives that provide insight into each stage of business model development. The school holds an annual venture capital competition, during which aspiring entrepreneurs put their models to the test and receive feedback from established venture capital firms. It can even be competitive to get into some of the later-stage entrepreneurial classes, which require an application and a business plan.

Despite the accolades Kenan-Flagler has received for making improvements to its program, it still has a relatively low yield percentage. The admissions committee will take a close look at your application to see whether you are serious about attending the school. The school even offers an early action round (the first application deadline) for applicants who know that Kenan-Flagler is their first choice. Establishing fit with the school's mission and values is a great way to express your interest. An additional, more conventional way to do so is by visiting the campus. The admissions committee looks positively on applicants who visit the campus as a way to get to know the school and the learning model more intimately. Taking this step will express the level of commitment for which the school is looking.

Insider Information

In the past, Kenan-Flagler was criticized for its lack of focus on international business. It has since increased its global emphasis by offering global immersion electives, increasing study abroad opportunities, and adding language courses.

The school now actively looks for applicants who are interested in pursuing global careers, so if you have any experience or interests along those lines, make sure to bring it out in your application.

Schools That Call for a Similar Approach
- Cornell University (Johnson)
- Emory University (Goizueta)
- Vanderbilt University (Owen)
- Queen's University

University of Pennsylvania—The Wharton School
Philadelphia, PA   *www.wharton.upenn.edu*

Application at a Glance

Application due dates (1st, 2nd, 3rd round): Oct. 4, Jan. 4, March 3

Requirements

Essays: Four (between 300 and 700 words each)

Interview: By invitation only

Recommendations: Two, at least one from a direct supervisor

Resume

Application fee: $250

School at a Glance

Dean (start of tenure):	Thomas S. Robertson (2007)
Admissions director:	J.J. Cutler
Program size:	1,674 full-time
Acceptance rate:	17%
Yield:	68%
Mean undergraduate GPA:	3.5
Mean GMAT:	718
Middle–80% GMAT:	680–760
Average years of work experience:	5.0
International:	36%
Women:	38%
Minority:	32%

Your Wharton Application Strategy

Wharton used to sum up the school's positioning in two words: Wharton Innovates. Indeed, Wharton's stellar reputation and consistent appearance at the top of the rankings can be attributed to the school's ability to transform itself since its establishment in 1881 as the nation's first collegiate business school. Part of your challenge as an applicant is to get the admissions committee to think of your position as *Your Name Here* Innovates.

In support of this positioning, Wharton is boasts an impressive array of entrepreneurial-focused courses, initiatives, and symposia. The Small Business

Development Center features an opportunity through which students act as consultants to local aspiring entrepreneurs. As consultants, students assist with business model development, raising capital, and conducting feasibility studies. Wharton also hosts an annual business plan competition during which student teams compete for more than $100,000 in cash and prizes. After completing the business plan, students can utilize the Venture Initiation Program (VIP) to transform their idea into a business. VIP provides Wharton students with the support they need to complete the final part of the entrepreneurial process. If you have any entrepreneurial aspiration, discuss it in detail in your application and it will definitely catch the admission committee's eyes.

There is perhaps no other business school in the United States that is as international-minded as Wharton. Incoming classes represent more than 70 countries, most students speak a second language, and the learning model encourages students to look at business issues from a global context. The school offers premier global joint programs through Penn's Lauder Institute and Johns Hopkins University's Nitze School of Advanced International Studies. For students who are interested in a more traditional study abroad experience, Wharton offers exchange programs in 15 countries and the Global Immersion Program (GIP). GIP includes five weeks of studying a global region, followed by a four-week study abroad to that region. If you have any international experience, make sure to work it into your application, because it will probably be valued by Wharton more so than by other schools. If you haven't worked or studied abroad, demonstrate a global perspective in your professional interests or display an interest in developing one while at Wharton. Overall, Wharton is very serious about its international mission, and seeks applicants who aid and or benefit from that mission.

Wharton is often credited for having a top-notch finance curriculum, and its students are widely sought after for their finance capabilities. This means that the admissions committee will be paying close attention to your analytical abilities, as conveyed through your GMAT score, GPA, and professional activities. This doesn't mean that you have to come across as a quantitative guru, but it does mean that you have to show you can "hack it" in the classroom. Wharton has historically been friendly to applicants from non-traditional backgrounds, but that doesn't preclude analytical ability.

Though Wharton certainly is a "powerhouse" finance school, its strengths stretch far beyond finance. Wharton offers 17 majors and features nearly 200 electives, more than any other business school in the world. Students can specialize in everything from Real Estate to Health Care Management to Operations and Information Management to Strategic Management. Students are also allowed to create their own majors that focus on cross-functional learning paths. The seemingly unending options are like a smorgasbord of delicious foods. It would serve your application well to discuss a Wharton learning path and provide details on how it will aid you in achieving your professional goals.

Wharton also places strong emphasis on its students' teamwork capabilities. During their first year, students work on assignments in "learning teams," which are central to the learning model. Members of the Wharton community are quick to emphasize the benefits of learning from students with different professional backgrounds. As such, the school will be extremely interested in your ability to interact in a team-oriented environment. You should expect questions on this to come up during the interview. Additionally, Wharton is genuinely interested in knowing what type of person you are outside of the professional environment. A short discussion of your hobbies or community service activities will show that you are more than a resume.

Insider Information

During the last several years Wharton has progressively highlighted the more experiential aspects of its offerings, particularly within the context of leadership. Referred to as "Leadership in Action," Wharton hosts a number of leadership lectures, targeted conferences, and a notable social impact management initiative. A combination of an innovative spirit with a bent toward leading through action serves powerful positioning that aligns well with what the admissions committee is looking for in its applicants.

Schools That Call for a Similar Approach

- ▶ Columbia Business School
- ▶ MIT (Sloan)
- ▶ NYU (Stern)
- ▶ University of London (LBS)

University of Rochester—William E. Simon Graduate School of Business Administration
Rochester, NY   *www.simon.rochester.edu*

Application at a Glance

Application due dates (1st, 2nd, 3rd, 4th, 5th round):
Oct. 15, Nov. 19, Jan. 5, March 15, May 13

Requirements

Essays: One 500-word essay

Interview: Recommended

Recommendations: One letter of recommendation

Application Fee: $125

School at a Glance

Dean (start of tenure):	Mark Zupan (2003)
Admissions Director:	Gregory V. MacDonald
Program Size:	246 full-time
Acceptance Rate:	31%
Yield:	37%
Mean undergraduate GPA:	3.5
Mean GMAT:	682
Middle–80% GMAT:	620–740
Average years of work experience:	4.3

International:	40%
Women:	36%
Minority:	18%

Your Simon Application Strategy

Two hallmarks of the University of Rochester's Simon School are a quantitative curriculum and a small learning environment. The school's curriculum is unique in that it approaches most of the major academic disciplines from an economics perspective. Simon students study finance, marketing, and organizational behavior all through the lens of economic theory, and are encouraged to tie these subjects together by using basic economic principles. The school believes strongly in this approach to business training, and looks for students with the same point of view. Although you won't be expected to speak intelligently about price elasticity or supply and demand curves in your admissions interview, be prepared to demonstrate an understanding of this learning approach and to explain why it appeals to you.

Simon students are expected to take a rigorous, analytical approach in nearly every subject, and the school is careful to screen for analytical abilities in the admissions process. Don't worry: If you didn't study economics or engineering in college, Simon is still interested in you. The school will give you every opportunity to get up to speed before you enroll. If you haven't already taken at least one college-level calculus course, Simon recommends that you take one before enrolling. (That is, you don't necessarily need one to get into Simon, but plan on taking one before you enroll.) Beyond calculus, the school will look closely at your quantitative GMAT score and your college transcript for other evidence of analytical abilities.

Simon was on the cutting edge in terms offering students an integrated learning experience, which other school have since replicated in their own way. Utilizing economics as a common thread running through most Simon coursework helped enable tighter integration. The school teaches a common methodology for approach business problems called "F.A.Ct." (short for Framing a problem, Analyzing it, and Communicating the conclusion). F.A.Ct. places special emphasis on breaking down and solving complex, ambiguous problems. Another nice Simon curriculum feature is that it allows first-year students to get at least three electives under their belts before their summer internships. Simon's small cohorts of 40 students each and small study teams is reflective of its tight-knit community and underscores applicants' need to get be successful in diverse team environments. In a small environment such as Simon's, the ability to get along with your peers is a must, so think about ways to demonstrate an outgoing personality and knack for teamwork.

Students are also encouraged to get involved at the school, and part of students' learning outside the classroom—the VISION program, which teaches subject areas including corporate social responsibility and innovation—is actually run by second-year students. The school looks carefully for evidence that you are truly interested in Simon, and demonstrating your enthusiasm for these unique benefits can help convince them of your interest.

Simon is best known in finance circles, which is no surprise given its emphasis on economic theory and quantitative skills. Students can flex their finance muscles managing the student-run Simon Meliora Fund (originally started back in the mid-1980s) or gain further exposure to Wall Street heavyweights by taking part in Cornell's MBA Stock Pitch Challenge. Though nearly half of each class goes into finance, the school also attracts many consulting and manufacturing firms that are interested in students' analytical abilities. Simon offers 15 concentrations across a variety of disciplines, including operations management, finance, electronic commerce, business systems consulting, marketing, entrepreneurship, and health sciences management.

Insider Information

Simon looks for several traits in its applicants, all stemming from the school's definition of what a successful leader can do. Consistent with its new F.A.Ct. curriculum, the school looks for an ability to decipher a murky situation and choose a course of action. Simon also looks for people who understand how to persuade and motivate people. This is where the school's emphasis on teamwork and diversity comes into play. Finally, the school looks for an ability to recognize talents in other individuals and to encourage their skill development, which is reflected in Simon's emphasis on teamwork. Think about ways in which you can demonstrate these leadership abilities through past experiences, as you work on your Simon application.

Schools That Call for a Similar Approach

- ◪ Carnegie Mellon (Tepper)
- ◪ University of Chicago

University of Southern California—Marshall School of Business
Los Angeles, CA   *www.marshall.usc.edu*

Application at a Glance

Application due dates (1st, 2nd, 3rd round): Nov. 1, Jan. 15, March 15

Requirements

Essays: Three (one of 500 words and two of 750 words each)

Interview: By invitation only, with on-campus interview preferred

Recommendations: Two, at least one from a direct supervisor

Resume

Application fee: $150

School at a Glance

Dean (start of tenure):	James G. Ellis (2007)
Admissions Director:	Keith Vaughn
Program size:	458 full-time
Acceptance rate:	22%
Yield:	45%
Mean undergraduate GPA:	3.3
Mean GMAT:	690

Middle–80% GMAT:	640–740
Average years of work experience:	5.1
International:	22%
Women:	31%
Minority:	34%

Your Marshall Application Strategy

Positioned as more than an MBA program, the Marshall School of Business portrays itself as a life-transforming experience. This experience is referred to as the Marshall Advantage and is highlighted by an application-focused curriculum and special programs in entrepreneurship and international business. The experience is augmented by the Trojan Family culture, which emphasizes teamwork, integrity, and professionalism. Your Marshall application strategy should demonstrate your ability to leverage the Marshall Advantage in addition to displaying fit with the Trojan Family culture.

From the moment students begin the Marshall program, they notice a strong emphasis on career development and putting theory into practice. A majority of the Marshall faculty has significant professional experience. The professors work in teams to discuss ways to highlight the application of theory in the classroom. Not surprisingly, the Marshall Admissions Committee will closely evaluate your maturity dimension. The committee is in search of applicants who can contribute to the classroom based on their success in professional and personal endeavors. Examples that you can provide to impress the committee along these lines include promotions, discussions of passion for your work or community, tangible improvements made to your company, and leadership demonstrated in group settings.

Marshall owns bragging rights to being the first business school with a dedicated entrepreneurship program. That program, supported by the Lloyd Greif Center for Entrepreneurial Studies, is now recognized as one of the top in the nation. Students have the opportunity to compete in business plan competitions in addition to developing their own business models. Discussing your entrepreneurial ambitions is a good way to display fit with Marshall's commitment to this subject. Along with entrepreneurship, Marshall offers almost 20 concentrations in areas such as business of entertainment, corporate finance, general marketing, investments and financial markets, management consulting, real estate finance, and technology development and entrepreneurial e-business.

Marshall's commitment to international business is highlighted by the fact that all students are required to travel abroad as part of the Pacific Rim Education Program (PRIME). As part of the first-year curriculum PRIME is a five-week program, during which students become more familiar with the global aspects of business through lectures, casework, and a team project. Students can select from a number a countries including Chile, China, Japan, Singapore, Thailand, Cuba, or Mexico. PRIME has quickly become a favorite among students, and a majority of them actually accept internships in the countries that they select for the program. International opportunities outside of PRIME include study abroad programs that come in lengths of three weeks, four weeks, or an entire semester.

Marshall will continue to look for ways to make a name for itself in the international arena, and it is therefore important that you display knowledge of or a desire to gain knowledge of global business issues.

Teamwork rests at the core of the Marshall learning model. Shortly after students arrive, they are assigned to small teams of five or six and are expected to work closely together through out the program. The teams are reshuffled for the second semester as well as for PRIME. Students begin the program by participating in a one-week orientation program followed by a three-week "super semester" that provides summary reviews of a breadth of managerial disciplines including financial accounting, microeconomics, statistics, and strategy. Additionally, teams of six students participate in a series of case competitions, which call for students to come up with recommendations to real-world business issues and then present to faculty, classmates, and company representatives.

Insider Information

Despite the myriad offerings with which Marshall provides its students, it often plays second fiddle to UCLA (Anderson), Berkeley (Haas), and Stanford. Marshall is looking to become more competitive with these area schools by highlighting the quantitative rigor of the program. As such, the admissions committee will take a close look at your quantitative GMAT score in addition to looking at your transcript(s) for evidence of proficiency in numbers-intensive courses. If you don't have a quantitative-heavy background, consider taking an accounting, statistics, or calculus course. The admissions committee will also take a close look and evaluate the probability that you will accept an offer. You can increase your chances by displaying intimate knowledge of the Marshall learning model and passion for the school's mission and values.

Schools That Call for a Similar Approach

- ▶ Emory University (Goizueta)
- ▶ University of California at Berkeley (Haas)
- ▶ UCLA (Anderson)
- ▶ University of Michigan Business School (Ross)

University of Texas at Austin—McCombs School of Business
Austin, TX   *www.mccombs.utexas.edu*

Application at a Glance

Application due dates (Early, International, Domestic): Nov. 1, Jan. 14, April 1

Requirements

Essays: Three (between 500 and 900 words each)

Interview: By invitation only

Recommendations: Two letters of recommendation; at least one should come from a direct supervisor

Application Fee: $175

School at a Glance

Dean (start of tenure):   Thomas W. Gilligan (2008)

Admissions Director:	Christina Mabley
Program Size:	534 full-time
Acceptance Rate:	23%
Yield: 4	9%
Mean undergraduate GPA:	3.5
Mean GMAT:	681
Middle–80% GMAT:	620–730
Average years of work experience:	4.8
International:	22%
Women:	23%
Minority:	25%

Your McCombs Application Strategy

The McCombs School of Business offers a general management program in an innovative, hands-on learning environment. The school offers no formal majors, but it does offer a broad set of 19 concentrations that cover both traditional and emerging business functions and industries, including investment management, private equity, energy finance, healthcare, social enterprise, clean technology, consulting, supply chain & operations management, and high technology marketing. About half of all McCombs students choose to pursue a concentration.

Teamwork is a major emphasis at McCombs, with students doing most of their work in project teams. Students also spend their entire first year taking their core classes together in "cohorts." Naturally, the school looks for people who will thrive in this team-oriented environment, so be sure to demonstrate your experience in working with others to make things happen. McCombs is also a relatively small program compared to its peers, and boasts a student-to-faculty ratio of less than 6:1, one of the lowest ratios at any top school.

One example of McCombs's innovation is its MBA+ Leadership Program, an experiential individually tailored approach to building the leaders. The program combines "micro-consulting" projects with executive coaching and seminars in helping students to develop a personal leadership style. The consulting projects occur over a four- to 10-week period, as students operate in small teams to tackle significant business challenges. At the end of the project, the team reports their findings and recommendations to their client. The MBA+ Leadership Program exemplifies what McCombs is about, so if it appeals to you, make sure to communicate that in your application.

Several other programs also demonstrate the school's emphasis on hands-on experience, including the Venture Labs Investment Competition (formerly known as Moot Corp), the MBA Investment Fund, Texas Venture Labs, and the Venture Fellows program. Since 1984, the school has hosted the Venture Labs Investment Competition, one of the oldest and largest inter–business school business plan competitions in the world. The competition now attracts teams from dozens of schools around the world, and winning teams get $100,000 and a chance to start their business in the friendly confines of the Austin Technology Incubator. Be sure to get to know this program better if you plan on applying to McCombs as a prospective entrepreneur.

Each year, 20 students are selected to run the MBA Investment Fund, a $15 million fund that was created in 1994 as the first legally constituted, private investment company to be managed by students. McCombs students have an opportunity to apply growth, value, and fixed-income strategies to several portfolios. The student managers even manage a small part of the school's endowment, getting advice from professional money managers along the way. If you have an interest in investment management—or even just like the school's hands-on learning philosophy—you'll want to show your enthusiasm for it in your application.

Texas Venture Labs was launched in 2010 as a campus-wide initiative with an objective of facilitating and accelerating time-to-market for student entrepreneurs. Venture Labs provides students with a step-by-step framework for harnessing their innovations and commercializing them.

Finally, the McCombs Venture Fellows programs capitalizes on the school's location in start-up-heavy Austin, each year providing 20 students with semester-long internships with local venture capital or private equity funds. Few job sectors are more appealing right now for MBA grads than the venture capital and private equity fields, and this program can provide you with a great leg up in trying to land a coveted position with one of these firms. Outside of the typical finance-heavy schools, consider McCombs if you are serious about pursuing a career in venture capital or private equity.

Insider Information

McCombs is careful about selecting people who it believes have a sincere interest in its program. Whereas all schools look for this kind of interest and enthusiasm demonstrated throughout your application, McCombs specifically looks for it their essay questions. Invest considerable time in researching the school and finding out what kind of opportunities interest you (or could be added to the program). If you're really interested, then make sure to visit the school. Even more importantly, focus less on trying to pick out an obscure activity to impress the admissions committee, and focus more on writing about something that truly interests you and how you will pursue that interest at McCombs. If your interest isn't currently met by one of the school's activities, then you have a great chance to show your initiative by proposing how you would start an activity around that interest. The key is to write about something for which you truly have passion, and to show how you will bring that same passion to McCombs.

Schools That Call for a Similar Approach

- ▶ Indiana University (Kelley)
- ▶ Vanderbilt University (Owen)

University of Toronto—Rotman School of Management
Toronto, Ontario, Canada   *www.rotman.utoronto.ca/mba/*

Application at a Glance

Application due dates (1st, 2nd, 3rd): Nov. 15, Feb. 1, April 30

Requirements

Essays: Four (one of 500 words and three of 250 words each)
Interview: By invitation only
Recommendations: Two letters of recommendation
Application Fee: $175

School at a Glance

Dean (start of tenure):	Roger Martin (1998)
Admissions Director:	Cheryl Millington
Program Size:	534 full-time
Acceptance Rate:	44%
Yield:	54%
Mean undergraduate GPA:	N/A
Mean GMAT:	652
Middle–80% GMAT:	560–720
Average years of work experience:	4.0
International:	42%
Women:	33%
Minority:	N/A

Your Rotman Application Strategy

The Rotman School of Management ushered in an era of change in 1998 when Roger Martin left his consulting career to become dean of the school. Martin brought to Rotman a perspective that MBA programs generally had stopped evolving while the global economy was experiencing unprecedented transformation. In his view, innovative business solutions are generated when business leaders are capable of considering business challenges holistically, evaluating numerous approaches simultaneously, and understanding the tensions among the approaches. The result of Martin's push for a more holistic approach to business learning is referred to as "Integrative Thinking."

The essence of Integrative Thinking now sits at the core of Rotman's curricullum and is what Rotman considers to be its primary point of differentiation versus other MBA programs. Although students are certainly trained in all of the primary business fundamentals, Rotman attempts to go beyond simply teaching traditional disciplines by also emphasizing the interrelationships across the disciplines to maximize organizational success. In the first year of the curriculum, this approach manifests through two courses: *Foundations of Integrative Thinking* and *Integrative Thinking Practicum*. These courses walk students through a variety of decision-making models, and teach students how to respond to business change and evaluate a variety of business models. In addition to these courses, students can select from five second-year elective courses that extensively draw from the Integrative Thinking approach.

The faculty members at the school are very much bought into the approach as well and represent a vast array of research capabilities that focus on furthering Rotman's innovative approach to learning. The program actively seeks to maintain a balance of strong academic research with faculty members who bring strong professional experience to the school to ensure that students have access to progressive learning constructs that still have applicability to their budding careers.

Given the importance of Integrative Thinking to the Rotman curriculum, it's critical that applicants convey an understanding and appreciation for the approach. In particular, the ability to convey an understanding of how this skill would apply to your prospective career is highly valued. Rotman believes strongly (and graduates agree) that the principles of Integrative Thinking are wide-reaching, are applicable to all future career paths, and enable business leaders to have substantial impact in the marketplace.

The other major strength of the Rotman curriculum is its impressive focus on the world economy. With 70 percent of its faculty boasting international credentials, global themes find their way into most core courses and students may select from a range of international courses in their second year. To supplement these perspectives, students have the opportunity to participate in exchange programs for one full term during their second year. Rotman has established programs with more than 20 schools worldwide and also offers international study tours that provide students with direct opportunities to engage with the global markets. Certainly reflecting an international mindset or at least a desire to further your understanding of the global marketplace should be an important aspect of your application.

Insider Information

Another unique aspect of the Rotman curriculum is its emphasis on design. The school believes that design prowess is fundamental to innovation and that business leaders must be capable of thinking and acting as designers in order remain innovative and relevant in the market. In 2006, Rotman launched the Business Design Initiative under its Integrative Thinking umbrella. Through this initiative, Rotman has cultivated a close relationship with Stanford's Institute of Design and offers a Business Design internship program that places Rotman MBAs on teams together with design students to tackle a variety of business challenges. If you have an inclination toward product innovation or design, this aspect of the Rotman curriculum is definitely worth exploring further and more importantly discussing in your application.

Schools That Call for a Similar Approach

- ▣ Indiana University (Kelley)
- ▣ MIT (Sloan)
- ▣ University of Rochester (Simon)

University of Virginia—Darden Graduate School of Business
Charlottesville, VA   www.darden.virginia.edu

Application at a Glance

Application due dates (1st, 2nd, 3rd round): Oct. 14, Jan. 5, March 30

Requirements

Essays: Three (two of 500 words each)

Interview: By invitation only

Recommendations: Two; work-related recommendations are suggested

Application fee: $215

School at a Glance

Dean (start of tenure):	Robert F. Bruner (2005)
Admissions director:	Sara E. Neher
Program size:	642 full-time
Acceptance rate:	25%
Yield:	45%
Mean undergraduate GPA:	3.4
Mean GMAT:	701
Middle–80% GMAT:	650–740
Average years of work experience:	4.1
International:	31%
Women:	29%
Minority:	15%

Your Darden Application Strategy

Upon visiting Darden, you will be immediately struck by three traits: the stunning campus, the dynamic classroom interactions, and the academic discipline. Each of these traits is rooted in closely guarded tradition. Though many business schools have changed their models over time to keep up with the latest fads, Darden has remained true to the ideals that have kept its students highly regarded as general managers. Your application should clearly display your fit with the Darden philosophy.

The central tenets of the Darden philosophy are based upon the close-knit feel of the school and the respect among students and faculty. Every weekday morning "First Coffee" is held, during which the Darden community sits down and discusses topics that are pertinent to the school. Students consistently rave about the bonds that are formed throughout their years at Darden, and the alumni are among the most committed to their alma mater. Indeed Darden is known to have the highest endowment per alum of any business school. Although the class size has grown over the last two decades, the small-school feeling remains. If you intend to get accepted, you should indicate your desire to become a member of this community and provide examples of how you have and would be a contributing alum. A visit to the Darden campus and classroom is a great way to show commitment to the school; just be sure to mention the visit in your application.

The case study method still remains the major pedagogical tool through which the Darden learning model is taught. Professors select students through cold calls to initiate case analysis and then invite the entire class to participate in the dialogue. Students are placed in the role of the decision-maker and must have the ability to articulate and defend their positions in an insightful manner. Your ability to contribute to case conversations will most likely be tested during your

Darden interview. The interviewer will be evaluating your ability to provide cogent responses, your confidence level, and your professionalism. Your challenge is to position yourself as a candidate who can play both the student and the teacher roles within the case study framework. It should be noted, however, that although Darden is a case study school at heart, it has added other educational devices to its toolbox such as video cases, articles, simulations, and experiential activities.

Though the cases place you in the role of an individual decision-maker, case preparation is conducted in student learning teams. As a student, you would be placed in a learning team immediately after starting the Darden program. Teams are expected to meet every night, so discussing your ability to interact well with others should be an important piece of your application.

Darden expects its graduates to be leaders in their fields, but it also understands that leadership is learned through a path of progression. Your essays should show a progression in leadership and your recommendations highlight your potential to continue growing as a leader.

Darden is also well known for its strong emphasis on ethics. All students are required to take a course on the subject and ethical challenges often arise in cases throughout the rest of the curriculum. The Olsson Center for Applied Ethics supports Darden's continued examination of the ethical aspects of business. Don't be surprised if a question on ethics comes up during your interview. Make sure to review the approach to these types of questions that we outlined in Chapter 4.

Insider Information

Some modifications have been made to the Darden learning model to curb excessive work, though the academic experience remains intense. Although students don't take exams on Saturdays, as in the past, the Darden experience is anything but a two-year vacation. Perhaps for no other school is the analogy to drinking from a fire hose more appropriate. There are no days off at Darden, as students spend more time in the classroom than at any other top business school and conquer 13 cases a week on average. Students are expected to enter the program with a background in statistics, economics, and accounting. The benefit from such a rigorous learning model is that graduates truly feel that they've received value in return for their efforts. The intensity pays off in preparation. Focus on this benefit and your ability to succeed within the parameters of the learning model, and you will be on your way to establishing a good fit with the Darden traditions.

Schools That Call for a Similar Approach
- Cornell University (Johnson)
- Dartmouth College (Tuck)
- Harvard Business School
- University of Western Ontario (Ivey)

University of Western Ontario—Richard Ivey School of Business
London, Ontario, Canada   *www.ivey.uwo.ca*

Application at a Glance

Application due dates (Early action, 1st, 2nd, 3rd, 4th round):
May 3, Aug. 16, Oct. 12, Dec. 6, Jan. 10

Requirements

Essays: Three 250-word essays

Interview: By invitation only

Recommendations: Two or three letters of recommendation

Application Fee: $150 (Canadian)

School at a Glance

Dean (start of tenure):	Carol Stephenson (2003)
Admissions Director:	Niki da Silva
Program Size:	146 full-time
Acceptance Rate:	35% (estimated)
Yield:	60% (estimated)
Mean undergraduate GPA:	N/A
Mean GMAT:	672
Middle–80% GMAT:	600–740
Average years of work experience:	4.4
International:	25%
Women:	32%
Minority:	N/A

Your Ivey Application Strategy

The Richard Ivey School of Business made waves in management education when it announced in 2005 that it was transitioning from its traditional two-year MBA program to an accelerated one-year program. Although the format of the program has changed dramatically, Ivey's underlying focus remains: turning out business leaders with well-rounded general management skills.

The Ivey curriculum is composed of four different segments. The first segment—the preparatory knowledge program—begins before classes even officially start and serves as a four-week primer, reviewing economics, accounting, finance, and quantitative analysis. The second segment—business essentials—consists of two modules that are taught over a six-month period. These core courses emphasize traditional business disciplines, such as finance, accounting, marketing, operations, and strategy, and combine them with courses that focus on how to succeed as a general manager, such as communications, leadership, decision making with analytics, and career management. In this way, Ivey's program is unique because career-management concepts and tools have become a part of the core curriculum, rather than remaining as a second-year elective or as a separate service in the school's career management office. If this kind of practical learning appeals to you, be sure to mention it as a reason for why you are a good fit with Ivey.

The third segment consists of two elective periods that enable students to select from a suite of electives that are aligned with six different areas: corporate strategy and leadership, finance, marketing, entrepreneurship, international management, and health sector. These electives move deeper into business management concepts, relying heavily on the case study method to help students analyze business challenges and design practical solutions that take the whole organization into account. This segment also builds on the first two by opening up the discussion to business management and competition on a global scale, an incorporates an optional two-week study trip abroad to either India or China after the first elective period. Not surprisingly, Ivey is interested in applicants with international experience, or at least a global viewpoint.

After the elective periods have been completed, the curriculum ends with a capstone segment, called leading cross-enterprise. This one-month segment is effectively experiential in nature, challenging students to deliver solutions to complex real-world, global business problems. In addition to the case study format, which is prevalent throughout the curriculum, students participate in interactive assignments and a speaker's series.

Two aspects of Ivey's hands-on general management curriculum are the Ivey Consulting Project (ICP) and the Ivey New Venture Project (INVP). Students may select which of the two they would like to participate in with ICP students consulting for corporate managers and INVP students focusing on developing and launching a new venture. Both programs call for students to operate in teams of six to eight students over a six-month period. Demonstrating an understanding of these programs and the real-world value that they can provide will help show your fit with the school.

Ivey expresses an undying devotion to the case study method. Students typically spend one to three hours preparing for each case individually and in learning teams, and then discuss their opinions and analysis in class, with the professor directing the discussion. It's a rigorous approach to learning, and one that requires a certain kind of student.

Accordingly, Ivey looks for applicants with strong academic backgrounds, as well as those with a willingness to throw themselves into tough challenges. This is more important than ever, given Ivey's one-year curriculum. The school likes applicants who bring a unique perspective to class, in order to encourage consideration of a wide range of ideas in each discussion. Ivey also looks for people with polish who are not afraid to voice their opinions. Any way in which you can demonstrate a time when you had to persuade others to follow you, or when you had to make an unpopular decision, will help greatly. Finally, the school looks for people who will make good citizens in the classroom. The case method works best when everyone involved is willing to consider others' opinions, so be sure to bring out this trait in your application.

Insider Information

Ivey's transition to a one-year program means that its MBA students no longer have the benefit of a summer internship. Whereas many students—especially those who are returning to their old employer or at least their old industry—won't mind this, career switchers may find themselves missing out on one of the more attractive aspects of a full-time MBA programs. Ivey has gone out of its way to emphasize that students can still switch careers in the new program, citing statistics that show that an internship isn't necessary for a successful career switch. Ivey's program is one of the major changes in management education in the past 10 years, and many students will love it, but we still recommend that you make sure that you are comfortable with the tradeoffs if you choose Ivey over a more traditional two-year program.

Schools That Call for a Similar Approach
- ⊵ Harvard Business School
- ⊵ University of Virginia (Darden)

Vanderbilt University—Owen Graduate School of Management
Nashville, TN   *www.owen.vanderbilt.edu*

Application at a Glance
Application due dates (1st, 2nd, 3rd, 4th round):
Oct. 21, Nov. 15, Jan. 10, Feb. 28

Requirements
Essays: Two 500-word essays

Interview: Required

Recommendations: Two letters of recommendation

Application Fee: $125

School at a Glance

Dean (start of tenure):	James W. Bradford (2005)
Admissions Director:	John Roeder
Program Size:	360 full-time
Acceptance Rate:	37%
Yield:	55%
Mean undergraduate GPA:	3.3
Mean GMAT:	653
Middle–80% GMAT:	620–720
Average years of work experience:	4.8
International:	26%
Women:	26%
Minority:	13%

Your Owen Application Strategy
After overcoming a relatively rocky period in the 1990s—in which the school's dean died and about 20 percent of its faculty turned over—Owen has bounced back to carve out a reputation as a small business school with some very innovative academic programs.

That turnaround can largely be credited to William Christie, a finance professor who stepped into the dean's role in 2000. He brought a great deal of energy the dean's office, and worked hard to address concerns that the administration wasn't responsive enough to student's concerns. Christie was succeeded by James

Bradford in 2005 (Christie still teaches at the school), but the positive changes that he instituted have taken hold. Owen students tend to be a happy lot these days, citing the school's responsiveness and innovative, practical curriculum as strengths.

One thing that hasn't changed at Owen is its small size. The school enrolls an average of 200 students per class, and it takes its 10:1 student-to-faculty ratio very seriously. The school's curriculum emphasizes practical application of management knowledge, as evidenced by its market-driven curriculum. Owen maintains close relationships with leading business professionals to help maintain a pragmatic approach to education and the majority of the faculty have worked in the "real world" in roles that range from entrepreneur to CEO. This orientation toward hands-on learning manifests in myriad ways throughout the two-year program, but most prominent is the consulting engagements that students take on. Students work in teams to provide consulting services to a client, analyzing a business problem and presenting their recommendations in a final report and presentation.

Leadership is also an important theme at Owen. A key feature that underscores this theme is the Leadership Development Program (LDP), which focuses on personalized and customized leadership development. Owen defines effective leadership in three ways: 1) create the new and different, 2) figure out how to get it done, and 3) engage others to help get it done. Owen helps students become effective leaders by first helping them to identify their personal strengths and targeted areas for improvement. Students also participate in intensive workshops that provide the opportunity to drill down deep on leadership issues with case studies and discussions. Keep in mind Owen's definition of effective leadership as you reflect on your application positioning.

Beyond the core curriculum, Owen students can pursue career/industry specializations in areas such as brand management, corporate finance, investment management, health care, and operations management. Beyond these specializations, the school also offers several "concentrations" that are more focused on traditional business disciplines, including accounting, finance, marketing, operations and strategy. Lastly, students may select a career-focused "emphasis"—basically lighter versions of specializations that allow students to delve deeper into a particular industry of interest. The school's Health Care MBA actually started out as an emphasis offered through electives. This kind of continuous change and innovation in the curriculum is nothing new for Owen (it quietly eliminated an E-Commerce concentration after interest in the subject waned), and don't be surprised to see the school keep tweaking its program to keep up with the times.

Due in large part to its small size, Owen has a collegial, close-knit community where student involvement is high. Students are encouraged to voice their opinions on school-wide matters, and the administration works hard to accommodate them. The school likes hands-on students with a penchant for collaboration. Keep this in mind as you think about the aspects of your application that demonstrate your community involvement and teamwork experience.

As do other schools that appear alongside bigger names in the business school rankings, Owen looks for students who really want to attend the school. Owen is likely to sniff out someone who is just looking for a "safety school," so make sure that you demonstrate why you want to spend two years there. One way to do it is by demonstrating a sincere interest in one of its specialized programs.

Insider Information

Owen responded to the increasing importance of healthcare as business problem by introducing its Health Care MBA in 2005. The two-year program, a joint venture between Owen and the Vanderbilt University Medical Center, aims to produce MBA grads who are able to "hit the ground running" after graduation. Students still take the standard business school curriculum and earn a traditional MBA, but also take a series of healthcare-related courses and work on strategic projects for sponsor organizations. The program goes even further than its competition by putting students in hospitals, giving them real-world, clinical exposure and helping them see the day-to-day realities of healthcare. If you are interested in pursuing a career in healthcare after earning your MBA, give Owen's program a close look.

Schools That Call for a Similar Approach

- ▶ University of Maryland (Smith)
- ▶ UNC (Kenan-Flagler)
- ▶ University of Texas (McCombs)

Yale School of Management
New Haven, CT   *mba.yale.edu*

Application at a Glance

Application due dates (1st, 2nd, 3rd): Oct. 7, Jan. 6, March 17

Requirements

Essays: Three (two of 500 words and one of 600 words)

Interview: By invitation only

Recommendations: Two letters of recommendation

Application Fee: $220

School at a Glance

Dean (start of tenure):	Edward A. Snyder (2011)
Admissions Director:	Bruce DelMonico
Program Size:	429 full-time
Acceptance Rate:	18%
Yield:	44%
Mean undergraduate GPA:	3.5
Mean GMAT:	715
Middle–80% GMAT:	680–760
Average years of work experience:	5.0
International:	27%
Women:	35%
Minority:	19%

Your Yale Application Strategy

The Yale School of Management (SOM) aims to produce leaders who will make a difference both within their organizations and in their communities. The school's stated mission is to educate leaders "for business and society." Though nearly two-thirds of each class go into finance or consulting (as with most other business schools), there is a much greater emphasis on nonprofit and public sector lessons and opportunities at Yale than at most other schools. No matter what their career goals are, the candidates who most appeal to the admissions committee are the ones who demonstrate a broad perspective and an understanding of the importance of contributing to society at large.

Fittingly, Yale has one of the best-known non-profit programs in the United States. The school offers extensive elective options in nonprofit and public sector management, and also provides students with a variety of opportunities for getting involved in their communities outside of class. Yale's Internship Fund, established in 1979, provides financial assistance to students who take on non- or low-paying jobs in the nonprofit or public sector. Funds are raised from contributions from the Yale SOM community, and approximately 20 percent of the class receives some amount of funding in any given year. Even if you don't plan on pursuing a nonprofit job after school, demonstrating enthusiasm for getting involved in this type of program can help further show your fit with the school.

Entrepreneurship is also a focus at Yale, and students have several opportunities to get involved in building a business. Yale is one of the key partner schools in the Haas-led Global Social Venture Competition, giving students the chance to combine their entrepreneurial chops and their desire to do well in a competition versus students from across the globe. The school's Program on Social Enterprise (PSE) provides additional support and opportunities for students who are interested in the intersection between business and positive social impact.

Yale stresses the importance of understanding the interaction between the private sector and public sector, so you want to demonstrate a "big picture" view and a willingness to learn about how one affects the other, no matter what your career interest is. Yale especially looks for people who are comfortable with having their thinking challenged and are willing to take intellectual risks. The more you can demonstrate a willingness to "think outside of the box" both on the job and in your extracurricular activities, the better off you will be. Additionally, the school looks for applicants with integrity, so think about how you can demonstrate this as part of the maturity dimension in your application.

Further, Yale is looking for business-minded people who are just as comfortable talking about world politics as they are building an asset pricing model. You can show a fit with the program by demonstrating your knowledge of current events and a natural desire to get involved in your community. Although Yale's application no longer features an essay question that hits this head-on, the school still looks for people who are aware of the world around them and want to make a positive impact. No need to force it and promise that you're out to cure world hunger when you're not, but keep this in mind if you're serious about applying to Yale SOM.

Insider Information

Spend some time familiarizing yourself with Yale SOM's innovative core curriculum. Though many business schools these days are talking the talk about multidisciplinary approaches to problem-solving, Yale is really walking the walk with its new program. The curriculum eliminates the traditional core courses of finance, marketing, strategy, and so on, in favor of eight courses (called "Organization Perspectives") that each correspond to a certain role or stakeholder in an organization. Examples include the employee, the customer, the innovator, and the investor. The traditional management disciplines are still present and accounted for, but are taught together in the context of those eight organizational roles. Another addition to the core curriculum includes the international experience, a mandatory two-week trip abroad for all first-year students, making Yale one the first top U.S. business school to make overseas study a required part of the curriculum. Make sure you understand these unique aspects of the program as you develop your Yale application strategy.

Schools That Call for a Similar Approach

- ▣ Harvard Business School

- ▣ University of California at Berkeley (Haas)

 FAQs

I know it's never too early to start planning one's business school application, but at what point is it too late?

Planning for business school is a tremendous undertaking. From the onset, applicants should devise a realistic time line that allows them ample time to conduct their due diligence, which includes school visits, attending prospective students' events, and talking to students and alumni. In addition, they should devote ample time to doing well on the GMAT, developing well-structured essays, and soliciting solid letters of recommendation. If an applicant finds himself having to rush to complete any of these key application components by a deadline—for example, cramming for the GMAT while simultaneously trying to write his essays—then it's probably too late for that round. Remember that submitting a great application is the best thing you can do to maximize your chances, rather than rushing to get an application in by the Round 1 deadline versus Round 2.

What are some things that make an admissions officer say, "This applicant is going to do very well!" when reviewing an application?

In addition to some of the obvious factors such as academic and professional prowess, it's apparent that applicants will do well when they show obvious signs of introspection before and during the application process. This is apparent in their clearly outlined essays: They are asked why they are looking to go to business school, why does a particular school provide the perfect training ground for their professional and personal development, and which career paths—both short and long term—would they like to pursue after business school and the logical reasons why. It's also clear that applicants will do well

[handwritten margin note: links to my goals in life]

when they are able to effectively differentiate themselves from the rest of the applicant pool. When an admissions officer is able to identify something in an application that makes her say "Wow, that's really interesting…," that applicant has succeeded in standing out and will likely be successful in adding to the diversity of any business school program.

What's really the importance of community service to an MBA application?

We cannot emphasize enough how important community service is to the MBA application. When an applicant is involved in community service, it demonstrates several things: that they care about improving the lives of others, have a sense of civic duty and social responsibility, are committed to protecting the rights and welfare of others, have certain principles, and are selfless. All of these are tremendously important signs to members of admissions committees because it gives them some insight as to the level of commitment an applicant will display toward the betterment of society *and* the positive impact they are likely to have on campus, in their communities, and beyond. Community service is also valuable to the applicant who hasn't had the chance to take on a true leadership role at work. For instance, for someone who serves a technical, non-managerial role at work, leading an event at church or organizing a walk to raise money to fight disease is another great way to show leadership abilities.

Letters of recommendation are tricky because they're the part of the process that an applicant controls the least. What's the best advice for ensuring my recommendations are strong?

Letters of recommendation are critical in the admissions review process because they not only provide the committee with a third-party verification of the applicant, but, if done well, could very well move a borderline applicant into the "admit" pile. Therefore, it is important that considerable time and thought be put into the writing process and that an applicant follow certain minimum guidelines to ensure great letters from their managers. Guidelines follow:

- **Select your recommenders wisely.** Applicants should make sure that the people they are choosing have a tremendous amount of insight as to the type of person they are and can write to their strengths, abilities, contributions, and experiences. The letters should come from people who have worked on projects with the applicants or those whom the applicants have reported or currently reports to. Applicants should also choose people who would be in support of the applicants pursuing graduate business school.

- **Provide your recommenders with a packet of information.** First, provide a brief statement of purpose (up to one page), which should include why you want an MBA, why at this point in your career, and what you would like to do after graduating. Second, provide a page outlining the list of projects you worked on while under these people's supervision or while serving as a member of their team and your contributions. Third, provide a list of accomplishments or milestones reached in that position or while working on specific projects. Fourth, provide an updated resume. Fifth, provide a brief profile or primer of the schools you are targeting (outlining their strengths and why you believe you are a fit) so that your writers spend very little time, if any, researching them.

◪ **Give your recommenders ample time.** Recommenders need time to develop thoughtful and detailed responses, rich with examples and anecdotes, in your letter. Plan on this taking at least a couple of weeks, maybe even longer depending on how busy your recommenders are. It's important to also give them a deadline for when you need the letters by, and it helps to provide a gentle reminder in the week leading up to the deadline.

What advice is there for the otherwise strong applicant who just can't seem to get above 650 on the GMAT?

Making several attempts and still not getting your target GMAT score is one of the most frustrating aspects of applying to business school—but it doesn't need to be, because the exam is just one predictor of academic success. The GMAT is a significant piece of one's application; however, there are other important factors that can also be seen as predictors of one's success. Through essays, one should still illustrate how he or she possesses the strong analytical and verbal skills necessary to meet the academic rigor of that school. This is often evidenced by applicants responsibilities at work, specials projects they may have be assigned, courses they may have taken since graduating from college, and any extracurricular involvement that supports their potential. For example, someone with a GMAT in the low 600s, but strong grades in a post-college finance class and multiple examples of using analytical abilities on the job, can make a strong case that he really does have the ability to succeed in business school. And remember: It really is just one data point.

What is the definition of a safety or stretch school?

A safety school is a business school to which you have greater than a 90 per-cent chance of being accepted. Generally, safety schools are considered to be those that have 80th percentile of the school's GMAT scores and mean un-dergraduate GPAs that are lower than your scores. Additionally, you should ensure that you are no more than one year less than the school's average num-ber of years of work experience and that you can project a good fit before you assign the safety school moniker. A stretch school is considered to be any school where either your GMAT score or undergraduate GPA is less than the 80th percentile of the schools' scores. Of course, because the application pro-cess is about much more than just these numbers, you should only use these statistics as a rough guideline. You can also help yourself by meeting students and alumni from the schools in question and seeing how their experiences compare to your own. You will likely be able to get a good feel for whether or not a school is a stretch or a safety this way.

Do you recommend that someone apply to safety schools?

Applying to safety schools can be a sound strategy if you are willing to attend a lesser-ranked program in order to pursue your career goals. We've come across far too many applicants who apply to safety schools just to see if they can get in and when they gain admissions, they turn down the offers because they would still rather reapply to see if they can gain admission to their dream schools. At the end of the day, (applicants should only apply to safety schools if they are truly interested in the programs' offerings and will attend if acceptances to their dream schools do not materialize.) Also, by applying to safety schools that they would not ultimately attend, these applicants can effectively take spots away from other applicants who may regard the same schools as their dream schools. Keep in mind that many lower-ranked schools' admissions offices are very good at sniffing out applicants who are only applying to the program as a safety school. So, applying to safety schools is not necessarily a sure thing, as the business school admissions process is a highly subjective one. The most important thing here is to apply to a range of programs that will provide the best training given your goals and interests.

What would you say is the single most important thing about the business school application process?

The single most important thing about the application process is to put a tremendous amount of effort to crafting well-developed and effectively written essays. Why? Because business schools' essays are the applicant's single most important means of telling an applicant's story and in his own unique way. The essays serve as the foundation on which all other parts of the application are built. They also fill in the gaps. Essays are the applicants' opportunity to illustrate that through this potentially life-altering process they've gone through a highly introspective process, which has ultimately allowed them to:

- Be honest about who they are and who they ultimately aspire to be.
- Understand their reasons for wanting to pursuing business school.
- Share their passions and interests—critical to the career equation.
- Articulate the logical progression from their short- to long-term career goals.
- Share aspects of themselves that provide a vivid picture of who they are.
- Differentiate themselves from the rest of the applicant pool.
- Conduct adequate due diligence and show school fit.

In sum, excellent essays really can get you into a great business school!

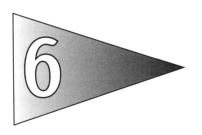

Assembling Your Game Plan

Your game plan is the culmination of your research and preparation efforts prior to actually "digging" into the application. The plan includes:

- ▶ A time line for the application process.
- ▶ Career goals.
- ▶ Information on your target schools.
- ▶ Professional background.
- ▶ Resume.
- ▶ Academic background.
- ▶ Personal background.

Together, these game plan components will serve as:

- ▶ The formulation of your strategy to get accepted by your target schools.
- ▶ A baseline in writing and reviewing your essays.
- ▶ A reference document for your recommenders.
- ▶ A point of preparation for your interviews.

Putting together a game plan is a time-consuming process, but it's an invaluable tool that is definitely worth the time. Since we published the first edition of *Your MBA Game Plan,* successful applicants have consistently told us that they referenced their game plan throughout the application process and that it played a key role in gaining acceptances. Recommenders also find these plans to be helpful in crafting recommendations that support the messages that you emphasize in other aspects of your application.

As an example, we'll now step through portions of a game plan that a successful applicant put together in her attempt to gain acceptance to some of the top business schools. As with other sections, we've added our comments to highlight the most important aspects of the document. We will present some sections in their entirety and others in summary form, depending on what we've already covered elsewhere in this book.

The applicant, Lauren, has an engineering background and worked at Hartman Energy for the last four years, assisting customers with their energy needs. She wants to go to business school in order to break into general management, study sustainable development techniques, and eventually assist corporations in pursuing environmentally sustainable business practices.

You'll notice that Lauren is a very strong applicant. The purpose of stepping through her game plan is not to emphasize her own individual strengths, but rather to show how useful creating application strategies can be. Keep that in mind as you begin to formulate your own game plan.

Lauren began her plan by addressing her recommenders, whom she viewed as the main audience. In addition to supplying the document to her recommenders, she utilized her game plan as a launch pad in executing her application strategies.

Lauren's Game Plan

Introduction

The purpose of this game plan is to provide you with information about me as a professional, student, and individual. Additionally, it will provide you with information on my application time line and background on the business schools for which you are writing recommendations.

The plan has been written in summary and with detail so that you can glean the information you feel is helpful in completing the recommendation forms. The process of writing this plan has helped me to gain a better sense of my story and to document it as I enter the application process.

The competition to get into the world's top MBA programs is fierce; the average acceptance rate at the top schools ranges from 10 to 25 percent. Top business schools receive thousands of applications from individuals with solid work experience, great GPAs, and outstanding GMAT scores. However, schools are looking for more from candidates than 4.0 GPAs, 700 on the GMAT, and work experience at reputable companies. Top business schools are looking for demonstrated leadership potential, ingenuity, the ability to work in teams, and a genuine interest in making a difference in the world.

Recommendations play an extremely important role in the application process. As the Stanford GSB admissions team has stated, "We have found that the most useful recommendations provide detailed descriptions, candid anecdotes, and specific evidence that highlights a candidate's potential for leadership. This kind of information helps us to distinguish the very best candidates from a pool of many well-qualified ones."

Thank you for your time and assistance with this process, and in general, for your support!

> Many recommenders won't understand how competitive it is to get into top business schools. It's important that they understand the vital role that they play in helping you get accepted.

Why business school and why now?

When I think about my future, I can picture myself moving into a role that is broader and that has a greater impact on society than my current operational position. In the short term, I definitely see myself returning to the energy industry. I truly enjoy the challenges, the fast pace, the chance to work closely with bright, dynamic individuals, the exposure to a wide variety of customers and business issues, and the constant personal and professional growth that a career of this nature affords. Given this intent, I believe that I am at a natural point in my career to pursue an MBA. While I feel that I am able to add a considerable amount to my joint Hartman/customer teams, I am anxious to contribute a great deal more. An MBA will give me an even stronger general business foundation and understanding of the "big picture," deeper knowledge of the business functions of particular interest to me, the opportunity to master concepts that are difficult or time consuming to master on the job (finance, accounting, statistics), thorough quantitative and leadership training, and added confidence in my abilities—all of which will make me a stronger professional and person.

> Lauren provides good reasoning for why she's at a point where she wants to make a transition.

In the long-term, I would like to assist companies in coming up with environmentally sustainable business practices that are beneficial to the companies and their constituencies. My background as an environmental engineer gives me some insight into potential steps companies could take, but I need to learn more about the intersection of business and the environment. My current role in operations limits my ability to have a broad impact on the direction of the company or our customers. I believe that the skills and knowledge that I will gain from a MBA program will afford me the career flexibility that I desire.

> Lauren presents interesting long-term goals that will certainly impact society and leverage her background. She has spent time reflecting on the direction in which she would like to go. Lauren also provided her recommenders with a draft of an essay that contained more details on her career goals.

Given my short- and long-term personal and professional goals, I plan to apply to general management programs that will allow me to develop a background in strategy, finance, and international business. I believe these areas of business will provide me with the tools that I need to analyze sustainable development opportunities and to "sell" companies on how these opportunities can fit in to their long-term visions. I strongly believe that the issues addressed by sustainable development are global in nature and I am therefore interested in how I could introduce solutions at an international level.

Which schools?

I am applying to four schools, all of which have strengths in the areas that I want to study, strong reputations and faculties, and academic environments that appeal to me. In deciding which schools I would apply to, I evaluated the top MBA programs based on: academic environment/culture, overall fit with my goals and personality, program reputation, international emphasis, teaching quality/style, program features, and location. Although I am equally enthusiastic about each of the four programs, the schools differ slightly in their areas of recognized expertise. I intend to incorporate program-specific messages into each application and hope that you will reflect those program-specific messages in your recommendations.

> Lauren demonstrates a good understanding of what she's looking for in a school and provides good reasoning for the selection of her target schools.

The four schools I am applying to are:

- ‣ The London Business School.
- ‣ Kellogg School of Management.

‣ Stanford Graduate School of Business.

‣ The Wharton School.

> She made the decision not to apply to a safety school, based on her needs.

Academic environment, culture, and fit with my goals and personality

The schools I've targeted have reputations for having supportive, team-oriented, and family-like cultures. All of the schools emphasize working in teams to enhance learning and developing leadership abilities. I have always enjoyed approaching problems in teams and believe that I am most effective when working within a collaborative culture. The schools I've selected provide the type of environment in which I would flourish.

The collaborative cultures that each of these schools engender supports the introduction of new ideas in the classroom and through extracurricular activities. Although each school has made some strides in terms of supporting the ideas of sustainable development, I would like to further this way of thinking at the school that I attend. I know that each one of these schools would welcome that and the possibility of (establishing a club or volunteer action team) would resonate positively with the admissions committee.

In general, I am seeking a relatively relaxed atmosphere (not overly academic or competitive) recognizing that all of the top schools are rigorous and will require my full, best effort.

Overall program reputation and international emphasis

The four schools selected are all widely regarded for their general academic excellence. Additionally, they are known for their particularly strong general management programs. In one case (London Business School) the international emphasis is obvious; the others offer specific programs or exchange opportunities to promote a global view of the business world for its graduates. Ideally, I would like to obtain an internship in France working on a renewable energy project and perhaps spend a semester abroad at one of the MBA programs in France (such as INSEAD or HEC). Each school on my target list would provide ample opportunity for me to achieve these goals.

Teaching quality and program features

These four schools also receive praise for the overall quality of their professors. Faculty members at my target schools (for both core and elective courses) are not only accomplished teachers, but are also renowned in the academic world for developing theory, authoring enduring textbooks, and advancing management thinking. The schools also have student-to-faculty ratios that allow for a great deal of student/teacher contact. Because professors at my undergraduate school were research-focused and had to deal with large class sizes, outstanding teachers and significant one-on-one time were the exception rather than the rule. I'm looking forward to a more exciting learning experience during business school.

Each school on my list utilizes a variety of teaching methods; class formats vary to best suit the subject and material covered. Whereas students at a Harvard or Darden use the case study method almost 100 percent of the time, students at my target schools benefit from a range of methods—theoretical, discussion, case study, simulation, role play, team project, and independent study. Based on my undergraduate work and work experience, I believe the varied approach better suits my learning style.

Location

I am generally looking at schools in major economic centers that offer plenty of real business opportunities within the local corporate community. These locations are also easy to travel to and from (for me, my friends, and family). Because my (soon-to-be) husband and I will possibly be living apart for two years, this is of significant importance to me.

I have attached a brief write-up on each of the schools with details about their programs, culture, teaching methods, and criteria for admission.

Timeline

The following time line lays out my plans in terms of the application process. Please note the submission due dates for your recommendations.

> The timeline is a great tool for you and your recommenders that helps ensure that all of the required activities get done on time.

Date	Action
December 1 – March 1	GMAT preparation / initial school selection
March 10	Take GMAT exam
March 15 – May 15	(Additional GMAT preparation, if necessary)
May 20	(Retake GMAT, if necessary)
June – July	School research / target school selection
August 1	Request transcripts from previous universities
August – September	Review application and provide recommenders with forms, Game Plan, and draft essays
September 20	Submit Kellogg application online
October 1	Submit Wharton application online
October 4	Submit London Business School application online
October 10	Submit Stanford application online
October – December	Cross fingers for acceptance!

> Starting early is key! Note, that if you have to take the TOEFL, you'll probably want to get started even earlier.

> Make sure to leave adequate time in case you need to retake the GMAT or GRE.

> Sign up for your interviews early, because slots go quickly.

> Set a due date for your recommenders that is earlier than the actual date by which you need them, so that you have a time buffer.

> Try to submit your applications at least one week before the deadline, to ensure that you don't face an 11th-hour crunch in which a Website isn't working or your paper application materials miss the deadline because of a delay in the mail.

Figure 6.1

Summary

My applications will have similar themes interwoven throughout them, but will be tailored for each school's unique set of evaluation criteria. What follows is background information on my work, academic, and personal experience. This background information will be used to support both my general and program-specific messages.

Work experience

My most meaningful work experience has been my four years with Hartman Energy. In describing my work experience to date, I will try to give details showing:

- A wide variety of experience in a relatively short amount of time.
- Performance at a high level (judged by my project managers and peers) in a team environment.
- My determination, intelligence, creativity, and leadership capabilities.

> These are all great attributes to express.

- Recognition (through rapid promotion) and accomplishments.

Community involvement

I truly enjoy giving back to the various communities to which I belong and have done so for as long as I can remember. In my applications, however, I will emphasize my community involvement since college, as business schools tend to focus their attention on post-university experience. When discussing my community involvement, I intend to:

- Demonstrate my interest in getting involved in my community, when and where possible, despite keeping a busy travel/work schedule.
- Highlight the leadership roles I have taken on (because engineers typically lack significant management experience).
- Show that I am the type of applicant who would take full advantage of the business school experience and would seek out ways to get involved in the MBA community.

> Again, great attributes to express. Admissions counselors love applicants who can demonstrate these traits.

Academic history

I have always loved school. Since I was very young, I have been driven (through positive reinforcement and support from my family) to excel academically. I have always worked extremely hard for my grades and because of this effort, am very proud of what I've accomplished. Schools look at an applicant's academic history as her best predictor of future performance. I will emphasize:

- My scholastic strength in a broad array of subjects in order to demonstrate my ability to handle the quantitative rigor of each program, as well as the "softer" subjects.
- My achievements in the broader context of involvement in my undergraduate school (extracurricular involvement, leadership positions, work experience). By doing so, I hope to demonstrate my energy, time management ability, and enthusiasm for getting the most out of every experience.

Personal information

I think the biggest challenge in the application process for most applicants is distinguishing themselves—I know this will be the case for me. Where possible, I will look to provide personal information about myself; as Stanford puts it, "the person behind the grades, test scores, job titles, and leadership positions." Through my applications, I hope to:

‣ Describe the unique set of experiences, interests, and perspectives that I would bring to the business school community.

‣ Share my influences, motivations, passions, values, interests, and aspirations.

‣ Paint a picture of a well-rounded, caring, approachable, motivated person who would contribute to the MBA community.

Appendix

The appendix to the game plan contains detailed information on the previously covered topics. The appendix serves as a reference for both the applicant and recommenders, so that they can easily provide supporting data in essays, recommendations, data sheets, and interviews.

Work Experience

The work experience section allows you to document all of your professional activities, so that you can select the most pertinent experiences for inclusion in your application. You should document your explicit functional or project work in addition to any work-related extracurricular activities in which you're involved. Additionally, try to include positive comments you've received during any of your reviews. These comments can be a great third-party reference that can be included in your essays or recommendations. You should also consider including a section that outlines your strengths and weaknesses. This will give your recommenders a reference point for a question they most certainly will be asked. At the end of the section, you should include a copy of the resume you put together for one of your target schools.

Academic Experience

For many applicants, it will have been several years since they thought about their college experiences. This is the section through which you can relive some of the positive ones. Specifically, you'll want to document your accomplishments and activities inside and outside of the classroom. To the extent possible, you want to project yourself as someone who is always willing to get involved and participate. Showing a history of doing so is a great way to display that trait. You'll also want to bring out any special skills that you developed while you were in school. For example, if you studied a foreign language or simply took a broad range of courses that helped improve your perspective on business issues, then be sure to include that here.

Personal Experience

The personal experience section is your opportunity to express that you're more than a paper-pusher. You should discuss the hobbies and interests in which you're involved outside of the work environment. This could include community service activities, sports, theater, or anything else with which you occupy your time. Knowing the personal side of you is always helpful to your recommenders, who might only know the professional you. Writing down this information will be helpful in preparing for your interviews, as your interviewer will often want to get to know the person behind the resume.

Which Schools?

In this section, you can provide detailed information on your target schools for the purpose of understanding how you will establish fit with each one. There are two types of information that you'll want to include for each target school:

1. Background information about the school, topline statistics, and your strategy for getting in. The majority of the information can be taken directly from Chapter 5.

2. A discussion of why the school is a good fit for you, which will help you nail down your story for each school before you tackle your essays and interviews.

We've included Lauren's approach to the second component as an example.

The London Business School

LBS's international make-up is one of the main reasons why I'm applying to it. In college, I participated in a study abroad program at the London School of Economics and was the only American in my class. The experience, although brief, was truly life-changing. I learned as much from my team members—about the world and about myself—as I did from the class. I am certain that LBS would offer similar learning and growth experiences.

Another appealing feature is the school's (deliberately) small size, and thus, its sense of intimacy. Students give the school high marks for its culture and friendly atmosphere. According to one second-year MBA, LBS isn't "quite as competitive as some of the U.S. schools. You don't have to get a good grade at the expense of someone else." This is exactly the kind of environment that I am looking for!

Finally, because of its global focus, all LBS students must demonstrate competence in at least one language other than English by the time they graduate. While some students might view this requirement as something they need to "get over with," I look at it as a golden opportunity to make significant strides towards my goal of becoming fluent in French.

Kellogg School of Management (Northwestern University)

One of the largest business schools among the Top 30, Kellogg enrolls some 600 students a year in its full-time program. Despite its large size, however, Kellogg is able to create a unique, family-like culture through its team learning philosophy—one of the school's biggest draws and differentiators in my opinion. I have always enjoyed a collaborative approach and have never needed a great deal of competition to motivate myself. For these reasons, I believe Kellogg is a perfect fit for me culturally.

Kellogg has an extremely well-balanced program. Although Kellogg is best-known for its marketing program, it actually offers one of the strongest arrays of functional departments available anywhere. Most Kellogg MBAs major in two or three functional areas and can also opt to specialize in an interdisciplinary major. I would most likely major in strategy and finance and specialize in international business. I would also take advantage of the Global Initiatives in Management (GIM) program. Students in this program create specially designed international independent study courses, and focus on a country of their choice. For each of the geographic areas, students work in groups to create a syllabus, book guest speakers, determine research topics, and identify key issues facing local industries. After coursework is completed during the winter quarter, students travel to the selected country over spring break for a two-week consulting project. Results are then presented to faculty and visiting executives in the spring. I would also take advantage of one of their exchange programs—most likely with HEC in France. Classes at HEC are conducted in both English and French, presenting an ideal opportunity for me to improve my foreign language skills.

Stanford Graduate School of Business

Supporting an entrepreneurial spirit, Stanford's curriculum is very flexible and allows students to select from an array of electives while forming a strong general management foundation. MBA students are not required to major in specific academic disciplines.

Stanford offers a supportive, intimate culture. The business school does not publicly post grades or include overall class rank on academic transcripts. Rather, the collaborative culture frees students to take academic risks and broaden their management and leadership skills. These features are particularly appealing to me. My undergraduate engineering curriculum was extremely grade-focused and, in my opinion, the emphasis only detracted from the learning experience.

Another strength is the school's global management focus. International issues are integrated into the core courses and approximately 25 percent of Stanford electives focus on international topics. Stanford also provides career resources, speakers, student clubs, and conferences to help students connect with global companies.

Many of the global initiatives are provided through the Global Management Program (GMP). The GMP offers an academic certificate in global management for students (like me) who want to focus even more sharply on global issues. To earn the certificate, students complete at least five GSB electives with an international focus. I would definitely take advantage of this option. I would also pursue the Global Management Immersion Experience (GMIX). This program combines a core course in global management, a research project, and a summer internship for students to gain international work experience.

Students can earn up to 16 credits in courses offered outside of the business school. This feature would give me a chance to take advanced French language instruction—something that is nearly impossible to do when working on an out-of-town project.

The Wharton School (University of Pennsylvania)

Wharton is known as a leader and innovator in the business school arena. It receives praise for its emphasis on international initiatives and creative approaches to teaching. Like Stanford, it has a nondisclosure grading policy, which helps to foster a team environment and allows students to concentrate more on their areas of interest.

The first year of the program is divided into four six-week quarters. Students move through their classes as part of a 60-student cohort—a kind of class within a class. Each cluster shares the same team of core professors who work together to integrate the coursework and coordinate student workload. As a member of a cohort, I would be in an intimate environment, without giving up access to resources that larger schools have.

Wharton offers a number of optional programs for its students. One option for first year students that looks particularly appealing to me is the Global Immersion Program (GIP). This program involves six weeks of introductory lectures on a country or region critical to the world economy, with a four-week overseas experience following final exams in which students meet corporate and government officials, tour local businesses, and attend cultural events. Students also submit a written assignment in the Fall. Another enhancement program that fits well with my overall career goals is the Multinational Marketing and Management Program. This program partners Wharton with business schools in Israel, Canada, and other locations to form multi-school MBA teams that design marketing strategies for companies hoping to enter the North American market. Finally, students can opt to spend a full semester abroad in one of more than 15 exchange programs with non-U.S. business schools. I am strongly considering a semester at the HEC School of Management in France.

Summary

As you can see, the game plan is a powerful tool that allows you to record and refine your story prior to attacking the applications. This type of preparation will be of great benefit to you and your recommenders as the application process drags on. In fact, you should sit down with your recommenders, and step through the plan and perhaps an essay or two that further describes your career goals. This will give them a broader understanding of the plan's purpose and ensure that they use it effectively.

Yes, assembling a game plan is time-consuming, but an admittance letter is well worth the additional hours. It's important, therefore, that you not only assemble a dynamic game plan, but that you also execute it.

10 Truths of the MBA Application Process

The one thing that every applicant comes away from the process with is stories. From the applicant whose computer crashed, wiping out all of his freshly written essays, to the applicant who was asked out by her interviewer, we all come away with something. Although the unique experiences are probably more interesting, the common ones are probably more useful to you in your application preparation. With that in mind, here are 10 experiences that will most probably find their way into your storybook.

1. **Your first interview will be your worst.** Even Michael Jordan looked a little rusty when he first came out of retirement, so you shouldn't expect to be in top-notch condition after not interviewing for several years. This isn't to say that you'll bomb your first interview, but generally, applicants need to work through the first one before feeling entirely comfortable with the process again. If you follow the interview advice provided in Chapter 4, then you should be fine, but if possible, set up your first interview with your safety school.

2. **Your last application will be your best.** Many applicants start off working on the application to the school in which they are most interested. More often than not, this is a bad move. By the time you move on to your third or fourth

application, you will be in prime application-writing mode. You will have a bunch of base essays from which to start and have already spent tremendous amounts of time revising them. This means that the last application will benefit from all of the knowledge you've gained by working through the first few. If time is not an issue, consider working on your highest priority-application last. Just be aware that fatigue may set in by the time you're on your last application. Even if you've become sick of the whole process, resist the temptation to recycle an old essay that doesn't quite fit with the application at hand.

3. **When it comes to essays, you shouldn't act on every single bit of advice that you receive.** We recommend that you always get one or two talented writers to review your essays, simply to have another set of eyes to catch mistakes and to help with clarity of communication. But be careful: Some well-meaning friends or "experts" may make suggestions that could alter your essays to the point where they no longer have your voice or say what you want them to say. At the end of the day, they're your essays, and they should reflect your own voice and ideas.

4. **Visiting a school is always a good idea.** Would you buy a car that you couldn't see? Probably not, so you should also strongly consider visiting your target business schools. You will be surprised what you pick up, and doing so will help you score big points with the admissions committee. What seems to be a fairly routine gesture will go a long way toward demonstrating your enthusiasm for your target schools.

5. **You will lose perspective and be tempted to make irrational decisions.** We know someone who decided to try to save a couple of bucks by sending in her recommendations via the regular mail only a few days before the deadline. As you might have guessed, her recommendations never arrived, and she had to apply to that school again in the next round. (Business schools have heard every excuse before; there's no story that can overcome a lost or late application.) If you continue to view business school as a long-term investment, saving a couple bucks while taking on significant risk becomes an obviously bad tradeoff.

6. **One of your recommenders will not meet the date with which you provide him.** We're busy people and so are our recommenders. Chances are, they'll accept your request to write a recommendation and then put it aside for a while. It's up to you to ask them early, follow up often, and maybe even more importantly, set a due date that is far in advance of the application deadline.

7. **Your friends and family will get sick of hearing about the process.** Applying to business school can be a time-consuming process that takes over your life for a whole year. From taking the GMAT, to researching schools, to writing essays, to waiting for responses, the process will seem endless at times. And you will, of course, share your experiences with your friends and family. Unfortunately, they won't be able to understand the trials and tribulations associated with the process unless they've been through it themselves. So, be prepared for their glassy eyes and hollow "uh huh's" as the months drag on.

8. **You will spend more money on the process than you would ever have imagined.** GMAT study guides, exams, and classes; essay consultants; $200 application fees; visits to schools; book on application strategy—none of these come for free (although we think the book on application strategy provides a great ROI!). As you get closer to receiving responses from your target schools, you'll notice the expenses piling up. Be prepared to make the necessary investment, because you won't want to go through it again.

9. **During the process you will meet other applicants who intimidate you with their credentials.** This is how it will happen: You will attend an information session for one of your target schools, maybe at a local hotel. While waiting for the session to start, you'll strike up a conversation with the person sitting next to you. He'll turn out to have gone to an Ivy League school, will have put in time with the Peace Corps or Teach for America, and will be shooting up the ranks at some bank or consulting firm that you've definitely heard of. (Don't sweat it. If he knew how prepared you are in this process, he'd probably be intimidated by *you*.)

10. **Receiving an admittance letter from your dream school will make it all worthwhile.** There are few more satisfying, fulfilling, and overall happy moments than receiving word that you've been admitted to your choice business school. Cartwheels, fist pumps, back flips—it'll all come out. Keep that in mind as your trudging through some of the more mundane aspects of the process!

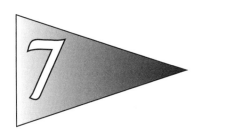

Game Over

What Happens Once You Submit Your Application?

As any good business manager would, you should design your product (your application) with your customer (the admissions officer) in mind. To that end, it helps for you to know what will happen to your application once the admissions committee receives it. No two schools are the exact same in how they process admissions applications, but what follows is a general example that will give you an idea of what a "typical" business school application goes through.

Once your application is received, it is usually held until all of your other materials are received (if they are sent separately), including recommendations or transcripts. Once all of these materials are received and the application is marked as ready for review, a reader will take it in a batch of applications, which can be as few as several applications and as many as dozens. At many business schools, the first reader will be a current MBA student; at other schools only admissions personnel review applications. The first reader will go through your entire application, including a transcript of your interview if you have already had one. The reader will look for evidence of the traits that the school seeks in every applicant (starting with the core dimensions that we outlined in Chapter 2) and will grade you on each of these traits. Based on how your application stacks up, it will receive a simple, high-level grade (such as Yes, Maybe, or No) or a numeric score, in the case of some schools. These grades may seem somewhat arbitrary, but for every application a reader fills out an extensive form to back up his decision, citing as many examples as possible or pointing out areas that call for further investigation.

Think about what this reader is faced with: a 2-feet-tall stack of applications that mostly look the same, a tight deadline, and the burden of having to decide whether each applicant should be admitted. You can help your cause by putting yourself in the reader's shoes and thinking about how you can make his life easier:

- ▷ **Keep it short.** We cannot emphasize enough how important it is to respect the word limits in essays and data sheets. You are not the most important applicant, nor the one with the most interesting experiences. So make life easy by keeping things concise.

- ▷ **Make it interesting.** Don't use gimmicks, but do remember that your application will be one of hundreds that your reader will see. An appropriately humorous paragraph or even whole essay will be appreciated, and will almost certainly be remembered.

▷ **Be organized.** If you don't follow instructions, don't expect a stressed application reader to contact you for missing information. Give yourself extra time to make sure that your application is totally complete.

▷ **Be clear about what you have to offer.** Present a focused message, one that your reader will easily understand. Stick only to examples and stories that highlight your core messages.

At most schools a second reader—who also may be a student but is often an admissions officer—will read your application and grade it based on the same exact criteria. The second reader almost never sees what decision the first reader has made on your application, so you can be sure that you will get a fair shake. The second reader will come to a decision and also back up her findings with an in-depth report.

Usually, a third decision-maker then comes into play, someone who is a little more senior in the process. It may be the admissions director, or it may be an associate director. If the first two readers agree that you are a Yes or a No, then your fate is quickly sealed, for better or for worse. If they disagree, then the third person will usually read the application herself and come to a final decision. There is sometimes spirited debate about a single application, but remember that everyone involved is trying to get through a huge stack of applications as efficiently as possible. If the third reader still can't decide, or the consensus seems to be "Yes, but..." then often that is when you will placed on the waitlist.

Contrary to what it often seems, application readers and interviewers are not just looking for reasons to reject you. More than anything, they're looking to find out who you are and how well you embody each of the traits that they look for in an applicant. This sounds simple enough, but it can be especially challenging for a reader when faced with dozens of applications that all look the same. To this end, stay focused on your core messages of who you are and what you can offer to the program. This will make your application readers' jobs much easier, and will greatly improve your chances of admission.

The 5 Response Types

Years ago, you could infer a business school's response to your application based on the size of the letter. The traditional belief held that if you received a thick letter in a manila folder then you were in, and if you received a thin letter in a business envelope then you were out. Now, business schools are much more responsive and generally contact applicants via phone, e-mail, or secure Web page before the letter is even sent. Although the communication vehicle has changed, what hasn't changed is the type of responses you can expect to receive.

There are five types of responses that you could receive:

▷ Direct admission.

▷ Admission with requirements.

▷ Admission with postponement.

▷ Waitlist.

▷ Denial.

Direct Admission

Hopefully, at least one of your target schools will fall into this category. If this is the case, then pat yourself on the back and celebrate, because you've accomplished what many applicants failed to do. After all, acceptance rates at most top schools are in the 7-percent to 20-percent range. But of course, no sooner than you receive your good news will you have to face a whole new crop of deadlines and decisions. We'll tackle some of the most common ones in the pages that follow.

Deciding Which School to Attend

This is one of the more pleasant decisions that you will ever have to make. Even though you may dread having to actually make the decision, don't forget that this is a dilemma that few others have the luxury of facing.

If you find yourself torn between two or more schools, take an inventory of what mattered most to you when you initially applied. How do you feel about these criteria now? Visit the schools (we highly recommend attending each school's on-campus events for admitted students) and get a feel for your potential future classmates. After all, these are the people with whom you may spend the next two years. Sit in on a class (even if you already did so months ago) and ask yourself if you could see yourself participating in the discussion. Yes, this sounds subjective, but your experience in business school will largely depend on how well you fit the culture, and vice versa.

Of course, there are more tangible attributes to consider as well, such as how many grads each school places in your desired career path, its location, and how much money it offers you in scholarships or grants. First of all, don't become too obsessed with rankings. If two schools are close to one another in rank, then this is a moot question. Don't fool yourself into thinking that two or three notches in a magazine's rankings mean a thing in the real world. However, if you are deciding between a top-five school and a top-30 school, for example, we recommend that you place as little emphasis on scholarship dollars as possible. Even if the lower-ranked school offers you a free ride, the money shouldn't be your main reason for enrolling there. Yes, mountains of debt can be scary, but you really need to think long-term and ask yourself which school will help you the most down the road. Greater career opportunities in the future are surely worth more than a few thousand dollars today. The same goes for other factors, such as geography. Remember that business school is just two years, but the benefits that you take away will be with you for the rest of your life. So, don't sell yourself short.

That's not to say that you should always enroll in the higher-ranked school over the lower-ranked one. Far too many applicants make their decision solely on the basis of rankings, and they really aren't being true to themselves. There may very well be a legitimate reason why the top-30 school appeals to you more than the top-five school does, including strength in certain academic fields or unique career opportunities. If that's the case, don't let anyone lead you to believe that you're making the wrong choice. Go where your heart tells you to go. We simply urge that you make your decision for rational reasons, not for the short-term convenience of having less debt or living in a sunnier climate for two years.

Remember: You won't ruin your life by making the wrong decision! The business school you attend won't determine your lot in life. The fact that you were able to gain admission to more than one of these schools is a good indicator that you'll be successful. Where you are 20 years from now will depend much more on your ambition and skills than on whether you choose to attend the number-seven-ranked or number-10-ranked business school right now. Go where you think you will get the most out of the MBA experience, and the rest will take care of itself.

The Deferment Question

varies by school, but gaurranteed admission to uni, but wait a year later to start (only if app succ.)

All schools discourage admitted students from deferring their enrollment, and many explicitly state in their application materials that they don't allow deferment *for any reason*. Still, even those business schools who purport that they don't al-low deferment will generally consider it under certain circumstances. And there are some reasons why you may want to delay the start of your business school experience. The most common reasons for an applicant wanting to defer for a year usually have to do with a professional opportunity or a change in personal circumstances.

If your company offers you a big promotion or a once-in-a-lifetime opportunity to take on a new project, then you may want to think about pushing off business school for a year. The biggest question to consider is whether it's an opportunity that will come along again anytime in the near future. If you believe that your new role would allow you to gain rare new skills and experiences that will help you down the road, then seriously consider it. If, however, your company is just trying to keep you around for another year by offering you more money or a better title, don't be so quick to defer your enrollment. Yes, the money can look good, but maintain a perspective that extends 20 years into the future. Earning those extra bucks today pales in comparison to the opportunity cost of waiting another year to accelerate your career.

Some people face personal reasons for wanting to defer their enrollment, such as the birth of a child or an illness in the family. If you are faced with a situation that you believe will make it hard to devote 100 percent of your energy to your MBA, then consider deferring. Remember, though, that it's easy to think of *any* time as a bad time to start business school (something always seems to come up). So, only defer if you are sure that your personal circumstances will look signifi-cantly different in a year.

If you have decided that you want to defer, and your school will consider let-ting you do so, then you will have to build a strong case for why it makes sense to wait a year. When it comes to professional reasons, an admissions committee will ask questions along the lines of what we raised previously: What is it about this new opportunity that will make you that much better able to contribute to your class a year from now? Be prepared to argue your case using a framework similar to what you employed in your original application. If you can craft a convincing story that is consistent with your overall application theme, you will stand a chance of gaining a deferment. Remember, though, that a deferment is never guaranteed.

Schools tend to be a little more willing to listen to personal reasons for deferment because they know that business school will consume your life once you arrive. Honestly let the school know your situation and explain why you are afraid that it may interfere with your business school experience. Schools will usually be very understanding, and will work with you to find a solution. They may not offer you a deferment, but they may at least be able to help in other ways, such as suggesting a transfer to a part-time program, or connecting you with people or resources that can make your situation a little easier.

In any case, be prepared to do some convincing, both via letter and over the phone. Even though many schools tend to be a little more lenient than they let on, many applicants who ask for deferments are not granted them. The school may test your commitment by asking that your reapply the following year with a wink and a nod, indicating that if next year's app is as solid as this year's, you can expect to be admitted. If not, you will definitely be expected to submit your initial tuition deposit (usually on the order of $2,000 to $5,000) now in order to hold your spot in next year's class. There's no clearer signal that you really do intend to matriculate than handing over a signed check. Keep in mind that this deposit is non-refundable, though, so be prepared to kiss it goodbye if you decide next year that business school isn't in your plans after all.

Financial Aid

Once you're admitted and you know which school you will be attending, then you need to worry about how you're going to pay for the whole affair. Most schools will send financial aid information along with your admittance letter, or will send it shortly after admitting you. You will need to submit information about your financial status, both to the school and to the federal government. The latter will receive the information that you enter into your Free Application for Federal Student Aid, or FAFSA (accessible online at *www.fafsa.ed.gov*). Get familiar with these forms as quickly as possible, especially because some schools call for your old tax returns dating back as many as three years. If your jaw just hit the floor when you read that last sentence, don't worry. You can contact the IRS to get these copies (look for IRS Form 4506).

You should submit your financial aid application as early as possible, because most schools work with a fixed amount of money to dole out to incoming students. Just as applying earlier in the admissions process makes things easier because there are more seats to be had in the class, applying earlier for financial aid gives you a better chance of getting more aid. Although being the first one to apply won't necessarily get you a significant amount more, you definitely don't want to be among the last to apply, because the money may already be spoken for by then. In fact, if you're reasonably confident that you will receive admission to at least one of your target schools, then you should consider actually filling out your FASFA forms even before you get your responses. Also, you should still apply if you feel like your situation will make you ineligible for grants given by your business school. Many applicants across all types of situations get a small amount of aid. You'd be crazy to not at least try for this free money, even if the odds seem to be against you.

After you have filled out the requisite forms, your school will usually get back to you quickly enough to ensure that you have enough time to arrange for other sources of aid, if needed. Some schools offer (merit-based aid, some offer need-based aid, and some offer both.) Most of this aid will be in the form of grants (money that you don't have to pay back). Whatever the case is for your school, the amount that the school offers is rarely negotiable. Some students have had success negotiating what aid they get, but need-based aid is hard to negotiate (because it tends to go by a formula that takes your assets into consideration), and a majority of merit-based aid decisions will likely have already been made by the time you contact the school. It's worth a shot, but don't expect to get very far in negotiating with the financial aid office.

Assuming that you will need an external source of loans (most students do), there are a few programs in place that make it relatively easy to get money for your education. Your financial situation may not qualify you for grants from the school, though you may be eligible for Stafford loans from the federal government. These come in two types: subsidized and unsubsidized. Although you won't have to start paying off either type of Stafford loan while you're in school, subsidized loans are preferable, because interest doesn't accrue until you graduate. Naturally, subsidized loans are harder to qualify for. How much you're eligible to receive and the type of Stafford loan you can get depends on your financial situation, as dictated by your FAFSA results.

Who actually services your Stafford loan (that is, who cuts the check) can be anyone from your school to a third-party bank such as Sallie Mae (SLM Corporation). Shopping around and consolidating your Stafford loans can help you save significantly on fees and interest rates. In recent years, intermediaries such as Graduate Leverage have been established to attempt to achieve lower rates through collective bargaining. These intermediaries represent thousands of students simultaneously and thereby achieve favorable incentives and borrower policies. Don't worry about settling on a third-party bank or intermediary imme-diately, though, because this is a decision that can be revisited closer to the end of your time at business school when your loans are actually about to be serviced.

Consolidation of federal loans can often be advantageous, because it offers you the opportunity to lock in a low interest rate over a long period of time (30 years in many cases). This can result in a very reasonable payment plan that isn't subject to the vagaries of interest rate hikes.

You also might need to get private loan options. Many schools partner with a major bank such as Citigroup to offer preferred student rates on loans. They are usually fairly competitive, although with some shopping around you can often find a better deal on your own. These loans are usually structured so that you don't start paying them back until you graduate. For American students, these loans tend to be very easy to qualify for, but international students generally have to provide detailed, verifiable proof of assets in order to qualify.

Private loans are often linked to the prime rate. The prime interest rate represents the interest rate charged by banks to their most creditworthy customers and is almost always the same among major banks. You can anticipate that the payment for your private loans will actually fluctuate with the prime rate. Consolidation of private loans is also an option and may include the possibility of locking in an interest rate. Unlike federal loan consolidation, however, your lock-in rate is likely to be higher than the prevailing prime rate to ensure that the private loan issuer is protected against future interest rate hikes.

The bottom line is that business school is expensive, but practically no one has to turn down the chance to attend because the costs are too great. Be prepared to fill out lots of forms, patiently research loan options, and take on debt. Just remember: This is a long-term investment!

Scholarships, Fellowships, and Teaching Assistantships

Outside of taking on loans and receiving a business school grant, graduate business students have it pretty tough in terms of finding sources of income for tuition purposes. The prevailing belief is that we're all going to be rich someday, and therefore aren't in dire need of financial assistance. Although scholarships aren't plentiful for aspiring MBAs, there are definitely some opportunities that exist. Rather than searching for one-off scholarships, check out *www.fastweb.com*. The FastWeb Website will ask you a number of questions in regard to your general background, demographics, and area of study. After completing the detailed questions, you will receive a report that cites the scholarships for which you can apply. Each scholarship has different application requirements and time lines, so you can select those scholarships that suit you best. FastWeb will also continuously send you updates as the year progresses and new scholarships become available.

In addition to these "external" scholarships, there sometimes are additional funding opportunities internal to MBA programs to which you may not have access until you actually attend a school. Some of these scholarship opportunities are part of the application process, and you have to specifically write an essay and apply for them (which we recommend!), but many business schools will offer their students the opportunity to apply for additional scholarships, fellowships, or teaching assistantships after they start classes. Keep these additional sources in mind, and make sure to ask your school about them, so that you can take advantage later down the line.

Admission With Requirements

You may find that you're offered a conditional admission to your target school. Don't worry: This is not an insult. In fact, it speaks pretty favorably of you if the school was willing to admit you despite an obvious weakness. Look at it as an opportunity to get a head start on your MBA experience, or at least to brush up on your weaker subjects.

Most frequently, a school will require you to successfully complete a pre-MBA course in a quantitative subject such as statistics or a business-related course such as accounting. Some schools offer these programs before your first semester begins, but most will ask that you complete this coursework at a local accredited college. Your business school will usually be very willing to work with you to help make this happen.

There are two things to be aware of, though. First, because you don't know what schedule your local college operates on, start researching your options as soon as possible to avoid missing an enrollment deadline. The sooner you can take a class to pass your requirement, the better. Second, you should know that you will have to take these courses on your own dime. So, add these costs into your budget as you plan for business school.

Admission With Postponement

This decision usually applies to undergraduates and those who have very little business experience. Though it is still somewhat rare, we have seen this type of admission become much more common in recent years as top business schools increasingly compete with one another (and with other types of graduate programs) for the cream of the crop among college students and recent graduates. Whereas some MBA programs have introduced specialized programs such as the HBS 2+2 Program and Yale's Silver Scholars, others will simply admit a young applicant on the condition that he complete a couple of years of full-time work experience before enrolling.

Your school may tell you that it likes what it sees in your application, but that it wants you to work for a year or two more before you enroll. Even though this may be frustrating, it's still much better than a rejection, so take heart. Also know that if the school feels strongly enough about your application to offer you this rare opportunity, then they probably have a point. In the cases with which we're familiar, the applicants have said that the extra work experience helped them get more out of their business school experience.

Waitlist

Finding out that you've been placed on the waitlist is a melancholy moment. After all of your efforts and patience, you've essentially been asked to wait some more. The immediate question that comes to an applicant's mind at this point is: *What are my chances of getting off the waitlist and into the school?* Generally, your chances of getting off a school's waitlist are directly related to that school's yield percentage. If, for example, a school has a 90 percent yield, your chances of getting off the waitlist are probably pretty slim. Other factors that will play a role in determining your chances of winning a spot include the total number of applicants accepted and the size of the business school class, as well as the number of applicants who were placed on the waitlist. Although it's nice to know the initial factors that will determine your chances, these numbers differ greatly from school to school and year to year. Regardless of what the chances are, there are a number of steps you can take to greatly increase your chances of turning a waitlist into an admission.

The first step you should take is to understand your target school's policy on the waitlist. Many schools will provide you with a point of contact within the admissions office who will hopefully be your main advocate in helping you gain admissions. If you haven't already guessed, it's important to get this person to like you, so use tact in your communications. The second step you should take is to review all of your application materials in order to evaluate *why* you weren't directly admitted. The fact that you've been placed on the waitlist means that the admissions office *could* see you attending the school, but they didn't quite see enough to take you over the hundreds of other applicants. At least not yet.

Run down this list of questions when evaluating what your weaknesses might be:

- ▶ Are my career goals defined effectively?
- ▶ What problems will I solve through achieving my career goals?
- ▶ Who will I affect through achieving my career goals?
- ▶ Is it clear how attending business school will help me achieve my career goals?
- ▶ In what ways do I emphasize fit with the business school in my application?
- ▶ How do I demonstrate leadership, innovation, maturity, and teamwork abilities?
- ▶ Did I effectively demonstrate my ability to perform well academically through my GMAT, GPA, transcript, and professional experience?
- ▶ How does my application differentiate me from others with a similar profile?
- ▶ Did I communicate passion for the MBA program's mission?
- ▶ Did I do enough in terms of visiting the school, and speaking with current students and alumni?

After running through the list, if you're still not sure what your weakness is, consider having a friend, student, or alum read through your application, asking the same questions. (This is where having an experienced set of eyes review your application can be especially helpful.) Sometimes having an outside perspective can help you recognize weaknesses of which you were previously unaware. For example, you might think your career goals are crystal clear, whereas others who read your application are confused about what you're trying to communicate. Naturally, this sort of analysis should be done even before you submit your application, but it can be extremely helpful in crafting your messages when trying to get off the waitlist.

Once you've identified the areas that you would like to strengthen in the eyes of the of the admissions committee, you should select the methods you would like to utilize in your approach. Some of the methods that successful applicants have utilized include:

▷ **Follow-up calls to an admissions officer.** Having semi-frequent conversations with your contact in the admissions committee is a great way to keep your name at the top of his mind. By following up and asking if there are any further developments, you will be able convey your strong interest in gaining admittance. Admissions officers want to make sure that anyone who is admitted from the waitlist will accept, so in these conversations, you can underscore the fact that officer's school is your top choice. Of course, there is a fine line here between sounding interested and becoming annoying. Daily calls or badgering the admissions officer is great way to ensure that you never get off the waitlist. Sometimes the officer will give you guidance in terms of when you should check back in, but in lieu of that guidance we suggest a call every three weeks.

▷ **An additional recommendation.** Sending an additional recommendation can be a great way to emphasize character strengths that the target school values. Coming from a third party, it contains all of the benefits that your initial recommendations contained. Having reviewed your application for potential weaknesses, you can work with the additional recommender in focusing on those perceived weak areas. If, for example, you think that the admissions committee might question your quantitative abilities, your recommender could discuss a rigorous analytical analysis that you recently completed. Ideally, this recommender is an alum of the school. Because it's a more targeted recommendation than the originals, it is not a necessity that the recommender know you as well. What you're shooting for is a recommendation that persuades the admissions committee that you have the requisite abilities and that you would be a great addition to the culture. Certainly an alum can speak most effectively to the second objective. Of course, if you don't have access to an alum, a targeted recommendation from someone who can write convincingly about your qualifications is adequate. Finally, if you know someone with a lot of clout at the school (for example, a significant donor), now is the time to call in a favor. Even if admissions officers downplay the benefit of this type of activity, having an influential alum or donor pull strings for you is never a bad thing.

▷ **A business course or an improved GMAT score.** Depending on when you hear back from your target school, this method may or may not be option. Given time, however, you might want to consider taking a business course or retaking the GMAT if you get the sense that the school has some reservations about your academic ability. In some cases, a school will actually allude to the fact that you will need to display more academic prowess in order to get off the waitlist. (We've known applicants who have been explicitly told by an admissions officer: "I would love to see you get your GMAT 40 or 50 points higher." There's no clearer signal of how to get admitted from the waitlist!) If you go down either or both paths and perform well, this is a great way to push yourself over the top.

▷ **Dialogue with a faculty member.** This method has the least predictable results and therefore is somewhat risky. The goal is to find a faculty member with whom you have similar interests and engage her in regard to those interests. Faculty members tend to like to discuss the topics that they've dedicated their lives to, so they are often open to discussing them. Your hope is that as a result of these brief conversations, the faculty member will enjoy the dialogue enough to approach the admission committee and request that you be admitted. Of course, admissions committees take faculty input very seriously, so if you can get a professor to speak up on your behalf, then you're in good shape. The trick is getting that far. Just as contacting the admissions committee does, contacting a faculty member holds the possibility that you will annoy her. In fact, there is a greater possibility of this result because the faculty member isn't expecting you to contact her. As such, you should proceed cautiously when selecting this method. For one thing, don't go after the world-renowned faculty member. Chances are that Harvard's Michael Porter isn't going to freely swap e-mails with you. Rather, go after a young faculty member who appears open to being engaged in such a manner. Students can help point you to the professors who fall into that category. Also, make sure you know what you're talking about. The point is to find someone with whom you truly share interests, so it's important that you can speak intelligently about those common interests. Indiscriminately contacting faculty members and blabbering about how you need to get off the waitlist is a great way to get off that list—and on to the rejection list.

▷ **A follow-up letter.** The follow-up letter is a great method to use in that it is the least risky and the method over which you have the most control. As a result, a well-written letter can be one of the most effective methods to utilize in getting off the waitlist. Follow-up letters generally provide the admissions committee with information about your activities since you've applied. In some cases, you might not find out that you've been placed on the waitlist until more than three months after you sent in your application. That means there are plenty of new experiences to discuss that would improve your candidacy in the eyes of the admissions committee. Additionally, the follow-up letter is a great method to use to pin-point the weaknesses that you uncovered in your application evaluation. Finally, the follow-up letter can highlight your fit with the MBA program's culture and your passion for the school's mission.

What follows is an example of a follow-up letter written by a successful applicant who, after evaluating his application, decided to communicate several messages that he felt would resonate positively with and admissions. The letter is written to the applicant's contact in the admissions committee. Although the applicant is very strong in terms of credentials, he failed to adequately highlight his own strengths in his application. In this follow-up letter, he focuses on demonstrating his abilities, discussing his career goals, and establishing fit with the target school. This was a very effective combination and won the applicant a spot in the incoming class.

Sean's Follow-Up Letter

The purpose of this letter is to further support my candidacy for admission to Top Business School (TBS). In short, attending TBS would be the perfect "next step" as I progress toward my long-term goals. Because fit with any institution is a two-way street, I will focus my comments on my professional progress, business model development, global perspective, community service involvement, and natural affinity with the TBS curriculum. These are all activities and attributes that would allow me to become a dynamic member of the TBS student community and eventually a leading member of the TBS alumni community.

> Nice introduction that lets the admissions officer know exactly what to expect from this communication.

Professional progress

Since submitting my application to TBS, I have played key roles on two additional assignments that have strengthened my professional background. These roles have also provided me with additional experiences that I would bring into the TBS classroom.

As highlighted in my application, I am interested in increasing my knowledge of finance and marketing so that I can develop business cases for technological innovations. The roles that I've played on these assignments have helped start me in that direction.

I recently completed a project involving an IT value assessment of a large pharmaceutical company. I played an integral part in determining the economic value added (EVA) of the corporation's IT expenditures. In order to determine how to better manage IT costs and enhance value to end-customers, I instituted a process that allowed the team to analyze IT cost drivers and distinguish between non-core and core IT functions. After careful review of the client's current technical solution evaluation processes, I developed a standard technical solution implementation methodology tailored to the demands and requirements of the company. To further enable the client to effectively manage IT expenses while maintaining market share, I created an IT competitive positioning strategy.

> Sean does a nice job of putting his additional professional experiences into perspective in terms of his career goals rather than simply listing what he's done since submitting his application.

Currently, I am working with a core team of employees who recently formed SimTech's pharmaceutical group. In the last few months, my group has released Pharmtek. Pharmtek is a pharmaceutical industry-specific information technology solution package that is expected to experience rapid market growth over the next five years. To maximize our relationships with potential customers who might be interested in the Pharmtek solution, my team is focused on generating sales, recruiting and training skilled resources, developing external marketing campaigns, and generating support materials for sales teams. One of my primary tasks on this project has been to conduct research on major pharmaceutical industry trends. My research has focused on Customer Relationship Management (CRM), supply chain management, and the financing of research and development. Gaining a deeper knowledge of the activities of each functional area has given me a better understanding of our customers' strategic directions and the way in which technology can enable those directions. An added benefit, from a long-term perspective, has been that I have gained further insight into how I can activate a business model in the pharmaceutical industry.

Business model development

In my application to TBS, I stated my long-term ambition is to develop a global electronic exchange through which a select group of pharmaceutical and biotechnology companies can dynamically exchange research techniques and knowledge of various compounds. Through extensive research and a better understanding of the pharmaceutical industry, I have altered my concept to focus on purchasing trends of hospitals. My objective is to create a national exchange that allows hospitals to consolidate their purchasing power, reducing healthcare costs for hospitals and for patients.

> Sean mentioned that he felt one of the weaknesses of his application was confusion around his career goals. Certainly this section helps the admissions officer understand the direction in which he's going. Sean actually followed up this letter by submitting an initial draft of his business plan to TBS.

Over the past six months, I have spent numerous hours developing a business plan that details the intricacies of my target market, business operations, and financials. The plan's pro forma financial statements indicate that there is a significant opportunity for such offerings both in the United States and in Europe. In the near term, I would like to improve my understanding of finance and marketing, while refining my business model. I also intend to submit my plan to a variety of local investment capital programs, such as the TBS Venture Fund and other lending institutions for financing.

Global perspective

The globalization trend continues to integrate information flow across nations. Having an understanding of globalization is therefore vital to the success of business leaders. A strong global perspective is an attribute that I have been able to impart in both my professional and personal endeavors. On a professional level, a global perspective has allowed me to provide insight in SimTech's analyses of clients who have outsourced operations to East Asian nations. Additionally, being bilingual and maintaining a strong network in Taiwan has been essential to my interactions with our global customers.

Community service involvement

One important component of my personal interests that I was not able to fully convey in my application is my involvement in community service activities. Upon graduating from Adams University, I decided to participate in the Big Brothers Big Sisters (BBBS) program, which pairs adults with at-risk children from single-parent households. In January of 2008, I was matched with twins. As a Big Brother, it is impossible to count the number of ways that I had an impact on my Littles' lives. During the course of our relationship, I have tried to instill the value of education and the desire to achieve a college degree. In addition to the impact that I have had on the boys, they have taught me not to always take myself so seriously. I would say that it has been a mutually beneficial relationship.

The desire to create opportunities for others led me to establish a scholarship program in February 2008 at my alma mater. The scholarship is awarded each year to two entering freshmen who graduate from an inner city high school. The scholarship is given based on academic performance, community involvement, and an essay.

Most recently, I participated in School to Work Day, an annual SimTech team event in which we host local high school students. The day focused on connecting the academic world with the business world. Students were exposed to three different modules: resume building, public speaking, and a business case. As the lead for the public speaking module, I organized the material to be presented and coordinated the session. Each student had the opportunity to practice his or her public speaking skills and learn useful speaking tips that would be useful during presentations under myriad conditions.

Involvement with community outreach will continue to play a large role in my activities. I intend to establish foundations in both the United States and Taiwan that will assist underprivileged children in gaining access to educational opportunities that would otherwise be out of reach.

> Sean made a big mistake in his application by not referencing any of his community service activities even though he's quite active. Certainly this section demonstrates to the admissions committee that he's involved with the community.

Natural affinity with TBS

As stated in my application, I believe that I would learn a great deal from TBS's cross-functional approach and "hands-on" style of teaching. The curriculum is very strong in the areas of finance, marketing, and international business. I have only become more convinced that TBS is the best place for me to pursue an MBA through discussions with current students and alumni, additional visits to campus, and further research on the curriculum and faculty. Moreover, my academic focus in computer science, combined with my professional experiences in high tech, have given me a solid background from which my TBS classmates would benefit and on which I would continue to build. Finally, the team atmosphere that TBS cultivates is inviting, as it reflects the emphasis on teamwork that is inherent within SimTech.

> Sean is tactful in the way that he implicitly says that he'd accept an offer from TBS if it was given.

Upon graduating from TBS, I would like to spend a few years further honing my finance and marketing skills by getting on the front lines pitching the added value of technological innovation, all while continuing the development and refinement of my business plan. I am certain that TBS is the best institution for me in terms of preparation for such roles.

Below I have listed additional specific TBS resources from which I could benefit.

Faculty with similar professional interests:

- Professor Ivy E. Lester—Professor of Finance.
- Professor Davíd Aguliar—Professor of Technological Innovation and Entrepreneurship.
- Professor Anupam Kumar—Professor of High Technology Marketing.

Classes of interest:

- Marketing Management.
- Marketing Technology.
- Financing Your Start-up.
- Selling Technical Innovation.
- Strategic Marketing Planning.
- Preparing Your Business Plan.
- Entrepreneurial Management.
- International Marketing Management.
- Sources of Venture Capital and Private Equity.
- Principles of Corporate Finance.

Activities of interest:

- Asia Business Conference.
- Global Projects Club.
- Entrepreneurship Club.
- Entrepreneurship and Venture Capital Club.

> Simply listing a school's resources isn't all that impressive, but after gaining an understanding of Sean's background and goals, having these lists helps show how TBS will help Sean achieve his career goals.

I am pleased to have been placed on the waitlist and can

assure you that if I am admitted to TBS, my unique background and strong spirit in the areas of culture, professional knowledge, academics, and community involvement will supplement the TBS environment and experience. I look forward to joining you in August.

Sincerely,

Sean

. . . .

The secret to coming up with a successful strategy for getting off the waitlist is to put together some combination of the five methods that addresses the weaknesses of your application. In Sean's case he contacted the admissions committee from time to time, submitted an additional recommendation from an alum, and of course sent the follow-up letter that you just read. Clearly, getting off the waitlist is no easy task, and much of what determines success or failure is out of your control. However, if you are committed to the process and are willing to put together a targeted strategy, you will be able to greatly increase your chances of success, just as in the initial application process.

Denial

It feels just like a punch in the stomach. "The Admissions Committee has thoroughly evaluated your application and regretfully cannot offer you a spot in the incoming class." Suddenly you don't want to face any of your friends, family members, or peers at work. Although getting denied by one or more of your target schools can certainly be a humbling experience, there is a lot to be learned from it.

First, it's important to realize that the world isn't going to come to an end. Applying to top business schools is inherently a competitive process, and odds are that you will receive at least one denial. Second, you should take some time to evaluate your application using the questions in the section on the waitlist. It's important that you identify how you went astray in case you decide to reapply. Along those lines, some top MBA programs offer personalized feedback to rejected applicants. Take advantage of that even you'd prefer never to hear the school's name again. Many applicants find these feedback sessions to be useful and those that incorporate the feedback into the following year's application often achieve admittance.

Don't be surprised, however, if you find the feedback to be somewhat generic. Vague comments along the lines of "We wish we had seen a little more career potential" or "We had questions about your focus" may simply indicate a general lack of "oomph" in your application that would have spurred the admissions committee to admit you. We talk to many applicants who come away from these feedback sessions complaining that they didn't learn anything new. That may indicate a lack of preparation on the part of the admissions officer who offered the feedback—there's a good chance that she just quickly looked at the notes on your application before talking to you—but it also probably means that there was no single "smoking gun" that killed your chances. Rather, admissions officers just didn't see enough to put you over the hump and give them a reason to pick you instead of the hundreds of other applicants who looked a lot like you.

This is undoubtedly the tougher situation to face. Though specific feedback may be daunting (for example, "If your GMAT score were a lot higher, you'd be a very competitive candidate.") at least it lets you know where you stand and gives you something specific to attack before you reapply. Vague feedback doesn't help you map out a reapplication plan of attack, and can even lead to larger feelings of self doubt along the lines of "Maybe I just don't have the 'it' that admissions officers are looking for." Don't psych yourself out, however; every year hundreds of re-applicants get into the world's top business schools after more research, introspection, and preparation.

With respect to reapplying, you may face a situation in which you are admitted to one of your target schools but are still considering reapplying to a school that was higher on the list. If you are confronted with this situation, then you should ask yourself whether the business school to which you've been admitted will provide you with an opportunity to achieve your career goals. If the answer is no, then you shouldn't have applied to the school in the first place. Just make sure that you don't pass on an option that would allow you to achieve your goals so that you can potentially attend a "more prestigious" MBA program in the future.

If you do decide to reapply, make sure that you fully understand the weaknesses of your initial applications and that you attack them tirelessly using the techniques we've outlined in previous chapters. With another year to prepare yourself, your application should shine with polish.

Certainly the goal of this book is to help you avoid facing the prospect of receiving denials. We feel strongly that if you closely follow the strategy and the steps we've outlined, you will be in a much better position to receive the proverbial "thick letter" once decision day comes.

. . . .

Closing Thoughts

The one person who controls your application's fate more than anyone is you. Sure, it's difficult to send your application into the abyss not knowing the final outcome, but by the time you're done you will have spent months maximizing your chances for success. Fit with your target school will be obvious. Your uniqueness will be clear. And your thick letter will be on its way. Let us know when you succeed by reaching out to us at twitter.com/MBAGamePlan.

All the best!

Additional Admissions Essays

Here you will find additional sample essays (arranged alphabetically by school) with associated commentary to provide you with more examples that can help as you refine your own essays. Unlike the essays highlighted in Chapter 4, which only provides examples of strong admissions essays, these run the gamut from excellent to "needs a lot of work." The associated commentary should help you see what admissions officers look for when evaluating essays.

SAMPLE ESSAY: "MARK" (BOOTH SCHOOL OF BUSINESS) ◄

If you could be present at any event in time, what would it be, and why? (500 words)

If given the opportunity to be present during any event in time I would choose maximize the benefits of said opportunity, by choosing to witness an epic event which had a tremendous, and continuing, impact on modern society; an event, shrouded in uncertainty and the subject of prolific debate. Given these criteria, and after careful consideration, I would choose to be present during Moses' receiving of the Ten Commandments.

My motivation for witnessing this event is based on a fascination with human societal development rather than personal religious soul-searching, though there certainly would be potential for me to experience a dramatic religious epiphany. I consider religion to be an integral part of the development of human societies throughout the world, as well as a major underlying theme behind numerous events and conflicts throughout human history, such as the Crusades, the Jewish holocaust in World War II, and the present-day conflicts in the Middle East. By witnessing Moses' receiving of the Ten Commandments, I would be witnessing one of the critical events which led to the moral foundation for the laws and religious practices of the billions of followers of the world's three most populous religions: Christianity, Judaism and Islam.

I admit to not knowing exactly what lessons I might learn from witnessing this event, but I am confident that whatever information I could gain would have a tremendous impact on a personal, or possibly global, level. Perhaps I could bear witness to some previously unrecorded historical and religious details, which could give me a new perspective to the substance and development of the present day religious beliefs for the world's major religions. Perhaps I could learn something that could aid in the reduction of religious conflict in the world. At the very least, I would expect to gain a new perspective on present day conflicts, to say nothing for the possibility of personally experiencing a religious epiphany from witnessing a miracle, or the direct manifestation of God. If you're going to see an event in time, it may as well as be a big event… and you can't get much bigger than seeing the Almighty! On the other hand, maybe what I witness would make atheists rejoice, and complete undermine the basis (if not the wisdom) for the modern Judeo-Christian based ethics.

The historical facts behind the legends and miracles in religious history are a heatedly debated topic by theologians and historians, the religiously faithful and skeptical. It would seem impossible that any major topic of religious debate or question could possibly be resolved. Given the opportunity, I for one would like to make the impossible, possible.

· · · · · · · · · · · · · · · ·

Comments

▷ This is one of those essay questions that we refer to as "personal philosophy." Although many applicants believe such essay question exist merely to annoy them, the purpose of these essays is to allow the admissions committee to gain a quick insight into how you think and what motivates you. Rather than viewing this essay as an annoyance and writing about the first thing that comes to mind, you should use it to your advantage by discussing something that supports the theme(s) you developed in the rest of your application.

▷ For the most part, Mark's writing is strong. It is clear, crisp, and colorful. This allows the reader to move through the essay easily and understand the main points that Mark is trying to convey. In one or two places he gets a little more wordy than he needs to be (for example, "I would choose to maximize the benefits of said opportunity by choosing..." in the very first sentence). Having someone else review his essay can help him "trim the fat" in a couple of places.

▷ Mark does a nice job of establishing up-front what his criteria are for selecting the event he would like to attend. From there he discusses why he'd like to attend the event, providing the reader with a detailed account of his motivations.

▷ Many applicants are gun-shy when it comes to writing about something as personal as religion. Our advice is simple: If it matters a great deal to you, then there's no reason not to write about it in your business school applications. Whenever we have seen applicants do it badly, it has been when their writing comes off as an attempt to proselytize too much, which makes MBA admissions officers wonder how well that person might fit in a class full of people from various backgrounds and beliefs. As long as you make the essay about you and can clearly explain why the subject matters to you (whether it's religion, running, painting, or anything else), we don't think you should shy away from writing about what's important to you.

▷ Not having seen the rest of Mark's application makes it difficult to provide specific advice for essay improvement (especially because the essay is well written). We would suggest, however, that Mark makes sure that his chosen event and the themes he expresses in it are reflective of the messages he would like to send to the admissions committee. For example, if other parts of his application touch on the theme "making the impossible, possible," then this is an excellent addition. That theme could work really well in conjunction with career goals and an overall personal philosophy that aligns well with the essay.

▷ Note that Booth no longer uses this essay question, but we decided to include it here since it is still very valuable for applicants to review.

SAMPLE ESSAY: "MELANIE" (COLUMBIA BUSINESS SCHOOL) ◄

What are your short-term and long-term post-MBA career goals? How will Columbia Business School help you achieve these goals? (750 words)

My diverse professional experience since college has included financial brokerage, commercial banking and defined contribution consulting. My goals have evolved through experiencing in those diverse settings, and my goal now is to obtain my MBA from the Columbia Business School and to join a prestigious finance organization with the eventual goal of owning my own consulting firm.

In selecting a career I have always been told to figure out what you like to do and then make a career out of it. Eight years ago, armed with this bit of philosophy, I set out to find out what I like. Before entering college, I came to the realization that my interests lay in business. My courses in business were the ones I always look forward to, and my business projects and presentations were the most challenging and rewarding of all my undergraduate course work. Upon graduating, I interviewed with, and was offered several enviable positions with well-known firms in New York City. I forewent those offers and decided to join Anderson & Stevens as defined contribution analyst.

As a defined contribution analyst with Anderson & Stevens and The Johnson Companies for the past two and a half years, I have developed a solid foundation in teamwork, analytical and problem solving skills. I work in a group that currently has four members. The success of the group relies on the extraordinary amount of cooperation from each of us. As a junior member of the team, I am able to the contribute to the group in several ways including, managing and accurately completing multiple requests with short turnaround times, gathering and conveying information from client, collecting and calculating data, maintaining databases, and strengthening my own foundation of knowledge to be used as a resource. However, while I am an excellent team player, these experiences provides expansive career opportunities in consulting, I have reached a plateau in developing the analytical and management skills necessary to achieve my goal.

Being a successful leader of an organization, I have to learn all aspects of organization outside of defined contribution such as marketing or system administration. I have found that I need to overcompensate for my "soft" appearance in order to get my point across. By attending Columbia Business School, I will gain exposure to both theories and practices in the world's financial centers. I will attain a deeper understanding of management concepts and be able to apply those concepts to real life situations on the job. I hope to improve to negotiating skills and to gain more experience in getting group members to carry their own weight. At the same time, I do not want to be a tyrant. To be effective, it is important for a manager to maintain the proper balance of power and compassion. Only in this way, will I be able to lead a team of people to realizing the goals of the firm.

Following a successfully completion of my MBA program, I would like to seek a position in a prestigious finance organization. Because of the excellent preparation of the basics Columbia will have provided me, I will excel among my peer and eventually climb up the corporate ladder. After excelling in all aspects of the defined contribution, I would like to start with consulting in the area of retirement services and eventually expand my business to other areas of consulting such as actuarial and life insurance. Initially, I would like to concentrate my clients within United States. Eventually, I would like to expand my client base oversea starting with the Asia market where the foundation of the defined contribution is still very weak and unfounded. The ability to converse in Chinese and an understanding of Chinese and American Culture, It will give me a top advantage to initiate my business in the Asia market.

Furthermore, an effective manager in the 21st century must be well-versed in international business. Unfortunately, my desire to gain this broader understanding of the increasing interdependent global economy remains unsatisfied at the current position. Columbia Business School is located in the heart of the New York City. The students of Columbia Business School have the advantage of being able to study in one of the top school in the dynamic and cosmopolitan city where most of the multinational corporations are located.

My professional experiences thus far have enabled me to gain much confidence in my ability to set very high professional goals because I know I will maintain the personal dedication and hard work necessary in achieving them. I feel that these diverse experiences have prepared me well to receive an education from Columbia just as a MBA from Columbia will undoubtedly help me reach my short-term goal along the line proceeds to that end point.

· · · · · · · · · · · · · · ·

Comments

▷ This essay suffers conversation flow and grammatical issues. Melanie would benefit from using headers in the essay, because of its longer length. Melanie should also make sure that she has someone with a strong background in academic English review the essay.

▷ The focus of the essay is three parts: 1) short-term goals, 2) long-term goals, and 3) where Columbia Business School fits in. Unfortunately, Melanie doesn't cover any of these adequately. The reader knows that she wants to join a "prestigious finance organization" upon graduation, but she doesn't explain why that is a goal of hers.

▷ The last sentence in the third paragraph is confusing. It indicates that she's reached a plateau in terms of the analytical and management skills that are required for her to reach her goal. If she's reached a level that allows her to reach her goal, then why does she need business school? That's unclear. It's also unclear what the goal is that she is mentioning here.

▷ The second part (long-term goals) is addressed more completely. The fifth paragraph is the best paragraph in the essay. Melanie describes her goal to start her own consulting firm decently. More details on why she her venture will be successful would be helpful. Additionally, Melanie should create a link between her short-term and long-term goals. Finally, some more details on the Asia market and why her venture would be successful there would also be helpful.

▷ The last part (Why Columbia?) needs some work. Melanie should tie her goals to what Columbia would provide. She should write much more specifically about Columbia's clubs, networks, curriculum, mission, classes, students, faculty, and so on, and present a case that establishes fit with the school and her goals.

▷ In the third paragraph Melanie mentions several positive attributes. These attributes would be much more believable if she provided actual examples of the attributes in action.

▷ Overall, Melanie should really focus on the basic structure of the essay and make sure that she covers the three parts adequately.

Sample Essay: "Brian" (Darden School of Business) ◀

The Darden MBA program expects students to actively participate in learning teams, the classroom, and the broader community. Please share one or two examples from your past experience that best illustrate(s) how you will contribute to this highly engaging and hands-on learning environment. (500 words)

I had only been at Marathon Securities for four months, but already I knew we had a big culture problem. No one believed that our goals were even remotely achievable, and worst of all, no one felt that it was worth it to try to correct the situation. I had joined the company because leader of my department was a sharp and charismatic person, but he had left the company before I started, and it felt like the department was a rudderless ship. Walking into my boss's office and seeing her working on her resume in Microsoft Word was the last straw. Someone had to do something, and if it had to be me, then so be it.

I first met with my boss and described what was going on among the associates on the team. "My advice to you is to keep your head down and just put some points on the board.

Once you have accomplished a few things, then you can try to stick your neck out. Or you can find another job." That was her advice. At that moment I knew she would not be part of the solution.

I decided to first garner support among my fellow associates. Together we could at least agree on a course of action to take this black hole of energy and turn it into a bright shining star to light the way for the entire organization going forward. I called a meeting of the 26 associates to get the ball rolling. It started out uncomfortably since we didn't all know each other, and we were always openly encouraged to compete against one another (which was part of the culture problem), but after an hour people started to open up. It felt like a dam finally broke, with everyone starting to share their fears and concerns.

As a team, in several meetings over the next month we generated a list of ideas for how we could improve morale in the group. These ranged from relatively easy things, such as Thursday happy hours, to some tough ones, such as management committing to reset our goals since they were so unrealistic. Then the trick was presenting these tougher ones to management. As a group we decided that another associate, Anita, and I would get a meeting with our division's managing partner and take him through our recommendations. That meeting came ten days later.

The night before the meeting I remember sleeping no more than two hours, because I was just so nervous. The company's culture problems were no secret, but the party line was simply to pretend they didn't exist, and to leave if we hated it that much. Even my own boss had old me as much. As far as I knew, I would leave the meeting with the managing partner without a job.

Fortunately, that couldn't have been further from reality. Anita and I calmly and constructively took him through the six main issues we had identified, and proposed a solution for each problem. Ten minutes into the meeting our managing partner cleared his calendar for the next three hours, and he dug right in, asking us questions, kicking around additional ideas, and giving his candid feedback on each proposal. By the end of the meeting we had a list of four concrete ideas that we all agreed were worth pursuing, milestones for implementing them, and the managing partner's commitment to fully support these ideas with the rest of the partners in the firm. We had done the right thing, and it was already starting to pay off. I am now leading the implementation of several of the ideas.

I plan on bringing this same enthusiasm and unwillingness to accept the status quo to Darden. Even when it means putting myself in an uncomfortable position or going against the grain, if I see a way to contribute to Darden's learning environment, I commit to doing the right thing and helping everyone around me.

• • • • • • • • • • • • • •

Comments

> Brian has a very interesting story to tell, and it's one that admissions officers will certainly be interested to hear. This is a classic leadership story presented in the SAR (Situation, Action, Result) format—a very effective formula for a business school admissions essay.

> Brian's choice of topic may seem a little odd because this essay prompt doesn't specifically ask for him to describe a time when he took an uncomfortable stand or faced a difficult situation in a group. This can be risky, because Brian doesn't want it to look like he's simply shoe-horned in an essay from another application, one that doesn't really answer the question. However, this is a great story from Brian's background, and because Darden doesn't provide another essay that gives him the opportunity to write about it, we think he made the right choice here. We recommend

that he put a bit more thought into how he ties it back to Darden at the end of the essay, but the theme of this story—Brian doesn't stand idly by when he sees a way to make things better—is a terrific one for him to use here.

▷ Brian's writing is very clear and concise, with clean grammar and a nice voice throughout. There are a few moments where he really helps the reader imagine what he was experiencing, such as when he sees his boss polishing her resume as she plans to leave the company. However, there are one or two places where he gets a little too ambitious with his attempt to use descriptive language (for example, "a course of action to take this black hole of energy and turn it into a bright shining star"). Brian's writing is strong enough that he doesn't need devices like this.

▷ One obvious weakness is that this essay is well over the word limit right now. Even if he uses all of his 10% margin of error, Brian still has to cut 100 words from this essay. Normally, in an essay like this an applicant devotes too many words to the situation setup and not enough to the action and results. We do think the first paragraph could shed about a dozen words or so, but this is a case here the editing will need to be sentence-by-sentence, paragraph-by-paragraph. There is no one obvious paragraph that Brian should significantly chop down. One possible exception is the paragraph that starts "The night before the meeting," although we think it's important for Brian to emphasize to the reader that this was not an easy thing he was about to do. Overall, we think Brian will have to get down to 550 words (or fewer) with some "nip and tuck" throughout the essay.

▷ Although this may seem to contradict the above point, we would like to see Brian include a few more specifics in this essay. Right now he tells an interesting story, but the essay falls short of perfection because it mostly describes the issues in generalities. For example, when he describes the meeting with the managing partner, it may be more effective for him to focus in one particular problem, especially one that seemed riskiest to Brian to discuss. We don't think this will be hard while he's also trying to cut down his word count, because we think Brian can simply swap out a few of his general, sweeping statements (for example, the sentence that starts with "Ten minutes into the meeting our managing partner cleared his calendar...") with more specific ones.

▷ Right now this is a very promising essay. If Brian can cut down the word count, work in a few more specifics, and tie the essay back to Darden a bit better, he will have an essay that admissions officers will be very eager to read.

SAMPLE ESSAY: "SANDRA" (FUQUA SCHOOL OF BUSINESS) ◀

How will your background, values, and non-work activities enhance the experience of other Duke MBA students and add value to Fuqua's diverse culture? (two pages)

I recently asked my friends to describe me with three words. A number of them used the word "different." They explained that they could not think of another word to describe my seemingly subconscious ability to not fit into some of the norms or molds of society. They also noted that I did this without conflicting with my environment. This was not surprising to me because for many years friends and family have called me "different." I believe this is because I handle things in a different manner to those around me. I always question whether there is a more effective way to do something or whether a tradition is worth keeping. To accomplish a task, I tend to seek unconventional way to "Get It Done" faster or more efficiently.

I was born in Canada, I grew up in Trinidad and Tobago, and I completed college in the United States. I have experienced both developed and developing country environments. I am very aware of how their economies differ and affect the quality of life (access to sufficient healthcare, education, food, and other facilities) of their citizenry. However, I believe my detailed understanding of diversity and disparity came from my experiences at a predominantly black college called Tobias University (TU).

The rich heritage of TU has really impressed me with its legacy from great African-American figures who were different in their own fields, like the Tobias Corps; a successful World War II Army unit and Randolph Elliot; a simple farmer who made numerous scientific and agricultural discoveries and inventions. Tobias' prestige is built upon the perseverance to succeed against the odds (whether due to discrimination, lack of resources, etc). Many of my achievements at TU resulted from similar determination to succeed against many of the challenges I faced as active student. TU has given me the track record and the confidence of a successful leader.

I believe that my personality, my experiences, and my legacy are sufficient to get me on the path to success. I know that once there, I have the determination and the support I need to endure to the finish. I can't wait to share these qualities with my classmates at Fuqua.

. . . .

Comments

▹ The essay's second and third lines really grab the reader's attention. We immediately read that Sandra is different, and are curious as to what exactly makes her different.

▹ The rest of the paragraph doesn't give readers many specifics as to how exactly Sandra is different. She writes that she does things differently and accomplishes tasks more efficiently, but an illustration using an example is needed here.

▹ Most of the next paragraph tells us more about Sandra's undergraduate school than about her. What exactly does this add to her theme? We recommend cutting most of this out, as it is precious space in which she could write about herself.

▹ The theme of overcoming adversity to succeed, which she covers later in this same paragraph, is a powerful one. However, Sandra again only mentions this in passing without providing an example to illustrate how she has done this. With the space that she could save by cutting out the material about her school, she could provide a nice, concise example here.

▹ There are some typos that need fixing. For example, "it's" in the third paragraph should be "its." Also, the punctuation in that same sentence needs work. (Although we recommend eliminating this sentence, anyway.)

▹ Finally, Sandra needs to devote more effort to explaining exactly how she sees herself contributing to the Fuqua community. She sounds like an interesting person, and it looks like she has a good deal of material in her background that she can work with to paint the portrait of someone who will add something different to Fuqua's culture. However, she doesn't quite "close the deal," merely mentioning Fuqua at the very end of the essay. What is it about her that will make her a unique and welcome addition to Fuqua—her "Get It Done" mentality, her experiences at TU, or something else entirely?

▹ Overall, Sandra has a promising theme, which she sets up the right away. She should work on building the entire essay around these first two sentences (assuming she keeps the "different" theme), keep the focus on herself, and devote more words to explaining what exactly she can bring to Fuqua's culture. If she can do all of those things, she should have a compelling application essay.

Sample Essay: "Logan" (Harvard Business School) ◀

What would you like the MBA Admissions Board to know about your undergraduate academic experience? (400 words)

When I first got to Pinewood College, I couldn't believe that they had a club for every single interest I could imagine. Rock climbing? Check. Filmography? Definitely. Ultimate Frisbee club? Of course. A capella singing? Yes...three different men's groups, in fact. I was like a kid in a candy store.

Cut to a scene of me on the phone, assuring my parents that the "Academic Letter of Concern" that they just received wasn't a big deal. Somehow, they didn't buy this argument.

Now cut to me sitting in the math department director's office, explaining why I thought I could succeed as a math major despite my 2.2 GPA after one year in college. As much as I loved all of those clubs, I clearly had been spending too much time exploring everything Pinewood had to offer *except* what went on in the classroom. Now I found myself having to convince the math department to take me as I prepared to declare my major.

Next scene: Logan wandering through the gymnasium at the course registration fair, trying to decide whether to enroll in a fifth class at the start of my sophomore year. I didn't feel like I needed to prove it to myself, but I needed to prove to everyone else that I could not just survive, but even excel at Pinewood. "What the hell, Logan," our protagonist says as he strolls up to register for a differential equations course. "A capella can wait. This is what you need to do."

Fast-forward to the end of sophomore year: Logan is in the math department director's office almost exactly one year after their last meeting, showing the director the 3.89 GPA he got over the past year. "So you decided you wanted to stay at Pinewood, huh? Keep it up," the director says as he hands over the signed card making Logan's status as a member of the math department official.

I got off to a slow start in college because I was 18 years old and assumed that every day had 30 hours in it. When those last six hours never materialized, schoolwork was what went out the window, but that habit died quickly by the end of my freshman year. For my last three years at Pinewood I earned a 3.8 GPA in a very challenging major. I am certain that this is more indicative of my true ability and dedication to learning. I will bring this discipline to Harvard Business School.

· · · · · · · · · · · · · · ·

Comments

▷ Logan uses this essay (an optional one in the HBS application) to address an issue that many business school applicants must overcome every year: dealing with a low undergraduate GPA. Given how common this story is, admissions officers are very used to hearing the typical "I just was immature when I got to college and eventually grew up" story, which Logan tells here. Because his undergraduate grades got better as time went on, all he has to do is tell this story in a convincing fashion and then move on. If his grades got worse or stayed bad over the course of his career, he would have a much harder story to tell here. (See our comments on overcoming weak undergraduate grades in Chapter 2.)

▷ We think this essay already works quite well except for one thing: Logan tries to use the "movie director" device throughout the essay because he's mentioned in other parts of his application that he's very interested in film and the entertainment industry. However, here we think it's a bit clunky and distracts some from his real mission, which is to put to rest any questions admissions officers might have about his college transcript. Though we like that he's thinking about spicing up his essays and making them more interesting to read, this may not be the best essay in which to use it.

▹ If Logan insists on keeping the "movie director" device, then the only way it will work is by doing it entirely throughout the essay, not only in the middle four paragraphs. Right now he jumps back and forth between first- and third-person perspectives. He needs to commit to one and stick with it. Again, though, we think it might be better if he saved this device for another HBS essay prompt.

▹ Logan has a nice, tidy story here: It took him a year to realize that he needed to apply himself in the classroom. We think he's a few nips and tucks away from being ready to submit this essay to Harvard.

SAMPLE ESSAY: "PAUL" (HARVARD BUSINESS SCHOOL) ◀

What are your three most substantial accomplishments and why do you view them as such? (600 words)

My three most substantial accomplishments came in three different facets of my life that all matter a great deal to me: sports, my career, and my family. Each one represents a moment when I chose to "go for it" instead of shying away from a challenge, making each one an important marker in my growth.

The first accomplishment was is when I made a significant impact on my college soccer team. At the end of my junior year, I was named captain of the Hamilton University soccer team. Although I didn't even realize it at the time, I was the team's first ever African-American captain. While my teammates were always very accepting and race never once came up within our locker room, it was hard not to think about the issue when opposing players would shout insults during matches. My teammates would always rally to my defense, and for much my first year I would try to stop them, saying, "No, I can handle this myself." But finally I realized that I didn't *need* to handle it myself, because we were a team, and we faced adversity of any kind as one unit. After I embraced this notion and realized that race was no cross that I had to bear on my own, I increasingly found myself being more outspoken in the locker room, taking younger players under my wing, and keeping everyone positive at all times. When I was named captain of the Hamilton soccer team, it had nothing to do with race and everything to do with the fact that my teammates felt that I had come to symbolize the meaning of "team" better than anyone, which was the most meaningful compliment I had ever received.

My second most substantial accomplishment came at work, when I was named lead analyst of the Tanner Consulting Class of 2008. When I first started at Tanner I felt lost; the company's training program was much more "on the job" than I realized, and mistakes on any client-facing work could be very costly. The consultants seemed to speak a completely new language to me, and I sometimes felt like I had no idea of what they were asking me to do. Instead of shying away from the challenge, I threw myself into my work, taking on every client-facing assignment I could. Even when it meant long nights and weeks that blended right into the weekends, I made myself the "go-to analyst" for any request that a partner had. In less than a year, I earned their trust, and at the start of my second year I was named the lead of our group of seven junior analysts. While others complained that they weren't being trained enough, I simply jumped in and got the job done. I made a few mistakes along the way, but by just jumping in and doing it, I was able to prove my mettle.

My third accomplishment came from a very unexpected place: my own sister, Jackie. While we had never been particularly close while growing up (she is eight years older than I am), our jobs took both of us to Philadelphia, and we started to finally grew as close as siblings should be. During that tough first year at Tanner Consulting, my sister began divorce proceedings against her husband, which was tough on her and on her two-year-old daughter, Lilly. Jackie and Lilly were going to be better off in the long run, but poor Lilly didn't understand why she wouldn't see Daddy every day. I found that being Uncle Paul was not only good for Lilly, but it was a tremendous release for me whenever I was able to get away from work. On weekends I would take Lilly to the park or the zoo, just me and her. As much as she needed a father figure in my life, I realized that I really needed Jackie and Lilly in my life, and so I opened up and let it happen. Lilly is almost five years old now, and while she lives alone with Jackie, I see the two of them just about every week. Lilly will always be my niece, but she means even more than that to me now, and I know I am more to her than just an uncle.

. . . .

Comments

▷ Paul has chosen three distinctly different stories for this essay, which is a good idea. Although you are certainly not required to go this route with Harvard's "three most substantial accomplishments" essay, it's a good place to start because it gives you a chance to get multiple application themes on the table. If two of your stories come from one facet of your background, this is absolutely fine, but you do want to ensure that the three stories don't overlap with one another in terms of what application dimensions they highlight.

▷ Overall, Paul has a good essay here. It just needs some work to tighten it up and be sure that he delivers on the themes he describes at the start of the essay. We like how he sets the stage in the first paragraph, describing his decision to "go for it" instead of shying away from challenges. Even though these are three different stories from various parts of his life, that overarching theme is a great way to tie them together. However, as it stands now, the third story (which we like overall) doesn't quite seem like an example of how he "went for it." We think what he's describing here is how he decided to embrace the concept of family and be a better brother and uncle, but what was his alternative? To ignore Jackie and Lilly? We think a more effective way to tell this story is to describe how it was hard for him to embrace his sister and niece, perhaps because he was so busy at work or because he and Jackie were never close to begin with. This is one case where his course of action seems obvious in hindsight, but a few details can help the reader better appreciate his decision to "go for it" and be a better uncle to Lilly.

▷ The second story, which describes his success as an analyst in his first job, is probably the weakest of the three right now. Adding a few more details would make it much more effective. It sounds like it was a tough "sink or swim" job, but right now Paul only describes it in generalities (for example, "mistakes on any client-facing work could be very costly"). Our advice to applicants in this situation is to just pick one example that was indicative of the "what" the applicant faced at the time, and include details from this example to help bring the story to life for the reader. Also, Paul should remember that any details that he's not able to include here can always go into his letters of recommendation. He can suggest these stories to his recommendation writers when he recruits them for the job.

▷ Paul is well over the word limit right now. This essay is notorious among applicants for being incredibly difficult to do well within the 600-word limit. We can identify at least one or two sentences within each story (particularly in the first story) where he can save a few words here and there. We estimate Paul could trim about 75 words from this essay without significantly rewriting it, which would bring him to within 10 percent of Harvard's word limit.

▷ Finally, some applicants include a brief concluding paragraph at the end of this essay, but we don't feel that it's necessary here, particularly given the tight word limit. Paul's introduction helps set the stage, and the three stories (especially after some editing) stand on their own.

▷ We like this essay, and think that Paul can make it a great one with some smart editing and by including a few more details to help the reader feel what Paul felt as he achieved each of the accomplishments described here. He's on his way to having a strong essay for his Harvard application.

SAMPLE ESSAY: "KURT" (INSEAD) ◀

Discuss your career goals. What skills do you expect to gain from studying at INSEAD and how will they contribute to your professional career? (500 words approx.)

I was not born with a love for economics nor was it my forte in college. Technology was always the hidden "thing" in me. A decade later since earning my bachelors, I have therefore struck a well-maintained balance of acquiring technical prowess and an international work experience. Thus far I have been extremely successful.

By the summer of 2001 however I had begun reflecting on my career till date and where I wanted to take it. It was when I was leading a technical team of engineers in my first job and we were amidst designing a fixed telecommunication network for an operator in Sri Lanka. Placing a technically sound and highly competitive offer, my best guess was a few rounds of price negotiations and the deal was ours. Surprisingly that was not to be. It took an external consulting firm to assess the worth of that business opportunity for our company, a complete financial analysis of the operators' annual report, a tough call on whether to use debt or equity to fund the prospect and endless meetings convincing Goldman Sachs to secure a financing loan. Towards the end we clinched the business but the experience was an eye opener and brought to light how much more there was to learn about business in general. The anecdote also brings to forefront my short and long-term career goals.

Today I believe I have chalked up some solid professional experience in all my previous positions as technical sales and planning lead and have also achieved significant international exposure to how telecom business is conducted around the globe. I now strongly feel that to advance further I need to consolidate what I have learnt and the three elements of business—strategy, technology and finance. I want to have a multifaceted role of an operational business manager, relationship manager, strategy planner and a business developer. From the current responsibilities as a senior planner, a career in account management or business development manager in telecom therefore fits perfectly for me as the next logical step in career growth. This also formulates my short-term career goal.

Most managers in an organization are identified with a particular business discipline. The most common are operations, finance, marketing, information and human resource. To achieve my goals I must communicate effectively and work productively with people from these disciplines. At INSEAD I want to learn the "language" of each of these functional specialties. I want to learn how to analyze a financial report of a company; how to price an option; what does shareholder value really mean; what makes the stock market tick; what does Alan Greenspan do; what are the implications of an interest rate cut by the European Central bank; what an investment banker really does. At INSEAD, I believe such core courses as Financial Markets & Valuation and Prices & Markets can teach me the business funda-mentals while subjects like Strategy and Managerial accounting can equip me with core functional skills that make me a business developer.

As environment of organizations-including economic, political, competitive, regulatory, and cultural factors-becomes more complex, there will be an increased need for manag-ers with the necessary skills, understanding, courage, and energy to tackle the difficult de-mands facing organizations of all kinds. These general managers would organize the work of others and decide on the course of action an organization must take.

After a few years of experience in account management or as a business development manager and armed with an MBA, I intend to set foot into general management. With a punishing work schedule and a rigorous curricula that imitates the pressures on our time in real world, with a global perspective and reach, with real life case studies in classroom where one can instantaneously apply the theoretical skills in a context of constraints, opportunities and alternatives I truly believe INSEAD can help me transform into a corporate leadership role—something I envisage as my long-term career goal. Also in Johanna Hellborg's own words, "INSEAD can develop general management and entrepreneurial skills that many 'techies' don't have when they arrive at B-school."

Probably a decade from now, en route to the big corner office, I would stop and ponder how I enhanced my knowledge, how I raised my visibility and built a strong personal network and thank INSEAD came my way.

. . . .

Comments

▷ Overall, Kurt does a good job of weaving his interest in INSEAD into the essay. Although many applicants leave school-specific material for a tell-tale "modular" paragraph toward the end of the essay, Kurt makes this essay stronger than most by talking about INSEAD throughout the essay.

▷ The second paragraph is probably the weakest part of this essay. Kurt tells this story to illustrate how he first became interested in business matters, and this makes sense. However, the reader doesn't have enough information to fully appreciate what happened, yet adding more info would just take the essay off topic. Also, it's not clear what exactly Kurt did in this situation. It may be best for him to take out this paragraph entirely.

▷ Right now Kurt is over the suggested word limit by more than 200 words. Though INSEAD only asks that the essay be "approximately 500 words," we recommend that Kurt get the word count down to 550 or less, which would put it within 10 percent of that limit. (Remember that admissions officers perpetually feel worn down while reading one long essay after another!) Eliminating the second paragraph would save him 173 words immediately, and the essay wouldn't be any worse off without it.

▷ Another part to trim might be the fifth paragraph. This is one part of the essay that doesn't focus on Kurt at all. We consider it to be expendable.

▷ Although we're looking for places to save space, one way that Kurt could bolster his essay is by going into more detail about why he wants to do business development after attending INSEAD. He mentions this career at the bottom of the fourth paragraph, but doesn't explain why this career path appeals to him.

▷ Kurt has a few small grammatical mistakes in his essay that he still needs to clean up (for example, the fifth paragraph starts "As environment of organizations..." but should read "As the environment..."). Having a native English speaker give it a quick read will help Kurt a lot here.

▷ One more small point: The "corner office" comment in the last paragraph can probably be left out. Kurt may have meant for it to come across as somewhat whimsical, but he doesn't want it to make him sound like someone who is too self-important or has unrealistic expectations about what an INSEAD MBA will bring. He may be ambitious, but he doesn't want to come across as being arrogant or out of touch.

▷ Overall, a good essay that just needs to be tightened up some. We suggest that Kurt evaluate each sentence and make sure that it's answering the question asked, and that it keeps the focus on him. If he does that, he should do well.

SAMPLE ESSAY: "EMERSON" (JOHNSON SCHOOL OF MANAGEMENT) ◄

Describe your greatest professional achievement and how you added value to your organization. (400 words)

It was my first day at American Technologies Corporation (ATC). I was shown my allotted cubicle. It was barely eight-by-eight feet in size. I looked around. Similar-sized cubicles were everywhere. Dilbertism might not be a myth after all.

Within six months of joining ATC, I became one of the principal architects driving the development of the award-winning, state-of-the-art ATC's software platform. But it was not enough to bring ATC's flagship technology, neural network personalization, to mainstream. Studying the adoption of similar technologies, I concluded that we needed to connect with the "early adopters" of this technology.

I discussed my plan with colleagues in the marketing department. Despite sharing my enthusiasm, they were non-committal due to lack of resources. It was clear. If my proposal were to see the light of the day, I would have to go beyond the call of my duty. I decided to take the plunge.

Through an online forum, I started reaching out to the small community of "early adopters." From handholding the novice developers to answering the complex questions of the expert developers, I started a process of demystification of the technology. Slowly but surely, the online forum started to create a buzz in the developer community. Having understood the nuances of neural network personalization, the entrepreneurial developers started to discuss how it could be used to solve the intricate business problems. Business plans were developed and a lot of small ventures were floated.

The unexpected response to the online forum attracted the interest of our Marketing team. And this time they acted. The Marketing team soon became a regular to various trade shows and industry conferences. I was the technology expert at most of these sessions. The developer community grew rapidly and in no time boasted of 15,000+ developers from 25 different countries.

The online forum, which started out as a technology dissemination forum, established ATC as the leader driving the adoption of neural network personalization. It became the sales channel through which ATC got most of its enterprise customers. Today, these customers account for 15% of ATC's total revenue. The feedback that we gathered from the developers also helped streamline our Product Development process. There was a marked shift from "build and they will come" approach to a more customer-centric approach, which proved beneficial in the long run as lots of costly mistakes were avoided up-front.

My efforts in building this community were recognized in an influential book on neural network personalization. As the technology became ubiquitous, I felt proud that I had played my own small role in its commercialization. And what about my cubicle? Thanks to its three-and-a-half walls, which always defined my boundaries accurately so that I could continually scale those boundaries.

• • • • • • • • • • • • • • •

Comments

▷ Any applicant who writes about technology runs the risk of confusing or boring his audience, but Emerson does a good job of briefly explaining why the technology was important to ATC without getting bogged down in details.

▷ The only real weaknesses in this essay come in the first and last paragraphs. They seem somewhat disconnected from the rest of the essay. Although Emerson's "Dilbert" comment in the first paragraph is good in that it shows he has a sense of humor, the tone that he sets in this paragraph (one of a faceless, monolithic corporation) doesn't carry through the rest of the essay. Also, the very last sentence doesn't make sense as it's written right now; perhaps Emerson got a little too ambitious with the poetry here. We suggest that he think about other ways to start and end this essay, or that he try reworking the middle to give it more of the feel that the first paragraph currently has. Either way, the last paragraph needs more work to help avoid the feeling that Emerson is hastily trying to end the essay.

▷ Along the same lines, Emerson goes from describing this world of cubicles to describing what sounds like a pretty big set of responsibilities in the second paragraph. Was this the job he was initially hired to do? If not, how did he work his way into this position?

▷ Emerson is well over the 400-word limit right now, so he will need to find a way to shave off at least 20 or 30 words. He may be tempted to cut out the first paragraph, but we like how it sets the stage for the essay. We think a little "nip and tuck" in the third through sixth paragraphs should be enough.

▷ Emerson is rightly proud that his efforts were mentioned in a book! He should even go a step further and mention the name of the book. Doing so will help the accomplishment seem more real.

▷ Overall, this is a good story that clearly demonstrates the impact that Emerson has had on his employer. If he can improve the last paragraph and better tie the first paragraph to the rest of the piece, this will be an excellent essay.

Sample Essay: "Larry" (Kelley School of Business) ◄

Please discuss your post-MBA short- and long-term professional goals. How will your professional experience, when combined with a Kelley MBA degree, allow you to achieve these goals? (two pages)

"Engineers make devices, marketers make products" notes William Davidow, a high-profile venture capitalist. However, when dealing with techies, a marketer is forced to adapt the role of an engineer. Partly due to overcompensating for not having a technical degree, when marketing a product, I am known to hide behind product specifications. The concept of price, product, place, and promotion are used in the tech world, but very loosely. This sentiment is the driving force behind why I want an MBA: to become a classically trained marketer. I asked a friend what he valued most from his freshly minted MBA, entering marketing the marketing realm. He adamantly replied, "Structure."

In the high-technology field, an MBA is not needed for career progression. On occasion, even the lack of a bachelor's degree is accepted. In fact, I noticed that none of my supervisors are equipped with an advanced degree. But I realized, that is exactly why I need one; something is lacking. My supervisors were very qualified to go about their daily tasks, but if taken out of their zone, they did not know how to function as managers.

Ultimately, my goal is to start my own company. The idea of creating something with my own hands is my lifelong dream. There is no greater desire than to create a product, raise capital, and take a company public. This is my path, no matter how or when I get there.

While I see myself as a budding entrepreneur, a couple more years of being redeployed in the tech world after matriculation would be good to understand the dynamics of a corporation and more importantly, how the company is interweaved. Most companies fail not because of a lack of technological vision, but rather from failure to execute. Armed with an MBA, I would like to take the next step in my corporate career in the role of product management, with tasks including taking product from cradle-to-grave, managing P&L responsibility, and creating an advertising campaign.

Business schools are not created the same, in terms of content, faculty, and peers. When I took a Wharton Executive Education course, I realized the glaring difference between regional colleges and a top-caliber university. The faculty was more knowledgeable and the course content more relevant, which helped to create a fruitful ongoing dialog with my peers. The ability to discuss business matters outside the scope of the classroom is what made the experience most rewarding. Indeed a major portion of business school is the network gained, something especially relevant when engaging in any entrepreneurial venture.

What attracted me most to Kelley is that a majority of the students I met during my visit had a marketing interest in consumer-packaged goods. The focus of the program is apparent with Academies dedicated to disciplines like packaged goods and retail. Sitting in Professor Alexander's first-year marketing class left me with the impression that marketing involves more psychology than I previously thought. Last, out of all the MBA schools I visited, Indiana University had the most friendly and caring student body, a camaraderie, resembling that of a family. Kelley also prides itself on an integrated curriculum. This fits in my future plans of running my own business. Seldom are small businesses composed of silos, as corporations do by the creation of departments. A manager's mindset should span across multiple disciplines, as this holistic approach instills new methods of problem solving. Hailing from Silicon Valley is a double edge sword because I see much technological innovation, but limited educational perspective. Emphasis On basic, business fundamentals are lost because of the push that technical skills take precedence. For instance, many managers cannot draft a proper letter or have very poor speaking skills. I made a conscious effort not to apply to any West Coast schools, with the fear of this very limited perspective.

A few years ago, I would not have been ready for an MBA. It took me time to grasp the fundamentals building blocks of the technology industry. This oversight, by a majority of people, of not learning the industry basics led to an onslaught of failure of companies associated with the "new economy."

Intelligent, they could translate their intelligence into tangible products, rather selling vaporware. It is now time for me to take the 40,000-foot view in my industry.

· · · · · · · · · · · · · · ·

Comments

▷ Larry has all the content he needs for this to be a great essay. He starts off well by framing the essay with a quote that supports his desire to attend business school. He follows that by adequately describing his future goals. Finally, he does an excellent job of describing his attraction to Kelley. Mentioning his visit makes his argument for Kelley all the more compelling. The essay does, however, have several weak points that should be addressed.

▷ The essay does not flow very well in several places. Larry writes "a marketer is forced to adapt..." (first paragraph) rather than adopt. He writes "There is no greater desire than to create a product..." (third paragraph). And he writes "...how the company is interweaved" (fourth paragraph). These are all examples of sloppy writing and make the essay more difficult to process. Larry should seek out a friend who is well versed in writing.

▸ Also, we're not quite sure why Larry points out his technical deficiency. The essay focuses on his desire to become a marketer. Noting a lack of technical prowess without addressing that weakness probably isn't a smart move. We suggest that he adjust that part of the first paragraph.

▸ The essay ends on a weak note. We're not quite sure what Larry is trying to communicate at the end. He should work to put together a succinct, powerful ending that relates back to his previous statements.

▸ Finally, the essay is a bit long for the two-page requirement. Larry should consider trimming it down. He could start by evaluating whether the fifth paragraph adds anything to the essay other than additional length. With a little bit of work, this will be a very solid essay.

SAMPLE ESSAY: "MICHAEL" (KELLEY SCHOOL OF BUSINESS) ◀

Describe an ethical dilemma that you faced in your professional career. How was it resolved and what did you learn from the experience? (two double-spaced pages)

Another stop traffic sign on my way home. Another orchestrated routine of braking, stopping, looking sideways and proceeding. But as I pulled into the garage, it all became too obvious. I discovered the solution to my conundrum.

It all started when I was inspecting a software module. The deadline of the all-important software project was a couple of weeks away. I discovered that our source code was strikingly similar to one of my earlier open source projects. After confronting him, my colleague confessed that he had copied the code but he did not realize that his acts had legal repercussions. I went into turmoil.

I had two choices: report the incident or ignore it. Delving into the issues, I discovered that the software's open source license required that any derivative software be released under the same license. By releasing a software product under our proprietary license, we would not only corrupt the spirit of the open source but also infringe on its copyright. I realized then that this was an elementary case—we could not use the open source code.

As I strolled through my teammates' cubes, the half-eaten slices of pizza, towers of empty Pepsi cans, and carelessly strewn pillows reminded me of their tireless dedication over the previous six months. The new version of our software product was poised to put us years ahead of our closest competition. By reporting the incident, I would jeopardize the product release and undo all of their labor. I recognized that my issue was with my colleague's action rather than the colleague himself, and that by reporting him I would not only destroy the project, but also put his job at risk. With the ethical debate reopened, I subscribed to the dichotomy of my ethical watchdogs.

From my readings of Immanuel Kant's categorical imperative, I reasoned that any moral person would choose to report the coworker. My understanding of Mill's utilitarian approach, however, taught me that morality is not about rules and duties, but consequences.

In this confused state of mind, the stop traffic signs, on my way home, showed me the way. Like the stop signs, our moral and ethical values serve as signposts in our life. A failure to observe these signposts at seemingly unimportant occasions can very well manifest into a deep-seated habit. A glance at the corporate world revealed that all unethical business practices started out as minor violations to observe these signposts; Gradually, these unethical methods became the way the business was run. In the short-term, failure to report the incident would have resulted in a smooth release of our product and bring happiness to my team. In the long-term future, however, there were sure to be repercussions to both my teammate's actions and my decision, as order and accountability were defenestrated.

I was convinced that reporting the incident was not only the right choice, but also the only choice. I reported the incident to my manager, but made sure that the ignorance of my colleague was also highlighted. My manager was very cooperative and instantly formed a special team to develop our own solution to the problem and replace the offending code. After a lot of hard work, we managed to finish the new coding shortly before the project deadline.

. . . .

Comments

▷ Overall, Michael's writing is strong. He uses an interesting metaphor that captures the reader's attention and then moves into his ethical dilemma and how he went about resolving it. He also does an excellent job of capturing his options and taking the reader through his thought process, showing that he didn't necessarily have an easy decision on his hands. The fourth paragraph is especially powerful, as it reflects the fact that his decision had implications for the entire team.

▷ At first glance there appears to be little wrong with the essay, but a quick examination reveals that Michael can significantly improve this essay in a couple of ways. First, note the last part of the essay prompt, which asks "What did you learn from the experience?" Right now, the fifth and sixth paragraphs of the essay read a bit more like a college lecture by Michael on the relative merits of Kant and Mill. Although none of this is overwhelmingly off topic or out of the bounds of the essay, admissions officers want to know that they're getting the real Michael they'll see on campus every day, not the Michael who likes to ruminate about philosophy. This is a relatively minor point in the grand scheme of things, however. If Michael chooses to keep this part of the essay as it is now, we can't fault him too much.

▷ Also, right now there is a bit of a disconnect between Michael's estimated downside of doing the right thing ("I would jeopardize the product release and undo all of their labor") and what finally happened ("My manager was very cooperative...we managed to finish the new coding shortly before the project deadline"). As is often the case when an applicant needs to trim words, he wraps it up a bit too neatly, which leaves the reader thinking that it may not have been such a tough decision to begin with. We urge Michael to try to fit in one or two more details about the pain the he and the team endured to do the right thing. Doing so will help the reader appreciate that this was not an easy decision that Michael made.

▷ Overall, this is very strong for a first draft. With a few minor tweaks Michael will have a knockout admissions essay about ethics.

SAMPLE ESSAY: "ELEANOR" (KELLOGG SCHOOL OF MANAGEMENT) ◀

Describe an instance where you encountered resistance in a professional team setting. How did you address the situation? (400 words)

The Rogers Oil environment encapsulated into one word is "diversity." My conservative Chinese background coupled with Rogers Oil's extremely diverse groups of people, with different degrees, ethnicities, and positions have created continual challenges. We work in hostile, remote environments, with life-threatening operations and materials (e.g., radioactives), under long working days and strict deadlines. Each member is crucial to an operation; a small failure can lead to financial costs of billions, market share erosion and most importantly physical harm or death. Therefore, significant pressure exists to ensure efficient group processes.

In the field, where a team comprises of executives, engineers and the "muscle-men" rig operators, speaking a common language to connect, understand and maintain respect is important. Everyone's objectives are aligned and a sense of confidence instilled even amongst those most different. Although I struggled initially, I slowly devised strategies to manage diversity including ensuring clarity of communications, holding meetings, and supervising effectively. I standardized daily operations reports while working in remote locations to ensure support from higher management even in emergencies. During conflicts, I acted as mediator to relate to the rig crew, engineers, client and Rogers Oil management.

Due to complexities associated with group decision-making amongst a diverse group, where each person is crucial to safety, our team faced difficulties involving appropriate people in decision-making. Hence, I identified at initial stages of group operations the roles, capabilities, and weaknesses of each member through external social interaction.

In dealing with diversity, values of individual group members will be different. I was required to be flexible in changing priorities of work and life balance depending on deadlines for projects whereas my Mexican counterparts gave equal priority to both at all times. As a result, strong emphasis was placed on efficient processes, achievable deadlines, and effective project management.

In the male-dominated oil industry, I recognized my uniqueness. Many times, I was the first female member, leader or supervisor that my group had worked with. Initially, I proved credibility and influenced people at strategic points. I utilized interpersonal, relationship-building skills to resolve emotional conflicts while incorporating technical strengths to gain confidence. I depersonalized machismo remarks of male members, responding with professionalism and strict command over project issues.

I adapted to different demands of diverse managers while accommodating varying needs of other team members. I have worked under seven managers within five years, typical at Rogers Oil where international employees frequently change assignments. Identifying different work styles and motivating factors of team members, which varies substantially from one culture or individual to the other, is critical in such an environment.

· · · · · · · · · · · · · · ·

Comments

▷ Eleanor does a good job of clearly spelling out the content of the essay at the very beginning. Applicants are often tempted to craft a "poetic" intro at the expense of helping the reader understand what the essay will be about. Especially when you're only working with a few hundred words, we urge you to choose clarity over flashiness.

▷ After the initial description, the essay starts to get a little muddled. Eleanor discusses some challenges that she faced and how she dealt with them at a high level (for example, being a woman in a male-dominated field), but she never goes into many specifics to show how exactly she encountered resistance. A more impactful way to tell her story could be by focusing on just one or two things and providing specific details about a specific challenge that she faced. For example, she could talk about how uncomfortable she felt the first time a coworker made a crude remark, and then discuss how she dealt with it and improved the situation. Admissions officers will be looking for specific evidence of how Eleanor overcame these teamwork obstacles.

[Handwritten margin note: How? Show, not Tell!]

▷ This question invites a classic SAR essay: What was the problem you encountered? What did you do to solve the problem? How did it turn out as a result of your actions? In this essay, we recommend that Eleanor use the first paragraph to "set the stage" and let the reader know that the oil industry a rough, dangerous one where very few women are found. She should then get right to describing a specific instance where she encountered resistance because of who she was. Then, ideally with more than 250 words still to go (remember that the bulk of a "SAR" essay should be devoted to the action you took), she should describe exactly what she did to overcome this resistance. The last 50–100 words can describe the (hopefully positive) outcomes that resulted from her actions.

▷ Even though the commonly accepted rule of thumb is that going over a word limit by up to 10 percent is okay, we encourage Eleanor to work on getting this essay closer to 400 words. After making the changes described in the previous points, Eleanor should be able to shorten this essay to 400 words and not lose any of its key messages.

▷ Eleanor has a very unique story to tell, because she has a lot of experience in what has traditionally been a male-dominated industry. If she can focus her story around one topic and provide some more specific examples, and work the essay into a clearer "SAR" format, she will have a very compelling essay.

Sample Essay: "Christine" (Krannert School of Management) ◀

Discuss your long- and short-term career goals, how these goals developed, and what you hope to gain from graduate study at Krannert. (500 words)

My 10-year career goal is to become a premier research partner to provide business modeling and marketing research services for multinational companies in China with global management and business perspectives.

I started out in my profession as quantitative research analyst for the industries ranging from media to telecommunications to healthcare while I completed my undergraduate studies. I learned quickly and effectively and was promoted as project supervisor twice within three years to assume greater responsibilities and leadership for a variety of multinational companies. During three years of analytics, marketing and modeling experience, I recognized huge market opportunities in media and high tech industry in China. Besides, China's accession into WTO enhanced my confidence in these opportunities. Therefore, I pursued my master studies in marketing and media management at Purdue University, and I feel this has prepared me for research and analysis in this industry.

However, over two years of master studies and practical training in graduate school at Purdue University, I realize that to achieve my long-term career goal, I need to continue to learn, to grow into a highly effective management professional with cutting-edge analytical skills, sound business knowledge, complete and effective communication and presentation skills. The unique accelerated Krannert's one-year MSIA program is absolutely an ideal program to train me into such an entrepreneurial.

In this demanding program I'll thoroughly develop and enhance my interpersonal and communication skills in a multicultural environment, as well as my ability to make decisions under risk and uncertainty. I'll take full advantage of core courses to advance my finance knowledge and quantitative business methods.

In addition, I'll keenly participate in the unique Krannert executive forum to shape my global business and management perspectives as well as to develop networks with accomplished top-level corporate executives. I'll line up with a business plan team to attend the 2005 Burton D. Morgan Competition to demonstrate entrepreneurship and marketing skills. Furthermore, I'll take an active part in graduate student clubs like Krannert Graduate Marketing Association and Krannert Asian Business Club to improve my leadership and interpersonal skills.

After one-year of training in quantitative methods, marketing, finance, effective management and leadership, I propose to join a global business modeling and marketing research corporation. I believe that team working skills, analytical ability and management of technology will enable me to get such a job. Ideally, over a period of three to five years, I should be able to work in different sectors of the industry (business modeling providers, marketing research suppliers, etc.). In this time, I aim to achieve a leadership role within a sector/geography combination that will enable me return to China.

As an international student, with a different culture, I firmly believe attending the MSIA program will smooth the path to these goals. Moreover, my personal dedication and hard work as well as professional experience will undoubtedly help me achieve these career plans.

· · · · · · · · · · · · · · ·

Comments

▷ Christine has put together a strong essay. She briefly explains her background and the choices she has made until now, why she wants an MBA from Krannert, and what she will do with her degree.

▷ She has already attended Purdue as a graduate student, and it is clear that she is familiar with the school and what Krannert in particular has to offer. She does a good job of demonstrating her interest in the school. Rather than sounding like a standard essay with Krannert's name used in place of another school's, this essay reads like one that was written specifically for Krannert. This is what every applicant's essay should sound like.

▷ Christine also writes convincingly about what she wants to do in the next five years. She comes across as someone who clearly knows what she wants to do with her career. Admissions officers will appreciate this.

▷ Probably the single biggest weakness of this essay is in the third paragraph, where Christine starts to explain why now is the time for her to pursue an MBA. She says that she needs "to continue to learn, to grow into a highly effective management professional with cutting-edge analytical skills," and so on. While this is probably true, the language is still rather general. In this part of the essay, Christine could get into more specific details and explain why exactly she needs these skills. Ideally— without taking up too much space, of course—she could provide an example or two from her past experience, explaining why she believes that these skills are necessary.

▷ Like most other international students, Christine has made some grammatical mistakes that a native English speaker should be able to help her fix. For example, she writes "The unique accelerated Krannert's one-year MSIA program is absolutely an ideal program to train me into such an entrepreneurial," while it should be "Krannert's unique, accelerated one-year MSIA program is an ideal way to train me as an entrepreneur."

▷ Overall, Christine is in good shape. Her sincere interest in Krannert and her professional maturity come through in this essay, which will give her a good chance for success.

SAMPLE ESSAY: "ANDY" (LONDON BUSINESS SCHOOL) ◄

Give us a brief assessment of your career progress to date. In what role do you see yourself working in immediately after graduation and what is your longer term career vision? How will your past and present experiences help you to achieve this? How will the London Business School MBA Programme contribute to this goal? Why is this the right time for you to pursue an MBA? (750 words)

I aspire. I plan. I execute. Cliché or not, this has been the cornerstone leading me from a fledgling student to a business professional, fully prepared to pursue my MBA at London Business School.

My alma mater launched, upon matriculation, an orientation program that offered new admits consultation on academic study, and more importantly, early career plan. Tested to possess great potential in business, I pinpointed MBA as an ideal master degree to pursue following several years' solid work experience. Even more heartening was the fact each year our university boasted a cohort of alumni admitted by top programs including LBS, Harvard Business School, and Chicago Booth.

With plans made, I embarked on the trek by opting to minor in international finance, in addition to taking a broad spectrum of business-related electives including intermediate accounting, economics and banking. Unfortunately, most of the teaching materials derived from the communist time while teachers still resorted to the stale methodology of indoctrination. Final exams required students to memorize theories mechanically and took the form of multiple choices in lieu of more subjective case-based analysis. Though less stellar than my core course grades, they further solidified my plan to acquire a formal business degree.

My liberal arts background proffered me great latitude in engaging in a variety of functions requiring disparate skill-sets, thanks to my versatility as well as knowledge build-up. After all, I position myself as a generalist instead of a specialist typified as an accounting or software programmer. In retrospect, I have been progressing on a rolling project basis, with each stage building upon the previous one.

My peers at each organization are mostly three or four years senior to me; nevertheless, my performance has been well on par with, if not better than, that of others. Unfortunately, to assume that my road to Rome has been plane and wide all along would be too premature a conclusion to jump at.

While my project at International Media Corporation, my second employer, was in high gear, the financial crisis reduced international travel to a near standstill. As if this were not enough, the ensuing fiber-optic scandal in which International Media Fiber Optics was involved, worked perfectly as the last straw—our parent company suspended its China-based operation including my project. The unemployment seriously undermined my career planning and mercilessly shattered my blueprint. I did not burn money; neither had I cooked books, yet was victimized by the irrational and irresponsible human nature.

The ensuing half a year was to bring my career aspiration out of the murky. Six months with the UN initiative were also a time when I reflected upon the world at large. Obviously it is no perfect world, but should it behave like this? What is my next career stop, or is there still one? A victim of the corporate ethics meltdown, I could not help feeling frustrated and disoriented—MBAs apparently played a large role in scandals. Consequently, this experience, allowing me to contribute to society, constituted a break from the mercenary world to seek rationalization.

Originally my career plan was simple: to excel at workplace, get an MBA, and then work as a top strategy consultant before settling down as an executive at a corporation. My work relationship with the UN program manager, an LBS graduate, substantially changed all this. This time, I started to perceive MBA from a new angle—first and foremost, MBAs must be socially responsible before they can aspire to reap professional achievements; otherwise they are still doomed to failure however smart they are. This was again solidified by my acquaintance and mentorship, at the UN conference, with an investment-banker-turned-social-good-doer, also the founding chairman of the US-based Green Earth Institute. There were, and are, responsible people and organization after all.

Six months on, I headed back to the corporate world, confidence recovered. National Data Systems (NDS) seemed an ideal place to start my career anew—I knew so the minute I saw the receptionist for interview—in lieu of charming girls, a pygmy handled the task. Later I learned this deep-rooted culture resulted from NDS's strong advocacy of handicapped-hiring. As for me, I further extend it to hiring veterans in my department. Not only do I commit social obligations, but the department actually benefit from their ultra reliability and diligence. Besides, I volunteered as the department representative of the corporate environment, office health and safety initiative.

Mid 2004 will witness my department's consummation of a worldwide business transformation project, to which I have been contributing from the operations perspective. I deem it an optimal time to start pursue my MBA, which, at this stage, will be conducive to my career aspiration.

Upon graduation, I will join a top-tier IT corporation and rotate in different functions in its leadership/executive development program at mid-management level. In ten years I aspire to be a senior executive and strategy-setter.

Meanwhile, I will devote myself to helping the underprivileged in China. Consequently, I plan on establishing an IT-based NGO in the long run. My business acumen will render me better positioned to contribute to this scenario—applying cost-effective technologies (only possible through my experience with an elite technology firm) to drag the poor out of the social and economic abyss plaguing generations for decades, if not centuries. After all, the betterment of the entire nation cannot hinge upon the prosperity of but a number of regions or cities. I believe that managing an NGO shares much synergy with running a for-profit business: leadership experience developed and social connections established in the business arena should be most conducive to my long-term career aspiration. The end of my achievements in business will ultimately find their way in the social cause. Admittedly, financial standing is an important yardstick, against which personal success is judged; however, it will be even more fulfilling if I can share this success with the needy and bring benefits to them.

As one of the leading MBA programs in the world, London Business School incorporates the many lectures in addition to cases that prepare students for all kinds of real business challenges and opportunities, which caters well to my career aspiration. I trust LBS is where I can attack my weak link by brushing up my financial skills, which I believe are indispensable to my career advancement later on. "He is a sharp cookie, a natural leader just waiting to burst out of his shell", goes the comment on my first performance review. My communication with LBS students and alumni has fully attested to my belief that LBS is the very school that will transform me from a candidate to a bona fide leader in the future.

· · · · · · · · · · · · · ·

Comments

▷ Andy's message of wanting to develop into a socially responsible manager is a good one, and for the most part it comes across as genuine. The beginning of the essay might be more powerful if he were to explicitly call out this theme. The current opening paragraph doesn't seem consistent with the rest of the essay. For example, it starts with "I aspire. I plan. I execute," but the reader is left searching for examples of how Andy planned and executed in his career. We recommend changing the intro to make sure that it highlights what will follow in the essay.

▷ Andy's biggest job will be to find about 300 words to shave from this essay. Although that's more than a quarter of the essay, we actually don't think it will be that hard. The essay prompt asks for a "brief assessment" of Andy's career progress to date, yet he devotes close to 250 words to what happened before he entered the full-time workforce. We don't think he needs to eliminate every last word here, but he should only *briefly* touch upon his undergraduate experience to set up the context for his first post-university job (especially if he feels he needs to explain an unusual career choice) and then move on. We believe he can save about 200 words simply by doing that.

▷ At times it is difficult to follow Andy's career progression. For instance, in the sixth paragraph he discusses his project at International Media Corporation, but this is the first time the reader hears about this company. How did Andy end up there? Headers may help to make these transitions smoother.

▷ Make sure to spell out any acronyms. For example, the first time he writes "NGO," Andy should in fact write "non-governmental organization (NGO)." Andy can simply use "NGO" from that point on.

▷ Andy only devotes two sentences to what he wants to do immediately after he graduates from LBS (in the 11th paragraph). This will almost certainly raise some eyebrows (not in a good way!) among admissions officers; they may wonder how much thought he's given to this. This is an opportunity for Andy to expand his essay and show that he truly understands how LBS will help him in his post-MBA career.

▷ The next paragraph (about helping the underprivileged in China) is good, but can probably be reduced to make more room for the preceding paragraph.

▷ Some of Andy's language could be simplified (for example, "proffered me great latitude in engaging in a variety of functions requiring disparate skill-sets..."). Remember that the goal is to get across your main ideas as efficiently as possible, not to show off your knowledge of the English language.

▷ Along those lines, Andy's English is clear, but he does have some grammatical mistakes. We recommend that Andy have at least one or two more native English speakers review his essays before he submits them.

▷ Overall, a promising theme from an obviously intelligent applicant. We recommend that Andy focus more on the "socially responsible" theme, spell out his career goals more clearly, cut out much of the pre-career content, and make it easier for readers to follow his career progression up to this point. The result will be a much stronger essay.

SAMPLE ESSAY: "CAROLINE" (ROSS SCHOOL OF BUSINESS) ◀

Is there anything else you think the Admissions Committee should know about you to evaluate your candidacy? (500 words)

To support myself through college, I began working various part-time jobs beginning in my first semester. At one time, I held three separate jobs while maintaining a full course-load. In my second semester, I started working at the Eastern University Johnstone School of Business in their technology group. I found my broad learnings from that job to be even more interesting and applicable to my future goals in consulting than the computer programming that I was studying in class. I took this job very seriously and often spent 30–40 demanding hours each week—well beyond the 20 hours per week stated in the job description. During my two years of employment, I earned a series of quick "promotions" and almost a threefold increase in salary.

Recruiters from consulting firms confirmed my belief that I was growing by leaps and bounds when they expressed far greater interest in my work experience than in my undergraduate coursework or my GPA. Despite competition from applicants with higher GPAs, I landed a highly coveted internship with Farley Technologies, and later a full-time position with Myers Consulting. In fact, I was the only intern that Farley hired on campus (from over 100 applicants). In signing on with Myers, I was the only hire given the option to relocate to the highly competitive New York office—a golden opportunity that I seized with great relish.

Beyond my success in a highly demanding part-time job, I rounded out my education and my experience in a new country through various extracurricular activities. I founded two organizations (Society of Software Consultants, which helped Computer Science majors find consulting jobs, and, the teen-counseling organization Helping Hand) while in college. I was also actively involved in numerous others. Additionally, I attended college during the dot-com boom: a pervasive entrepreneurial spirit abounded and, inspired by the possibilities, I devoted a substantial amount of time to create a business plan for an outsourcing business. Unfortunately, at the peak of my involvement, health issues during my second year forced me to abandon the idea—as well as to drop four classes.

I trust that my highly analytical focus as a professional, my strong 730 GMAT score, and my "A" grades in calculus, microeconomics and computer science courses will dispel any doubts about my quantitative abilities. My undergraduate grades reflect the choices I made and the challenges I faced—not my abilities or potential.

. . . .

Comments

▹ Caroline has used Ross's optional essay to address what many applicants believe to be their biggest weakness: their undergraduate GPA. With this kind of essay, it's easy to be too sensitive about the matter and find yourself making too many excuses. However, Caroline avoids this trap pretty well. She stays focused on the positives of her undergraduate experience (which are impressive). She obviously accomplished a lot, and makes clear that those accomplishments were possible as a result of a tradeoff that she decided to make.

▹ There are just a couple of suggestions we would make here. First, we'd recommend that Caroline be a little more explicit at the start of her essay about her stance on her undergraduate grades. Just adding something like "I do not believe that my undergraduate GPA reflects my academic potential, and here's why..." would make the intro a bit smoother. As it is now, she jumps right into story-telling mode, potentially prompting the reader to ask, "Where is she going with this?" She's well under the word count right now, so adding an additional sentence or two (that's all she needs here) won't cause any problems. ✓

▹ Our other suggestion is that, though we like the fact that Caroline doesn't sound apologetic or embarrassed by her undergrad GPA, she could probably go a bit further in making clear that she will take her academics seriously at Ross. She doesn't even need to suggest that she'll do things differently this time around—just that she appreciates that classes are important in business school. ☆

Sample Essay: "Denise" (Sloan School of Management) ◄

Please describe a time when you convinced an individual or group to accept one of your ideas. (500 words, limited to one page)

In my workplace, GlobalPharm, the exclusive distributor of Medico Drugs in Chile, the situation turned complicated when the company incurred in losses. Moreover, in an environment where the possibilities of diversifying the variety of products were scarce, reversing the situation depended on a cost-oriented strategy, a task for the Financial Office. However, since this task was very delicate, the team was reduced to four members: the CFO, the interns under my charge, and myself. Even though we had been working on some information to make some proposals of this nature, this time the shareholders had demanded to reach a profit level never obtained in the company's history. The hard work consisted of doing this optimally.

My role inside the team was to elaborate the proposals, to discuss them with the CFO, and to coordinate with the interns the generation of relevant data to sustain these initiatives. Broadly, the task was divided in two parts: the administrative reorganization of the business and the analysis of the rest of operational expenses.

Because the first part was strictly confidential by its own nature, only the CFO and I dealt with it. Hands-on, we could identify some positions with a relatively costly and others not indispensable. There was also the case of some positions that whereas necessary, presented increasing remunerations based on the sole fact of the amount of time in charge, fostering an undesirable culture of conformism and obsolescence. All of this framed inside a philosophy of cost-competitiveness, which consisted of lightening the structure of the company, but maintaining a group of key positions, each prepared to have more personnel under charge. Likewise, lower-rank positions were meant to be occupied in an increasing proportion by young, proactive, and creative people.

The Board almost completely approved the administrative restructuring, being quite close to reach the shareholder's objective (we cut labor costs nearly a 30%). However, we still needed to identify other sources to improve, thus I convinced the group to take the accounting information to classify it in categories that reflect more familiarly the cost drivers, avoiding the obstacles inherent to the accounting technicalities. With this information, we could obtain revealing information, among the most important issues, was the cost-optimization of imports by using bigger containers and avoiding the consolidated cargos, lowering these expenses between 2% and 3%. This happened because in prior times there was a severe excess of inventory, which made the management be aware only of the amount of imports but not of the container-efficiency.

In addition to this topic, I treated the case of the commissions charged for the banking management of letters, which were extremely expensive because of the huge number of minor amounts; however, we just used this scheme since it was the "standard." In the end, the administration determined that there was no need to face these charges, and that the company could do it by its own, managing to obtain a banking commission's reduction of about a 20%.

In conclusion, my participation in this effort was important to revert the financial situation of the firm and to maintain it competitive in spite of the falling incomes. My initiatives were mostly accepted and I managed to compromise those under my charge, involving them actively in the project and highlighting the importance of their labor.

· · · · · · · · · · · · · · ·

Comments

▹ Unfortunately, right now Denise's story lacks the drama that this essay needs to grab the reader's attention. This question asks Denise to describe a time when she convinced someone to accept one of her ideas. The word *convince* is a dead give-away that the admissions committee wants to see evidence of leadership and persuasion. The ideal scenario would be one in which Denise was certain she had a better way to go about solving a problem, but the rest of her team was skeptical. The essay would then largely be about what she did to win over her team to her way of thinking. However, here she talks about her participating in a team effort to control costs in her company—mostly dry stuff that risks losing the reader's attention by the time she mentions doing any convincing in the fourth paragraph.

▷ Even when she does describe the "convincing" that she had to do, she addresses it so quickly and cleanly that it sounds like she merely had a good idea, the team all agreed to go along with it, and then it was quickly implemented. Unfortunately, there's very little drama here or cues that can help admissions officers see Denise as a potential leader who can win over employees and colleagues.

▷ Denise also falls into the trap of providing not enough detail in some parts of the essay and too much detail in others. In the first part of the essay (where she describes the situation) the reader maybe could use a little more detail. Was Denise given a specific goal, such as reducing fixed costs by 25 percent or more? Were thousands of jobs on the line if the team couldn't find enough cost savings outside of labor costs? Some details such as these would help the admissions committee appreciate the magnitude of the problem.

▷ Meanwhile, in the fourth paragraph (right where she buries the "here's the convincing I had to do" part of the story) Denise seems to include too many details. Information such as why the container issue was previously ignored, and why the company used standard costing for commissions, could probably be trimmed down. Denise wants to keep the focus on her actions as much as possible, rather than on the nitty-gritty details of her job.

▷ Denise probably should start over here. Right now this essay is a rather dry description of some accounting procedures; what she really should do is tell the story of a team under pressure that needed a junior member (Denise) to step up and show the team a better way to get things done. If there are other examples she can share of how she changed the status quo, overcame organizational obstacles, or dealt with difficult people, even better. Ideally, Denise can present herself as a budding leader who makes things happen, rather than as an effective cost accountant who follows his boss's lead all the time.

▷ The language and tone that Denise uses are also fairly formal and dry. This may partly be the result of Denise not being an English speaker, but it contributes to the feeling that this is a really dull essay for an admissions officer to read. Once she rewrites the essay, we suggest that Denise have a native English speaker read it to help her perfect the tone.

▷ Denise has a unique experience to share; not many young professionals get to work with the CFO on a major cost-cutting project. If she can make this less of a story about accounting procedures and more of a high stakes story about how she *convinced* the team to go against what was traditionally expected for the company's benefit, she will have a story that Sloan admissions officers will want to read.

SAMPLE ESSAY: "NIKOS" (SLOAN SCHOOL OF MANAGEMENT) ◄

Please describe a time when you convinced an individual or group to accept one of your ideas. (500 words)

During the last two years, I have been working as an Analyst in Lystl, a small electronics manufacturer employing 300 persons. My main duty has been the completion of a Business Process Reengineering project, initiated by the new major shareholder Torence Group. The project involved the detailed recording of the business processes and organizational structure at the time of the buyout, the polishing of what we felt was wrong or could be done better, along with the implementation of an ERP (Enterprise Resource Planning) software suite to assist business. The whole project and its purpose was no secret in the company and the majority of the staff was hesitant regarding this matter. In fact, a negative reaction was expected, since people are usually unwilling to change. Particularly, there were certain people who feared that their "power" would lessen. For example, the master user of the old proprietary software (a custom home-developed solution) had until then been the main gateway through which most of the information used to pass. He was the one to prepare many reports and there was a company-wide feeling of dependency on his work. This was by no means justified by the nature of his work, which, under the new ERP system, would be curtailed to a purely supportive role. In addition, there were a lot of technophobe people, who feared that they couldn't rely on computers and that their work would not be done successfully under the proposed system.

Although the senior management had already approved the installation of the ERP suite, we could not just proceed and ignore people's fears and resistance. After all, these very people would be the main users of the ERP suite.

My challenge was to convince these people (as well as everyone in the company) that the whole change was for their own benefit. The new ERP system would simplify most tasks and, since top management had already decided that no staff reduction would arise from the ERP, there was nothing to worry about.

I had to come to their level then and persuade them (rather then enforce the opinion) that the new system would prove beneficial to everyone. I isolated and cited what I thought were their biggest worries about the imminent change. I figured that everything is absolutely explicable and understandable. I then broke down their initially huge worries to the lowest level of detail regarding the handling of single processes. I explained how the new ERP software would affect each and every process from the view of the actual user. I persuaded them that their power would increase, since power did not arise from the machine or the software itself but purely from their work. Since their work would be made easier, their impact and usefulness to the company would be leveraged.

After several weeks of endless discussions, most of the initially protesting staff became in fact supporters of the ERP suite, even before they actually see it live. And this proves extremely valuable in the currently ongoing implementation of the project.

· · · · · · · · · · · · · ·

Comments

▷ This is a classic case of adding too much detail to the situation part of the essay. As we explained in the essay section of this chapter, the situation portion of the SAR framework should be succinct and just long enough to give the reader a good background of the event. Here, Nikos provides an over-abundance of information, which leaves the reader in a state of confusion. The third sentence runs on with details of his responsibilities, including details around a buyout. The rest of the essay focuses on issues that occur as a result of the ERP implementation. As such, Nikos should really focus his attention on the setting up the ERP implementation.

▷ From that point on, Nikos does a fair job of describing the fears that the employees had in regard to the implementation, discussing the steps he took to counteract those fears, and what the results were of his actions. Unfortunately the reader is still trying to process the information that Nikos presented in the situation section. Therefore, it is imperative that Nikos align that section with the rest of the essay.

▷ Although Nikos does a fair job of describing his actions and what resulted from those actions, he could do a better job in discussing specifics in both areas. For example, it would be nice if Nikos provided an example of one of tough interactions that he had with a fellow employee in regard to the implementation. That would provide the reader with a better feel for exactly how difficult it was for Nikos. Similarly, it would help if Nikos discussed a conversation with an employee after that employee had been convinced of Nikos's position. That would reinforce Nikos's success in the minds of the reader. As a general rule, providing succinctly written specifics over elongated generalities is almost always better.

▷ Overall this is a good situation to select and relatively easy to show how a difficult interaction was overcome. With some polishing and additions of examples, this essay should be solid.

Sample Essay: "Nick" (Stanford GSB) ◄

What are your career aspirations? What do you need to learn at Stanford to achieve them? (450 words)

Over the past four years I have progressed from Technical Support Analyst to Customer Support Lead to Product Manager. I have taken on increasing responsibility at every stage, advancing to now manage people and control budgets. Career progress has been exceptional by every company metric.

In the near future I envision myself in a senior general management position at hi-tech industry, such as VP of Product Management VP of Strategy or VP of Business Development. In the longer term the biggest dream is to establish a technology company of my own, especially in the Silicon Valley, the beautiful, wonderful heart of the world's hi-tech industry.

When I count what I have done and what skills and abilities I have, I realize that there are plenty of things I have to learn to get there. I have gotten to where I am today based on my unmatched technical prowess, but I have limited knowledge about finance and economics; I have virtually no experience or knowledge in marketing and sales; I have to study a lot about human resources and organizational behaviors; my strategic thinking isn't developed enough; and that's only the beginning of the list!

But most of all, I feel that I lack knowledge and experience in two crucial aspects of general management, especially in the hi-tech industry: a) the ability to assemble a team of talented professionals which will work together and cover your relative incompetence in a certain field necessary for developing your business (after all, one person cannot be an expert in everything), and b) the rare ability to foresee things before they become obvious to everybody and exploit such vision for your success. I can try to acquire some of these experiences and skills by the try-and-error method on the workplace. However, I still expect this will leave me with large holes in my knowledge.

Because of my focus in the hi-tech industry management, it is no wonder that Stanford GSB is the ideal choice for me. Stanford's outstanding connections with the hi-tech industry through its Career Management Center and strong alumni network also plays an important role in my decision.

In addition, the intellectual excellence and the diversity of the student body, Stanford open-minded and informal attitude towards MBA students (expressed in the "Take a Professor to Lunch" program), and the social life in Stanford and the Bay Area assure that, if I will have the honor to study in Stanford, my MBA years will be meaningful and enjoyable ones.

But the most important factor that makes me choose Stanford is his unique and strong emphasis on the entrepreneurial studies. I regard entrepreneurship as one of the most important qualities of a hi-tech manager; I also think that this quality is the hardest to acquire by other means rather than elite MBA program. Stanford's outstanding entrepreneurial program provides an opportunity to acquire entrepreneurial skills necessary for a success in the hi-tech industry with an active help and guidance from the best and brightest in the field.

· · · · · · · · · · · · · · · ·

Comments

▷ One of the hardest things about this essay is deciding how much to talk about your professional background. Stanford offers no essay prompt that explicitly asks you to describe your career progress to date, so many applicant feel the need to at least briefly describe their professional backgrounds in this essay, to provide enough context when describing their future career plans. Nick avoids the trap of using up too many words to describe his work experience to date (which admissions officers will be able to judge from other parts of his application). He covers it very briefly and then moves on to where he wants to go next. If Nick were desperately looking for words to cut he could even possibly discard his opening paragraph, but we think he can safely keep it.

▷ The other challenge that we frequently see with this essay is that the question doesn't ask "Why Stanford?" but rather "What do you need to learn at Stanford?" Many applicants read this question and think they see the former, and end up listing multiple reasons why the school is a good fit for them. Nick does fall into this trap in this draft. Notice how the last three paragraphs (nearly 200 words) are devoted to Nick trying to show fit with the school by rattling off all of the Stanford GSB programs and features that he's read about. Though it is indeed imperative that he show knowledge of the program, he could easily cut this down to focus on just one (or no more than two) reasons why Stanford GSB is the best fit for him. We think the entrepreneurship focus of the last paragraph makes that one the most promising to keep, and Nick can discard much of the other two paragraphs to help get the word count down.

▷ Nick is an international applicant, and although his written English is good, there are some places where his word choices are awkward. For instance, he refers to his "exceptional" career progress and his "unmatched technical prowess." These phrases may give the impression of someone with a huge ego, which we don't think is the case with Nick. And, referring to Silicon Valley as "the beautiful, wonderful heart of the world's hi-tech industry" is probably a bit much. There are also a few places where he simply makes the wrong word choice, such as using the wrong pronoun or preposition. These issues are all easily fixable, and we advise that Nick have at least one native English speaker read his essay to catch unusual word choices such as these.

▷ Overall, Nick is on the right path, although we think he can cut down much of the last part of the essay and even devote a few more words to truly answering the question: What does he *need* to learn at Stanford GSB to reach his career goals? Embedded in that answer can be cues that show that Nick really has done his homework and has good reason to believe that he'll be a great fit at Stanford. If he can tweak the essay to put a little more emphasis there—and fix some of the grammar and word choice problems—Nick will be in good shape.

SAMPLE ESSAY: "RITESH" (STERN SCHOOL OF BUSINESS) ◀

Think about the decisions you have made in your life. Answer the following (750 words):

(a) *What choices have you made that led you to your current position?*

(b) *Why pursue an MBA at this point in your life?*

(c) *What is your career goal upon graduation from NYU Stern? What is your long-term career goal?*

I secured 9th rank amongst half a million students in 12th grade examination. All premier institutions in India were within my reach. A chemical plant in the town always fascinated me. Vehicles, electronic devices, cement kiln developed a passion for engineering in me. After weighing pros and cons of all options and extrapolating myself into all possible roles, I decided to pursue chemical engineering as it offered me the diverse opportunities. I selected Punjab Technical University (PTU), as it is one of the best colleges for chemical engineering in India. By virtue of its experienced faculty, challenging atmosphere, and exhaustive curriculum, PTU has delivered wonderful results over decades.

PTU is known as a gateway to USA. Over 50% of its students pursue MS/Ph.D. at reputed schools in USA. My goal was different; I wanted to be an Entrepreneur. I realized that working with good companies and then pursuing an MBA at a reputed school was the best path to follow. India Chemicals Corp. (ICC), where I was selected in the campus recruitment program, suited my requirements as it promised me a wide exposure and high responsibility. I went through a well-structured training program and started working as a process engineer. I got an opportunity to apply my technical skills for resolving practical problems. I was instrumental in devising several profit improvement schemes. Because of these accomplishments, I was entrusted by the management to lead a team of ten engineers for increasing capacity of the plant. I did a good job as I successfully lead my team in designing and implementing the project.

Though I worked on technical assignments at ICC, I approached work in a very holistic way. I studied role of other departments, looked at the human aspects, and interacted with colleagues in other fields like finance and marketing. As I gained experience, I felt the need to consolidate my technical and functional knowledge. I applied for MBA program at few schools and received good response. Stern school interviewed me in January '02. After a fruitful discussion, I was advised and encouraged to gain more experience and apply again. Meanwhile, the reputed schools in India like IIM and ISB selected me but I was firm on gaining more work experience and pursue MBA at one of the best schools in USA.

I joined Universal Petroleum Company (UPC) as Senior Engineer in March '02 as it offered me a management position. Over the past year, I have lead team of engineers and business experts in objectively evaluating business decisions taken during the past months. We call it a Retro-analysis. Retro-analysis has helped UPC in improving profits. Our linear programming model has helped in crude selection, optimizing operating conditions and product pattern. I have developed strong understanding of oil economics and have used it to our advantage at UPC.

Over past 4 years I have worked in different companies, on different projects and in different roles. I started as a Process Engineer and I am an Assistant Manager today. I have understood the various technical, economic and humane aspects of the manufacturing industry in general and chemical industry in specific. I have understood the interrelation of various entities in an organization. I now need tools to help me understand this correlation. I need formal training and professional degree that will enable me to take higher responsibilities and grow as a professional.

I aspire to be an entrepreneur and lead a chemical manufacturing organization. I need knowledge of finance, marketing and business strategy. I must also be able to raise the resources and deploy them in the most effective and efficient manner. I am sure that the Stern MBA will provide me with all these skills. With its experience faculty, competitive environment and thorough curriculum, it is one of the best places to do MBA. I intend to specialize in the areas of entrepreneurship and financial management. NY exposure, the Berkeley Centre for Entrepreneurial Studies, the CEO series, international exchange program, varied student organizations and business plan competition attracts me to Stern. The school team-building focus fosters the type of environment in which I will excel. I am certain that I will gain a great deal from my fellow students and contribute to their experiences at the Stern.

After graduation, I plan to work for about 2 years with an organization where I can apply the knowledge and skills gained during MBA. I envisage this organization to be a successful startup venture. This will give me hand on experience in starting and running an organization. Also a medium sized organization will ensure that I am exposed to variety of work areas and be able to apply business education effectively. My association with this organization should give me credibility as a professional and a business leader. At appropriate time and with resources, I will start my own venture. I will identify and analyze good ideas and capitalize on them.

· · · · · · · · · · · · · ·

Comments

▹ Ritesh suffers from a common problem among business school applicants: He speaks in generalities when one or two facts will help him tell his story so much more effectively. In the second paragraph, Ritesh mentions "devising several profit improvement schemes." Here is a natural place where an essay reader will ask: "By how much?" If Ritesh can back this up with some numbers (even rough ones), that will help. The same goes for the fourth paragraph. (Note: applicants are sometimes bashful about their achievements because "achieved a 3% reduction in costs" may sound insignificant. But don't worry; admissions officers won't scoff. They'll appreciate your making the accomplishment more tangible.))

▹ In the same paragraph, Ritesh states that he successfully led a team in implementing a project. This is another great place to provide more detail. It is exactly this kind of leadership example that can help set Ritesh apart from the competition. Plus, because Stern suggested that he needed more professional experience, it is even more critical that he point to success on the job. If he needs to take something out in order to make room for these examples, he could take out some of the description of his school (which isn't very important, because admissions officers would rather know more about Ritesh than his school).

▹ We recommend that Ritesh work on the last paragraph to make his post-Stern career goals more clear. He describes his first post-Stern company as a "successful startup," but then goes on to say that he wants to work for a medium-sized organization. Is this the same company?

▷ Also, why does he only want to spend two years at his first job? It might seem un-reasonable to an admissions officer that Ritesh can learn all that he wants to learn in this relatively short amount of time.

▷ Note that some applicants are successful by breaking up this essay and explicitly an-swering each of the three questions. However, that's not necessary, as Ritesh shows here. Either way can work.

▷ The paragraph about Stern isn't bad, but this paragraph could fairly easily be swapped out and replaced by a paragraph for Wharton, for Columbia, and so on. (Of course, a lot of applicants do just that.) If he has time, we recommend that Ritesh try to work his Stern theme into the whole essay. This should be fairly easy, because he already talks about teamwork and entrepreneurship in other parts of the essay. Note that, although part (b) doesn't explicitly ask why Ritesh wants to pursue a Stern MBA, he should assume that's what the admissions committee really wants to know.

▷ Ritesh's grammar is mostly good, although there are a few places where he needs to make some small fixes. We recommend that he have at least one native English speaker proofread his essays before submitting them. Again, this is the kind of thing that will help set him apart from the thousands of other Indian applicants, which is critical for him.

▷ As an aside, many international applicants have a reputation for talking about their test scores and statistics more than their "soft and fuzzy" attributes. Unfortunately for Ritesh, he reinforces this stereotype by starting off the essay discussing his class rank in the very first sentence. Any additional way that Ritesh can show that he is more than just an engineer with good test scores will help him a lot.

▷ Overall, there is work to be done here, but Ritesh has the makings of a good essay. If he can bring out leadership examples some more, and make a slightly more convincing case for why Stern makes the most sense for him, he will be in much better shape.

SAMPLE ESSAY: "ADE" (TUCK SCHOOL OF BUSINESS) ◀

Why is an MBA a critical next step towards your short and long-term career goals? Why is Tuck the best MBA program for you? (500 words recommended)

October 2000—Logos, Nigeria—After three consecutive years of drought, the residents of Logos had spent their lifetime's savings, and accumulated debt sufficient to last a lifetime. The local moneylender charged an interest of 5% per month while taking their property as collateral. (This was at a time when the Prime Lending Rate was less than 10%.)

August 2003—Umtata, South Africa—Foodworld (an affiliate of Dairy Farm, Hong Kong) had opened 50 swanky self-service supermarkets. Family grocers have seen a 30% drop in revenue and understand consumer preference for an open store format. They do not know how to raise the capital to make a transition.

A ringside spectator of these two situations, I believe both these instances illustrate the scope for growth in the African financial sector. I strongly believe that availability of finance holds the key to development. Innovation in this sector can unleash the potential for progress. About fifteen years from now, I intend to attain a position where I can drive innovation in the African financial system. This will enable me to make a positive impact on the lives of a large number of people.

After completing my engineering degree, I wanted to do an MBA. During my 6-month internship at INSEAD, Fontainebleau, France I discovered that diversity of students and prior work experience greatly enhanced the learning one got at a business school. So, I decided to work for a few years, understand the working of an industry and then move into finance after an MBA.

I chose to join the rotational training program at Revel Consumer Goods (RCG). During the last three years, my assignments have included designing a system to track profitability of brands across RCG, evaluating the impact of development projects on social cohesion in villages in Logos and setting up a vendor managed inventory system at RCG, Greece. My most important learning at RCG is that a customer centric approach is imperative for sustainable, profitable growth across industry sectors.

On the surface, finance may appear to be a strange shift in career direction from my current role as a manager in a consumer packaged goods company. I made my first investment in the stock market as a 13-year-old. For the last 12 years, I have been participating (profitably!) in the African stock markets as an investor. As African interest rates drop, I have advised family, friends and colleagues on solutions to ensure a good income from their investments. I have taught myself the theory behind futures and options to enable me hedge my portfolio. A move to finance will unite my passion for finance with my desire to enable people to improve their lives.

Exposure to different industry sectors and an in depth understanding of the working of the financial industry are critical for me to move into the financial services industry. I need to understand the analytical techniques that are used in finance. I want an understanding of the theory of what makes an enterprise tick. Since I lack sufficient work experience in finance, I also desire an opportunity of a summer internship to strengthen my credentials. An MBA will give me a theoretical foundation in finance as well as the practical exposure necessary to build a strong career.

My application to Tuck is the first step toward realizing my goal of delivering innovative financial solutions in Africa. After my MBA, I propose to join a global financial services corporation. I believe that team working skills, analytical ability and customer centric approach will enable me to get such a job. Ideally, over a period of six to ten years, I should be able to work in different sectors of the industry (municipal finance, mortgage and pension funds). In this time, I aim to achieve a leadership role within a sector/geography combination that will enable me return to Africa.

The J & G Distributors case was my first exposure to Tuck. This case was part of the operations module of the 1-month management program for RCG trainees. Hence, Tuck was one of the first schools I looked into, after I started researching schools for MBA programs. Tuck's focus on general management and depth in finance fit in well with my career goals. The Tuck Leadership Forum will help in all round development of my leadership skills. I expect to benefit from the opportunity to interact closely with top-notch faculty members facilitated by the small class size.

My undergraduate university is 170 miles from the nearest city. The rural setting of the Tuck school and the collaborative nature of the community promises to be a déjà vu of sorts for me. The prospect of returning to an environment where everybody knows each other energizes me immensely. As an international student, from a different culture, my active involvement in activities in and outside the classroom will help me contribute to the richness of the community. I look forward to building lifelong friendships fostered by the small scale and residential environment. The prospect of learning skiing and ice hockey is icing on the cake!

. . . .

Comments

▷ Ade does a nice job of providing the reader with some background as to why he wants to pursue the career that he discusses. The opening paragraphs give us a nice glimpse into his thinking and into events that have clearly impacted his worldview. These are powerful vignettes and would be terrific to bring up again during the interview.

▷ The second event, however, could be a bit clearer. We're not sure what "understand consumer preference for an open store format" means without reading it over a few times. To make sure that vignettes such as this one are poignant, they need to be straightforward and free of industry jargon. This is one place where it can be especially helpful to get a proofread from a friend or family member from outside the workplace.

▷ Ade also does a nice job of linking his professional and personal experiences to his career goal of delivering innovative financial solutions to the African continent. It would be nice if Ade could provide an example of one such innovative solution that interests him. This would help crystallize his goal and help show its potential for impact.

▷ The third piece of the essay, Ade's discussion of "Why Tuck," starts off well, but could be made stronger. Ade begins by referring to his first exposure to Tuck, which is a nice lead it, but then almost makes it sound as though he's applying to Tuck mainly because it was one of the first business schools to which he was exposed. Rather then leaving that impression with an admissions officer who's always think-ing about yield numbers, Ade really should talk more about his first exposure to Tuck and how that left a lasting impression that Tuck is truly the place for him. From there the rest of his discussion in terms of what Tuck has to offer would flow nicely.

▷ We really like how Ade's ending conveys his enthusiasm for Tuck. And it always helps to make the admissions representative smile at the end of the essay.

▷ This essay's biggest weakness is that it's a bit on the long side. Though Tuck has no official word limits, the school hints that 500 words is the most appropriate length for its admissions essays. The first three paragraphs of the essay (where Ade provides a glimpse into what he saw unfold in Africa) and the middle paragraph (where he brags about his successful investing experience) are two places where Ade can perhaps save some words. These parts of the essay aren't necessarily weak, but we expect Ade could save at least 100 words by trimming these down and keeping the essay more a bit more focused.

SAMPLE ESSAY: "DIANA" (THE WHARTON SCHOOL) ◀

Describe a failure that you have experienced. What role did you play, and what did you learn about yourself? How did this experience help to create your definition of failure? (600 words)

Out of our team of seven people at Bank USA, the managing director heading my group was the first one to notice the mistake. But it was too late. We had already faxed a client the pages on a new equity issue, only the pages had the name of the wrong client in the corner. Not only did we make a careless mistake, but we also unwittingly let our client know that we were presenting the same idea to one of their competitors. To make matters worse, I felt responsible because I was the one who sent the fax.

The pitch was to a very important client, hence the number of people on the team. There were four people from my group, Integrated Financial Services, and three from the International Equity Group (IEG). From the beginning, we made the mistake of not making IEG feel like a part of the team. Perhaps it was because they weren't even located in the same building we were. Instead, we included IEG solely because of their strong knowledge of equity issues, without familiarizing them with our history with the client. The head of my group didn't even know the names of the junior IEG people who joined us on a conference call. I firmly believe that had we made IEG feel more a part of the team, they would have understood the importance of the presentation and taken more care to focus on the project and ensure the accuracy of their work.

Another reason why our team failed was poor communication within our group and with IEG. On the night the fax was sent, IEG e-mailed us the pages they put together, without explaining what they were for. I didn't know what the pages were for, but my Vice President looked them over and told me to fax them to the client. I later found out that he requested the pages from IEG; only he didn't clearly explain to them what the pages were for. As busy as I was, I didn't ask him about them and instead I quickly created a cover sheet and sent them off. I should have asked my VP what the pages were for. Had I stopped to ask and realized that they were for a conference call with the client, I would have been more cautious about sending them out. With better communication between all parties, we may have avoided our mistake.

I wish I had looked past the first page and noticed the wrong client name. But I didn't, and that was my fault. I learned that one of my roles on the team was to take one last look at what was being sent out, as it was usually the analysts who did the faxing, printing or e-mailing. I learned the hard way not to assume the accuracy of anyone else's work, and that, whether or not I made the mistake, letting it go through was a big failure on my part. This unwillingness to "go the last mile," regardless of whose job it is or how important it seems, became my yardstick for failure from that point forward.

When the head of my group turned beet red and screaming mad, my VP taught me an important lesson about accountability. Though it may have been easier to deflect some of the blame to IEG, he didn't blame them at all. He realized that we had a role in the mistake, and he accepted responsibility. At first I thought it unfair for us to bear the brunt of our managing director's diatribe, but my VP's example helped me realize that accepting responsibility and learning from mistakes is far more desirable than shifting blame to others. I will be sure to do this from now on.

· · · · · · · · · · · · · · ·

Comments

> Diana's choice of a failure to discuss is easy to understand and relate to. She doesn't try to do too much. Rather, she focuses on a story that everyone can understand. Most of us have probably made a mistake very similar to this at some point in our lives, which makes it very easy to relate to his story.

> Additionally, she does a good job of quickly setting up the problem. After just four sentences we understand what happened and who was involved.

> One area in which the essay could be improved is by making it a little clearer how and why this was an important mistake. Naturally, sending the wrong client name is a huge mistake, but what was the fallout? Was the client upset? Did Diana's bank lose the deal because of it? Without adding much length, a few more details like this could help add a bit more depth and make the reader care a bit more, which is always a good thing. (If it turns out that there was no fallout with the client, then Diana could focus a bit more on the managing director's reaction. Did this mistake have any consequences?)

- Also, although we don't think a complete re-write is in order, Diana should think more about the emphasis that the question places on Diana, rather than on her team. As it stands now, this seems like it may be an essay that Diana tried to reuse from another school's application, because it misses the mark a bit on answering the exact questions Wharton asks. There is a lot of story-telling about who did (or didn't) do what, how others handled the situation, and so forth. Much of this is relevant and can stay in the essay, but Diana should put more emphasis on what she did, what she learned, and how her definition of failure changed as a result.

- A small stylistic point: Diana could possibly create a little drama by explicitly describing what feelings ran through her mind the moment she was confronted with the mistake. Admissions officers like to see this kind of introspection. But, Diana would need to make room for it in this essay right now.

- One other thing for Diana to think about is what main lesson she wants to communicate in this essay. She talks about three things: how her group should have gotten IEG more involved, how communication within the group was lacking, and how she learned about the value of holding oneself accountable.

  1. The first theme (about IEG) could use a little work, because right now it's not immediately clear to a reader whether getting IEG more involved would have really prevented the mistake. Would it have? Or is this a separate failing of the team?

  2. The second theme (communication) is a potentially good one, but again, Diana should think about how lack of communication directly led to the mistake. As mentioned, would better communication really have prevented the mistake?

  3. The third theme (accountability) is a strong one. If Diana wanted to focus on just this, though, she would need to devote more words to the managing director's reaction, the consequences that Diana faced, and so on. This may end up being the better theme to focus on, especially if Diana decides that the first two themes don't directly connect to the failure. But the essay would require a fairly significant reworking if she chose this route.

- Overall, we like where this essay is headed. If Diana can put more emphasis on what she learned (and ideally how she put these lessons to work in a later challenge, rather than a future hypothetical situation), she can take this from a promising essay to a very strong one.

SAMPLE ESSAY: "GREG" (YALE SCHOOL OF MANAGEMENT) ◄

What achievement are you most proud of and why? (500 words)

Growing up, I always had an intense fear of public speaking. I remember my first-grade teacher, Miss Hamilton, telling me that she loved my Christmas story and asking me to read it aloud for everyone's parents at the school's Christmas play. I immediately burst into tears, begging her not to make me speak in front of so many people. She finally relented, but even as a six-year-old I recognized the concern in her voice. This fear continued through my early teenage years. At various times I would be asked to give a presentation or make a speech, and I would always find an excuse to get out of it. I would rarely even speak up in class for fear of embarrassment. I couldn't imagine how I would ever overcome my fear of public speaking.

By the time I reached college, I had become more comfortable with speaking in a group. Things had changed for me. The difference was that I was no longer thinking about what I was going to say to the point of paralysis. I was just speaking my mind. Still, I couldn't imagine myself actually speaking in front of a large audience. What would happen if I finally got up in front of a crowd? Would I freeze up? Would I even be able to bring myself to get up in front of that crowd? When would the right opportunity present itself?

That opportunity came in my junior year of college, when I decided to run for the office of treasurer in our student government. I had always had strong opinions about how the school could be improved, and this was my chance to make a difference. I wanted to get more students involved in all areas of the student government. Of course, running for office meant making a speech in front of my university's 8,000 students. The old Greg would never have done it, but when I realized that a five-minute speech was what stood before me and the possibility of becoming my student body's treasurer, I refused to let it stop me. That day I walked up to the podium and delivered my speech without thinking about that large audience at all. I simply said what I wanted to say, only glancing at my notes once or twice. I stumbled a few times at first, but by the end of the speech it all felt very natural to me, to the point where I didn't want to leave the stage!

Everything had changed. I no longer worried about what I would say, what my voice would sound like, or how people would react. I learned that effective communication didn't have to be perfect, as long as it was sincere. And I realized that there was no secret to public speaking. Great speakers simply have confidence, and I have since gained this trait. I have gone on to speak in front of crowds in academic, business, and informal settings, and each time I have just relaxed and let myself speak. And it always feels as good as it did that day in front of 8,000 fellow students, when I conquered my fear of public speaking.

· · · · · · · · · · · · · · ·

Comments

▷ The intro paragraph is great. Greg provides a nice illustration of how intense his fear of public speaking was, and how it had been with him since childhood. ✓

▷ In the second paragraph, Greg could try to describe an example of how he was starting to become more comfortable with the idea of speaking in a group. Even just one sentence would help give the reader an idea of Greg's evolution as a speaker, and maintain the vivid story-telling that Greg established at the start of the essay.

▷ All of the questions at the end of the second paragraph can probably be removed. Greg mentioned to us that he was looking for ways to cut this essay down to the 500-word limit. We recommend striking these questions completely. No need to try to stir up drama in such a short piece.

▷ The third paragraph moves the story along well, although we'd advise taking out the second and third sentences. They aren't relevant to the story that Greg is trying to tell. This is another opportunity to shorten the essay.

▷ Terrific ending. We wouldn't change a thing in that last paragraph.

▷ Although the question doesn't explicitly ask him to relate his achievement back to the school, Greg could help himself by mentioning how his achievement and his speaking ability will help him contribute at Yale. This is something to consider adding, as long as it doesn't end up sounding forced.

▷ Overall, Greg is much further along than most applicants are after one draft. We just recommend that Greg tighten up the middle part and keep only what's relevant, adding one more vivid example (that helps illustrate how he changed over time) if possible. That would take this essay from very good to excellent.

Sample Essay: "Manoj" (Yale School of Management) ◀

Describe an accomplishment that exhibits your leadership style. The description should include evidence of your leadership skills, the actions you took, and the impact you had on your organization. (500 words)

In 2001 Integrity Applications was hired by Regency Financial to build a content syndication system. This was to be the first system of its kind, which the client desired to have in place in a very short time frame. I was appointed technical architect of this project and was to lead a team of relatively inexperienced developers. This was going to be a tough assignment, requiring long hours of work and extra effort from every team member.

My first step was to identify the strengths and weaknesses of different members and assign them tasks accordingly. I kept the toughest and most critical task for myself. As we progressed through the initial stages of the project, there were a number of times, when one or more member appeared dispirited at being stuck with a problem. Some other showed signs of fatigue. It was difficult for me to mentor each one individually, as we were racing against time. So I introduced a new communication concept called "lessons learnt." Each evening, over a coffee break, the team would get together at a "lessons learnt" meeting to discuss what they learnt that day. Everyone brought up their problems, and how the same were overcome or not. In the latter case, we would collectively suggest solutions.

Most of the times, "lessons learnt" related to work and helped teammates learn from each other. Occasionally however, we would indulge in lighthearted banter—once a member shared his "lesson learnt" that taking Haver Street down to the office rather than Leverly Drive took him 437 seconds longer! (Yes he actually used a stopwatch to time himself.) Such interactions acted as amazing stress busters and we would all get back to work feeling refreshed. My teammates now seemed motivated and put in that extra effort, mainly because they realized they were learning and growing professionally through this effort, leading to a successful delivery and a highly satisfied client.

I, too, had some vital "lessons learnt" from this entire experience, which have helped me grow as a leader. Foremost amongst these was the importance of keeping your team motivated through effective communication. Secondly, I learnt how important it is to lead by example. I was able to quickly gain the respect of my team members because I took on the most difficult portion of the project myself. I also learnt about the importance of managing available resources optimally, in this case inexperienced technical developers.

I have led teams through many difficult projects but the teamwork and productivity of this team is something I am especially proud of.

. . . .

Comments

▹ This is the classic leadership question, which can be approached by focusing on describing the situation, your specific actions, the results, and what you learned. Overall Manoj covers all of those bases, providing a good overview of his role, impact, and the lessons he learned.

▹ We would, however, have liked to seen more specificity. For example, Manoj points out that he kept "the toughest and most critical task for himself," but never mentions what that task was. Additionally, he shares a light-hearted example about the "lessons learnt" sessions, but doesn't provide an example of a more straightforward lesson that he learned.

▹ Finally, it would have been helpful if Manoj included some numbers that give the reader an idea of the size, scope and magnitude of the project on which he worked. Note how the question is phrased—it specifically asks for the impact the applicant had on his organization. Manoj needs to go into more specifics here. How many people was he managing? How much in terms of dollars was the project worth to the company? What metrics did he meet?

▸ The SAR approach was tailor-made for this essay! If Manoj can apply that technique and include more details about his actions and the impact they had on his organization, this essay will be much stronger.

SAMPLE ESSAY: "ROBINSON" (YALE SCHOOL OF MANAGEMENT) ◂

What is the most difficult feedback you have received from another person or the most significant weakness you have perceived in yourself? What steps have you taken to address it and how will business school contribute to this process? (500 words)

"Rob, you're making it impossible for this team to get anything done. You need to work with us. I don't have the authority to fire you from the team, but if you keep it up, I can't work with you anymore. I'm going home now."

As soon as Lisa finished saying this, she headed right for the door and exited the conference room. I was alone, and I sat there for 15 minutes, silent, thinking about how the whole project had unraveled over the past month. Our team has been tasked with developing an improved workflow for custom-built software solutions. On the team were someone from the sales department, two people from project management, and me, who represented engineering team.

Before long, we found ourselves in an "us vs. them" situation, where I would shoot down everything that sales wanted, and Lisa and the other project manager wanted nothing to do with my solutions. One reason I volunteered for the team was because I always enjoyed working with people from other groups, but everyone on this team seemed to be protecting his or her own agenda. Things came to a head when a late-night meeting was adjourned early after we couldn't agree on anything. That was the night Lisa delivered her stinging feedback.

As I sat there, I realized the pattern I had fallen into. Early on the sales representative had made some jokes about being sorry to see someone from engineering on the team, since everything would be a "No" answer from me. Rather than joking back or working to prove him wrong, I let that put me on a defensive footing. Every time he asked for an inch, I was certain he was trying to take a yard, and I would think of five reasons why his request or suggestion was a terrible one. He started to do the same, the project managers started shooting down others' ideas, and the cycle repeated itself until that fateful night, when we almost left the project for dead.

After giving Lisa's feedback a lot of thought during a restless night, I asked her if I could meet with her over coffee the next afternoon—"On neutral turf," I joked. She obliged, and we then spent two hours having a frank discussion about how everything had gone wrong. We were both so relieved to clear the air.

There was no turf to protect, I realized. We were all on that team to improve how the company operated and to make it more competitive. When I thought I had been doing my own team a favor, I had in fact been hurting the company overall. I committed myself to re-convening the team and approaching the opportunity as a CEO would. When the sales guys teased me, I joined in the fun and teased them right back. More importantly, when someone put forward a new idea, I first thought about how much it would help the company, not how much work it would create for the engineers.

Within two months our team created an entirely new, far more effective workflow for new orders, and we were congratulated with generous gifts from our leadership team. I knew I was one step closer to being the CEO I knew I could be.

• • • • • • • • • • • • • • •

Comments

▷ Writing about weakness or failure is always tough for an applicant, although it can make for an incredibly effective essay. Here Robinson demonstrates some vulnerability by admitting that he contributed to his team's unhealthy environment, which in turn affected the overall effectiveness of the team.

▷ Nice introduction. It grabs the reader's attention, and immediately sets the tone for the rest of the essay.

▷ This is a good place to use the SAR framework described in Chapter 4. This is one area where the essay can be improved, and probably shortened just a bit: Robinson devotes more than 330 words to describing the situation, fewer than 170 words describing the action he took to make it better, and just two sentences to the result. He has the right structure here, but we believe he could cut down the situation setup by at least 50 words and not lose anything. For example, the third and fourth paragraphs could be combined, and he could devote fewer words to explaining exactly how the problem started (for example, that the salesperson teased Robinson, which also may make Robinson sound overly defensive or immature).

▷ Tightening the situation set-up would give Robinson a little more room to describe exactly how we went about thinking and acting differently. Perhaps he could include an example of an idea that the salesperson suggested, and describe exactly how he treated that idea differently than he would have just one month earlier. A few more specific here will help admissions officers better visualize Robinson's transformation. This is the one place where the essay needs some additional "meat."

▷ It's fine that he devotes only a couple of lines to the result, but the very last line is awkward. Many future MBAs think they'll one day be CEO or even king of the world. No need to get into that rhetoric here.

▷ We believe Robinson is off to a good start. Often the story itself makes or breaks the essay, and he has chosen a good story to work with here. While it's not quite finished yet, Robinson is not far from having a strong essay.

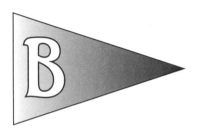

Additional Resumes

In this section you will find five additional resumes with associated commentary that should help give you a sense of what admissions counselors look for when evaluating this application component. As with the additional essays, there is a range of strong to weak resumes, which should help you as you evaluate your own.

SAMPLE RESUME: "MARIELENA" ◀

Marielena L. Morris
2412 Miskinis Rd.
Trenton, NJ 08611
(555) 695-9534

EXPERIENCE

Engineer II, Cingulon, Trenton, NJ   **04/2010–Present**

Responsible for the design and performance of a cellular phone and data network. Led local, regional, and national projects resulting in a 20% improvement in quality performance. Designed and commissioned 32 new cell sites resulting in cell phone and data coverage for an additional 200,000 people.

- Developed and implemented procedures for 15 Cingulon markets, automating a common engineering practice that took 70% of engineers' time. Trenton alone had a 10% reduction in the number of customer dropped calls (unwanted cell phone disconnects) due to automating this procedure.

- Saved Cingulon 750 hours of engineering man-hours by developing a value analysis tool that allows engineers to quickly transfer engineering metrics to a format usable for financial analysis. *Received an Excellence Award for this achievement.*

- Authored an engineering software program maintenance document. These steps resulted in faster and more reliable performing computers allowing for enhanced metrics analysis. *Received an Excellence Award for this achievement.*

- Derived a new model for measuring, forecasting, and reporting engineering metrics. This analysis raised the bar for metrics analysis amongst Cingulon engineers. *Received an Excellence Award for this achievement.*

- Developed a document on carrier utilization procedures for Cingulon markets. These procedures helped engineers efficiently utilize engineering hardware, resulting in cost savings that were diverted for new cell sites, increasing cell phone coverage.

- Trained 45 engineers across the country on several of the above mentioned processes.

Engineer I, Cingulon, Trenton, NJ   **04/2008–04/2010**

Responsible for the design and performance of a cellular phone and data network. Improved local network quality by 22%. Designed and commissioned 35 new cell sites resulting in cell phone and data coverage for an additional 400,000 people.

Wireless Engineer, Cingulon, Trenton, NJ   **01/2006–04/2007**

Responsible for the construction of 26 new cell sites. Activities included: managing construction timelines, lowering costs, and interfacing with city governments, landlords, contractors, and several Cingulon departments.

- Developed a local database for construction engineers, radio frequency engineers and other departments to enter and store cell site information.
- Wrote site procedures for three different departments.
- Saved Cingulon $180,000 by reducing the amount of fencing used around cell site leased areas in the Trenton market.
- Compiled a training manual for wireless implementation engineers.

EDUCATION

Rutgers, Newark, NJ

Bachelor of Science in Electrical Engineering

Graduation Date—December 2005

COMMUNITY

2003–2005—Global youth leader for Habitat for Humanity. Construction projects in Lima and Botswana.

2004–2005—New Jersey state robotics championship—grand prize.

PERSONAL INTERESTS

Ran three marathons, world travel, camping, home improvement, professional pianist.

· · · · · · · · · · · · · · ·

Comments

▷ Marielena does a nice job of spelling out the tangible impact of her efforts. Most resumes fall short in that area, simply listing statements without quantifying impact. Still, Marielena could make the resume stronger by highlighting not only what improved but the impact of those improvements. For example, how did customers' experiences improve as a result? What did this really mean for the broader company and its objectives?

▷ Marielena gives the impression that she has managed a number of people in her roles, but she never explicitly states that. It would help show her leadership abilities if the resume highlighted her role as a manager a bit more. As an engineer, this would be particularly beneficial.

▷ The amount of career progression that Marielena has experienced over the years is questionable based on this resume. While it is clear that she has been promoted over time, it is less clear exactly how her roles and responsibilities have been expanded over time. If career progression has indeed been minimal, this is something Marielena should actively address in her essays and interview. Indeed, it could be part of the answer to the "why an MBA?" question. The response being that she has consistently delivered terrific results, but has found her career progression to be limited.

▷ The community and personal sections are interesting. They should serve as good fodder for conversation during admissions interviews.

SAMPLE RESUME: "ALEXIS" ◀

ALEXIS M. DUNCAN

Address: 3242 Hitus Ave #232, New York, NY 10012

Phone: (555) 941-7994

E-mail: aduncan@coldmail.com

PROFESSIONAL EXPERIENCE

Marketing Communications Department Manager, *Salvatore International,*
New York, NY   02/2010–Present

‣ Supervise corporate global print and web marketing campaigns in 4 sales regions, resulting in an increased corporate image retention and company/product exposure rate by 250%.

‣ Manage process of industry exhibitions worldwide, including new product presentations, support documentation, booth construction/upgrades supervision, and exhibition schedule development.

‣ Oversee daily marketing agenda, including product documentation, product packaging, and case studies.

‣ Developed corporate branding strategy, including brand booklet and rules for use and placement of Salvatore brands in advertising, exhibitions, stationery, and customer marketing materials.

‣ Created global marketing communications department from scratch on a limited budget of $230,000, while re-evaluating existing processes to create more efficiency and re-claim 9% of first year budget

‣ Impacted organizational thinking and processes by creating new marketing-centric focus of company, resulting in closer collaboration of Sales, Marketing, Production, and R&D departments globally.

Product Manager   5/2008–02/2010

‣ Managed and made more efficient the security product development processes between R&D in New York and production facilities in Bangalore, India.

‣ Managed company product and international standards documentation and version control.

Sr. Technical/Marketing Writer, *Lattis Technical Writing, New York, NY*   11/2006–4/2008

‣ Produced hard-hitting marketing communications and technical documents for clients in consumer products, software, and medical industries.

‣ Supervised FDA approval process for biotechnology client's cancer therapeutic, including heading the team of writers to develop the 20-volume set of data and declarations. Worked with internal FDA consultant and scientists to ensure precision and direction under time constraints.

Project Manager, *The York High Tech Group, New York, NY*   3/2006–11/2006

‣ Worked with entrepreneurs to develop business plans, product feasibility reports, market research, and financial projections at various stages of company start up.

‣ Wrote four business plans for entrepreneurs and assisted in securing seed, first and second-round investments in excess of $25 million.

‣ Assisted entrepreneur clients with documentation needs, including presentations for VC and BOD audiences.

‣ Assisted Director of New York Commerce Department in Australia with business development of investment and strategic partnerships between Australia and New York local businesses.

Freelance Business Consultant, *New York, NY*   12/2005–2/2006

- Worked closely with entrepreneurs to develop business plans, product feasibility reports, market research, and financial projections at various stages of company start up.
- Supported executive staff in development of logos, product documentation, and marketing strategies.
- Coached entrepreneurs in fund raising and giving presentations to VCs and Board of Directors.
- Assisted CEOs with location of real estate for overseas office and professional PR agency in the same city.

Product Manager, Business Development, *Bluecloud, Inc., Lansing, IL*   11/2003–6/2005

- Administered software development products for automotive and warehouse management industries, which included close contact with customers to development of product specifications, budget, and implementation.

Product Manager, Software Developer, *Interactive Systems, Inc., Detroit, MI*

9/2002–11/2003

- Managed development of time-keeping software product line for healthcare and transportation industries, including market research and technology evaluations, cost estimations and project funding.

Project Manager, *Miev-Langon, Detroit, MI, USA*   9/2001–9/2002

- Developed electrical designs and programming of automation systems for manufacturing of consumer products for Felnis Consumer, while managing team interaction between office and factory.

EDUCATION

BS in Electrical Engineering, Michigan State University, East Lansing, MI

1996–2001

5-year program including three 6-month internships.

One of only 200 students who participated in 2-year pilot engineering program funded by National Science Foundation to interlace subject areas, a new teaching paradigm.

ACTIVITIES

2010–2011

Member of Board of Directors—Golden Rule—a non-profit organization focusing on the interaction of neighboring countries to create a working dialogue through group involvement in community projects and self-evaluation.

- Head continued re-organization processes with research into organization and implementation of developed business plan, marketing plan and branding, and financials.

PERSONAL

Interests: Salsa dancing, kayaking, sky diving, rock climbing

∙ ∙ ∙ ∙ ∙ ∙ ∙ ∙ ∙ ∙ ∙ ∙ ∙ ∙ ∙

Comments

▷ Alexis clearly has a number of terrific experiences to highlight and does a fair job of detailing those experiences in a meaningful and tangible way. She should consider cutting out some of the short stints, such as when she operated as a "freelance business consultant" and focus on her most important (recent three) positions. This will make for a more succinct resume and help keep it down to one page.

▷ For each of the most recent three positions, it would help if Alexis led with a non-bulleted statement that summarized her activities and the impact those activities had on the organization. She's headed in the direction already with the first bullet for each of these positions, but there are a few things she should consider:

▷ It would be helpful to get a sense of the magnitude of her leadership responsibilities. How many people is she currently managing?

▷ Alexis gives a tangible number in terms of the increase in exposure rate, but what does that mean exactly? How does that impact the company and what did she do to drive that increase?

▷ Similarly, in the first two bullets of the next two positions, Alexis needs to more effectively provide tangible estimates of the impact she had as well as the result of her actions in a summarized statement.

SAMPLE RESUME: "TOBY" ◄

TOBY S. WALKER

PROFESSIONAL EXPERIENCE:

Stealth Solutions (Management Consulting), New York, NY

Associate   2010–Present

Client: Insurance Company, Midwest U.S.

- Analyzed print spend, identified savings opportunities, bid print jobs to vendors, and produced savings of $22M annually
- Created business unit to centralize print production
- Developed process maps and job descriptions, assisted in hiring and training new staff, organized metrics to measure success, and trained staff on metrics reporting

Client: Credit Card Company, Eastern U.S.

- Managed the communication and training needs of a change management initiative intended to address new regulatory concerns
- Developed live training materials, trained compliance trainers, and organized training for six thousand employees
- Oversaw the creation of web-based training curriculum to be used for the remaining 24,000 U.S. employees
- Wrote the curriculum, selected and managed the content vendor, and brought training live within two months

Internal Involvement

- Co-chair of social committee, running monthly events at venues across New York City
- Organizing on-campus recruiting initiative for Brown ('05–'06) and Northwestern ('06), and interviewed business analyst, associate and senior associate candidates

BMB (Management Consulting), New York, NY

Business Analyst   2008–2010

Client: Investment Banking Firms, Eastern U.S,

- Participated in several market data rationalization projects for all divisions
- Interviewed employees on market data needs and usage, analyzed usage data, proposed and implemented savings of 55% on market data costs

Client: Market Data Provider, Eastern U.S.

- Performed market size and share analysis for securities industry in the U.S. and Europe, providing guidance on new market entry

- Led to further investment in commodities and foreign exchange derivatives
- Conducted and presented an analysis of the Order Routing and Order Management business for acquisition targets, leading to client bid

Internal Involvement
- Organized on-campus recruiting initiative and interviewed business analyst candidates
- Spearheaded marketing efforts for the firm, including corporate brand image and brochures

Easton Bank–Private Client Group, New York, NY

Summer Analyst   Summer 2005 & 2006
- Aided in prospecting and developing new business clients through regular cold-calls; sold $6.5M in new business loans
- Assisted Senior Financial Advisor in development of investment strategies for clients using portfolio analysis concepts

COMMUNITY CONTRIBUTIONS:
Brown Excel Board of Trustees, New York, NY

Vice Chair   2006–Present
- Developed, financed and managed the Excelerate campaign, a bar-code keytag that students carry and scan when they attend events, providing a quantitative barometer of organizational success
- Led finance committee, overseeing the budget and forecasting based on annual donations (nearly $900,000 today)
- Manage IT committee, overseeing the website, student program, Excelerate database, and donor databases
- Created and led the Student Life committee, providing donors and student leaders a forum for communication and mentorship

Brown Image Committee, Providence, RI

Co-founder   2007–Present
- Coordinated efforts with the university to update the logo, brand color, website and marketing brochures
- Encouraging further change in university class size and communication to enhance its brand image

Brown Entrepreneur Organization, Providence, RI

President   2007–2008
- Managed networking opportunities for students and alumni, coordinated and ran student and local entrepreneur forum

EDUCATION:
College of Engineering–Brown University, Providence, RI

BS in Operations Research and Industrial Engineering, 2008

· · · · · · · · · · · · · ·

Comments

> Toby does a nice job with this resume, highlighting a number of contributions despite a relatively short amount of time in the professional work environment. Although it would be nice to know a little bit more about *how* he's executed these activities, he does a good job of using tangible figures to give an idea of magnitude of impact. The reader can also see a nice progression in his career over time.

▷ Toby's professional experiences are also nicely supported by his community contributions. He's clearly an active and engaged, which will resonate with the admissions committee, as he will likely contribute a great deal to whichever program he attends. It would be nice to hear more about his role as president of the entrepreneur organization, particularly if he sees entrepreneurship in his future. The one bullet he does have there is relatively generic for an organization that should impart a high degree of excitement.

▷ Toby could also spice things up a little bit by adding a personal section and highlighting a couple of hobbies/interests that could serve as discussion points.

SAMPLE RESUME: "ASHISH" ◀

ASHISH KUMAR

KG BANK	**New York, NY**
Senior Manager, Division	*March 2007–Present*

Manage organizational development, strategic change programs, talent development and retention. Responsibilities include setting up goals, managing expense, budgeting and supporting organizational initiatives on data center consolidation, managing product life cycle and reporting performance metrics to infrastructure director.

‣ Promoted from an engineering team lead to infrastructure senior Manager.

‣ Managing system engineering resources in 32 technical projects.

‣ Completed merger and acquisition related projects accounting for $15 million in 2009.

‣ Led multiple programs to reduce operating expenses. Achieved cost reduction of $750K in 2009.

‣ Consistently received highest ratings for departmental audit and recipient of two service star awards.

GEOMETRIC CORPORATION	**Atlanta, GA**
Senior Consultant	*January 2005–March 2007*

Provided technical expertise in requirement analysis, architecture and design, testing and implementation. Developed and enhanced procedures to reduce cost, risk and exposure. Improved service delivery and operating efficiency. Instrumented process improvement, resource planning and reporting, disaster recovery, business continuity and resiliency planning.

‣ Managed 15 engineering resources with a supporting staff of 10 in application support area.

‣ Accomplished 35% revenue growth in two years.

‣ Finished two major upgrades in KG Bank in less than six months saving approximately $300K.

‣ Provided technical consulting to increase sale of the in house software application by 125%.

‣ Reduced incidents in the production environment by 50% with improved proactive support procedures.

FREEDOM TECHNOLOGY SERVICES	**Chicago, IL**
Engagement Manager	*November 2002–January 2005*

Managed consulting operations. Responsibilities include achieving customer satisfaction in service delivery, evaluating budgetary impact, interacting with sales personnel to develop proposals and pricing, producing monthly project status reports for senior management, building team to provide quality and cost effective consulting deliverables.

‣ Managed 25 onsite and offshore consultants.

‣ Built two offshore teams to realize cost savings of $750K in year 2003–2004.

‣ Achieved a growth of 27% in the company's consultancy revenue in 2004.

‣ Recipient of best employee award in 2004.

BIRLA CONSULTANCY SERVICES   International

Senior System Analyst   *February 2000–November 2002*

Worked as on site project manager. Directed engineering resources in issue escalation and problem solving.

‣ Managed 21 engineering resources on site. Provided aggressive marketing and resource management skills to achieve a six-fold increase in revenues in Star Capital, USA.

‣ Achieved 250% increase in consultancy head count at the client account in Haiku Technology, Japan.

‣ Presented the latest Y2K product in Platinum Life Insurance in Belfast, Ireland. Won $2 million Y2K project contract.

‣ Reduced software delivery time by two months realizing a saving of $75K in International Data Bergen, Norway.

UNVERSITY OF TECHNOLOGY   Jaipur, India

System Manager and Lecturer in Computer Science and Engineering

February 1996–February 2000

Managed computer center resources. Represented college in World Bank projects, worked as a student advisor on the Dean's committee. Responsibilities include billing and budgeting, architecture and design of the computer networks, managing hardware procurement and teaching courses in Computer Science and Engineering.

‣ Managed a team of four people overseeing the hardware procurement in the college.

‣ Achieved an increase in the number of midrange computers from 107 to 167 and users from 200 to 500.

‣ Increased data center funding by 200% with the World Bank approval for two critical projects.

‣ Created computer consultancy cell (RSTART) with an annual profit close to 300K rupees.

ORION COMPUTERS   Mumbai, India

Assistant System Analyst   *July 1995–February 1996*

Analysis, design and coding of software for Mumbai traffic police. Trained six new hires in software development process.

EDUCATION
UNIVERSITY OF TECHNOLOGY   Jaipur, India

Bachelor in Computer Science and Engineering   *September 1991–July 1995*

‣ Graduated with first class marks.

‣ General Secretary of the student's Union.

‣ Best all rounder of the year award in 1990, Captain of the University Cricket and badminton team.

. . . .

Comments

▷ Ashish has a long professional history and plenty to talk about. Perhaps too much to talk about. He could improve the resume by focusing a bit more on being succinct and achievement oriented. His summary statements read more like job descriptions than a brief review of the scope of his work and his accomplishments. Although it can be difficult to balance those two, the resume would be more powerful if he didn't list his responsibilities, but rather told the reader what he accomplished in executing against his responsibilities.

▷ There are a number places in this resume where we can clearly see Ashish leading and managing. It would be helpful for Ashish to be able to communicate in his essays and interview what type of leadership style he maintains as well as what he's like to work with on a team. This type of introspection would be helpful in setting him apart from peers who might produce a similar-looking resume.

▷ An abbreviated "personal" section would be nice and allow the reader to see that Ashish has interests outside of work and could serve as additional discussion pieces.

SAMPLE RESUME: "CHARLES" ◄

CHARLES STANLEY

EXPERIENCE

VINSON HOLDINGS, INC.	**Seattle, WA**	03/09–Present

Cash Manager

‣ Direct treasury and cash management operations for Fortune 1000 national homebuilder.

‣ Execute short-term investment strategy for corporate, charitable foundation and in-house insurance agency investments with combined assets of $200 million; exceeding benchmarks on investment yields.

‣ Cultivate 27 separate banking network relationships while allocating appropriate shares of banking and investment business.

‣ Supervise compliance with financial guidelines and reporting covenants on $1 billion Senior Debt and Medium Term Note programs.

‣ Created and maintain cash forecasting models which improved accuracy by 20% on $8 billion annual receipt and disbursement projections, freeing up excess cash.

‣ Improved liquidity management on $1.25 billion corporate credit facility, decreasing annual interest expense by more than $75,000.

‣ Modernized cash management and information exchange platforms and established internal operating controls ensuring compliance with new Sarbanes-Oxley regulations.

‣ Established DVC Community Involvement Task Force, receiving executive management approval to grant employees paid time off to volunteer at local charities.

IVHR HEALTH INITIATIVES	**Seattle, WA**	06/08–03/09

Associate Treasury Analyst

‣ Monitored asset management for national non-profit health corporation.

‣ Employed strategies to optimize cash resources on $5 billion operating and pension investment portfolios.

‣ Automated and designed efficient operational controls reducing daily allocation and reconciliation time commitment by 25%.

BRIDGESTONE TRUST　　　　　**Seattle, WA**　　　　　03/07–06/08

Cash Management Analyst

- Managed $100 million in daily cash activity for S&P 500 Real Estate Investment Trust.
- Implemented enhanced liquidity strategy to reduce annual deposit float cost by 37% on annual revenue receipts of $1.5 billion.
- Coordinated efforts to reduce service charges by 18% through seeking and evaluating competitive pricing proposals from current and new banking partners.

EDUCATION

University of Arizona, Tucson, AZ

Bachelor of Science, December 2002

Double Major: Finance & Marketing

- Minor: Economics
- GPA 3.5, President's Award
- President, Delta Chi Phi—Dean's Award for Chapter of the Year
- Interned at JP Goldman—Private Client Portfolio Management, 1998–2002

ADDITIONAL

- Certified Treasury Professional (CTP)
- CFA Level I Candidate
- Colorado Treasury Management Association, Education Committee
- Volunteer, Project Angel Heart—Meals with love for people living with HIV/AIDS
- Volunteer, Hands on Denver—Enhancing the quality and character of Denver's parks
- Interests include softball, hiking and snowboarding

· · · · · · · · · · · · · · ·

Comments

- Charles presents a clean, succinct activity-focused resume with plenty of quantitative measures that allow the reader to evaluate his success.
- Although there aren't any glaring weaknesses, sometimes applicants with strong finance backgrounds submit applications that are devoid of passion. They are often somewhat staid and fail to provide the admissions committee with insight into what really motivates the applicant. To the extent that Charles can avoid that in his essays and interview, it will help balance a resume that is largely about the numbers. Being about the numbers isn't bad. It should just be balanced with personality.
- It's good to see that Charles has some community service activities to point to here. These activities should be mentioned again in one of the other application components.

Index

About *the* **Authors**

SCOTT SHRUM and **OMARI BOUKNIGHT** have been helping applicants get into the world's most competitive business schools since 2003, when they published the first edition of *Your MBA Game Plan.* In 2005 they co-founded the MBA Game Plan essay and resume evaluation service, which later merged with Veritas Prep's admissions consulting business (*www.veritasprep.com*). Scott and Omari both now serve as directors of the Veritas Prep family of admissions consulting services. They have assisted thousands of applicants in achieving admission to top business schools, regularly give talks on the subject of MBA admissions, and have been interviewed by a number of media outlets including *Bloomberg Businessweek, The Wall Street Journal, Forbes, U.S. News & World Report,* and *The Financial Times.* Bouknight is a graduate of Harvard Business School and resides in Fremont, California. Shrum is a graduate of the Kellogg School of Management at Northwestern University and resides in Westlake Village, California.